Reshaping Organizational Management and Workplace Culture With AI

Sajjad Ahmad Baig
National Textile University, Pakistan

Muhammad Mohsin
Hunan University of Humanities, Science, and Technology, China

Rab Nawaz Lodhi
University of the Punjab, Pakistan

Ghazia Batool
National Textile University, Pakistan

IGI Global
Scientific Publishing
Publishing Tomorrow's Research Today

Vice President of Editorial	Melissa Wagner
Director of Acquisitions	Mikaela Felty
Director of Book Development	Jocelynn Hessler
Production Manager	Mike Brehm
Cover Design	Phillip Shickler

Published in the United States of America by
IGI Global Scientific Publishing
701 East Chocolate Avenue
Hershey, PA, 17033, USA
Tel: 717-533-8845
Fax: 717-533-7115
Website: https://www.igi-global.com E-mail: cust@igi-global.com

Library of Congress Cataloging-in-Publication Data

Names: 1 Baig, Sajjad Ahmad, 1978- edi | 1 Mohsin, Muhammad, 1989- edi | 1 Lodhi, Rab Nawaz, 1985- edi | 1 Batool, Ghazia, 1989- edi
Title: Reshaping organizational management and workplace culture with AI / edited by: Sajjad Ahmad Baig, Muhammad Mohsin, Rab Nawaz Lodhi, Ghazia Batool.
Description: Hershey PA : IGI Global Scientific Publishing, [2025] | Includes bibliographical references. | Summary: "The objective of this book is to give leaders, managers and researchers the theoretical knowledge necessary to make effective use of AI in various organizational contexts through real-life examples as well as practical tips. It investigates the interface of artificial intelligence (AI) with management, examining how AI technologies are transforming traditional management practices"-- Provided by publisher.
Identifiers: LCCN 2024055164 (print) | LCCN 202405 (ebook) | ISBN 9798369389607 (hardcover) | ISBN 9798369389614 (paperback) | ISBN 9798369389621 (ebook)
Subjects:
Classification: LCC HD30.2 .R476 2025 (print) | LCC HD30.2 (ebook) | DDC 658/.0563--dc23/eng/20250214
LC record available at https://lccn.loc.gov/2024055164
LC ebook record available at https://lccn.loc.gov/2024055165
British Cataloguing in Publication Data
A Cataloguing in Publication record for this book is available from the British Library.

Table of Contents

Detailed Table of Contents

evolving landscape. By adopting AI, organizations can transform operations and achieve sustained growth.

In this chapter we will discuss the collective impact of machine learning on business decision-making, this chapter emphasizes the capacity of AI to improve efficiency, increase accuracy, and provide better insights for business decision-making. It begins with the basics of machine learning principles; and discusses how organizations can use data-driven methods to improve decision-making processes and get advantages over other businesses. The major issues such as ethical implications. Data quality and technical complexities. In this chapter, we will also consider. Strategies for. Effective adoption of machine learning and highlighting the objectives and interdisciplinary collaborations For the implementation of machine learning in business decision-making and improving the existing models. The chapter then concludes by discussing the upcoming trends including automation and, integration of advanced technologies, etc.

This chapter consists on the definition of KMP (Knowledge management process) and digital technologies by different authors. Further, there is in-detailed concept of knowledge management process is elaborated along with its dimensions. The main dimension such as Knowledge utilization, Knowledge application, Knowledge dissemination, Knowledge store, Knowledge sharing, Knowledge creation, Knowledge accessibility and Knowledge organizing. This chapter will be very beneficial for the reader to get deep knowledge about the KMP and digital technologies and its implications in different sectors.

This chapter examines how technology and artificial intelligence (AI) are revolutionizing several industries by enhancing company processes' accuracy, speed, and trust. When combined, they assist companies in automating, augmenting, and achieving authenticity in their workflows. For example, blockchain and artificial intelligence (AI) in financial services increase the speed and accuracy of procedures like loan approvals. This combination increases accuracy, decreases manual labor, and fosters consumer trust. Better care and treatments are possible in the healthcare industry thanks to blockchain's secure record-keeping and artificial intelligence's data analysis capabilities, which give clinicians access to patient records while maintaining patient privacy. AI manage inventory, optimize routes, and even monitor carbon emissions for sustainability. Early success of AI indicates a bright future, despite certain obstacles like maintaining correct data and keeping AI tools current. By utilizing these solutions, businesses may enhance customer happiness, data security, and save time.

The purpose of this chapter is to examine the effect of financial technology on economic performance in the context of emerging economies. By utilizing modern technologies, "fin tech" refers to the supply of efficient, automated, and user-friendly financial services. Fintech enables businesses, business owners, and consumers to better manage their financial affairs, procedures, and lifestyles via special software and algorithms that are used on computers and smartphones. The study objective is to assess how financial technology may affect economic performance using the panel data. The results of this study were aid researchers and professionals in their understanding of the development of fintech. The data gathered from sample of 20 emerging economies with the help of world development indicators and many other sources. The main result of this study is that there is a positive impact of financial technology on economic performance. The findings of this would be helpful to concerned stakeholders.

As technological advancements continue to reshape industries, AI has become this kind of wild force, forcing workplace practices to change and fostering innovation. However, SMEs for adopting innovation need substantial capital, but the access of funding through traditional sources is a major barrier. So, crowdfunding emerges as a great alternative solution to finance their AI-driven inventions of the workplace. This chapter investigates the role of crowdfunding in facilitating the adoption and deployment of AI solutions within SMEs, focusing on various crowdfunding models and identifying which are most suited for AI projects. Factors that influence campaign success or failure will be discussed, and, according to expertise in the subject, how crowdfunding serves as a funding mechanism for projects but also as a market validation and feedback instrument. Crowdfunding, therefore, assists SMEs to test and fine-tune their AI products since enabling businesses fosters innovation and enhances capabilities.

In recent decades, the incorporation of AI in the strategic planning process is revolutionized the business model by improving the efficiency of decision-making, operations, and customer relationship management. AI provides the means for organizations to handle large volumes of data almost instantaneously allowing for the generation of predictive analytics that enhances forecasting and flexibility. It replaces manual labor for low-level duties and assigns humans the responsibility of higher-ranking tasks. On the other hand, there are challenges in AI development and deployment valuation such as a massive cost associated with technology purchase and data management. Integration can only be achieved if both artificial intelligence and the purpose of the firm's activities are harmonized while developing an environment where decision-making is collective and involves the use of AI as well as humans.

Artificial Intelligence (AI) has changed the way of management in organizations and workplace culture. Machine learning, natural language processing, and robotic process automation AI technologies have transformed decision support, operational efficiency, and human resources, enabling the move from traditional hierarchical management to an AI enhanced process. In this paper, we examine how AI facilitates data driven decision making, increases productivity by automating tasks and allows for human–AI collaboration in the workplace. This study examines AI's relevance to customer service, supply chain management and recruitment, showing how AI is becoming an ever more important business imperative for modern organizations to stay ahead in an increasingly isolated world dominated by digital. Also, implications of ethical AI adoption are discussed making the importance of the adoption of AI

Preface

INTRODUCTION

In today's rapidly evolving business landscape, the integration of artificial intelligence (AI) has become a transformative force, reshaping the very foundations of organizational management and workplace culture. From streamlining operations to enhancing strategic decision-making, AI presents organizations with unprecedented opportunities to thrive in an increasingly complex, data-driven world.

Reshaping Organizational Management and Workplace Culture With AI is a timely exploration of how AI is profoundly influencing traditional management practices. Authored by Sajjad Baig (National Textile University, Pakistan), Muhammad Mohsin (Hunan University of Humanities, Science and Technology, China), Rab Nawaz Lodhi (University of the Punjab, Pakistan), and Ghazia Batool (National Textile University, Pakistan), this book serves as a critical resource for leaders, managers, and researchers seeking to understand and harness the innovative potential of AI within their organizations.

CHAPTER OVERVIEW

Reshaping Organizational Management and Workplace Culture With AI offers an in-depth examination of how artificial intelligence is transforming businesses, leadership, and workplace dynamics across industries. Each chapter builds a comprehensive understanding of AI's role in contemporary management practices:

Chapter 1:

This chapter explores the rapid technological advancements, focusing on how AI and digitalization are reshaping businesses. It outlines the conceptual framework of AI, discusses digitalization, and provides sector-specific examples of digital transformation, predicting continued AI integration into business operations.

Chapter 2:

Highlighting strategies for leveraging AI to streamline operations, enhance customer experiences, and create new revenue streams, this chapter presents a roadmap for AI adoption. It emphasizes fostering an AI-centric culture and shares case studies demonstrating AI's transformative power in business models.

Chapter 3:

This chapter delves into how machine learning improves efficiency, accuracy, and insights in decision-making. It discusses ethical challenges, data quality, and technical issues, while proposing strategies for successful machine learning implementation and exploring emerging trends like automation.

Chapter 4:

Offering an extensive discussion of the Knowledge Management Process (KMP), this chapter covers key dimensions such as knowledge sharing, creation, dissemination, and accessibility. It provides critical insights into the role of digital technologies in knowledge management across sectors.

Chapter 5:

Investigating the combination of AI and blockchain, this chapter shows how these technologies enhance accuracy, speed, and trust in industries like financial services and healthcare. It discusses early successes, challenges, and future prospects for AI-driven operational improvements.

Chapter 6:

This chapter assesses the impact of fintech innovations on economic performance using data from 20 emerging economies. It highlights how fintech drives efficiency, automation, and financial accessibility, offering valuable insights for researchers, policymakers, and industry stakeholders.

Chapter 7:

Focusing on the funding challenges faced by SMEs, this chapter examines how crowdfunding supports AI innovation. It analyzes various crowdfunding models, success factors, and the dual role of crowdfunding as both a funding mechanism and a tool for market validation and product refinement.

Chapter 8:

This chapter explores the integration of AI into strategic planning, enhancing decision-making and operational efficiency. It also addresses challenges such as high costs and the need for harmonized human–AI collaboration to successfully embed AI into organizational goals.

Chapter 9:

Examining the impact of AI on organizational structures and processes, this chapter discusses the transition from hierarchical management to AI-enhanced operations. It highlights AI's role in customer service, supply chain management, recruitment, and ethical adoption considerations.

Chapter 10:

This chapter focuses on AI's transformative role in CRM, enabling hyper-personalization, predictive insights, and automation. It also addresses challenges such as data privacy and algorithmic bias while envisioning future trends like emotionally intelligent CRM systems.

Chapter 11:

Offering a foundational understanding of leadership, this chapter discusses key definitions, types of leadership, and major theories. It emphasizes the evolving role of leaders in organizations, focusing on strategies to guide employee development, opportunity recognition, and goal setting in a technology-driven workplace.

CONCLUSION

Drawing on real-world examples and practical insights, this text bridges the gap between theoretical knowledge and practical application. It provides readers with the tools needed to effectively integrate AI technologies into various organizational contexts, thereby fostering efficiency, strategic growth, and a forward-thinking workplace culture.

We invite readers to explore the dynamic intersection of AI and organizational management, and to discover how embracing these technological advancements can drive meaningful transformation in today's competitive environment.

Sajjad Baig
National Textile University, Pakistan

Muhammad Mohsin
Hunan University of Humanities, Science and Technology, China

Rab Nawaz Lodhi
University of the Punjab, Pakistan

Ghazia Batool
National Textile University, Pakistan

Chapter 1
The Role of Digital Transformation in Businesses Under the Influence of Artificial Intelligence

Hilal Celik
https://orcid.org/0000-0003-2227-5462
Beykent University, Turkey

ABSTRACT

In the recent period there have been rapid and great technological developments. Especially the developments in information technologies have brought solutions that make human life extremely easier. The purpose of this study is to explain the role of artificial intelligence and digital transformation in businesses and its impact on sectors. In the first part of the study, artificial intelligence and the relevant conceptual framework are included. In the second part, the issue of digitalization is mentioned. In the last section, the role of digital transformation in businesses is mentioned by giving examples from the sector. As a result, it seems that artificial intelligence has developed rapidly in recent years. Many businesses have transitioned to digital transformation in the work done by their employees and started to outsource their work to artificial intelligence robots. It is predicted that the importance and intensity of artificial intelligence in businesses will continue to increase with digitalization in the future

DOI: 10.4018/979-8-3693-8960-7.ch001

INTRODUCTION

In the last years, there have been rapid and great technological developments. Especially the developments in information technologies have brought solutions that make human life extremely easier. In this way, many businesses have now included a significant part of the work in their production processes with error-free robots. Many banks have started to transition to digital transformation in the work done by their call center employees and outsource their work to artificial intelligence robots. It is predicted that the importance and intensity of artificial intelligence in businesses will continue to increase with digitalization in the future.

The purpose of this study is to explain the role of artificial intelligence and digital transformation in businesses and its impact on sectors. The study conducted for this purpose was carried out using the document analysis technique, one of the qualitative research methods. As a result of the research, it is seen that artificial intelligence has developed rapidly in recent years. As a result, it is understood that digital transformation under the influence of artificial intelligence, a product of human intelligence, will continue to manifest itself in many areas of our lives in the near future.

DEFINITION OF ARTIFICIAL INTELLIGENCE

When we look at the definitions of artificial intelligence in the historical process, it can be said that the definitions of the concept vary depending on people's perspectives, the diversity of artificial intelligence in its application or the area of focus of the relevant discipline, and therefore there is no commonly accepted definition of artificial intelligence yet.

Artificial intelligence definitions are about what is expected from artificial intelligence (Acar, 2020, p.8). John McCarthy, who established artificial intelligence on a conceptual basis and conceptualized artificial intelligence in 1955, argues that the purpose of artificial intelligence is "to enable a machine to behave in a way that is similar to a human behavior and can be called intelligent." In this context, it is possible to say that what is expected from artificial intelligence is to behave like a human and exhibit intelligent behavior. For this reason, it seems that the first studies in the field of artificial intelligence were based on the idea of creating machines that can imitate human intelligence. In the majority of studies, the aim is to establish parallelism between artificial intelligence and human intelligence.(Zawacki-Richter et al., 2019, p.9). Based on this, a general definition of artificial intelligence can be made. Artificial intelligence is "the branch of science that examines how we can make artificial systems perform every cognitive activity that natural systems can do at even higher levels of performance" (Say, 2018, p.83). In this definition, with the expression "every cognitive activity", it is emphasized that artificial intelligence is not limited to certain tasks (playing chess, solving puzzles, using vehicles), on the contrary, artificial intelligence has developed to cover different and broad cognitive activities today. As a matter of fact, artificial intelligence is classified as weak-narrow intelligence and strong-general intelligence according to its evolutionary stage (Haenlein and Kaplan, 2019, p.6). Narrow artificial intelligence is a type of artificial intelligence that performs only one or a part of human cognitive abilities and is used for single tasks. Broad artificial intelligence, also known as strong artificial intelligence, is the ideal type of artificial intelligence that, unlike narrow artificial intelligence, can imitate human cognitive abilities and can be used outside of certain tasks.

Artificial intelligence; It is used in studies on developing systems with human-associated features such as reasoning, making sense, self-learning, and generalization (Copeland, 2019, p.1). In these definitions, it is seen that artificial intelligence is approached from a more technical perspective and the process of transferring/introducing human characteristics to artificial systems is touched upon. In this context, artificial intelligence can be defined as the ability of machines, computers or robots to act, think, make decisions or react like humans as a result of various complex processes. As artificial intelligence technologies develop, the number of these abilities increases and the difference between humans and machines decreases day by day. Therefore, the definitions of artificial intelligence are also increasing in diversity. This makes it possible to classify definitions. (Russell and Norving 2016, cited in Gülşen, 2019, p.410) examined various definitions of the concept under four groups:

Table 1. Classification of artificial intelligence definitions

Systems that think like humans	Rational thinking systems
"It is the automation of activities associated with human thought, such as decision making, problem solving and learning." In this group, artificial intelligence systems that can think like humans have been defined.	"Perception, reasoning, etc. "to make research in the field of computers to make it possible." In this group, artificial intelligence forms that can reason, make inferences or perceive calculations like humans are defined.
Systems that behave like humans	Systems that behave rationally
"It is the attempt to enable computers to do things that humans are currently better at." In this group, types of artificial intelligence that can act in a human-like manner are defined.	"Artificial intelligence is an effort to exhibit intelligent behavior through artificial neural networks." In this group, systems that can analyze designs and calculations are defined.

Source: Gülşen, İ. (2019). İşletmelerde Yapay Zeka Uygulamaları ve Faydaları: Perakende Sektöründe Bir Derleme, Tüketici ve Tüketim Araştırmaları Dergisi, 11(2), 407-436.

It is seen that Shankar's definition of artificial intelligence includes the concepts of software and algorithms, which are not used much in other definitions. According to Shankar (2018, p.6), artificial intelligence is "algorithms, software, systems or machines that make up artificial intelligence". Salehi and Burgueno (2018, p.170) similarly define artificial intelligence as computer science that develops machines and software with human intelligence.

In the report published by IBM and NRF (2019, p.2), artificial intelligence is defined as "the ability of machines to think logically, remember information, identify and learn new information through data discovery."

According to the Organization for Economic Development and Cooperation (OECD) (2019, p.6), artificial intelligence is "machines that can perform human-like cognitive functions and a machine-based system that affects real or virtual environments for defined goals and can make suggestions, predictions or decisions."

The definitions above, the definition of artificial intelligence may vary from person to person, institution to institution and even discipline to discipline; Therefore, it is difficult to say that there is a common definition for the concept. However, by examining the definitions, common points between the definitions can be determined. In this context, common points in the definitions are; AI can be a computer, machine, robot or software. At the same time, these systems are associated with the characteristics that make humans human because thinking, perception, reasoning, calculation, learning, decision-making; It is stated that it may have the ability to move and speak. Zawacki-Richter et al. (2019, p.1) examined 146 studies on artificial intelligence in order to identify the common denominator in the definitions and found that the authors define artificial intelligence as; They made a determination that computer systems are defined as intelligent agents with features that make humans human, such as perceiving, memorizing and using information and understanding human natural language. Although current definitions give an idea of what artificial intelligence is and what it is not, it is considered important to take a closer look at the history of artificial intelligence, whose development spans a long period of time, goes through seasons (artificial intelligence seasons) and shows its impact in many areas with the technologies it is integrated with today, in order to better understand the concept. .

Regarding this issue, science historian Mayor states that the idea of creating artificial life and robots began to appear in ancient myths long before technological developments made it possible to make self-moving devices (Margaryan, 2019, p.1). Also Mayor; B.C. with early artificial intelligence, robots and self-propelled objects. He emphasizes that it is also encountered in the works of Ancient Greek poets Homer and Hesiod, who are estimated to have lived between 750 and 650 BC. In his study, McCorduck discussed Homer's Iliad; He gave examples representing artificial formations that serve humans and have various human characteristics (Mc-

Corduck, 1977, p.951). Because Descartes sharply separates mind and matter and puts forward the idea that the animal body is no different from a machine (Quoted by Ünal and Kılınç, 2020, p.55). In other words, he sees animals as machines rather than living creatures.

Table 2. Studies effective in the development of artificial intelligence

Heron ve El Cezeri	**"Automatic machines developed using water and water spring"**
Schickard	"A calculator that can perform four operations mechanically"
Leibniz'	"Binary counting system that operates with 0 and 1"
Samuel Butler	"In his novel "Erewhon," published in 1872, the idea that future machines will have the potential to have consciousness at some unspecified point"
Karel Capek'(in)	"In 1921, he discussed the concept of robots, that is, artificial humans produced in factories for the first time, in his theater play, etc."

Source:https://stringfixer.com/tr/Timeline_of_artificial_intelligence, 19.03.2023.

The first strong steps based on scientific foundations were taken in 1943 with the work of McCulloch and Pitts, who described brain cells mathematical models . In their studies, McCulloch and Pitts not only showed whether neurons fire or not, but also showed how these brain cells can learn and change their actions over time (Warwick, 2012, p. 2). artificial nerve cells brought about the possibility of assigning various features to robots, and thus the first steps of single-arm robots in factories were taken (Aydın and Değirmenci, 2020, p.21).

Watson, another artificial intelligence system in which IBM competes with human intelligence, has competed under equal conditions in the popular game show known as "Jeopardy" in America and "Big Risk" in Turkey, and by answering questions quickly, it has competed with the two great champions of the game, "Ken Jennings". " and defeated "Brad Rutter" (Sarıel, 2017. p.24; Bostrom, 2018, p. 30). With its natural language processing, perception and ability to comprehend written information, Watson has become a turning point in artificial intelligence.

In the first months of 2016, Google's Deep Mind company developed an artificial intelligence system that works with the deep learning technique and thus can learn on its own. As can be guessed from its name, this system, known as Alpha Go, is assertive in the GO game and has the ability to learn the game on its own and improve itself. Alpha Go has once again demonstrated that artificial intelligence can be superior to humans in certain areas by defeating its world champion opponent in the Go game, which is much more difficult and complex than chess (on a 19x19 board). Especially in recent years, developments in big data, cloud computing, machine learning and deep learning, and the capabilities that come with other new techniques have greatly increased the usability, growth and therefore power of artificial intelligence. In addition, technological advances, affordable sensors and the increasing volume of big data have been effective in the rapid development of artificial intelligence (OECD, 2019, p.21). Autonomous driving systems, face detection and recognition, natural language processing, prediction and reasoning systems and chatbots/digital assistants (Siri) can be cited as examples of the advancements of artificial intelligence systems in various fields. At this point, it can be said that different techniques and algorithms are effective in the development of artificial intelligence technologies.

ARTIFICIAL INTELLIGENCE TECHNIQUES

When we look at the development process of AI, it is seen be there are techniques and algorithms with different content and level of development (Görener and Toker, 2020, p.7). Artificial intelligence techniques are the basic elements that make artificial intelligence AI. Just as there are indispensable parts and areas for the brain, such as neurons and cerebral cortex, similarly, there are techniques and algorithms that must be present in artificial intelligence. These techniques and algorithms ensure the correct functioning of artificial intelligence (Şahin and Kaya, 2019, p.107). Expert systems, genetic algorithms, artificial neural networks, fuzzy logic, deep learning and machine learning are the main techniques and algorithms of artificial intelligence (Jarrahi, 2018, pp. 577-578; Görener and Toker, 2020. p.79.

Figure 1. Object recognition example

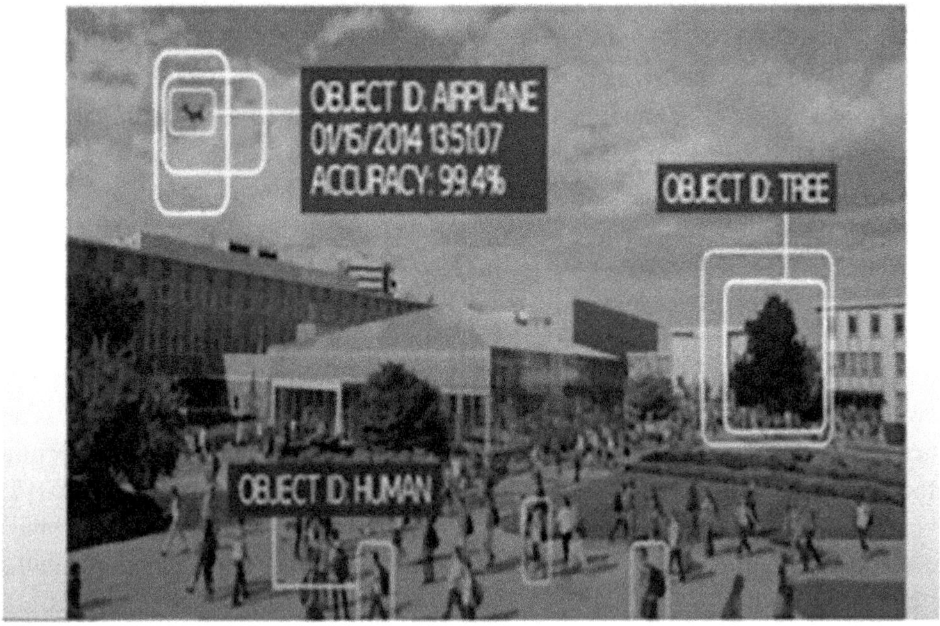

Source:*Pala, F. K. (2020). Makine Öğrenmesi ve Eğitim Sistemine Getirdikleri. Nabiyev V. ve Erümit, A. K. (Ed.). Eğitimde Yapay Zekâ: Kuramdan Uygulamaya İçinde. Ankara: Pegem Akademi Yayıncılık, 233-257.*

Here, the term coding refers to the process of converting the information possessed by developers into a form that machines can understand and apply. The point that makes this approach weak is that a significant part of the knowledge that humans have has a structure that cannot be explained. For example, it seems unlikely that a person could write instructions that would enable another person to ride a bicycle or similarly recognize a friend's face. In machine learning, it is not necessary to teach anything step by step and write instructions; Machines can learn and improve themselves by observing, classifying, and even failing, just like humans do. With artificial intelligence algorithms that learn from experience, the developer's obligation to re-write rules for new data is eliminated. When machine learning reaches sufficient data, it can identify objects in the photo or learn how to solve a problem, as seen in Figure 1 (Pala, 2020, p.233).

USAGE AREAS OF ARTIFICIAL INTELLIGENCE

AI is an interdisciplinary field of study and the diversity of techniques and algorithms used is effective in influencing various sectors. Artificial intelligence technologies have many types according to the use of algorithms like "expert systems", "fuzzy logic", "genetic algorithms", "machine learning" and "artificial neural networks" (Jarrahi, 2018, p.577-578). Therefore, knowing which artificial intelligence technology will be used in which field is very important in order to obtain efficiency from artificial intelligence. Because each technology has a specific task group on which it focuses. For example, machine learning provides good results in face, image, speech recognition and accurate decision making (Davenport, 2020, p.9-10).

Today, artificial intelligence; It is widely used in the fields of health, transportation, communication, production, security, agriculture, politics (Eşitti, 2020, p.265) law, education, finance, insurance and telecommunication. In addition, there is an increase in the number of institutions starting artificial intelligence infrastructure studies in order to achieve their corporate goals. According to the Deloitte (2018) report, 47% of the institutions participating in the research believe in the importance of algorithms and modeling in business processes, and 24% use artificial intelligence technologies in daily work. Turkish Artificial Intelligence Initiative (TRAI), the impact of artificial intelligence used in Turkey on sectors was examined, it was concluded that the banking, telecom and media sectors are the sectors that will be most rapidly affected by artificial intelligence (Telli, 2019, p.193). In a report published by Price Waterhouse Coopers, it is estimated that the Global Gross Domestic Product will increase by 14% by 2030 due to the use of artificial intelligence (Alkan, 2020, p.5). As can be seen, the effects of AI tecnology is felt in daily life and the business world, and are also reflected in research reports.

Büyükgöze and Dereli (2020, p. 3) similarly state that artificial intelligence and robotics are used in the field of health for "early diagnosis, diagnosis, treatment, decision-making, education, research, protection and maintenance of health". In the report titled "Advanced health technologies I - Identifying health problems with smart health applications and data analysis" published by STM ThinkTech in 2019, AI explained as "Use of artificial intelligence for administrative purposes in health" and "Use of artificial intelligence for clinical purposes". It was examined under 2 headings;

Table 3. Use of artificial intelligence in healthcare

Use of Artificial Intelligence in Health for Administrative Purposes	Use of Artificial Intelligence in Health for Clinical Purposes
General Health Management	Public Health Management/Prevent
Documentation Management	Early Diagnosis and Emergency
Efficient Use of Hospital Capacity	Response
Remote Preventive and Complementary Health Services	Post-Treatment Clinical Decision Support
Cost and Quality Management	Care for the Patient in the End Stage of Life

Source: STM ThinkTech Research Report, 2019.

Considering the purposes of use of artificial intelligence, it can be commented that the impact of these technologies is not limited to doctors and patients only, but also many stakeholders can be affected by these technologies. IBM WatsonPaths is an example of artificial intelligence applications used in the field of healthcare. WatsonPaths by IBM; It is a project designed to enable doctors to make fast, conscious and accurate decisions and to facilitate their analysis of electronic medical records (EMR) (Ceylan, 2018, p.1). Factors that make Watson stand out in the field of healthcare: It produces personalized solutions by processing real-time data, predicts a person's possible diseases based on health records, and provides models that improve public health in a more general context (Uzun, 2020, p.84). As another example, Babylon Health in the United Kingdom enables patients to interact with the application called artificial intelligence doctor with the artificial intelligence chat bot it designed (Büyükgöze and Dereli, 2020, p.5).

Within the scope of the "Health Transformation Program", which was implemented in Turkey in the first period of 2003 and continues today, artificial intelligence applications are used in many areas, especially hospital automation and public health monitoring. Today, surgical robots and other technological tools that can perform medical interventions are used in many hospitals (STM ThinkTech Research Report, 2019, p.6). Finally, while the use of artificial intelligence in the field of healthcare increases day by day around the world, it also brings with it some issues of concern. In order to eliminate these concerns, which generally arise within the framework of the concepts of reliability and ethics, ethical standards are needed regarding how artificial intelligence will be used.

Use of Artificial Intelligence in the Field of Law

Related to the existence of law in every aspect of life, every situation in which artificial intelligence technologies interact with humans also finds reflections in the field of law. In addition, just like other fields, law itself needs solutions brought by artificial intelligence (Istanbul, Ankara and Izmir Bar Associations Workshop Report, 2019, p.10). In this case, the law is in a position to both regulate artificial intelligence and benefit from artificial intelligence (Erdoğan, 2021, p.184). Law differs from other disciplines with this position it has

Today, artificial intelligence; gathering information, classifying the text, making summaries, examining similar events and following the patterns by using decision data taken before the events (An AI Now Institute Report, 2018) and making a decision or recommending a decision (at the appeal stage) (Heikkinen, 2019, p.25). It is used to perform different tasks such as: Although these tasks using artificial intelligence seem simple, they are very important in terms of reducing the workload of people working in the field of law and allowing them to focus their energy on their profession. An example of artificial intelligence applications used in the field of law is the artificial intelligence-supported software called "System 206", which started to be used in the hearings of a case involving murder and theft in China. This system, which can identify witnesses and defendants, can also work as a stenographer and transfer everything to the digital environment (Wei, 2019, p.1). It is stated that with this method, which started to be used in 2019, more than three million cases were handled in a short period of 7 months. The social media platform called WeChat is used in hearing these cases (Kartal, 2020, p.83). One of the examples of the use of artificial intelligence in the field of law is Ross, developed by IBM. Designed with Watson software, Ross was hired in a law firm in the USA in 2016 and started assisting 50 lawyers. This system, which has natural language processing, can conduct legal research and answer questions through documents (Yılmaz, 2020, p.45).

Another important impact of artificial intelligence is on "private life and rights" (Kızrak, 2019, p.19). With the integrated use of artificial intelligence with mechanical systems, the possibility of people encountering new social and inter-societal problems increases. At this point, the question of what level of savings the legal rules regulating social relations will have on artificial intelligence applications becomes important (Kartal, 2020, p.154). In the current situation, legal status and liability issues regarding legal personality are two issues that the law seeks solutions for artificial intelligence. In this context, it can be said that modern law is trying to find a formula for determining the legal status of artificial intelligence and granting a legal personality to these technologies. Because the intersection of the natural and the artificial necessitates legal determinations. (Atalar 2019, p.50)

Use of Artificial Intelligence in Education

In today's world, education is among the areas that will be significantly affected by artificial intelligence technologies. It is predicted that the artificial intelligence market for the education sector will grow at an annual rate of 43.36% worldwide in the period covering the years 2018-2022. At this point, artificial intelligence technology has developed day by day and has become a teaching system rather than a learning system. Recently, with the integration of artificial intelligence systems into the field of education, it is seen that they have formed the basis for significant developments in the field (Chen, He and Zhong, 2018, p.62).

The environments in which students carry out their learning activities are shifting more and more each day from learning environments equipped with technology to "smart learning environments". Today, many applications supported by artificial intelligence are widely used by students and educators. In this context, with the use of artificial intelligence, it becomes possible to continue education independently of space and time. In addition, by integrating artificial intelligence applications into education systems; Options such as project-based learning, personalized learning and free choice can be added. Today, it is seen that artificial intelligence applications are widely used in education, generally in the fields of "distance education", "online learning", "augmented reality" and "virtual reality" (Tuğluk and Gök-Çolak, 2019, p.306). In this sense, the concept of school recently; It has begun to be defined as the environment where students and teachers come together virtually or physically in order to participate in educational activities (Timms, 2016, p.703).

When the issue is approached from the perspective of educators, educator administrators; It can be said that they have started to use "smart education management information systems" through systems that provide information that will support their decisions and data obtained, processed and well-arranged through the use of artificial intelligence. In this sense, educational artificial intelligence can be seen as "the intersection of artificial intelligence and educational sciences" (Chen, et al., 2018, p.63).

In recent years, artificial intelligence applications have begun to be used in student support processes, especially in higher education institutions. As a matter of fact, today some higher education institutions have students; It is seen that they use artificial intelligence applications to keep track of their attendance, homework and even behavior. Some of the applications used support students in automatically planning their course load. Additionally, these applications can make recommendations based on how students have performed in previous years, based on similar data profiles. An example of this is that a person studying in the arts can recommend data visualization. In addition, in higher education institutions, artificial intelligence-supported/based libraries can contribute to the development of a better learning experience (Cox,

Pinfield and Rutter, 2019, p.1). On the other hand, artificial intelligence systems can change lessons from day to day to adapt to different levels of student participation, thus making student learning more individualized.

As a result, with the use of artificial intelligence applications in the field of education, it is expected that both schools and teachers will contribute to education more than ever (McNeil, 2019, p.1).

DIGITAL TRANSFORMATION STRATEGY AND ROADMAP

Digital transformation strategies are the strategies of the entire business, not just one unit in the business. These strategies focus on product, service and business model implications as a whole. The goals of these strategies are customer experience, business transformation, and re-planning of business models and operations. It has no temporal interval and strategies are continuous. It uses models which create technologies and ensure harmony between networks, and aims to have a competitive advantage with the ability to think and adapt (Güvener 2019, p. 10).

For the success of digital transformation, the roadmaps determined by the business's digital transformation strategies must be compatible and measurable. Digital strategies enable the creation of new income sources by combining information and existing resources (Gobble 2018, p. 66).

Microsoft has grouped its digital transformation roadmap under 4 main headings:

1. It is necessary to interact with customers and provide them with personalized services.
2. Environments should be created to empower employees and continuously improve their competencies and knowledge.
3. Optimization of operations and optimization of business processes by gathering the entire operation under IT is necessary.
4. Adaptation of products is the restructuring and design of products according to digital production processes.

Schallmo and Williams (2018) suggested that the first steps regarding digital transformation should be taken carefully and explained the elements that need to be taken into consideration with a Venn Diagram as in Figure 2 (Schallmo and Williams 2018, pp. 16-17):

Figure 2. Digital transformation roadmap venn diagram

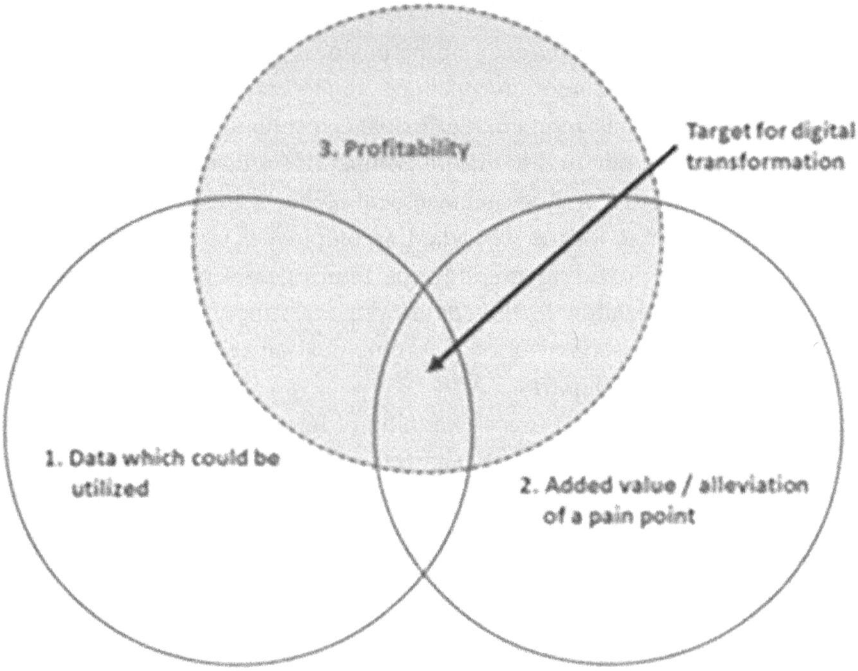

Source: *Schallmo, D. R. A. and Williams, C. A., 2018. Digital transformation now. USA: Springer International Publishing, ss. 41-42.*

The area where these three criteria overlap (circle 1), benefit for stakeholders (circle 2) and profitability (circle 3) is the area where maximum efficiency can be obtained during digital transformation by using the potential, the process of initial brainstorming. Since non-profit institutions work with limited resources, they and their stakeholders have to use their budgets as efficiently as possible. Therefore, even though their goal is not to make profits, they need to determine road maps to increase efficiency (Schallmo and Williams 2018, p. 42).

Digital Transformation and Human Resources Management Under the Influence of Artificial Intelligence

The concept of human resources was used for the first time in 1954 by Drucker in his work titled "The Practice of Management". Drucker focused on using the term human resources for managing and directing managers, employees, and organizational activities. The concept of human resources is defined as the management or division of labor responsible for managing employees and resources in businesses.

In other words, human resources is defined as a set of planned or systematic functions designed to provide the opportunities necessary to meet the job demands of business employees. (Kırmizisaç, 2021, p.158):

It is aimed to increase the efficiency of the business in human resources management, where activities such as recruitment of employees, determination of their personal rights, placement, assignment, performance evaluation and remuneration are determined or carried out, and to ensure competitive advantage by increasing the quality of work. Human resources management includes areas such as selecting employees who are suitable for the job, adapting employees to the organizational culture, motivating them, providing training opportunities, preventing or eliminating conflicts within the organization, leading developments, supporting employees' career plans, creating an intra-organizational communication system and developing employees. (Bayarçelik, 2020, p.61).

Basic functions of human resources; planning of human resources, creation of staff, provision and development of necessary training, evaluation, reward, training, protection, industrial relations and information systems. Since human resources management serves as a consultancy between units, it ensures harmony and coordination of work between units (Calp and Doğan, 2019, p.391).

Digital Transformation and Marketing Under the Influence of Artificial Intelligence

Digital marketing first emerged in the 1990s with the use of personal computers and the expansion of internet usage. Digital marketing is considered to have started with the first clickable banner internet advertisement made by AT&T on the website "Hotwired.com" in 1994. Many large companies such as Yahoo, HotBot, LookSmart and Google have entered digital marketing. Digital marketing began to gain importance thanks to cookies that began to be used through browsers in the mid-1990s (Gökşin, 2017, p.2). New marketing sites that emerged with the developing technology after the 2000s have been the pioneers of the development of digital marketing. The majority of marketing today is done through technological products. The concept of digital marketing is defined by the digital marketing institute; It is defined as the use of targeted and measurable communication to reach the desired target audience with the help of digital technological tools.

Digital marketing provides consumers; It offers important privileges in terms of transportation, time and space. When evaluated from the perspective of businesses, it allows the development of relationships with consumers through one-on-one and interactive communication. Businesses can improve or develop the products and services in question by evaluating feedback from consumers about their products or services through digital tools. Businesses can communicate with consumers with personalized messages. Thus, digital marketing allows customers to gain experience. It provides benefits in terms of labor, time and cost by reaching targeted audiences through different communication channels (Mert, 2018, p.1303).

Digital Transformation and Leadership Under the Influence of Artificial Intelligence

Digital leadership can be defined as creating an innovative vision by effectively using technology in management stages or processes for the formation of a culture of sustainable change in organizations (Ordu and Nayır, 2021, p.78). Digital leadership; It envisages a structure that will operate in an environment of communication, thought and science, with priority on reasoning, generating ideas, solving problems and discipline. Digital leadership has features such as encouraging followers, having a different perspective, empathy, being innovative, behaving differently, trying new approaches, continuous learning, being future-oriented and abandoning stereotyped practices. The digital leader should be able to act as a silent leader, facilitating, inspiring, motivating, providing innovative opportunities and avoiding unnecessary conversations and time wasting of others' activities (Özmen et al., 2020, p.58).

Table 4. Examples of successful digital transformation and leadership experiences

Firm	Leadership	Leadership Secrets
Toyota	Zack Hicks	-Do not leave dead bodies while you are awake, Work with people who will not let you down, It is important who is with you when you reach the finish, You cannot succeed alone, Unleash diversity, Build a team to deal with fires, Correct the mistakes, Pay the necessary prices to enter the market, Being able to predict problems in advance important, right at the right time It is important to use what is available, Know your job well, Create your own path, Do not act like old leaders did.
Google	Joris-Merks Benjaminsen	*Digital champion, going beyond technical knowledge. *Collaborator, thinking beyond your department or location. *Customer first, evaluating events with empathy. *Being innovative, going beyond what you haven't done.*Measurement-Proof is the measurement or proof that something will definitely work.
IKEA	Babara Martin	*Reviving customer contact points *Ideas that will affect customers' experiences *Teamwork *Acquiring missing skills in employees through training and developing existing skills *Creating a digital business culture *Strengthening digital DNA *Test-Create-LearnFeedback-Analysis of data *Clearly explained vision * A dynamic and flexible structure.
Starbucks	Adam Brotman Curt Garner	*What do customers need and how do we reach these needs *At what points can digital contact be established with customers *Security of work-speed-platforms *Improve ordering and payment methods *Being innovative *Ability to communicate with customers *Senior leadership team *Predict and discuss the future *The way Evaluate the map *Find short-term opportunities *Team focus and team collaboration
L'oreal	Chiristia Monnoyeur	*Agility is everything; innovation, personalization, minimizing time to market, being agile in quality and trust *Digitalization means personalization; transform data into information, advertising, customizations, data-driven business approach, automation, artificial intelligence, collaborative robots and using computer visions *There is a fascinating future ahead; Encouraging collaboration and innovation, freeing the contacts of the digitalized customer to ensure communication between producers-suppliers-consumers through digital means
Apple	Tim Cook	*Take risks *Listen carefully to the people you communicate with and focus on them *Trust those around you *Innovation is important *Admit your mistakes *Do your job well *Be humble *Be faithful and transparent *Don't act like others, be yourself *Create your own rules

Source: Çelen, A. İ. (2020). A Rising Value in the Digital Transformation Process: Digital Leadership. Proceedings e-book, 449-461.

THE ROLE OF ARTIFICIAL INTELLIGENCE IN FIRM PERFORMANCE AND INNOVATION

Businesses need new information technologies to be more efficient and act in accordance with the needs of the age. For this reason, businesses more easily adopt new technologies and adapt to these technologies. Various theories are used to determine the ability of business employees and managers to adopt innovations, to be open to change and to adapt to new technologies. TOE, one of these theories, is important for development.

TOE (Technology, Organization and Environment) Model

TOE (Technology, Organization and Environment) Model is important for revealing the status of the organization structure's digital transformation and innovation adoption and how these transformation applications are viewed. Tornatzky and Fleischer (1990) presented the TOE (Technology, Organization and Environment) Model in order to reveal the factors that are effective in the adaptation of innovations to organizations. TOE was included in the research model because an organization feels digital technologies as a need, researches and examines these needs and determines the elements of use in business processes. In his study, Rogers (2003) touched upon the issue that "the acceptance of innovation sometimes occurs in a short time and sometimes requires a long time."Innovation" is an idea, practice or object perceived as new by the individual or adopting units (Rogers 2003, p.12). Therefore, innovation can be an object or a process. While some innovations spread in 5-6 years, others require longer periods. In order to explain these differences in spreading periods, Rogers (2003) stated that individuals' perceptions of innovation should be examined in terms of the characteristics of the innovation

Dynamic Capabilities Theory

Dynamic capabilities (Teece & Pisano, 1994) have been discussed as a new strategic framework since the mid-1990s, with the understanding expanded paradigm was needed to explain how firms can gain competitive advantage. The concept of dynamic capabilities, which first came to the fore in the field of strategic management with the article "Dynamic Capabilities and Strategic Management" published by Teece et al. in the Strategic Management Journal in 1997, states that firms need to develop their own dynamic capabilities in order to gain competitive advantage and sustain this advantage, especially in dynamic/turbulent environmental conditions.

The dynamic capabilities framework (Teece et al., 1997) aims to explain how and why certain firms create competitive advantage under conditions of rapid change.

Teece, who is both the father of the concept of dynamic capabilities and a pioneer in the development of the sub-dimensions of the concept over time with his studies, shaped the sub-dimensions of dynamic capabilities in his conceptual article titled "Explicating Dynamic Capabilities: The Nature and Microfoundations of (Sustainable) Enterprise Performance" published in 2007. In his article, the author addressed dynamic capabilities in three dimensions as perceiving (and shaping), capturing and restructuring. It is possible to say that many different "capabilities" associated with dynamic capabilities in recent years have been associated with these three basic dimensions and accepted as dynamic capabilities. Teece, the most cited author of the dynamic capabilities literature, has published numerous articles, books and papers on dynamic capabilities since his first article in 1997. Many theoretical and empirical studies have been conducted in which Teece and his colleagues determined the framework of dynamic capabilities and accepted dynamic capabilities as abilities or skills (Camisón-Zornoza et al., 2020)

Resource-Based Approach RBV

Business managers and academics have become increasingly interested new approaches and techniques for sustainable competitive advantage. Especially after the 1980s, the subject of providing competitive advantage has generally begun to take shape around two types of approaches. While some academics and practitioners emphasize external factors in providing competitive advantage, others emphasize internal factors more. The first of these is the industry-based competitive approach, more commonly known as Porter's competitive strategies (Industry Attractiveness Model), while the second is the Resource-Based View (RBV), which focuses more on the firm's core competencies. The Resource-Based Approach was first put forward by Wernerfelt in 1984 and was developed particularly by Barney (1986; 1991).

According to the Resource-Based Approach, resources must have certain critical features in order to be used as a certain core competence. These critical features constitute the assumptions of the Resource-Based Approach. According to Barney (1991), Dierickx and Cool (1989), first of all, resources must be valuable and non-substitutable. In other words, resources must be able to create value for a long time in order for the firm to gain or maintain a competitive advantage and must not be easily obtained from alternative sources. Secondly, according to Barney (1991), resources must not be easily found and must be specific to the firm, that is, they must be rare. In other words, they must not be widespread among other firms in the industry and their transfer or trade must be very difficult or impossible. Thirdly, resources must not be easily imitated. This means that the resource is specific to the organization and is not easily distinguishable and is socially complex.

Digitalization and Energy Systems

The European Commission defines digital transformation as the integration of physical and digital systems as a result of advanced technology processes, resulting in innovative business models, new processes, and smart products and services (European Commission, 2018). Reduction in costs, increase in efficiency, sustainability, elimination of human errors, consistency, and ability to analyze can be counted as the benefits of digital transformation (Han and Sarı, 2021). Digital technologies are also changing the competitive environment of the energy sector.

Energy components are digitalized with technologies such as the internet of things (IoT), 3D printers, artificial intelligence (AI), big data, cloud computing, robots, cybersecurity, cryptology, blockchain and simulation. As a result, efficiency-enhancing elements such as smart grids, microgrids, hybrid grids, remote control, and virtual power plants emerge in the energy sector. The benefits of the digital transformation of the energy sector from an economic perspective can be listed as fast and accurate estimation, reduced production costs, reduced distribution costs, sustainable energy systems, reliable energy systems and flexible energy systems. At the same time, as a result of the digitalization of automation, efficiency is increased in issues such as reduced faulty production, reduced work accidents, increased production speed, reduced distribution and production costs. With the social digitalization of the energy sector, efficiency is provided in terms of affordable energy supply that everyone can access, flexibility in national and international policies, reduced product and service costs, increased welfare and opportunities for equalizing income distribution (TMMOB, 2021).

Obstacles Encountered in the Digitalization of the Energy SectorWhile the digitalization of the energy sector has great potential, some obstacles may be encountered in this process. These obstacles can be listed as security and cyber attacks, energy consumption of data centers, distrust of new technologies, inappropriate formation of markets, unexpected changes in nature, unexpected changes in the climate and decreasing energy costs increasing consumption. Detailed explanation of the obstacles is as follows (TMMOB, 2021)

Artificial Intelligence Law

The world's first artificial intelligence (AI) law, adopted by the European Parliament on March 13, 2024, is a significant step forward in the regulation and governance of AI technologies (European parliament, 2024). The law aims to address the challenges posed by AI by establishing clear guidelines, standards and accountability mechanisms. It emphasizes ethical considerations such as fairness, transparency, accountability and privacy to ensure that AI is compatible with societal values and human rights. The law requires collaboration with a range of stakeholders, including governments, industry, academia, civil society and the general public. The global impact of the law is significant and sets a precedent for other countries to establish their own AI regulations, potentially leading to further harmonization and standardization of AI governance frameworks. The law must remain dynamic and adaptable as AI technologies evolve and societal expectations evolve.

By taking a comprehensive and inclusive approach to AI governance, the Act sets a precedent for responsible AI governance in the digital age and serves as a blueprint for future regulatory efforts around the world.

Company Strategies Using Artificial Intelligence

Since the resource-based approach is related to transaction costs and internal accumulation of assets, it can benefit from the synergy of resources while creating a strategy at the company level. As it is known, transaction costs are the control, time and cost pressure that economic actors have to endure during the exchange of goods and services. The company's boundaries will be drawn accordingly. Because the company cannot produce everything. Its resources are limited. But it will want to use the resources in the most efficient way. The size of the company provides economic scale. It will want to achieve this by mobilizing the resources it is best at. The most fundamental problem in determining the company strategy is related to how much the company will diversify. In general, diversification is derived from the Resource-Based Approach (Peteraf 1993,p.188). According to this approach, it is based on the use of some resources as substitute resources that can provide support in the production of different types of products. For example, a brand can support other products.

Eastman Kodak is a good example of diversification through overcapacity in its core competency in photographic technology (Peteraf 1993,p.188). Growth in a particular market was limited by its high market share and antitrust concerns. Kodak saw an opportunity outside its core market to fully exploit its R&D capabilities. This was possible because the application area of photographic technology extended from the film industry to the X-ray industry. Kodak had a 35% share in the US amateur photography market in 1975. In this case, the firm's resources were not in this market despite overcapacity in that particular market. Kodak gained a significant advantage in the photographic market.

Penrose's work on the growth of firms pioneered a broad examination of the resource-based view. Penrose states that a firm is not a managerial unit but rather a collection of effective resources allocated by different users, and that the time for defining a firm by managerial decisions is over (Penrose, 2003,p.27). Later, this concept was used again by Welnerfelt, who offered an alternative for the diversification of the resource-based view (Welnerfelt, 1984:119). In recent years, this model has attracted great interest from scientists investigating the sources of competitive advantage (Amit and Schoemaker, 1993,p.33)

Amit and Schoemaker further expanded these factors and identified eight basic factors, including complementarity, scarcity, low marketability, inimitability, limitedness, substitutability, compatibility, durability, and integration with strategic industry factors. (Amit and Schoemaker, 1993,p.45)

The world's four largest auditing firms, PwC, Earnst&Young, KPMG and Deloitte, have also conducted studies on artificial intelligence.

- **PwC:** It has organized a global artificial intelligence study. As a result of the study, it is stated that by 2030, 45% of the income will be generated by artificial intelligence applications together with the diversification of consumer demand.
- **Earnst&Young:** This auditing firm has established its first artificial intelligence center in India by bringing together experts from many different fields.
- **KPMG:** KPMG has been using artificial intelligence techniques in its auditing processes since 2015. KPMG also uses IBM's cognitive computers.
- **Deloitte:** It uses an artificial intelligence application called "Kira Systems" to improve its own security activities. In the banking sector, HSBC bank uses artificial intelligence to prevent fraud. Morgan Stanley also provides investment recommendations to its clients based on real-time market data using artificial intelligence (Wilson and Daugherty, 2018).

Global AI Usage on the Rise

People Are More Concerned About the Impacts of AI According to a survey conducted by Ipsos, the percentage of people who think that AI will dramatically affect their lives in the next 3-5 years has increased from 60% to 66%. In addition, 52% stated that they are concerned about AI products and services. This rate was 39% in 2022. According to Pew Research Center data in the US, the percentage of people who are more concerned about AI has increased to 52%. These concerns about AI can be solved by better understanding people's AI awareness and better understanding of AI. In a society where AI is better understood, the demand for explanatory and ethical AI will also increase, and more studies will be conducted in this area.

According to Statista's global AI adoption rate file from 2017 to 2024, AI adoption, which was 55% globally in 2023, has made a big leap forward to 72% in 2024. This increase covers many regions and sectors, with the most significant increase seen in the professional services sector. • According to a global survey conducted by McKinsey, 65% of organizations reported regularly using productive AI in at least one business function. This rate has doubled from the previous year. Usage has increased significantly in marketing and sales functions in particular.

Economic Impact • Market Value: The global AI market is expected to be valued at approximately $142.3 billion in 2023 and approach $2 trillion by 2030. This represents a compound annual growth rate (CAGR) of approximately 36%. • Investment in AI Startups: In 2023, more than 25% of US venture capital investments were directed to AI-related companies. This rate was around 12% in the 2018-2022 period.

CONCLUSION

Digital transformation under the influence of artificial intelligence facilitates production to respond to rapid consumption in popular culture. Within popular culture, artificial intelligence is depicted in different ways. Some studies humanize artificial intelligence excessively. Emotions, desires and desires are given to artificial intelligence-supported robots or systems, making them almost indistinguishable from humans. This is a false portrayal of AI technology. Artificial intelligence is a tool. It does what is necessary as people program it. Digital transformation under the influence of artificial intelligence and the technologies produced by humans are actually related to humans' efforts to exceed their own performance limits through their minds. Despite this, depicting AI in pop culture is a way to introduce the technology to a wider audience. It is a way for us to explore the concerns and hopes of this exciting technology.

Because AI systems learn from data in addition to programmed rules, unexpected situations that the system is not trained to handle and uncertainties in human-machine interactions can lead AI systems to exhibit unexpected behavior that poses safety hazards for their users. In order to minimize the negative risks of artificial intelligence as well as its benefits, governments around the world need to better understand the scope and depth of these risks. There is a need to re-evaluate the effectiveness of traditional governance practices such as regulations, taxes and subsidies, which may be inadequate due to lack of information and constant changes. New versions and combinations of all kinds of products are produced using new technologies in order to achieve rapid consumption in the context of popular culture in society. Thanks to new technologies, there are constant changes in products and services. Each new change is presented to society as an innovation in popular culture. While the capitalist system produces a popular culture based on consumption, it also causes unlimited capital accumulation. This system creates individuals with an unlimited need for consumption. In the consumer society with popular culture, every individual is a loyal consumer and a loyal producer of the ideology of the social structure.

Buying, owning and using for short periods of time has become permanent. Differentiated new versions of products in popular culture are only at the level of innovations in design. These small innovations strengthen the image of the product and create a new purchasing need. Artificial intelligence makes purchasing easier day by day. Robots and artificial intelligence are used effectively in the world of science fiction, and it seems undeniable that robots and artificial intelligence depicted in popular culture can affect people's attitudes towards artificial intelligence. In Western culture, robots and artificial intelligence are shown as a future where people are harmed by technology. Artificial intelligence-supported technologies also enable digital transformation under the influence of artificial intelligence to increase new production opportunities in popular culture and encourage people to consume. Artificial intelligence-supported robots and unmanned vehicles make people's jobs easier, but on the other hand, the rapid development of robots and their acquisition of new skills cause concerns in society about the future of artificial intelligence.

As a result, it is an undeniable fact that artificial intelligence will significantly interfere with human life; The point we need to underline here about artificial intelligence is; Although artificial intelligence has a mental ability beyond human intelligence, it will not be possible for it to compete with humans in terms of emotional intelligence, because each person is a different individual in terms of both their genetic codes, the environment they live in, cultural background or occupation, attitudes and behaviors. However, it is also a fact that artificial intelligence applications and digital transformation provide convenience in the work of employees, companies and professionals in different sectors.

The growth trend of the AI market is expected to continue in 2025. Projections predict that AI will reach a global market value of nearly $2 trillion by 2030. It is thought that investments in productive AI and autonomous systems in particular will continue to trigger this growth.

REFERENCES

Acar, O. (2020). *Yapay Zekâ Fırsat Mı, Yoksa Tehdit Mi?* [Is Artificial Intelligence an Opportunity or a Threat?]. Kriter Yayınevi. [Kriter Publishing House]

Alkan, D. (2020). *İnsan Kaynakları Yönetiminin Yapay Zekâ Teknolojileri ile Dönüşümü [Transformation of Human Resources Management with Artificial Intelligence Technologies]. Oyunu Değiştiren Güç Yapay Zekâ* İçinde [The Power That Changes is in Artificial Intelligence]. İstanbul. 269-295.

Amit, R., & Schoemaker, P. J. (1993). Strategic assets and organizational rent. *Strategic Management Journal, 14*(1), 33–46.

Atalar, G. D. (2019). *Teknolojinin gelişimi ve hukuktaki yansımaları* [The development of technology and its reflections in law]. Ankara ve İzmir Baroları Çalıştay Raporu.

Aydın, İ. H., & Değirmenci, C. (2020). *Yapay Zekâ* [Artificial intelligence]. Girdap Kitap.

Barney, J. B. (1986). Strategic Factor Markets: Expectations, Luck and Business Strategy. Management Science, Vol. 32, No. 10, ss. 1231-1241.

Barney, J. B. (1991). Firm resources and sustained competitive advantage. Journal of Management, Vol. 17, No. 1, ss. 99-120.

Bostrom, N. (2018). *Süper Zekâ, Yapay Zekâ Uygulamaları, Tehlikeler ve Stratejiler [Super Intelligence, Artificial Intelligence Applications, Dangers and Strategies].* Koç Üniversitesi Yayınları [Koç University Publications].

Butt, J. (2024). Analytical Study of the World's First EU Artificial Intelligence (AI) Act. *International Journal of Research and Publications, 5*(3), 7343–7364. DOI: 10.55248/gengpi.5.0324.0914

Büyükgöze, S., & Dereli, E. (2020). Dijital sağlık uygulamalarında yapay zeka [Artificial intelligence in digital health applications]. VI. Uluslararası Bilimsel ve Mesleki Çalışmalar Kongresi-Fen ve Sağlık [6th International Scientific and Professional Studies Congress-Science and Health], 7(10).

Calp, M. H., & Doğan, A. (2019). Insan Kaynaklari Yönetiminde Dijital Dönüşüm [Digital Transformation in Human Resources Management].

Camisón-Zornoza, C., Forés-Julián, B., Puig-Denia, A., & Camisón-Haba, S. (2020). Effects of ownership structure and corporate and family governance on dynamic capabilities in family firms. *The International Entrepreneurship and Management Journal, 16*(4), 1393–1426. DOI: 10.1007/s11365-020-00675-w

Çelen, A. İ. (2020). Dijital Dönüşüm Sürecinde Yükselen Bir Değer: Dijital Liderlik [A Rising Value in the Digital Transformation Process: Digital Leadership]. *Proceedings E-Book*, 449-461.

Chen, K. Q., & He, Y. ve Zhong, G. Q. (2018). The Information Literacy Connotation Transformation and the Orientation of AI Education in the Perspective of Artificial Intelligence: Also on the Al Curriculum and Teaching Implementation Path in the Basic Education Stage. *Journal of Distance Education, 36*, 61–71.

Copeland, B. J. (2019). "Artificial Intelligence". https://www.britannica.com/technology/artificial-intelligence. 21.03.2023.

Cox, A. M., Pinfield, S., & Rutter, S. (2019). The intelligent library: Thought leaders' views on the likely impact of artificial intelligence on academic libraries. *Library Hi Tech, 37*(3), 418–435.

Deloitte. (2015). "Global Power of Retailing 2015: Embracing Innovation",https://www2.deloitte.com/content/dam/Deloitte/global/Documents/Consumer-Business/gx-cb-global-powers-of-retailing. pdf

Deloitte. (2020). Artificial Intelligence Innovation Report. https://www2.deloitte.com/content/dam/Deloitte/de/Documents/Innovation/Artificial-Intelligence-Innovation-Report-2018-Deloitte.pdf

Dierickx, I., & Cool, K. (1989). Asset stock accumulation and sustainability of competitive advantage. *Management Science, 35*(12), 1504–1511.

Erdoğan, G. (2021). Yapay Zekâ ve Hukukuna Genel Bir Bakış [An Overview of Artificial Intelligence and Its Law]. *Adalet Dergisi [Justice Magazine]*, (66), 117–192.

Eşitti, Ş. (2020). *Sosyal Medya ve Yapay Zekâ* [Social Media and Artificial Intelligence]. Artificial Intelligence Transforms Disciplines–Are We Ready for Change.

European Commission. (2018). DigComp into action: Get inspired, make it happen. JRC Science For Policy Report, EUR 29115 EN, Publications Office of the European Union, Luxembourg. http://publications.jrc.ec.euro-pa.eu/repository/bitstream/JRC110624/deguidemay18.pdf

European Parliament. (2024), Artificial Intelligence Act: MEPs adopt landmark law. (website). https://www.europarl.europa.eu/news/en/press-room/20240308IPR19015/artificial-intelligence-act-meps-adoptlandmark-law Accessed 7 October 2024.

Gobble, M. (2018). Dijitalleşme, Dijitalleşme ve Yenilik [Digitalization, Digitalization and Innovation]. *Araştırma-Teknoloji Yönetimi [Research-Technology Management], 61*(4), 56–59.

Gökşin, E. (2017). *Dijital Pazarlama Temelleri [Digital Marketing Fundamentals].* Abaküs Yayınları [Abacus Publications].

Görener, A., & Toker, K. (2020). Yapay zekâda evrimsel algoritmalar: Lojistik sektöründe bir genetik algoritma uygulaması [Evolutionary algorithms in artificial intelligence: A genetic algorithm application in the logistics sector]. Oyun Değiştiren Güç Yapay Zekâ [Game-Changing Power: Artificial Intelligence], (Editörler: Mustafa K. Yılmaz, N. Öykü İyigün), Beta Basım Yayım Dağıtım, 1-40.

Gülşen, İ. (2019). İşletmelerde Yapay Zeka Uygulamaları ve Faydaları: Perakende Sektöründe Bir Derleme [Applications and Benefits of Artificial Intelligence in Business: A Compilation in the Retail Industry]. *Tüketici ve Tüketim Araştırmaları Dergisi [Journal of Consumer and Consumption Research], 11*(2), 407–436.

Güvener, A. (2019). *Dijital dönüşüm sürecinde çalışanların teknolojik hazıroluş seviyelerinin belirlenmesi. Yüksek Lisans Tezi [Determining the technological readiness levels of employees in the digital transformation process. Master's Thesis].* Bahçeşehir Üniversitesi SBE.

Haenlein, M., & Kaplan, A. (2019). A brief history of artificial intelligence:on the past, present, and future of artificial intelligence. *California Management Review, 61*(4), 5–14. DOI: 10.1177/0008125619864925

Han, F. Ö., & Sarı, E. B. (2021). Enerji Sektörünün Dijital Dönüşüm Projeleri-ni Yürüten Araştırmacıların Dijital Yeterliliklerine Yönelik İçerik Analizi [Content Analysis of Digital Competencies of Researchers Carrying Out Digital Transformation Projects in the Energy Sector]. *Scientific Journal of Innovation and Socia Sciences Research, 1*(1), 1–25.

Heikkinen, T. H. (2019) "How Does the Use of Artificial Intelligence Affect the Concept of Fair Trial?", Faculty Of Law Lund University, Master Thesis-International Human Rights Law, Lund, https://lup.lub. lu.se/ student- papers/search/publication/8980709 (03.04.2023).

Jarrahi, M. H. (2018). Artificial intelligence and the future of work: Human-AI symbiosis in organizational decision making. *Business Horizons, 61*(4), 577–586. DOI: 10.1016/j.bushor.2018.03.007

Kırmızısaç, E. (2021). Yeni Nesil İnsan Kaynakları Yönetiminde Dijital Dönüşüm [Digital Transformation in New Generation Human Resources Management], *European Journal of Educational and Social Sciences, 6*(2), 156–169.

Margaryan, P. (2019). Antik Yunan Mitlerinde Yapay Zekâ [Artificial Intelligence in Ancient Greek Myths], Arkeofili. https://arkeofili.com/antik-yunanmitlerinde-yapay-zeka/

McCorduck, P., Minsky, M., Selfridge, O. G., & Simon, H. A. (1977, August). History of artificial intelligence. In IJCAI (pp. 951-954).

McNeill, S. (2019). Artificial intelligence in the classroom. Education Blog. https://educationblog.microsoft.com/en-au/2019/01/artificial-intelligence-in-theclassroom/ (03.04.2023).

Mert, Y. L. (2018). Dijital Pazarlama Ekseninde İnfluencer Marketing Uygulamaları. *Gümüşhane Üniversitesi İletişim Fakültesi Elektronik Dergisi* [Influencer Marketing Applications in the Axis of Digital Marketing. Gümüşhane University Faculty of Communication Electronic Journal*], 6*(2), 1299–1328.

Morgan, B. (2019), "The 7 Best Examples of Artificial Intelligence to Improve Personalization", Forbes. https://www.forbes.com/sites/ blakemorgan/2019/01/24/the-7-best-examples-of-artificial-intelligence-to-improve-personalization

OECD. (2019). Hello, World: Artificial Intelligence and its use in the Public Sector. [OPSI]. *OECD Observatory of Public Sector Innovation*, *36*, 1–148.

Ordu, A., & Nayır, F. (2021). Dijital Liderlik Nedir? Bir Tanım Önerisi [What is Digital Leadership? A Proposed Definition]. E-International Journal of Educational Research, 12(3).

Özmen, Ö. N., Eriş, E., & Özer, P. (2020). Dijital liderlik çalişmalarina bir bakiş. Süleyman Demirel Üniversitesi İktisadi ve İdari Bilimler Fakültesi Dergisi [A look at digital leadership studies. Süleyman Demirel University Faculty of Economics and Administrative Sciences Journal], 25(1), 57-69.

Pala, F. K. (2020). *Makine öğrenmesi ve eğitim sistemine getirdikleri. Eğitimde Yapay Zeka Kuramdan Uygulamaya içinde*. Pegem Yayıncılık. [Machine learning and what it brings to the education system. In Artificial Intelligence in Education: From Theory to Application. Ankara: Pegem Publishing]

PENROSE E. (2003). The Theory of The Growth of The Firm. In Nicolai, J. (Ed.), *Resources Firms and Strategies: A Reader in the Resource-Based Perspective, Oxford Management Readers*. FOSS.

Peteraf, M. A. (1993). "The cornerstones of competitive advantage: A resource-based view", Strategic Management Journal, Vol. 14, No 3, ss. 179-191.

Rogers, M. E. (2003). *Diffusion of innovation* (5th ed.). The Free Press.

Şahin, E., & Kaya, F. (2019). *Pazarlamada Yeni Dönem Endüstri 4.0. Yapay Zeka ve Akıllı Asistanlar*. Çizgi Kitabevi. [New Era in Marketing Industry 4.0. Artificial Intelligence and Smart Assistants: Konya: Çizgi Bookstore]

Salehi, H., & Burgueno, R. (2018). Emerging Artificial Intelligence Methods in Structural Engineering. *Engineering Structures, 171*, 170–189. DOI: 10.1016/j.engstruct.2018.05.084

Sarıel, S. (2017). *Günümüzde Yapay Zekâ*, İstanbul Teknik Üniversitesi Vakfı Yayını, İnsanlaşan Makinalar ve Yapay Zekâ [Artificial Intelligence Today, Istanbul Technical University Foundation Publication, Humanized Machines and Artificial Intelligence], 75.

Say, C. (2018). *50 Soruda Yapay Zekâ*. Bilim ve Gelecek Yayınevi. [Artificial Intelligence in 50 Questions. Science and Future Publishing House]

Schallmo, D. R. A., & Williams, C. A. (2018). *Digital transformation now*. Springer International Publishing. DOI: 10.1007/978-3-319-72844-5

Shankar, V. (2018). How Artificial Intelligence (AI) Is Resha- ping Retailing. *Journal of Retailing*, *94*(4), 5–11. DOI: 10.1016/S0022-4359(18)30076-9

Smith, A. (2018). "Three Ways AI Can Help Build Customer Relationships", Forbes. https://www.forbes.com/sites/anthonysmith/2018/03/12/

STM ThinkTech. (2019). "İleri Sağlık Teknolojileri I Akıllı Sağlık Uygulamaları ve Veri Analizi İle İle Sağlık Sorunlarını Tanımlamak" [Identifying Health Problems with Advanced Health Technologies I Smart Health Applications and Data Analysis]. https://thinktech.stm.com.tr/uploads/docs/1608905321_stm-ileri-saglik-teknolojileri-1.pdf

Teece, D. J. (2007). Explicating dynamic capabilities: The nature and microfoundations of (sustainable) enterprise performance. *Strategic Management Journal, 28*(13), 1319–1350. DOI: 10.1002/smj.640

Teece, D. J., & Pisano, G. (1994). The dynamic capabilities of firms: An introduction. *Industrial and Corporate Change*, *3*(3), 537556. DOI: 10.1093/icc/3.3.537-a

Telli, G. (2019). Yapay zeka ve geleceğin meslekleri. Yapay zeka ve gelecek içinde [Artificial intelligence and the professions of the future]. (ss. 186-197). İstanbul: Doğu Kitapevi.

Timms, M. J. (2016). Letting artificial intelligence in education out of the box: Educational cobots and smart classrooms. *International Journal of Artificial Intelligence in Education*, *26*(2), 701–712. DOI: 10.1007/s40593-016-0095-y

Tornatzky, L. G., & Fleischer, M. (1990). *The processing of technological innovation*. Lexington Books.

Tuğluk, M. N., & Gök-Çolak, F. (2019). Sanayi toplumu ve eğitimi. Eğitimde ve endüstride [Industrial society and education. In education and industry], 21, 305-335.

Ünal, A., & Kılınç, İ. (2020). Yapay zekâ işletme yönetimi ilişkisi üzerine bir değerlendirme. Yönetim Bilişim Sistemleri Dergisi [An evaluation on the relationship between artificial intelligence and business management. Journal of Management Information Systems], 6(1), 51-78.

Warwick, K. (2012). *Artificial Intelligence: The Basics*. Routledge.

Wei, J. (2019). China uses AI assistive tech on court trial for first time. https://www.chinadaily.com.cn/a/201901/24/WS5c4959f9a3106c65c34e64ea.html (11.04.2021).

Wernerfelt, B. (1984). A Resource-Based View of the Firm. *Strategic Management Journal*, *5*(2), 171–180. DOI: 10.1002/smj.4250050207

Wilson, H. J., & Daugherty, P. R. (2018). Feature Collaborative Intelligence: Humans And AI Are Joining Forces. *Harvard Business Review*.

Yılmaz, A. (2021). *Yapay Zekâ*. Kodlab Yayınevi.

Zawacki-Richter, O., Marín, V. I., Bond, M., & Gouverneur, F. (2019). Systematic review of research on artificial intelligence applications in higher education – where are the educators? *International Journal of Educational Technology in Higher Education*, *16*(1), 39. DOI: 10.1186/s41239-019-0171-0

Chapter 2
Transforming Traditional Business Models With AI-Powered Strategies

Dhartiben Neelkumar Patel
https://orcid.org/0009-0009-4109-9055
Indukaka Ipcowala Institute of Management, India

Reshma Gunaji Sable
https://orcid.org/0000-0002-4119-2761
Indukaka Ipcowala Institute of Management, India

ABSTRACT

AI advancements offer traditional businesses transformative opportunities to boost efficiency, drive innovation, and gain competitive advantages. This chapter explores strategies for leveraging AI to streamline operations, enhance customer experiences, and create new revenue streams. Key steps include evaluating business readiness by assessing data, workforce capabilities, and organizational alignment. A strategic roadmap is developed, highlighting AI use cases, timelines, and success measures. Fostering an AI-centric culture that emphasizes learning, risk-taking, and collaboration is essential for success. Case studies show how AI reimagines business models, driving value through innovation and operational optimization. AI enhances decision-making, personalization, and helps businesses thrive in a rapidly evolving landscape. By adopting AI, organizations can transform operations and achieve sustained growth.

DOI: 10.4018/979-8-3693-8960-7.ch002

1. INTRODUCTION

The power of Artificial Intelligence (AI) was not known to the world until the beginning of 21st century. As soon as the few businesses started adopting AI in its work processes, the world realised the revolutionary power of AI. Traditional business models were assessed for their limitations and started getting replaced with AI-driven automated models. The change though difficult and resisted initially now has become the only reason for existence of organizations in the field.

The purpose of this chapter is to reveal the power of AI, by focusing on its evolution, adoption and journey so far. It will focus on the process of transformation of businesses and the path-ways right from the readiness stage to the implementation stage. It also discusses the challenges in AI adoption, ethical considerations and few real life examples and cases for better understanding.

1.1 Evolution of AI in Business

In the last few decades, the evolution of artificial intelligence has progressed at breakneck speed, revolutionizing fundamentally the manner in which companies are run. Its initial incarnation saw AI mostly constituted by rule-based systems to execute simple repetitive tasks. In its early beginnings, business application was restricted to activities like entering data and minor customer support jobs that could be executed through pre-defined if then logic without needing any form of learning from data.

As the discipline improved, advances in machine learning and subsequently deep learning allowed for models that could accomplish more sophisticated and adaptive behavior. These new-fangled algorithms soon came to approximate elements of human cognition, supporting pattern recognition and predictive functions once beyond reach and significantly affecting business operations. (Russel & Norvig, 2020)

AI is now no longer about mere automation but has applications to a broad suite of advanced functionalities, including:

Data Analytics: New AI technologies can analyze and process large sets of data at rates and with levels of accuracy far beyond conventional approaches. This enables companies to discover insights, predict trends, and make informed decisions that improve competitive advantage.

Natural Language Processing (NLP): Progress in Natural Language Processing has transformed internal communications and customer interactions. Virtual assistants, AI-driven chatbots, and sentiment analysis software are now being employed regularly to support customers, optimize support services, and even drive marketing efforts.

Computer Vision: Computer Vision is considered as a key technology in industries like retail, manufacturing and healthcare which required controlling of quality and improving operational precisions.

Robotic Process Automation (RPA): AI-enhanced Robotic Process Automation systems improves efficiency of repetitive tasks and minimized human intervention by integrating learning and adaption thereby adding value to the entire process.

Together, all AI tools and capabilities have supported business to maximize the revenue, increase loyal customer base by improving operational capabilities for transforming the traditional business models.

1.2 Defining AI-Powered Business Models

Traditional business models rely on historical data and rigidly defines processes. They lack agility to adapt to the need of the hour. Whereas, the modern AI-driven models have ensured the integration of advanced technologies for automated decision making and future prediction. The AI-driven-customer centric approach has impacted to a great extent on various functions of the organization. (Chui et al, 2018).

1.3 The Imperative for Technological Integration in Businesses

The incorporation of advanced technologies into business models is no longer optional; it has become a tactical necessity for companies striving for sustainability and growth in today's digital economy. The increase of digital conversion and increasing consumer expectations for personalization and ease are pushing organizations to adopt new tools and systems to remain competitive. (Bughin et al, 2018)

Technology has started finding its place in almost all industries. As a result, certain businesses are experiencing significant changes in their work processes. For instance, sectors like Finance and Healthcare have undergone major transformations. In Finance, modern systems are used for risk assessment, fraud detection, and automated trading. In Healthcare, advanced diagnostic tools assist in identifying diseases at early stages, leading to improved patient outcomes. These examples highlight the potential of technology to disrupt traditional models and create more efficient, scalable, and innovative business practices.

1.4 The Shift from Traditional to AI-Enabled Business Ecosystems

Traditional business models are largely characterized by hierarchical structures, fixed processes, and a reliance on historical data for decision-making. These models often struggle to adapt to the volatility and complexity of today's markets. In contrast, AI-enabled business ecosystems are dynamic and adaptive. They leverage vast amounts of data collected from multiple sources such as social media, sensors, and customer interactions allowing businesses to gain real time insights and make proactive decisions. (Brynjolfsson & McAfee, 2017)

Let's take an example of Tesla, a company operating in an automotive industry and is leveraging Artificial Intelligence to create separate driving systems. By incorporating AI with vehicle sensors, Tesla not only develops the safety and functionality of its cars but also collects continuous data on driving patterns and conditions. This data is fed back into the system to improve the technology, creating a self-learning ecosystem that outdated automakers cannot easily reproduce.

1.5 The Role of Data in AI-Driven Business Models

Data is the heart of AI-based business models. The better the quality and quantity of data an AI works on, the better it is going to work. In the traditional model, data is isolated and underutilized, causing inefficiencies and missed opportunities. In contrast, AI-based businesses utilize data as a strategic asset. They employ data lakes and cloud computing platforms to store and process large volumes of information in real time to enable fast and informed decision-making.

2. CONNECTING THE POWER OF AI FOR BUSINESS TRANSFORMATION

Innovative technologies have become more powerful tools for transforming traditional business operations, enabling organizations to operate more efficiently, respond swiftly, and focus on customer needs (Gil et al., 2019). By leveraging technologies such as predictive analytics, automated decision-making, and data-driven insights, businesses can streamline their processes, improve customer experiences, and generate new revenue streams, positioning themselves as market leaders. This section provides an in-depth look at the use of these technologies in conventional businesses, reviews successful case studies, and outlines the technological requirements for implementation.

2.1 Application of AI in Traditional Businesses

AI has an application in predictable business, and its potential is increasingly being leveraged across industries. From finance and retail to manufacturing and healthcare, AI technologies are being employed to automate operations, forecast outcomes, and improve decision-making abilities. Major AI applications employed in business include predictive analytics, automated decision-making, and the creation of actionable insights using data-driven analysis.

2.2 Forecasting Analytics

Forecasting analytics employs historical information, statistical models, and machine learning algorithms to discover patterns and forecast future events. It is an important business tool for companies trying to predict customer activity, demand, and best practices. For example, in consumer retail, predictive tools can forecast inventory needs by analyzing customers' buying habits and seasonal trends, helping to avoid stock shortages and excess inventory. In finance, these tools are used to assess credit risks, detect fraudulent activities, and anticipate market movements.

Netflix is a prime example of a company that has effectively harnessed predictive analytics. By examining viewers' behaviours and preferences, Netflix recommends personalized content, boosting viewer engagement and customer loyalty. This feature is powered by algorithms that learn and adapt based on user patterns, making predictions increasingly accurate over time. Consequently, Netflix not only improves its user experience but also optimizes its content acquisition and production strategies to align with expected viewership trends.

2.3 Automated Decision-Making

Automated decision-making involves using advanced systems to make real-time decisions with minimal human input. These systems can handle vast amounts of data, evaluate multiple factors, and provide recommendations or take actions based on set criteria. This approach is particularly effective in industries requiring quick responses, such as logistics, finance, and manufacturing.

Let's take UPS as an example of a logistics company that has adopted a route optimization technology. It considers traffic patterns, weather conditions, and delivery schedules to determine the best routes for delivery trucks, minimizing fuel consumption and delivery times. In the manufacturing sector, decision-making systems can detect errors on production lines using computer vision technology and adjust processes to maintain product consistency, reducing downtime and increasing efficiency.

2.4 Data-Driven Insights

Today, businesses are using sophisticated data analytics tools to extract valuable insights from both structured and unstructured data. By analyzing data in real time, companies can better understand their markets, identify emerging trends, and make well-informed strategic decisions. This is particularly advantageous in marketing and sales, where analyzing customer data helps tailor marketing campaigns, optimize pricing strategies, and predict sales.

Starbucks provides a great example of using data analytics to improve its loyalty program and personalize customer interactions. Their system, known as the Digital Flywheel, gathers data from millions of transactions and customer interactions to understand customer preferences. This allows Starbucks to customize promotions and product recommendations for each customer, enhancing satisfaction and driving sales growth.

2.5 Case Studies: AI Integration Successful in Business

To evaluate the transformative potential of advanced technologies, this section showcases case studies of companies that have successfully integrated these tools into their operations, demonstrating enhancements in efficiency, customer experience, and revenue generation.

2.5.1 Amazon: AI-Driven Supply Chain Optimization

Amazon has set the benchmark for integrating advanced technologies into business, particularly in supply chain management and logistics. The company uses simple processes to optimize inventory management, predict product demand, and automate warehouse operations. Its robotic systems can efficiently sort, pack, and move products within fulfilment centers, significantly reducing the time needed to complete orders.

Additionally, Amazon's advanced algorithms continuously track customer preferences and purchasing habits, enabling the company to accurately forecast demand. This analytical capability helps Amazon maintain optimal inventory levels by cutting costs associated with excess stock or shortages. Integrating these technologies into Amazon's supply chain has led to faster delivery times, lower operational costs, and an improved customer experience, bolstering the company's competitive edge.

2.5.2 American Express: Fraud Detection through AI and Risk Management

In the finance sector, American Express has utilized advanced technology to improve its fraud detection and risk management processes. The company's system analyzes numerous transactions in real time, identifying patterns and anomalies that may suggest fraudulent activity. By employing machine learning algorithms, American Express's system continually enhances its accuracy in detecting fraud, enabling the company to take immediate protective actions. With automated fraud detection, customers experience fewer distractions and issue are resolved. Moreover, the company has employed advanced technology to better evaluate credit risks, enabling it to provide tailored financial products and services, thereby boosting revenue growth.

2.6 Requirements of Technology in AI Integration

While advanced technologies hold immense potential for transforming businesses, their successful implementation demands a robust technological infrastructure and digital preparedness. The following sections will explore the essential technological requirements for integrating these tools into business operations.

2.6.1 Data Organization

Effectiveness of AI is determined on the basis of the availability and quality of the data. For successful outcomes of AI solutions, organizations need large quantities of data from several sources viz. transactions of customers, data of dealings done on online platforms, network devices etc. It is equally important to create a structure for storing the data with the help of data lakes, cloud computing, data warehouses supporting real-time data analysis. The matter of data security also becomes of prime importance at this stage.

For technology to be effective, businesses must achieve a level of digital readiness that allows new systems to integrate smoothly with existing processes and legacy systems. Assessing digital readiness ensures seamless AI integration with current systems (Heyn et al., 2021). This may require upgrading IT infrastructure, modernizing software, and adopting cloud-based platforms that facilitate integration. For example, many organizations are transitioning to cloud-based enterprise resource planning (ERP) systems, which provide a scalable and flexible environment for deploying new applications.

2.6.2 AI-Enabled Workforce

Beyond upgrading technological infrastructure, businesses must also focus on developing a workforce skilled in advanced technologies. Successful integration requires employees with the technical knowledge about managing and operating these systems and also the ability to interpret the output generated through analysis. This may involve hiring new talent with expertise in data science, engineering, and cybersecurity, or providing training programs to upskill existing employees.

2.6.3 AI Power and Ethical Considerations

It is important to have the ethical governance framework in place for more responsible use of AI. This is possible only when the AI policies, AI standards for maintaining transparency, fairness and accountability is in place. Before adoption of AI organizations should focus on ensuring the regulatory and legal requirements considering the data sourcing, usage and transparency. Such framework will act as a guiding principles for organizations to operate in the dynamic field without losing the credibility and trust of the customers

3. EVALUATING BUSINESS READINESS FOR THE AI-POWERED TRANSFORMATION

Incorporation of AI in various functions of an organization a not an automatic process. It proceeds with evaluation of existing competencies of the organization, organizational hierarchy its infrastructural facilities and the strategic goals of the organization. Hence it becomes important to assess the organization's readiness for AI adoption by providing the detailed outline for enabling willingness appraisals and evaluation of the existing resources for AI implementation.

3.1 Evaluation Parameters for AI Readiness

The first step of AI adoption is assessment of the organizations existing resources and identifying the indicators of firms' preparedness for adoption of AI. It should be ensured that the basic building blocks are in place with minimum associated risk and maximum chances of effective implementation. The key criteria comprise of availability of data, skilled human resources, and technical know-how.

3.2 Data Availability

Data is the essence of AI systems. Organizations should get the access to huge volumes of good quality data in either structured, and unstructured form to train AI algorithms efficiently. Measuring data availability involves assessing whether the businesses have enough historical and concurrent data from various sources such as client interactions, transaction logs, sensor networks, and market analysis reports.

Organizations should also assess data integration capabilities, confirming that data isolations are minimized, and data from various departments can be amalgamated for analysis. Insufficient or compromised data quality can limit the efficiency of AI, causing wrong predictions, findings and insights. Hence, organizations must establish data management practices that are robust in nature. This includes data cleaning, authentication, and governance to maintain the quality of data.

3.3 Workforce Skills and Digital Competencies

AI empowered workforce is indispensable for executing and handling AI technologies. Organizations must assess whether their workforce holds the essential technical skills in data science, machine learning, AI engineering, and cybersecurity. This evaluation should also identify gaps in AI proficiencies and define the level of digital literacy throughout the organization.

Prerequisite for development of AI-ready workforce is none other than investment in training and upskilling programs for the organizational workforce. Workforces must be trained for operating the AI systems, interpreting the AI-driven outcomes so as to make them valuable resources in decision making processes. Furthermore, organizational leadership teams need to be polished on the strategic value of AI to effectively direct the business through the transformational change.

3.4 Technical Infrastructure

Any organization's technical set-up and supporting infrastructure is another crucial measure for AI readiness. AI technologies should be accessible and flexible. IT environments are generally sufficient to handle the computational demands of AI algorithms and the storage of big datasets. This comprises of the applications of cloud based platforms, unconventional networking capabilities, and high performance computing infrastructure. (Heyn et al, 2018).

Assessing technical setups will include investigating the organization's systems and networks and confirm that they are up-to-date and attuned with AI technologies. Organizations will require to invest in revolutionizing their IT infrastructures, integrate cloud based solutions, and implement data storage solutions like data warehouses with keen focus on data privacy and regulations.

3.5 Framework for Conducting AI Readiness Evaluations

An organized framework is crucial for companies to methodically assess their willingness for AI adoption by identification of existing gaps, alignment with business goals, and creation of a roadmap for implementation. The key components can include:

3.5.1 Define AI Objectives and Strategic Alignment

An organization needs to begin by aligning the AI initiatives with goals of business such as improved productivity, enhanced customer experience, and growth in revenue. With clarity in the objectives, organizations can identify areas where value addition can be done with the help of AI. For instance, personalized marketing in retail or predictive maintenance in manufacturing can be ensured with the support of AI.

3.5.2 Evaluate Existing Capabilities

After defining objectives, organizations should first assess their current capabilities related to data, workforce and existing infrastructure. A comprehensive audit can be conducted through a complete audit that can comprise of data audit, skills assessment and infrastructure reviews. Such audits can help organizations in identification of specific areas of improvement and can assist in the allocation of resources for training, technology upgradation and management of data.

3.5.3 Develop an AI Roadmap

On the basis of the findings from the AI-readiness evaluation, organizations should generate a dynamic and flexible AI roadmap clearly defining the steps necessary for effective implementation. The drafted roadmap should include the development of action plans for management of data, training programs for employees, and upgradation in infrastructure.

3.5.4 Pilot and Iterate

Before the implementation of AI solutions, it is advisable to test the projects on a small scale to uncover the underlying issues and establish support. Feedback can be used to redefining the strategies before the final implementation is initiate. This can further be a cyclic process of inclusion of feedback and future improvements.

3.6 Real-Life Examples: Best Practices and Lessons Learned

Several businesses have positively arranged resources for AI implementation. The examples include:

3.6.1 Procter & Gamble (P&G): An example of Data-Driven Transformation

P&G is a worldwide leader in consumer goods, and its methodology to AI adoption proves as a yardstick for other organizations. P&G held a widespread readiness assessment which focused on data availability and amalgamation. In the first instance P&G build a unified platform for data which was followed by data finding from various sources thereby enabling the AI algorithms to evaluate the dynamics of supply chain and customer behaviour effectively.

After successful assessment of existing state of being, P&G then continued with assessing the existing skill-set of the workforce in the areas of data science and AI and then comparing the outcomes with the required skill-sets, thus identifying the skills gaps. Such skills gaps were filled by launching the training and development programmes. Through this attempt of creating the AI enabled workforce P&G could achieve its strategic goals and at the same time its workforce achieved goals congruence. AI driven solutions like predictive-analysis and personalized marketing campaigns gave an edge to P&G over its competitors. This ultimately contributed in improved efficiency and revenue growth of the organization.

3.6.2 BMW: Example of building AI Competencies for Predictive Maintenance

AI readiness drive of BMW focused on enhancing its technical infrastructure by developing AI savvy proficient workforce through upskilling them through specialized training programmes. It adopted AI effectively for maintaining the manufacturing plants by identifying the defects in and improving the assembly line. BMW also gave preference to incorporating the predictive analysis, cloud based platforms and backing up the AI systems with the cutting-edge networking capabilities for dropping the equipment downtime and increasing the organizational productivity.

3.6.3 HSBC: Example of enhancing Fraud Detection with AI

HSBC is an example of focused data security and data compliance. Priority was given to real-time detection of fraudulent events through large volumes of transaction data. HSBC modernized the data infrastructure by adopting to the cloud-based solutions for data security. Well established AI governance policies also regulated the usage of data thereby maintaining the data transparency and data fairness. With adoption of AI in operational processes, HSBC could achieve detection of frauds, reduction of losses and enhancing customer trust.

4. DEVELOPING A STRATEGIC ROADMAP FOR AI IMPLEMENTATION

By incorporating the new technologies into the business, organizations need to carefully plan their strategies to ensure smooth functioning of the process. This section discusses in detail the necessary steps required for creating an integration plan, which includes setting the timelines, deciding Key Performance Indicators, managing risks, introducing pilot projects and their strategies.

4.1 Establishing the Foundation for AI Integration

Laying a strong foundation involves aligning AI initiatives with business objectives (Chui et al., 2018). The following things to be involved:

- **Setting Strategic Objectives:** Organization need to decide their objectives like, increase customer trust, improving the operation process, and their revenue growth. Through this initiatives business can ensure that new technologies add value and drive their growth.
- **Assembling a Cross-Functional Team:** To incorporate the different team for planning and execution, such as Marketing, Finance, IT, Human Resources and Operations for their point of view and expertise to take a decision.

4.2 Guidance of Step-by-Step to Developing the AI Integration Roadmap

A step-by-step approach ensures systematic AI integration (Davenport & Ronanki, 2018). Creating a roadmap involves several crucial steps to see the successful implementation.

Step 1: Evaluate Current Capabilities

In the beginning phase business should assess their current digital reliability. It includes data validity, clarity, system and skilled employees. This evaluation helps to identify any discrepancies that need to be remove before implementation.

- Readiness of Data: For smooth functioning of the processes, company should have access to sufficient quality data for smooth functioning of AI systems.
- System Assessment: Evaluate the current IT systems to ensure that they can support the new technologies like, Cloud computing platforms and solution of data storage.
- Assess the Workforce: By assessing the existing knowledge and skills of the workforce companies can determine the gaps existing the level digital literacy of workforce. This will help organizations to identify the training required to build the necessary capabilities for AI implementation.Step 2: Define Key Performance Indicators (KPIs)

Establishing KPIs necessary for monitoring the success of initiatives. These indicators should align with the business's strategic goals and be measurable and actionable. Some of the examples of KPIs for projects include:

- **Level of Customer Satisfaction:** For the objectives of an applications to enhancing customer experience, tracking customer satisfaction and retention rates can reflect the effectiveness of these solutions.
- **Metrics of Operational Efficiency:** By Tracking the process efficiency and its cost savings can help measure the impact of business operations.
- **Increase the Revenue Growth:** Through Monitoring the revenue from innovations, like new products or services, it can showcase the direct financial impact of these initiatives.

Step 3: Develop a Phased Timeline

A draftly roadmap needs a phased timeline that supports continuous implementation and regular scaling. The timeline should be realistic, with clearly defined milestones, pilot phases, and full deployment stages.

- **Initial Testing Phase:** To Begin with small-scale projects that are compare to low-risk and provide valuable learning opportunities. This approach enables businesses to test the reliability and effectiveness of solutions without major changes to current operations.
- **Review and Refinement:** After the initial testing phase, review the results, if requires refine the strategy, and expand based on the insights gained. This approach helps reducing the risks and ensures that whatever solutions are there it will be optimized before full-scale deployment.
- **Complete Rollout:** When the initial projects have proven successful, businesses can go ahead for the full-scale implementation. This phase involves monitoring ongoing performance.

Step 4: Implement Risk Management Strategies

When any new technology is implemented, various risks will arise such as data privacy concerns, technological challenges, and operational issues. To overcome these challenges business should create a risk management strategy.

- Recognizing Potential of Risk: Identify potential risks such as data breaches, system fraud, or resistance to change within the organization.
- Adaption Strategies: Adopt strategies like improving cybersecurity protocols, establishing contingency plans for system, and giving the training to employee to overcome this challenge.
- Continuous Oversight: By continuously supervising the system issues in performance can be detect and addressed promptly, thereby minimizing their impact on business operations.

4.3 Strategies for Pilot Projects and Phased Deployment

Introducing new technologies into a business it requires a careful approach to minimize risk. By implementing pilot projects and phased deployment strategies, organizations can test and refine solutions before full-scale implementation.

4.3.1 Pilot Projects

Pilot projects help in testing AI applications before full-scale deployment (Shrestha et al., 2019). To operative the Pilot Project following key are required to be present.

- **Choose an area of Pilot:** Select a business area or process where new technologies can offer significant value with minimal risk. Say for example, testing a recommendation engine in a specific product category allows you to evaluate its effectiveness without impacting the entire product line.
- **Define the objectives of Pilot:** Define the clear objectives and success criteria for the pilot, like increasing customer satisfaction, enhancing efficiency, and increasing sales. This approach helps assess the pilot's impact and determine its effectiveness.
- **Collection and Analysis of Data:** Collect the data during the pilot phase and assess the performance of the new solution. Use this data to make informed decisions and necessary adjustments for respective divisions.

4.3.2 Phased Deployment

Phased deployment strategies involve gradually rolling out new solutions in stages to manage risk and enhance learning.

- **Expansion Gradually:** Begin by implementing new solutions in a single business unit or location, then gradually expand to other areas based on the success of the initial phase.
- **Process of Feedback:** Initiate a feedback process to collect insights from each deployment stage. This iterative method enables the business to refine its strategy and enhance the solution's effectiveness before broader implementation.
- **Arrangements of Training Programs:** Implement training programs for employees at each stage to develop their skills with new systems, confirmed that they can effectively use and manage the new technologies.

4.4 High-Impact Use Cases for AI Integration

To maximize the impact of integrating new technologies, businesses should concentrate on use cases that provide substantial value. Some of the Examples of high-impact use included:

4.4.1 Personalization of Customer

New technologies can greatly improve customer experience by personalizing interfaces and recommendations based on customer choices and behaviour. This can include:

- **Intelligent Virtual Assistants:** Chatbots that offer real-time information and personalized assistance can enhance customer satisfaction.
- **Personalized Suggestion Systems:** Personalized suggestion systems can analyze customer data to customize products and services according to individual preferences, thereby increasing sales and enhancing customer engagement.

4.4.2 Operations Optimization

New technologies can streamline and enhance business operations, resulting in greater efficiency and cost savings.

- **Maintenance of Forecasting:** New technologies can forecast equipment failures and optimize maintenance schedules, minimizing disruptions and enhancing productivity.
- **Optimization of Supply Chain Process:** Advanced models can analyze supply chain data to enhance inventory management, optimize shipping routes, demand forecast, and increase operational efficiency.

4.4.3 Resource Management

Applications in resource management allow businesses to optimize the use of human and financial resources.

- **Scheduling of Workforce:** AI Algorithms can automate workforce scheduling, be sure that employees are assigned based on requirement and skill sets.
- **Strategic Financial Management:** For improving financial performance this models can forecast cash flow, oversee investments, and streamline budgeting processes.

5. AI-POWERED BUSINESS MODEL INNOVATION

AI has added value to the entire business ecosystem by expediting the processes of new product development and generation of new business and service models. By taking advantage of various data insights and automation, firms can innovate and acclimatize for meeting the evolving customer needs and opening new market opportunities, eventually leading to growth and competitive advantage.

5.1 Identifying New Market Opportunities

AI structures play a vital part in detecting new market prospects by scrutinizing huge quantities of data related to the trends in the market and behaviour of customers. Through predictive analytics, organizations can foresee the changes in customers' inclinations and proactively that may lead to development of a new idea. This data-driven approach can allow firms to be ahead of market alterations and exploit the new opportunities for growth.

Organization like Procter & Gamble (P&G), has maximized the benefits of AI-driven consumer insights for staying competitive in the changing times, by assessing the inclinations and buying patterns of the customers. Insights received through such intervention are incorporated into the product development process for encountering the developing consumer demands. By aligning the product development with customer demands, the organization has successfully managed to maintain its leading position in the dynamic marketplace there by improving dexterity and receptiveness to customer demands.

5.2 Developing Innovative Products and Services

In the dynamic time, AI has enabled invention of intelligent products and services acclimatizing the customer requirements. AI has enabled new novel product ranges in various categories such as automated and self-directed vehicles, custom-made healthcare solutions, smart home appliances etc. which has enriched the customer experiences by staying economical.

Tesla is one of the leading example of innovative products the automobile industry. The organization uses AI to augment the proficiencies of its electric vehicles, proposing structures like self-directed driving, concurrent navigation, and wireless software updates. These updates constantly develop vehicle performance and consumer experience without needing physical changes to the car. Tesla's AI assimilation not only separates it from old-fashioned automakers but also allows it to lead the way in the rapidly changing electric vehicle market. By taking the benefits of AI,

Tesla offers advanced solutions that suffices the contemporary customer outlooks for technology-driven accessibility and security.

5.3 Optimizing Operations for Profitability

AI solutions improves operating efficacy, decreases costs, and improves profitability across industries. (Bughin et al. 2018). By mechanizing procedures like scheduling of resources, optimization of logistics, and maintenance with predictive analytics, AI maximizes the utilization of assets and streamlines the workflows. For instance, DHL delpoys AI for predictive route optimization, reducing fuel consumption and planning efficient delivery routes, times, and costs. AI-driven predictive maintenance checks equipment breakdowns and minimizes downtime and expenses. These illustrations highlight the potential of AI to advance operations, boost resource allocation and lead profitability.

6. DESIGNING AN AI-CENTRIC ORGANIZATIONAL CULTURE

To achieve significant change, organizations should build a culture that values learning, inspiring innovative ideas and support their collaboration across different departments. By creating this kind of environment employees can explore the new tools, utilize the variety of skills and accept the technological changes, and become successful by completing the projects and increasing the growth of business.

Google demonstrates awareness of this approach by offering the internal education through workshops, online courses and hands on training. These creativities help employees to gain deep knowledge regrading new tools and practical application to promote a culture of research and innovation. Google not only equip its workforce by continuous learning but also create a more opportunities for their employee to handle any challenges or task easily.

6.1 Helping Collaboration Across Departments

Successful implementation of new technologies demands collaboration across all departments (Davenport & Ronanki, 2018). New technologies will benefit different departments like IT, Finance, Marketing, Operations by aligning with their business goals

The innovation Lab of Unilever has brought together the data scientists, strategies planners and the marketing and supply chain managers to develop new solutions. Unilever ensures that the new technology implementation has benefited to various functions. This has helped to enhance marketing campaigns that ensures personalized customer experience, and has optimized supply chain process through improved demand predictions and logistics management.

These strategies have boosted the efficiency of operations and increased customer satisfaction. The success of Unilever demonstrates how organization can achieve the significant result with diverse skills and view points in cross functional teams leading to effective decision making.

6.2 Forming Ethical Guidelines and Governance

Establishing ethical guidelines and governance is crucial for nurturing responsible AI use (Diaz-Rodriguez et al. 2023). Organizations need to prioritize preferences, data transparency and privacy by establishing the strong governance framework. For example, ethics boards can oversee the initiatives to ensure that they comply with standards and requirements as per the regulatory. Provide guidance to avoid the projects risks such as biased algorithms or privacy breaches. Let's take one another example of ethics board of IBM, it ensures data privacy, transparency and clarity in developing phase. To incorporate the ethical guidelines into projects, it will be help to build a trust with customers and stakeholders.

7. COMPETITIVE ADVANTAGES OF AI-POWERED BUSINESS MODELS

There are various benefits associated with incorporating AI into business models. AI integration leads to better decision making based on data-driven insights and the operational efficiency can also be improved by systematizing the processes with AI intervention. Organizations can also benefit from customised consumer engagement by moulding the customer experiences as per their needs and preferences. Such benefits enable the organizations to remain efficient in the dynamic competitive world and respond efficiently to growing market demands.

7.1 Enhanced Decision-Making Capabilities

Intervention of AI in various organizational processes is also justified due to its ability to process vast amount of real-time data sets and provide actionable insights and more learned choices adding in rapid strategic and operational decision making. (Lansiti & Lakhani, 2020). AI tools supporting natural language processing, machine learning and predictive analytics are proving extremely helpful in expedited, accurate and informed decision making. (Bughin et al., 2018). In the critical sectors such as finance AI can do wonders. Company like JPMorgan Chase uses AI in various ways such as assessing the market data, forecasting the trends, recognizing the future prospects, making rapid, strategic investment decisions with effective risk management. By including AI in decision making practices, JPMorgan won a competitive advantage due to monitored compliance and operative effectiveness. Inclusion of AI also improved the outcomes that drove profitability and reduced risks for JPMorgon in the dynamic data driven environments.

7.2 Efficiency and Cost Reduction

AI interventions have refined the efficacy of jobs by decreasing the costs of routine activities. This has resulted in huge savings in terms of time and resources. In the sectors such as retail, manufacturing and supply chain and logistics, AI has proven very effective. AI has enhanced the functioning of various processes by reducing the labour-intensive interference, refinement of workflows, optimization of resource allocations, resulting in faster cycles of production with minimum or zero defects or errors and considerable cost savings. (Dhamija et al., 2021)

Foxconn, a universal electronics manufacturer has integrated AI into its assemble lines. With the AI driven robotics repetitive tasks related to the product placements, operations and quality control etc. are now being taken care with minimum human interventions. AI-driven automation has decreased Foxconn's dependence on physical labour which resulted in considerable savings in labour costs, improved speed of manufacturing processes and augmented accuracies leading to lowered deficiencies and increased quality outcomes.

Automation of monotonous repetitive operational tasks at Foxconn has provided its workforce with room for more concentrated efforts. Employees could focus on more multifarious and ingenious tasks, leading to creative invention within the organization. With the help of AI, Foxconn has scaled its processes more effectively by meeting the increased customer demands and at the same time managing the operational costs. Foxconn is a best example of organization leveraging the power of AI for cost reduction, operational excellence, and a competitive market leader in the dynamic times.

7.3 Personalized Customer Engagement

AI has provided an opportunity to customers for personalization by evaluating and assessing the customer behaviour, identifying their choices through carefully studying the history of the purchases made in past. This tailor-made experience is very well accepted by the customers. AI-enabled suggestion or recommendation engines, chatbots and customer segmentation models are successful in enhancing the customer loyalty and satisfaction. (Chatterjee et al., 2021). The hyper-personalized marketing is possible due to real-time data analysis of customer behaviour and preferences. (Westerman et al., 2014).

An international beauty retailors named Sephora, could successfully demonstrate the customer satisfaction with the use of AI chatbots which guides customers in product selection and understanding their priorities, history and beauty routines. This has resulted in enriching the purchase experience of customers though expansion of Sephora's insights into their customer requirements. Improvement in sales is also attributed to significant personalized relationships maintained by Sephora, its customer ecstasy and retention.

8. CHALLENGES IN AI-POWERED BUSINESS TRANSFORMATION

Introducing new technology in the business leads to the challenges like accuracy of data, high level quality, managing these things into the existing systems. By helping the workforce incorporate the new technological process, will address these challenges with proper planning and check on the employee training and proper data management.

8.1 Management of Data and Issue of Quality

The main challenges in AI implementation is data management and quality of data. Artificial Intelligence depends on the data for proper training and their operation. If the quality of data was poor, then it's effect on the process of decision making.

To solve this issue, organization must establish a strong storage of data structure. These data structure includes the data repository, security, policy to evaluate the data. Based on the data framing the quality standard and conducting regular audit. During that process, system can easily bifurcate the high level quality data.

By incorporating effective data management, organizations can improve the consistency of their systems and generate clear data. This will help to take better decision and increase organization output.

8.2 Integration Complexity

Integration complexity is a important challenge when including AI into existing systems, because there are many changes into the existing system. Organization need to ensure that new technologies are comfortable with existing systems to protect discrepancies in operation process.

The experience of Walmart highlights that the challenges of incorporating the new technologies into the existing system. When the company objective to implement advanced logistic systems, it may be faced the challenges in integrating the new technologies with its existing operations. To address these challenges, Walmart took a continuous approach, starting from smaller pilot project to check the technology in a controlled setting. This approach allowed Walmart to identify issues and resolve them before expanding the new systems.

By systematically applying the pilot projects, Walmart was able to refine its integration process, ensuring that the new systems worked smoothly with their existing system. This approach not only reduced challenges but also maximized effectiveness of new technologies in increasing logistics efficiency, indirectly its leading to improved outcomes.

8.3 Resistance and Adaptation of Workforce

When we are adopting AI technology some of the common challenges are there like Resistance and adaption of workforce. Due to new technology arrival employees are worried about their job security. This impact on overall successful for implementation of AI in the business.

To incorporate these point business should arrange a training programme for employees to used that technology for better usage of resources. After successfully completed hands on training, employees build a confidence to use the AI technology. It is also required the clear communication when used the AI. Employers should highlight how technology can play job roles, simple tasks and create new opportunity for personal as well as professional growth.

By creating an environment where in which employees feel that technology as a helpful tool rather than fear, organization can remove resistance and develop a culture of innovation and collaboration. So this practical approach not only make it easier for employees to apply new technology but also empowers change and increase the demands of job.

9. ETHICAL CONSIDERATIONS AND GOVERNANCE IN AI INTEGRATION

In order to safeguard the responsible usage of AI, the organizations must incorporate AI into its models only after ensuring the ethical deliberations that needs to be addressed. Few of the key issues deals with factors like privacy and transparency of data and algorithmic bias which arises due to the accidental propagation of AI systems or intensification of the prevailing group biases. This results in an unfair judgment against certain clusters. This can further results in weakening of trust in AI technologies and consequently leading to damaged business brand.

For the dependency of AI systems on huge data which is individual specific and sensitive and is used for operations and training, data privacy becomes more serious issue to be addressed. Sound steps for protection of data is the only available solution for the businesses so as to protect the users' information. This requirement should be fulfilled by the concerned regulatory bodies. If the organizations fail to prioritize data privacy, this can lead to legal penalties and damaged of consumers trust.

Data transparency is also crucial in AI integration. Businesses should endeavour to make AI decision making methods comprehensible to customers and the business stakeholders. This involves giving clear information about operations of algorithms, the data being used, and the justification and rational for the decision made by them. Such transparent behaviour will foster accountability and will allow for informed public discourse around AI technologies.

To deal with such ethical concerns, businesses should document clear ethical guidelines and frameworks of governance that will always outline the organization's commitments to the responsible usage of AI. These structures should involve the doctrines for impartiality, responsibility, transparency, and instructions for observing compliance and handling the ethical apprehensions. Giving priority to ethical deliberations in integration of AI, businesses can develop trust with its stakeholders, improve the reputation of brand, and contribute to a better reasonable and accountable AI landscape.

9.1 Addressing Algorithmic Bias

Algorithmic bias in AI structures can result in prejudicial consequences, most often because of biased training data that replicates societal biases. Instances such as, recruitment processes which are AI enabled can have differentiation on the basis of ethnicity or gender of the applicants if biased data is used. The outcomes of such biased algorithms always leads to discriminatory outcomes. It can also lead to systematic inequalities if not managed carefully. (Mittelstadt et. al., 2016). In order to manage such issues, organizations should adopt to huge intensive datasets that highlights the numerous demographic details and consistently assess the AI systems for identification of biases. In order to mitigate the biases, fair algorithms that incorporated the proper ethical frameworks into the machine learning should be designed. (Binns, 2018). Market leaders such as Microsoft and Google are having established structures and procedures for collecting and evaluating data leading to confirmation of justice. This emphasizes the need of addressing the issues associates with algorithmic bias for developing inclusive and trustworthy AI solutions resulting into accountability and fair treatment for all users.

9.2 Data Privacy and Security

With the adoption of AI systems in workplace, one of the most important concerns for all organizations is data privacy and data security, due to the reason that AI systems progressively gathers and processes huge amount of personal data. (Floridi & Cowls, 2019). As large quantities of personal sensitive and transactional information are stored for analysis and insights, the concerns about user's consent, data protection and data risks for any possibility of data breach needs to be taken care of. Here the role played by authorities such as the General Data Protection Regulation (GDPR) become very crucial for regulatory compliance with frameworks. Non-compliance in such cases can lead to serious consequences such as financial losses and damage to the reputation of businesses. (European Commission, 2020).

9.3 Transparency and Accountability

In order to achieve the effective collaboration and develop trust between humans and machine, it is very important to maintain transparency and accountability in AI structures. (Jobin et al., 2019). Awareness of processes of decision making by AI systems among users is required, more precisely in the critical fields such as law enforcement, finance, healthcare etc. In the absence of the awareness of functioning of automated systems, customers may develop scepticism for the output generated by AI and can resist its usage in future failing to understand the benefits of these technologies.

The transparency of functioning of AI systems can be achieved through proper documentation depicting the traceability of AI models and its processes. (Floridi & Cowls, 2019). For this, detailed records of data source, algorithms and the entire decision making process with the use of AI systems should be carefully documented. Only through this mechanism, the organizations will be in positions to provide proper insights for the route taken by the AI models to recommend any particular decision or path of action.

Firm like IBM Watson Health, are no more an exception to this. This organization has taken remarkable pathways for achieving and maintaining the transparency of data in its AI models. The organization is always in position to provide a detailed *transparency records* about the patient's diagnosis and the plan of treatment that outlines the base for recommendations by the AI systems, enabling its important clients in the healthcare industry to understand the logic behind the recommended AI-driven decision. Such level of transparent communications has fostered the trust among IBM Watson Health's clients and users and has improved their confidence level in the usage of AI tools in cases where decision making is very crucial.

Furthermore, transparency boosts ethical AI processes and practices, as it enables the stakeholders to recognize the hidden biases or errors in AI systems. Through transparency and accountability, the organizations can build the trust and can improve the overall efficiency and acceptance of AI technologies in various field, resulting in more informed decision making and enhanced outputs.

10. REAL-WORLD CASE STUDIES OF AI-POWERED BUSINESS MODEL TRANSFORMATION

This overview highlights real-world case studies showcasing the successful integration of AI into business models, leading to substantial growth and enhanced efficiency.

10.1 Amazon's AI-Driven Fulfilment Centers

Amazon's fulfilment centers utilize automation to streamline sorting, packaging, and delivery. Advanced technologies like robotics and forecasting analytics boost efficiency, cut costs, and speed up operations, especially during peak seasons like Black Friday (Amazon, 2023). Robots handle repetitive tasks, reducing injuries and allowing employees to focus on complex duties (Dastin, 2021). Predictive tools help keep high-demand items in stock, minimizing delays and enhancing customer satisfaction (Chokshi, 2022). These innovations strengthen Amazon's market position and service quality, showcasing how technology transforms logistics. Overall, automation plays a crucial role in confirming timely, exact, and cost-effective fulfilment processes.

10.2 Tesla's Autopilot and AI-Driven Innovation

Tesla's Autopilot represents a leap forward in autonomous driving technology. By leveraging advanced systems and sensor data, Tesla cars can skilfully navigate traffic, change tracks, and manage complex road scenarios. The combination of real-time data from cameras, radar, and other sensors allows for quick decision-making, enhancing both safety and proficiency (Hawkins, 2021). Features such as automatic emergency braking and impact avoidance provide added protection for drivers, setting new benchmarks in the automotive industry (Lambert, 2023). Moreover, smart energy management helps extend battery life, promoting sustainable transportation. Tesla's regular software updates ensure that their vehicles stay at the forefront of technological advancements, solidifying their position as leaders in next-gen mobility.

10.3 Alibaba's AI-Powered E-commerce Ecosystem

Alibaba has transformed its e-commerce ecosystem by leveraging advanced technologies to improve logistics, customer service, and modified shopping experiences. By analysing real-time data, the policy can expect customer needs and streamline supply chain operations (Ni, 2022). Efficient inventory and shipping management, driven by demand forecasting and optimized delivery routes, are particularly evident during major events like Singles' Day. Virtual assistants efficiently handle customer inquiries, providing tailored support and product recommendations (Fannin, 2021). These innovations enable Alibaba to achieve quicker order fulfilment and greater personalization, distinguishing it in the global market and creating a scalable, future-ready retail model.

10.4 Arya.ag: AI-Driven AgriTech SME Transformation

Arya.ag, a New Delhi-based agri-tech company, transformed its business model by leveraging technology to simplify the post-harvest supply chain. Initially focusing on warehousing services, Arya expanded its offerings to include digital solutions like price forecast tools, risk valuation for loans, and a platform connecting farmers directly with buyers. Such a digital-change has lead into enhancement of reliability of operations, reduction in losses after the harvest is done, better financial accesses to farmers. This resulted in the success of Arya.ag as an important player in India's agri-business ecosystem (Arya.ag, n.d.).

11. EMERGING TRENDS AND THE FUTURE OF AI IN BUSINESS

AI has advanced rapidly after the onset of 21st century, and has provided huge amount of opportunities and challenges for organizations to stand in the dynamic world. Still with every day we can observe the changing faces and forms of AI which has impacted all sectors. Emerging trends are prominently visible in the form of automation, various software, natural language processing, data analytics and predictive analytics with a high regards to customer experience and data transparency and fairness.

AI can be seen integrating with the new technologies like IoT and block chain which enables the data collection in the real-times through improved transparency of supply chain. At one hand the companies are getting acclimatized with the issues like data security, quality, and ethics, and on other they have started focusing on leveraging full potential of AI and creating the innovation-driven culture.

11.1 Generative AI for Product Development

Fashion industry in no exception to adoption of generative AI. Atomization can be seen in prototyping and data-driven creativity for product modification or new product introduction. Generative AI tools like GPT and other generative models and applications are assisting to analyse the customer trends and generate customized designs.

Companies like Nike, uses generative AI to produce creative design for tailoring customized preferences. Though generative AI multiple creative designs can be created within fraction of times. It becomes better and better with collaborations with multiple teams working together on a single concept at the same time. By incorporating all thoughts into the prompt the creativity can take shape in the form of a new design. This has reduced the time of design-to-market cycle by improving the iteration rate based on real-time data.

11.2 AI in Edge Computing and IoT

The speed of decision-making is improved with the combination of AI with edge computing and IoT. The AI in edge devices have reduced the dependency on the cloud servers and can process the data locally and can be effective in time savings, mostly required in logistics and manufacturing industry.

Organization like Siemens, uses AI-powered edge computing for monitoring the machinery in real-time, with the help of embedded AI algorithms sensor data can be analysed for anomalies detection and required measures can be taken in real-time, thereby reducing the downtime and supporting quality production with operational reliability.

12. CONCLUSION

Transformative potential of AI is now being known to the world. Industries across the world have started capitalizing on the power of AI and at the same time is now preparing itself for meeting the ever changing demands. Realising the full benefits of AI requires more strategic approach.

Organizations should carefully all resources and establish the necessary flexible technological infrastructure. The focus should also be on developing the AI-enabled workforce and developing AI-driven mind-set. Additionally, companies should always be ready to address key ethical issues, such as data privacy and data bias, so as to ensure responsible and transparent usage. By implementation these strategies, organizations can position themselves as leaders in the driven future. They will not only gain a competitive edge through innovative products, services, and customer experiences but also ensure sustainable growth. As AI continues to evolve, those organizations that prioritize thoughtful implementation and ethical considerations will stand out, shaping industries and driving long-term success in the powered economy.

REFERENCES

Accenture. (2021). AI: Built to Scale – Unleashing the Power of AI across the Enterprise. https://www.accenture.com

Aeon, X. Digital. (n.d.). How Gopal Namkeen modernized its order processing system to improve dealer experience. https://www.aeonx.digital/how-gopal-namkeen-modernized-its-order-processing-system-to-improve-dealer-experience

Agrawal, A., Gans, J., & Goldfarb, A. (2018). *Prediction Machines: The Simple Economics of Artificial Intelligence*. Harvard Business Review Press.

Amazon. (2023). How Amazon fulfilment centers work. Amazon. https://www.aboutamazon.com/news/operations/how-amazon-fulfillment-centers-work

Amershi, S.. (2019). Guidelines for Human-AI Interaction. *CHI Conference on Human Factors in Computing Systems*. DOI: 10.1145/3290605.3300233

Arya.ag. (n.d.). *Arya agri-tech solutions.* Retrieved from https://www.arya.ag

Binns, R. (2018). Fairness in machine learning: Lessons from political philosophy. *Proceedings of the 2018 Conference on Fairness, Accountability and Transparency*, 149–159. DOI: 10.1145/3287560.3287598

Bock, L. (2015). *Work Rules!* Insights from Inside Google That Will Transform How You Live and Lead. Twelve.

Brynjolfsson, E., & McAfee, A. (2017). The Business of Artificial Intelligence: The Next Frontier for Competition. Harvard Business Review.

Brynjolfsson, E., & McAfee, A. (2017). *Machine, platform, crowd: Harnessing our digital future*. W. W. Norton & Company.

Bughin, J., Hazan, E., Ramaswamy, S., Chui, M., Allas, T., Dahlström, P., & Trench, M. (2017). *Artificial Intelligence: The Next Digital Frontier?* McKinsey Global Institute.

Bughin, J., Hazan, E., Ramaswamy, S., Chui, M., Allas, T., Dahlström, P., . . . Trench, M. (2017). Artificial Intelligence: The Next Digital Frontier? McKinsey & Company. https://www.mckinsey.com

Bughin, J., Seong, J., Manyika, J., Chui, M., & Joshi, R. (2018). Notes from the AI frontier: Modeling the impact of AI on the world economy. McKinsey Global Institute. https://www.mckinsey.com

Chatterjee, S., Rana, N. P., Tamilmani, K., & Sharma, A. (2021). The future of AI and customer engagement: A study of predictive customer behavior using machine learning. *Journal of Business Research, 124*, 353–365. DOI: 10.1016/j.jbusres.2020.11.048

Chen, H., Chiang, R. H. L., & Storey, V. C. (2012). Business Intelligence and Analytics: From Big Data to Big Impact. *Management Information Systems Quarterly, 36*(4), 1165–1188. DOI: 10.2307/41703503

Chokshi, N. (2022, November 25). How Amazon's logistics empire is preparing for Black Friday. The New York Times. https://www.nytimes.com/2022/11/25/business/amazon-black-friday.html

Chui, M., Harryson, M., Manyika, J., Roberts, R., Chung, R., van Heteren, A., & Nel, P. (2018). Applying artificial intelligence for social good. McKinsey & Company. https://www.mckinsey.com

Chui, M., & Malhotra, S. (2018). *AI adoption advances, but foundational barriers remain*. McKinsey & Company.

Coughlin, R. (2022). Designing Ethical AI Systems for the Future of Business. In Ethical, A. I. (Ed.), *Principles and Practice*. Springer.

Dastin, J. (2021, June 13). Amazon unveils warehouse robots to reduce workplace injuries. Reuters. https://www.reuters.com/technology/amazon-unveils-warehouse-robots-reduce-workplace-injuries-2021-06-13/

Daugherty, P., & Wilson, H. J. (2018). *Human + Machine: Reimagining Work in the Age of AI*. Harvard Business Review Press.

Davenport, T. H., & Ronanki, R. (2018). Artificial intelligence for the real world. *Harvard Business Review, 96*(1), 108–116.

Deloitte. (2023). State of AI in the Enterprise – 5th Edition. https://www.deloitte.comUse Case Examples & Business Practices

Deng, L., & Yu, D. (2014). Deep Learning: Methods and Applications. *Foundations and Trends in Signal Processing, 7*(3–4), 197–387. DOI: 10.1561/2000000039

Dhamija, P., Bag, S., & Debnath, R. M. (2021). Artificial intelligence (AI)-based digital transformation and dynamic capabilities: Mediating role of organizational agility. *Technological Forecasting and Social Change, 166*, 120636. DOI: 10.1016/j.techfore.2021.120636

Díaz-Rodríguez, N., López-Pernas, S., & Hernández-Leo, D. (2023). Responsible AI: Ethical principles and guidelines. *AI & Society, 38*(1), 12–28. DOI: 10.1007/s00146-023-01586-5

European Commission. (2020). *Ethics guidelines for trustworthy AI.* High-Level Expert Group on AI. https://digital-strategy.ec.europa.eu/en/library/ethics-guidelines-trustworthy-ai

Fannin, R. (2021, November 11). *How Alibaba redefined Singles' Day—and what it means for global e-commerce. Forbes.* https://www.forbes.com/sites/rebeccafannin/2021/11/11/how-alibaba-redefined-singles-day-and-what-it-means-for-global-e-commerce/

Floridi, L., & Cowls, J. (2019). A unified framework of five principles for AI in society. *Harvard Data Science Review, 1*(1). Advance online publication. DOI: 10.1162/99608f92.8cd550d1

Gartner. (2023). Top Strategic Technology Trends for 2024. https://www.gartner.com

Gil, D., Hobson, S., Mojsilović, A., Puri, R., & Smith, J R. (2019, September 22). AI for Management: An Overview. Springer Nature, 3-19. DOI: 10.1007/978-3-030-20680-2_1

Google Cloud. (2021). Edge AI and IoT: Transforming Industry. https://cloud.google.com/blogs, Books & Book Chapters

Gopal Snacks Pvt. Ltd. (n.d.). Infrastructure. https://gspl.7technosoftsolutions.com/infrastructure

Haenlein, M., Kaplan, A., Tan, C. W., & Zhang, P. (2023). Artificial Intelligence in Business: Myths, Ethics, and Reality. *Business Horizons, 66*(1), 85–96. DOI: 10.1016/j.bushor.2022.07.003

Hawkins, A. J. (2021, October 20). *Tesla's Full Self-Driving beta is here, and it's terrifying. The Verge.* https://www.theverge.com/2021/10/20/22735673/tesla-full-self-driving-beta-safety-issues

Heyn, H. M., Mohr, D., Neugebauer, R., Schumacher, A., & Weking, J. (2021). AI readiness in manufacturing—Toward a maturity model. *Procedia CIRP, 104*, 1256–1261. DOI: 10.1016/j.procir.2021.11.211

Hiniduma, T. A., Nguyen, T. H., & Dhinakaran, A. (2024). A strategic framework for evaluating AI readiness in SMEs. *Journal of Business Research, 172*, 114016. DOI: 10.1016/j.jbusres.2023.114016

Iansiti, M., & Lakhani, K. R. (2020). *Competing in the Age of AI: Strategy and Leadership When Algorithms and Networks Run the World*. Harvard Business Review Press.

IBM. (2022). AI and Ethics in Business: A Responsible Approach. https://www.ibm.com/research

Jobin, A., Ienca, M., & Vayena, E. (2019). The global landscape of AI ethics guidelines. *Nature Machine Intelligence*, *1*(9), 389–399. DOI: 10.1038/s42256-019-0088-2

Jordan, M. I., & Mitchell, T. M. (2015). Machine learning: Trends, perspectives, and prospects. *Science*, *349*(6245), 255–260. DOI: 10.1126/science.aaa8415 PMID: 26185243

Kordon, A K. (2020, August 1). Applied Artificial Intelligence-Based Systems as Competitive Advantage. DOI: 10.1109/IS48319.2020.9200097

Kumar, V., Dixit, A., Javalgi, R. G., & Dass, M. (2016). Digital transformation of business-to-business marketing: Framework and research agenda. *Journal of Business and Industrial Marketing*, *31*(8), 1151–1160. DOI: 10.1108/JBIM-12-2016-0276

Lambert, F. (2023, February 13). *Tesla pushes new safety features with software update. Electrek*. https://electrek.co/2023/02/13/tesla-pushes-new-safety-features-software-update/

Lee, J., Suh, T., Roy, D., & Baucus, M S. (2019, September 1). Emerging Technology and Business Model Innovation: The Case of Artificial Intelligence. Springer Science+Business Media, 5(3), 44-44. https://doi.org/DOI: 10.3390/joitmc5030044

Makridakis, S., Spiliotis, E., & Assimakopoulos, V. (2018). Statistical and Machine Learning forecasting methods: Concerns and ways forward. *PLoS One*, *13*(3), e0194889. DOI: 10.1371/journal.pone.0194889 PMID: 29584784

Marr, B. (2020). *Artificial Intelligence in Practice: How 50 Companies are Using AI to Grow Business and Solve Problems*. Wiley.

Microsoft. (2023). Generative AI: The Next Frontier in Product Innovation. https://www.microsoft.com

Mikalef, P., Krogstie, J., Pappas, I. O., & Giannakos, M. (2018). Investigating the effects of big data analytics capabilities on firm performance: The mediating role of dynamic capabilities. *Information & Management*, *55*(8), 103176. DOI: 10.1016/j.im.2018.03.004

Mittelstadt, B. D., Allo, P., Taddeo, M., Wachter, S., & Floridi, L. (2016). The ethics of algorithms: Mapping the debate. *Big Data & Society*, *3*(2), 1–21. DOI: 10.1177/2053951716679679

Mittelstadt, B. D., Allo, P., Taddeo, M., Wachter, S., & Floridi, L. (2016). The ethics of algorithms: Mapping the debate. *Big Data & Society*, *3*(2), 1–21. DOI: 10.1177/2053951716679679

Ni, V. (2022, July 14). *Inside Alibaba's tech-driven e-commerce empire. The Guardian*. https://www.theguardian.com/technology/2022/jul/14/inside-alibabas-tech-driven-e-commerce-empire

Nike. (2022). How AI is Changing the Future of Footwear. Nike Innovation Blog. https://news.nike.com

Open, A. I. (2023). Introducing GPT-4 Technical Report. https://openai.com/research/gpt-4

Poalelungi, D. G., Mu at, C. L., Fulga, A., Neagu, M., Neagu, A., Piraianu, A. I., & Fulga, I. (2023, July 31). Advancing Patient Care: How Artificial Intelligence Is Transforming Healthcare. *Journal of Personalized Medicine*, *13*(8), 1214–1214. DOI: 10.3390/jpm13081214 PMID: 37623465

Raisch, S., & Krakowski, S. (2021). Artificial intelligence and management: The automation–augmentation paradox. *Academy of Management Review*, *46*(1), 192–210. DOI: 10.5465/amr.2018.0072

Ransbotham, S., Khodabandeh, S., Kiron, D., LaFountain, B., & Kiron, D. (2020). *The Cultural Benefits of Artificial Intelligence in the Enterprise*. MIT Sloan Management Review and Boston Consulting Group.

Russell, S., & Norvig, P. (2021). *Artificial Intelligence: A Modern Approach* (4th ed.). Pearson Education.

Shrestha, Y. R., Ben-Menahem, S. M., & von Krogh, G. (2019). Organizational Decision-Making Structures in the Age of Artificial Intelligence. *California Management Review*, *61*(4), 66–83. DOI: 10.1177/0008125619862257

Shrestha, Y. R., Ben-Menahem, S. M., & von Krogh, G. (2019). Organizational decision-making structures in the age of artificial intelligence. *California Management Review*, *61*(4), 66–83. DOI: 10.1177/0008125619862257

Siemens. (2022). AI at the Edge: Transforming Industrial Automation. Siemens Digital Industries. https://new.siemens.com

Smith, J. The Impact of AI on Business Models. Journal of Technology Management, 15, 45-62.

Teece, D. J. (2018). Business models and dynamic capabilities. *Long Range Planning*, *51*(1), 40–49. DOI: 10.1016/j.lrp.2017.06.007

Tegmark, M. (2017). *Life 3.0: Being Human in the Age of Artificial Intelligence.* Penguin.

Wagner, D N. (2020, March 27). Strategically managing the artificially intelligent firm. Emerald Publishing Limited, 48(3), 19-25. https://doi.org/DOI: 10.1108/SL-08-2019-0119

Westerman, G., Bonnet, D., & McAfee, A. (2014). *Leading Digital: Turning Technology into Business Transformation.* Harvard Business Review Press.

World Economic Forum. (2020). AI Governance: A Holistic Approach to Implement Ethics into AI. https://www.weforum.org

Zhang, Y.. (2021). Edge AI: On-Demand Deep Learning Model Co-Inference with Device-Edge Synergy. [Industry Reports & White Papers]. *ACM Transactions on Computer Systems*, *39*(1), 1–27.

Chapter 3
Machine Learning in Business Decision-Making

Fahad Maiyah M. Alshammari
https://orcid.org/0000-0003-2099-5802
School of Distance Education, Universiti Sains Malaysia, Malaysia

ABSTRACT

In this chapter we will discuss the collective impact of machine learning on business decision-making, this chapter emphasizes the capacity of AI to improve efficiency, increase accuracy, and provide better insights for business decision-making. It begins with the basics of machine learning principles; and discusses how organizations can use data-driven methods to improve decision-making processes and get advantages over other businesses. The major issues such as ethical implications. Data quality and technical complexities. In this chapter, we will also consider. Strategies for. Effective adoption of machine learning and highlighting the objectives and interdisciplinary collaborations For the implementation of machine learning in business decision-making and improving the existing models. The chapter then concludes by discussing the upcoming trends including automation and, integration of advanced technologies, etc.

1. INTRODUCTION

The use of machine learning in various fields is swiftly emerging as an important tool in the industry that allows organizations to use big data for informed and better decision-making. Machine learning is a tool of artificial intelligence that enables computers to detect patterns from the data make decisions and enhance their perfor-

DOI: 10.4018/979-8-3693-8960-7.ch003

mance over time without programming for each specific decision it learns from its experience and improve its performance over time. Machine learning automatically enhances its capacity of automation to adapt based on the data in commercial setups where markets and conditions rapidly change, they were increasing their accuracy and swiftness. (Kraus et al., 2020).

1.1. Machine Learning (ML) within a Business Framework

The major applications of machine learning in the corporate sector include product aggregations customer segmentations risk assessment and predictive maintenance. These models are classified into different categories namely supervised learning unsupervised learning and reinforcement learning the details of which are provided in Figure 1. Each of those learning techniques allows the firm to meet different challenges with efficiency while implying algorithms that are tailored to their specific requirements and data architectures. Brighton lighting the historical data machine learning can make firm decisions for the businesses that are strategically data-driven and custom to the patterns. (Kraus et al., 2020; Lee & Shin, 2020).

1.2. Impact of Machine Learning on Decision-Making Processes

Machine learning can transform the commercial business decision-making processes by shifting from dependence on various intuitions to a more data-driven and more analytical approach. Machine learning Organizations can analyze a large amount of yeah to reveal correlations, and highlight various patrons and abnormalities that normally cannot be detected by human perception. (Khosravi et al., 2019). For example, machine learning predictions can facilitate the anticipation of a consumer need by enabling businesses to and then modify their inventory or production. The algorithms of machine learning can understand user behaviors, and easily this jails insiders there can facilitate Super personalized marketing and better consumer support, the data-driven design and help reduce risks expedite the decision-making processes, and improve accuracy which enhances operational efficiency and profitability (de Laat, 2018).

1.3. Significance of Machine Learning for Competitive Edge and Operational Efficiency

The application of machine learning allows businesses to have a competitive advantage by changing the existing setups by proving operational efficiency and enabling the Organizations to make forecasts and react to market situations proactively. By using ML-driven analytics it enables organizations to rapidly take my ears due to changes in rival activities external influences and changes in consumer behaviors, this ultimately leads to the in-house marketability of organizations' products or services and improved consumer loyalty. The applications of machine learning in automation can help optimize processes decrease expenses and enable human resources to better concentrate on more valuable tasks. It can optimize the workflows and provide actionable insights that enhance decision-making efficiency help promote a culture of innovation and enable the Organizations to maintain a competitive edge in their markets (Wuest et al., 2016).

2. CATEGORIES OF MACHINE LEARNING METHODS PERTINENT TO BUSINESS

Machine learning is several methodologies that can empower Organizations to meet a range of challenges by using data-driven insights these strategies can be classified into various groups and each group is tailored to the business requirements. The primary categories of machine learning business decision-making are given below. (Kotsiantis et al., 2006).

2.1. Supervised Learning

Supervised machine learning technique is one of the most commonly used machine learning methods commonly employed in the industry this method implies a training model that can label the data sets in which each input is associated with a specific output and the model acquires the ability to automate this process by associating the inputs with outputs and that helps in predicting outcomes for new and unobserved data. (Lee & Shin, 2020).

Applications in Business

As can be seen in Figure 1 the applications of supervised learning can be seen in various business aspects.

Figure 1. Applications of supervised learning in business

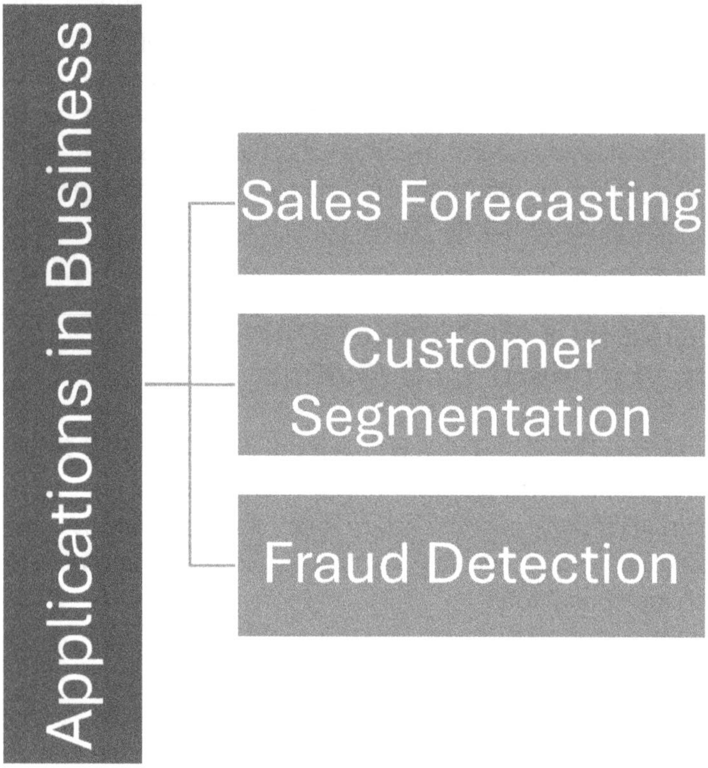

- ***Sales Forecasting:***

ML techniques can help forecast sales by analyzing the previous data and supervised machine learning models it may anticipate future and still trends and enable the Organizations to enhance their production and inventory management according to the situation.

- ***Consumer Segmentation:***

ML can also help consumer segmentation by supervised algorithms that can differentiate the customers according to the segments based on their purchasing behaviors preferences demographics and facilitate the focus marketing techniques adopted to situations.

- ***Fraud Detection:***

Definition organizations can employ supervised models in identifying the fraudulent transactions by analyzing the historical patterns of the frauds currently happening in the market are conducted in the past.

2.2. Unsupervised Learning

Alternatively, the unsupervised learning revolves around the unlabeled data. This method is very helpful in uncovering the hidden patterns and correlations in data and the clusters without results or predetermined categories. The unsupervised learning technique is very essential for better data and this is and enables organizations to summarize the data languages. (Lee & Shin, 2020).

Applications in Business

The various applications of unsupervised learning in business operations can be seen in Figure 2.

Figure 2. Applications of unsupervised learning in business

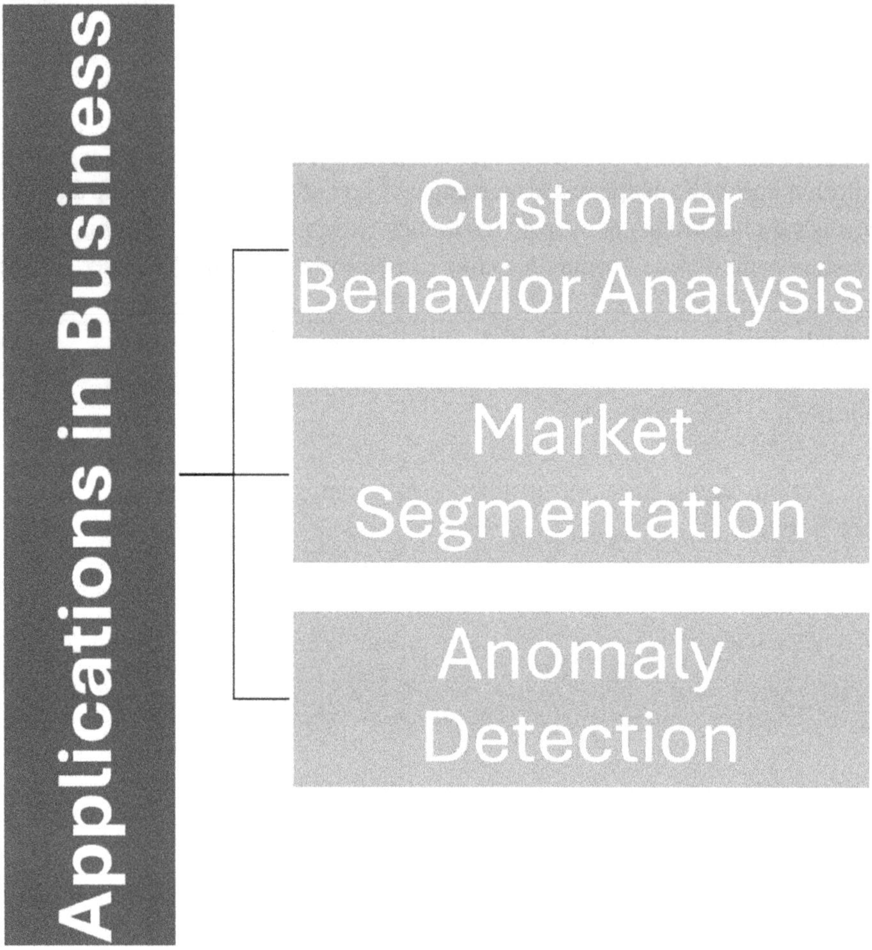

- ***Customer Behaviour Analysis:***

Organizations can analyze big data related to customers to help identify the behavioral patterns of consumers behavior and their purchase habits and in turn help product development, quality control, and setting up marketing plans.

- ***Market Segmentation:***

Unsupervised learning silicates the identification of various market segments by categorizing the clients according to their features and their shared behaviors and can enhance the precision of targeting.

- ***Anomaly Detection:***

Businesses can employ unsupervised models to help them in the identification of abnormal trends which may be significant in highlighting the operational problems and possible hazardous situations.

2.3. Reinforcement Learning

Reinforcement learning is one of the robust machine learning methods that emphasize learning by hit-and-drive methods in this technique the software acquires knowledge through interaction with the environment it obtains the rewards or penalties for its actions and thereby refines its behaviors to maximize the gains in the long term this method is very beneficial for dynamic and integrated decision-making processes in situations especially where the results are impacted by successive acts. (Lee & Shin, 2020).

Applications in Business

The various applications of reinforcement learning in business operations can be seen in Figure 3.

Figure 3. Applications of reinforcement learning in business operations.

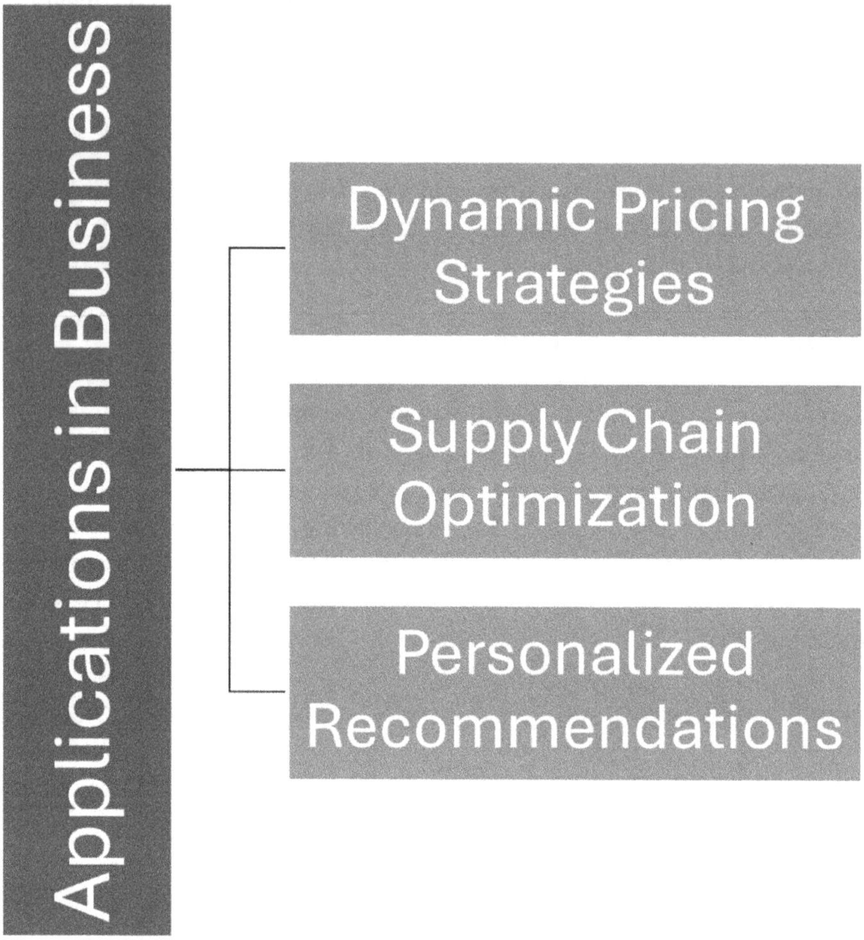

- ***Dynamic Pricing:***

Customized Recommendations: Streaming platforms and online marketplaces utilize reinforcement learning algorithms to personalize suggestions for users, enhancing engagement and conversion rates. By streaming the platforms and online marketplaces reinforcement learning can use the algorithms to personalize the suggestions for the users and improve engagement conversion rates according to the specific needs.

- ***Autonomous Systems:***

This reinforcement learning can also do drive system automations for example self self-driving vehicles robotics and other systems that require varied contexts.

2.4. Deep Learning and Neural Networks

Deep learning is a branch of machine learning that utilizes artificial neural networks to analyze the data in a manner that is analogous to the human brain. These neural networks are comprised of various layers of interconnected nodes that provide sophisticated data processing renters deep learning that is appropriate for various tasks such as natural language processing prediction analytics and image identification. (Lee & Shin, 2020) .

Applications in Business

- ***Advanced-Data Analysis:***

The deep learning methods can process big data sets to reveal the trends and forecast the results in applications such as analysis of various market trends and consumer sentiments.

- ***Customer Insights:***

By employing customer insights the analysis of social media content at the customer input deep learning models can enable the organizations to comprehend the client sentiment this can help in yielding insights for better brand management and quality product development.

- ***Image and Video Recognition:***

In retails at delves deep learning can facilitate in enabling their customers to locate products by uploading simple images nearby facilitating the visual search for improving the buying experience of consumers.

Each of these machine learning techniques is helpful in it was with his business settings, these techniques facilitate the organizations in making better-informed decisions based on data-driven approaches. By using these techniques Organizations can improve their customer experience, optimize their processes, and remain competitive in fast-changing markets.

3. UTILISATION OF MACHINE LEARNING IN CORPORATE DECISION-MAKING

Machine learning has various applications in different business sectors the first is to make more precise and informed decisions, by using these machine learning algorithms businesses can target their domains and enable themselves to enhance their procedures decrease their expenses, and elevate their client's satisfaction levels. Given below are the key utilities of machine learning in commercial decision-making processes.

3.1. Customer Relationship Management (CRM)

Machine learning can be very helpful in improving consumer relationship management by allowing businesses to obtain profound insights into their consumer behaviors potential hazards and preferences. By getting armed with knowledge organizations can anticipate client demands customize their interactions and cultivate robust partnerships. (Akash et al., 2024; Balarezo et al., 2023).

Applications in Customer Relationship Management

- ***Customer Satisfaction Analysis:***

These machine learning algorithms can improve the consumer interactions review to gauge the satisfaction levels provide feedback and enable the organizations to actively solve their concerns.

- ***Churn Prediction:***

By assessing consumer behavior patterns the Organizations can forecast which customers are prone to be lost and the algorithms can help execute the focus retention processes.

- ***Personalized Marketing:***

These machine learning algorithms can also be useful in personalized marketing in which the algorithms can suggest specific offers or items according to the specific preferences of the client thereby augmenting the customer engagement and loyalty.

3.2. Optimization of Sales and Marketing

That might influence sales then employers the machine learning techniques to enhance and improve their processes by forecasting the client reactions segmenting the demographics and automation in client campaign administrations these machine learning algorithms can examine the past data of sales and marketing and deliver improved insights that can help in enhancing their success related to different campaigns. (Kühl et al., 2020).

Applications in Sales and Marketing

- ***Targeted Advertising:***

In targeted advertising, the machine learning algorithms can make categories of the audiences and improve the targeted advertisements to most specific groups thereby optimizing their conversion rates and reducing unnecessary advertisements. (Yaiprasert & Hidayanto, 2024).

- ***Lead Scoring:***

By analyzing the past data on successful leads machine learning techniques can help rank the customers according to their conversion probability and this helps the sales teams to concentrate on leads that have high potential to be converted.

- ***Customer Segmentation:***

Machine learning techniques can help classify customers according to diverse attributes such as purchasing behavior demographics age and many others it enables marketers to develop specific campaigns for distinct segments.

3.3. Financial and Risk Management

Machine learning is becoming more crucial day by day in the financial sector, especially in areas in which high precision and timed decisions are important. These machine learning techniques then evaluate the financial data for risk management fraud detection defining the predictions identification of patterns and better decision-making. (Balasubramanian et al., 2022; Hui et al., 2024).

Applications in Finance and Risk Management

- ***Fraud Detection:***

Machine learning can help discover abnormalities in the transaction patterns thereby assisting their financial institutions in recognizing fraudulent activities.

- ***Credit rating:***

These machine learning algorithms can evaluate the credit history of lines including their spending trends and their transaction history and therefore can enhance the prediction of credit rating and reduce the risk of loss. (Schmitt, 2022).

- ***Investment Recommendations:***

Machine learning global advisors can evaluate the market trends and individual profiles of investors so that investment portfolios can be proposed specific to the distinct objectives and risk tolerances of the claims.

3.4. Operations and Supply Chain Administration

Interoperation and supply chain management machine learning techniques can help in optimizing the workflows enhance efficiency and decrease expenses these machine learning systems can assist businesses in their inventory management logistics optimization and demand forecasting through analysis of data from complete supply chains. (CR Carter, 2008; Islam & Amin, 2020).

Applications in Operations and Supply Chain

- ***Demand Forecasting:***

Machine learning algorithms can help evaluate historical patterns and seasonal fluctuations in the market help in forecasting future demands facilitate better inventory planning. (Jayanth Balaji et al., 2018).

- ***Inventory Optimisation:***

The machine learning algorithms can recommend battery inventory decisions they're providing ideal levels of inventory derived from the past sales and the projected demand thereby minimizing the shortages and excess stocks both at the same time.

3.5. Logistics and Route Optimisation

By analyzing the weather conditions traffic patterns and delivery limitations the machine learning models can help assist Organizations in optimizing their delivery rules and minimizing their costs in enhancing delivery efficiencies. (Simchi-Levi et al., 2008).

The machine learning ability can enable its applications in many business sectors each of which is characterized by data sources and distinct requirements. By integrating machine learning technologies organizations can make more efficient accurate and informed decisions which can result in enhanced outcomes in their organizations. (CR Carter, 2008).

4. ANALYSIS OF THE IMPACT OF MACHINE LEARNING ON BUSINESS PROCESSES

The use of machine learning in company operations significantly alters organizational functioning and decision-making processes. Machine learning may significantly enhance efficiency, accuracy, and strategic insight by improving decision-making capabilities and streamlining operations. This section examines the diverse effects of machine learning on business processes, emphasizing critical areas of transformation. (Howard et al., 2017).

4.1. Improved Decision-Making Velocity and Precision

One of the most renowned advantages of machine learning is the capability to expedite the decision-making processes along with enhancing accuracy. In business operations, the conventional decision-making processes frequently depend on manual analysis and intuitions of the employees which can be very laborious and can be suspected of errors. Whereas machine learning algorithms can evaluate large amounts of data sets very instantaneously and offer insights that can help organizations make informed and prompt decisions (Millo et al., 2024).

Accelerated Data Processing

Machine learning algorithms can analyze huge datasets significantly faster than human analysis and enable organizations to adapt to changing market brands and the demands of clients with great efficiency.

- ***Minimization of Human Error:***

Using data-driven approaches and insights instead of subjective management donations can decrease the errors in decision-making, which can result in more trustworthy outcomes of the decision-making process.

- ***Predictive Analytics:***

When playing the predictive models the Organizations can enable themselves to forecast future trends and make timed decisions to improve their efficiency and responsiveness.

4.2. Insights Informed by Data and Strategic Benefit

Machine learning techniques can enable organizations to improve their significant insights from their data that can enhance the style strategic objectives and help them in adding competitive advantages. The leveraging the data Organizations can get a more profound comprehension of their market dynamics and operations. (Ritala et al., 2024).

Actionable Insights

The logarithms of machine learning show the concealed patterns and explore relationships within data which can further yield deep insights and can be used to take a guiding strategy and increase creativity within an organization.

Client Insights

Machine learning can help organizations analyze the behavior and preferences of clients which can in turn allow them to customize their products improve their quality quality and foster customer experience.

Market Trends

By analyzing the data and the market indicators machine learning can help organizations explore the new trends and adjust their plans accordingly which can enhance their competitive positioning.

4.3. Transformative Results in Principal Sectors

By employing machine learning significant transformations can be observed in industries, and this can radically alter the corporate performances and value. The main sectors that are getting benefits from machine learning are given below. (Akash et al., 2024):

Retail Inventory Management

Retailers can use machine learning for the measurement of inventory personalized marketing plans and offer dynamic price pricing for their products all these can result in enhanced customer appeal and better sales. (Schmitt, 2023a).

Fraud Detection

In the financial does machine learning can improve fraud detection credit scores has been leading to increased efficiency and risk reduction.

Healthcare

The applications of machine learning in the healthcare sector our message which encompasses predictive analysis of patient outcomes and tailored treatment plans this can help enhance the operational effectiveness of hospital management and may lead to better patient care and cost reductions (Becker & Hoyer, 2024).

4.4. Lessons and Insights

The advantages of machine learning are that organizations must overcome a lot of hurdles to adopt these technologies successfully, the observations of Organizations that have implemented machine learning are given below. (CR Carter, 2008).

Quality of Data

The quality of data is very important for the successful implementation of machine learning applications organizations must allocate resources towards data optimization and noise reduction that can process the data to guarantee their models and can provide dependable datasets.

Continuous Improvement

The machine learning models must be upgraded from time to time there is a continuous monitoring and upgradation need so that the relevancy and efficiency of of machine learning applications in business environments can adapt to data change.

Collaboration is Essential

Effective implementation of machine learning requires frequent interdepartmental coordination and nearby living insights from different departments like data science business strategy, and marketing departments so that cohesive solutions that can fulfill the needs of organizations can be met best by summarizing the impacts of machine learning on decision-making processes and accepting the related challenges the Organizations can completely leverage these applications, equipping organizations for enduring success in a competitive environment. (Mitra et al., 2023).

5. OBSTACLES TO THE INTEGRATION OF MACHINE LEARNING IN BUSINESS DECISION-MAKING

The benefits of machine learning in business decision-making are huge but the deployment of machine learning technologies presents a huge set of problems organizations must first address several technical issues ethical issues and operational facilities to utilize machine learning properly in this section we will examine the potential issues and the factors that organizations can encounter when machine learning is implemented in their operations. (Balasubramanian et al., 2022). A few major examples of such obstacles are provided in Figure 4.

Figure 4. Obstacles of integrating machine learning models in business decision-making.

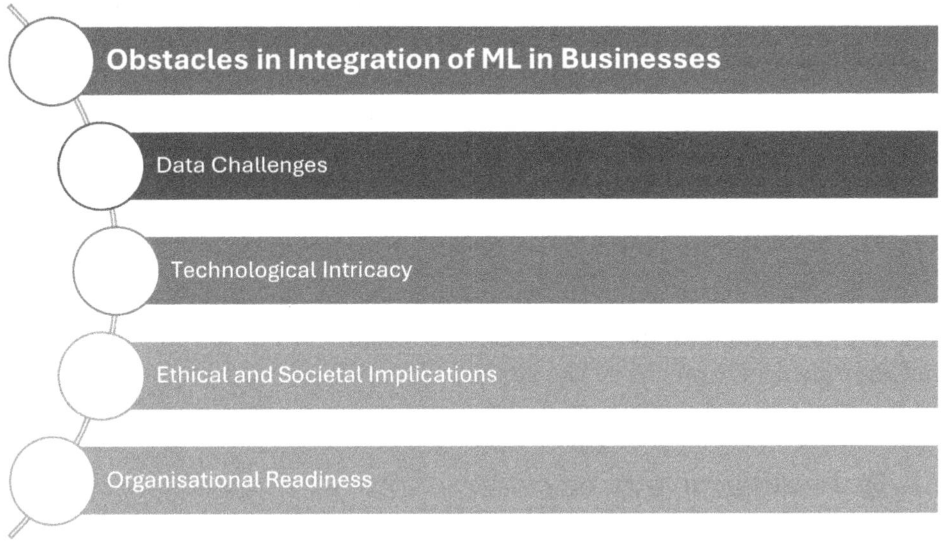

5.1. Data Challenges

The data plays the role of breaks in any machine learning application Organizations are frequently based on the number of problems related to data whenever they employ machine learning-based solutions (de Laat, 2018). To successfully adopt the AI model, businesses must overcome operational, legal, and technical hurdles, few major hurdles faced while implementing AI-based solutions are provided below.

Outdated Systems

Many organizations use outdated systems and software that are incompatible with machine learning models. Establishing compatibility between these two can be very time-consuming and may require huge investments.

Data Quality

The low quality and inferior data full of noises can erode the machine learning models and may provide wrong forecasts, organizations must show that the data being utilized for machine learning is pristine and is free from any pertinent and indicative problems.

Data Availability

Access to historical data is very important for training the machine learning models and several organizations' space issues while contending with data sets because the information is dispersed among different departments of the organization which hinders the creation of big data sets, data crucial for efficient learning of machine learning models (Clayton & Clopton, 2019).

Data Privacy and Security

The regulations of data privacy for example GDPR are intensifying and organizations must guarantee their data security and safety while meeting compliance whenever the data is processed or gathered for machine learning applications this need requires intense data governance and security protocols (Kushwaha et al., 2021).

5.2. Technological Intricacy

The implementation of machine learning solutions then frequently intricate technological problems that need specialized experience and knowledge (Cristofaro et al., 2025).

Model Selection and Tuning

This selection of appropriate machine learning algorithms and calibration for their parameters to attain better performance can be a big challenge organizations must require data scientists who are proficient in several machine learning methods to effectively navigate this process

Integration with Existing Systems

Then incorporation of machine learning into current business processes and intensive IT infrastructure presents huge challenges dog medications must show that novel machine learning solutions can be integrated without any problems in their existing systems whereas the workflows must be optimized to prevent disruptions.

Scalability

The organizations then expand, and the data volumes can rise. Machine learning models must be capable of handling larger amounts of data, which can further improve the analysis. This ensures the effective scalability of machine learning setups, which is very important for the sustainable success of organizations.

5.3. Ethical and Societal Implications

The implementation of machine learning has significant benefits but these benefits come at costs of ethical dilemmas that organizations have to face to uphold the responsibility and trust of customers (Balasubramanian et al., 2022). To maintain operations and reliability organizations must tackle various technical, operational, and ethical considerations. Few ethical considerations are mentioned below as examples.

Bias and Fairness

Machine learning models may be unintentionally biased or are inherently reinforced and endlessly while training in various datasets the results from such models are unreliable and may provide discriminating and inequitable results the organizations must ensure equity in their machine learning datasets by constantly checking the model's performance and adjusting these biases. One such example of these biases can be taken from an AI-powered tool for job applicant screening that favors one gender because the data dominantly includes resumes of one gender only. To navigate such challenges companies can use unbiased and diverse training data and perform regular audits of AI models.

Transparency and Explainability

The deep learning algorithms function like black boxes they can complicate the comprehension of decision making and the organizations must explore transparency and simplicity in their models to cultivate trust among all stakeholders. For example, many machine learning models make it difficult to understand how they made decisions and if a lack of transparency exists it can lead to irresponsible decision making. For example, a system that makes and recommends treatment options to the ambiguous decision logic and training data sets. The lack of transparency of the AI model however also makes it impossible even for the professionals to understand how the model concludes and reaches on such decisions. To counter such problems the AI-driven models should consist of human intervention to reach decisions, especially in risky decisions.

Impact on Employment

Machine building again displaces a huge number of Labor organizations that must reevaluate the ramifications of laborers and allocate resources toward teaching them new skills by introducing upskilling programs for their staff and changing their positions accordingly. Many multinational companies have incorporated AI-driven solutions that led to massive job displacement, although automation definitely improves efficiency but it creates economic inequities too especially when low-skill workers are easily replaced by AI-based solutions.

5.4. Organisational Preparedness

The efficient use of machine learning makes it important to make a cultural transformation in organizations that prioritizes data-driven decision-making and innovative approaches (Ritala et al., 2024) .

Leadership Endorsement

Roberts's decision-making and leadership endorsements are very important in implementing a culture of innovation and data-informed decision-making by using machine learning models the leaders must advocate for the machine learning applications and hello requisite resources for training and development of these models.

Cross-Functional Collaboration

What effective implementation of MLS it is required that corporations and organizations must increase collaboration among different departments within an organization like the operations department marketing data science and information technology department. Encouraging cross-functional teams can improve communication and facilitate good results.

Ongoing Learning and Adaptation

Applications of machine learning are advancing at a huge pace this necessity that organizations must upgrade themselves to perpetual learning and adoption by staying informed on new trends tools best practices makes them very essential for maintaining a competitive edge in the market (Kar et al., 2021). Decision-makers and even other employees may be reluctant to adopt AI-driven models because they may be afraid of losing their jobs. Promoting adoption, appropriate training to the employees, and mindset change often involving novel management techniques is crucial.

By addressing the issues and obstacles organizations can effectively use machine learning in their decision-making processes, spending the in-depth concepts and adhering to the ethical standards can enhance the success and sustainability of machine learning applications.

6. OPTIMAL STRATEGIES FOR INTEGRATING MACHINE LEARNING INTO BUSINESS DECISION-MAKING

The improve the machine learning models in business decisions organizations must follow good practices that can guarantee effective deployment and integration within the organization (Cohen & Levinthal, 1990). This section explores the essential steps for the effective deployment of machine learning models into business processes by highlighting the significance of cooperation continuous model oversights and stakeholder involvement (Grover et al., 2018).

Figure 5. Procedures for effectively integrating machine learning models in business

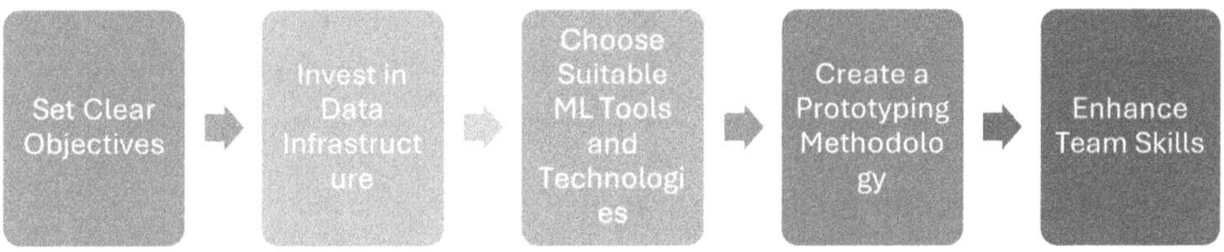

6.1. Procedures for Effectively Integrating Machine Learning Models in Business

To effectively incorporate machine learning models in an organization a multifaceted approach consisting of various steps should be followed as mentioned in figure 4.

Establish Explicit Objectives

Let's start by defining their goals for machine learning programs, this is dog repositioning the business cylinders that machine learning is required to go listen to his success measures that may further improve the effectiveness of machine learning in that atmosphere but everything their objectives the machine model machine learning models guarantee that all the objectives are synchronized and organizational properties are taken in account (Peng et al., 2023).

Invest in Data Infrastructure

Trusted and flexible infrastructure for machine learning endeavors is required for effective implementation in organizations therefore, organizations must prioritize collecting data storage definition of guaranteed availability of high quality and durable data without any noises or training the orders this establishes the data goodness protocols that can help ensure data integrity tell me open regulatory compliances.

Select Appropriate ML Tools and Technologies

The choice of relevant technologies and learning tools related to machine learning is very important in successful deployment and organizations must set their goals to access the machine learning platforms and file the frameworks according to their needs scalability demands and technical processes.

Establish a Prototyping Methodology

Employing a prototyping methodology enables organizations to evaluate ML models on a limited scale before comprehensive implementation. This aids in identifying possible concerns, validating their efficacy, and refining models, hence mitigating risks linked to large-scale deployment.

Developing and Enhancing Team Skills

Improving internal competency is very essential for the efficient use of machine learning in organizations so therefore they should allocate their resources to training their staff and improving their data competencies and machine learning concepts and the applications pertinent tools helping the teams with essential skills it can integrate a culture of creativity and sustained improvement in their machine learning projects.

6.2. Importance of Cross-Functional Collaboration and Stakeholder Buy-In

Interdepartmental collaboration is crucial for applying machine learning to business processes. Involving diverse teams from different departments fosters a rigirous approach to decision-making and enhances the overall success of ML initiatives (Kolkman et al., 2024).

Involve Key Stakeholders

The edification of key stakeholders for machine learning processes must be conducted throughout the organization and all the relevant departments for example data science operations and business leadership should be taken into account to ensure diverse viewpoints and added expertise in medicine and making processes this collaboration improves our mutual comprehension of goals and may help obstacles related to machine learning deployment (MURRAY et al., 2021).

Foster Transparent Communication

Wishing our transparent communication within an organization helps promote the exchange of feedback ideas and insights among all team members continuous meetings workshops and collaborations on different platforms can enhance the resumes thereby improving communication and can provide better solutions and effective outcomes

Encourage an Innovative Culture

The organizations must develop an environment of research and quality improvement and should drive the lessons from the failures this can help teams investigate new concepts and methodologies that can cultivate resilience and creativity in employees this is very important for the effective management of machine learning models

6.3. Ongoing Model Surveillance and Enhancement

After the deployment of machine learning models regular enforcement and monitoring is very helpful and are required to maintain the effectiveness and relevance of the model for this purpose various parameters are necessary some of which are discussed below (F. Balducci et al., 2018; Ritala et al., 2024).

Consistent Performance Assessment

Organizations should develop a monitoring strategy that can evaluate the performance of machine learning models regularly disk help in monitoring the precision accuracy recall at the KPIs to detect declining performance over time .

Feedback Loops

Implementation of feedback loops can help organizations collect valuable insights from end consumers and all the stakeholders while concerning the efficiency and influence of machine learning models by integrating the feedback loop the models can be improved and the refinements can be made thereby granting the alignment with business requirements (Toniolo et al., 2023).

Adaptation to Evolving Conditions

So the business environments are very transforming organizations must be ready to modify their machine learning models to accommodate any changing market dynamics and evolving trends or to accommodate any new data these adaptability and flexibility are the machine learning solutions that value retention and relevance over time

Continuous Training and Retraining

Cognitions must continuously update their models with new data so that they can ensure a sustainable accuracy and performance curve training programs in need build machine learning models to incorporate new data and adjust to ever-changing circumstances to secure sustainability (Ahmed et al., 2023).

Following the optimized practices in integrating machine learning in business decision-making, organizations can efficiently increase the information for successful machine learning models. An integrated strategy, alongside cross-functional collaboration and a dedication to ongoing enhancement, will empower organizations to fully leverage machine learning for innovation, efficiency, and competitive superiority.

7. EMERGING TRENDS IN MACHINE LEARNING FOR BUSINESS DECISION-MAKING

As machine learning technology advances, its uses for business decision-making will become significant. This section discusses the emerging trends and prospective future advancements in machine learning that organizations should prepare for to sustain a competitive advantage (Jordan & Mitchell, 2015). Figure 6 represents novel trends in ML for Business decision-making.

Figure 6. Novel trends in ML for business decision-making.

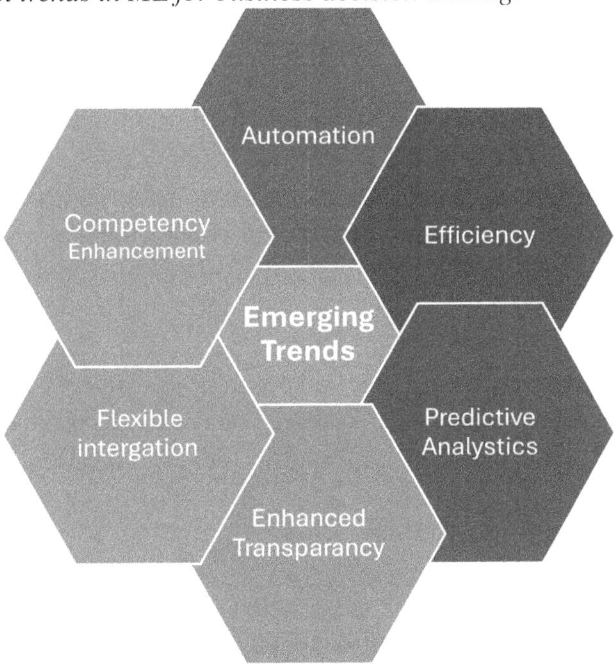

7.1. Enhanced Automation and Efficiency

The automation in company operations can improve due to progress in machine learning. As machine learning advances, organizations can anticipate enhanced efficiency in decision-making processes.

Automated Decision-Making

Organizations will progressively depend on machine learning algorithms to automate decision-making processes, omitting human involvement. This can result in expedited response times and improved performance.

Robotic Process Automation (RPA)

Employing machine learning with Robotic Process Automation can allow organizations to automate repetitive operations while utilizing ML for ongoing enhancement and optimization. This collaboration will optimize procedures and improve efficiency across multiple functions.

7.2. Advanced Predictive Analytics

Predictive analytics, driven by machine learning can offer organizations better insights into forthcoming trends and consumer behaviours (Bertsimas & Kallus, 2020).

Real-Time Analytics

The capacity to analyse data in time will become increasingly common, enabling organizations to make prompt decisions based on data flows. This feature will improve responsiveness in dynamic marketplaces (Schmitt, 2023b).

Improved Forecasting Models

Machine learning will facilitate the creation of better forecasting models that can integrate a broader set of factors and data sources, hence enhancing decision-making in domains such as financial planning, inventory management, and customer needs forecasting.

7.3. Explainable Artificial Intelligence (XAI) and Transparency

As apprehensions over the transparency of machine learning models escalate, the demand for explainable AI will intensify (Calvard, 2016). Organizations will prioritize the development of machine learning technologies that elucidate the decision-making process (de Laat, 2018).

Regulatory Compliance

As regulation on AI and machine learning intensifies, businesses must ensure that their models can adhere to standards of transparency and accountability.

Trust Development

By emphasizing explainability, organizations can cultivate trust with customers and stakeholders, meeting ethical concerns related to machine learning.

7.4. Integration with Alternative Technologies

The integration of machine learning with other novel technologies will create new opportunities for innovation and improved decision-making (Brewer et al., 2024).

Internet of Things (IoT)

The proliferation of Internet of Things (IoT) devices can yield substantial data, serving as valuable resources for machine learning applications. Organizations can utilize the data to, improve customer experiences, refine operations, and guide strategic decisions (Shrestha et al., 2021).

Blockchain Technology

The integration of machine learning with blockchain enhances data integrity and security, facilitating more dependable and transparent decision-making processes. This may be especially advantageous in industries like supply chain management and banking.

7.5. Focus on Ethical Artificial Intelligence

As organizations progressively adopt machine learning, the emphasis on ethical practices will become imminent. Businesses should prioritize, accountability, equity, and openness in their AI activities (Gong et al., 2024).

Bias Mitigation

Organizations should allocate resources to strategies and tools for identifying and resolving bias in machine learning models, so guaranteeing that the generated judgments are just and equitable.

Sustainable AI Practices

With increasing environmental awareness, Organizations will include sustainable practices in their AI initiatives, emphasizing energy-efficient algorithms and responsible data usage (B. Balducci & Marinova, 2018).

7.6. Competency Enhancement and Recruitment of Talent

The demand for talented professionals in machine learning will increase. Organizations must prioritize the acquisition and training of personnel to fully achieve machine learning benefits. Organisations can partner with universities and training institutions to develop programs according to industry requirements, to raise a pool of competent talent in machine learning (Batra & Keller, 2016).

As machine learning rapidly transforms commercial decision-making, organizations that adopt these technologies will enhance thier success in the current environment. By utilizing these technologies, enforcing ethical standards, and talent development, Organizations may fully benefit from machine learning to foster innovation and achieve sustainable success .

8. CONCLUSION

The use of machine learning in commercial decision-making highlights significant transformation that can enable organizations to function more efficiently, make informed decisions, and have a competitive advantage. This chapter discussed how machine learning can improve the decision-making process by increasing accuracy, speed, and the capacity to extract meaningful insights from extensive data sets. The utility of machine learning may impose several hurdles, such as technical complexity, ethical considerations, data quality, and the need for organizational readiness. Businesses should strategically address the challenges to completely avail the potential of machine learning while maintaining responsible and ethical considerations. The future of machine learning is promising the current trends indicate enhanced automation, sophisticated analytics, and explainable AI. As organizations implement machine learning with novel technologies, the demand for trained personnel and adherence to ethical standards will be very important. Adopting machine learning lets organizations promote a culture of data-driven decision-making and creativity, rather than merely using new technologies. Organizations that utilize machine learning may be positioned to lead in the business environment, by optimizing their productivity, improving their customer experiences, and attaining sustainable development.

REFERENCES

Ahmed, F., Hasan, M., Hossain, M. S., & Andersson, K. (2023). Comparative Performance of Tree Based Machine Learning Classifiers in Product Backorder Prediction. *Lecture Notes in Networks and Systems, 569 LNNS*, 572–584. DOI: 10.1007/978-3-031-19958-5_54

Akash, C. R., Vivekanandhan, P. K., Adam Khan, M., Ebenezer, G., Vinoth, K., Prithivirajan, J., & Kishan, V. J. P. (2024). Assessment of ridge regression-based machine learning model for the prediction of automotive sales based on the customer requirements. *Interactions (Cham)*, *245*(1), 289. Advance online publication. DOI: 10.1007/s10751-024-02132-4

Balarezo, J. D., Foss, N. J., & Nielsen, B. B. (2023). Organizational learning: Understanding cognitive barriers and what organizations can do about them. *Management Learning*. Advance online publication. DOI: 10.1177/13505076231210635

Balasubramanian, N., Ye, Y., & Xu, M. (2022). Substituting Human Decision-Making with Machine Learning: Implications for Organizational Learning. Https://Doi.Org/10.5465/Amr.2019.0470, *47*(3), 448–465. DOI: 10.5465/amr.2019.0470

Balducci, B., & Marinova, D. (2018). Unstructured data in marketing. *Journal of the Academy of Marketing Science*, *46*(4), 557–590. DOI: 10.1007/s11747-018-0581-x

Balducci, F., Impedovo, D., & Pirlo, G. (2018). Machine learning applications on agricultural datasets for smart farm enhancement. *Machines (Basel)*, *6*(3), 38. Advance online publication. DOI: 10.3390/machines6030038

Batra, R., & Keller, K. L. (2016). Integrating marketing communications: New findings, new lessons, and new ideas. *Journal of Marketing*, *80*(6), 122–145. DOI: 10.1509/jm.15.0419

Becker, B., & Hoyer, P. (2024). The anatomy of clinical decision-making: Aligning AI design with ICU routines. *Journal of Organizational Ethnography*, *13*(3), 427–451. Advance online publication. DOI: 10.1108/JOE-03-2024-0011

Bertsimas, D., & Kallus, N. (2020). From predictive to prescriptive analytics. *Management Science*, *66*(3), 1025–1044. DOI: 10.1287/mnsc.2018.3253

Brewer, J., Patel, D., Kim, D., & Murray, A. (2024). Navigating the challenges of generative technologies: Proposing the integration of artificial intelligence and blockchain. *Business Horizons*, *67*(5), 525–535. DOI: 10.1016/j.bushor.2024.04.011

Calvard, T. S. (2016). Big data, organizational learning, and sensemaking: Theorizing interpretive challenges under conditions of dynamic complexity. *Management Learning*, *47*(1), 65–82. DOI: 10.1177/1350507615592113

Carter, C. R., & Rogers, D. S. (2008). A framework of sustainable supply chain management: Moving toward new theory. *International Journal of Physical Distribution & Logistics Management, 38*(5), 360–387. DOI: 10.1108/09600030810882816

Clayton, P. R., & Clopton, J. (2019). Business curriculum redesign: Integrating data analytics. *Journal of Education for Business*, *94*(1), 57–63. DOI: 10.1080/08832323.2018.1502142

Cohen, W. M., & Levinthal, D. A. (1990). Absorptive Capacity: A New Perspective on Learning and Innovation. *Administrative Science Quarterly*, *35*(1), 128. DOI: 10.2307/2393553

Cristofaro, M., Giardino, P. L., & Barboni, L. (2025). Growth hacking: A scientific approach for data-driven decision making. *Journal of Business Research, 186*, 115030. Advance online publication. DOI: 10.1016/j.jbusres.2024.115030

de Laat, P. B. (2018). Algorithmic Decision-Making Based on Machine Learning from Big Data: Can Transparency Restore Accountability? *Philosophy & Technology*, *31*(4), 525–541. DOI: 10.1007/s13347-017-0293-z PMID: 30873341

Gong, Q., Fan, D., & Bartram, T. (2024). Algorithmic human resource management: Toward a functional affordance perspective. *Personnel Review*. Advance online publication. DOI: 10.1108/PR-01-2024-0099

Grover, V., Chiang, R. H. L., Liang, T. P., & Zhang, D. (2018). Creating Strategic Business Value from Big Data Analytics: A Research Framework. *Journal of Management Information Systems*, *35*(2), 388–423. DOI: 10.1080/07421222.2018.1451951

Howard, A., Zhang, C., & Horvitz, E. (2017). Addressing bias in machine learning algorithms: A pilot study on emotion recognition for intelligent systems. *Proceedings of IEEE Workshop on Advanced Robotics and Its Social Impacts, ARSO*. DOI: 10.1109/ARSO.2017.8025197

Hui, X., Reshef, O., & Zhou, L. (2024). The Short-Term Effects of Generative Artificial Intelligence on Employment: Evidence from an Online Labor Market. *Organization Science*, *35*(6), 1977–1989. DOI: 10.1287/orsc.2023.18441

Islam, S., & Amin, S. H. (2020). Prediction of probable backorder scenarios in the supply chain using Distributed Random Forest and Gradient Boosting Machine learning techniques. *Journal of Big Data*, *7*(1), 1–22. DOI: 10.1186/s40537-020-00345-2

Jayanth Balaji, A., Harish Ram, D. S., & Nair, B. B. (2018). Applicability of deep learning models for stock Price forecasting an empirical study on BANKEX data. *Procedia Computer Science*, *143*, 947–953. DOI: 10.1016/j.procs.2018.10.340

Jordan, M. I., & Mitchell, T. M. (2015). Machine learning: Trends, perspectives, and prospects. *Science*, *349*(6245), 255–260. DOI: 10.1126/science.aaa8415 PMID: 26185243

Kar, S., Kar, A. K., & Gupta, M. P. (2021). Modeling Drivers and Barriers of Artificial Intelligence Adoption: Insights from a Strategic Management Perspective. *International Journal of Intelligent Systems in Accounting Finance & Management*, *28*(4), 217–238. DOI: 10.1002/isaf.1503

Khosravi, K., Shahabi, H., Pham, B. T., Adamowski, J., Shirzadi, A., Pradhan, B., Dou, J., Ly, H. B., Gróf, G., Ho, H. L., Hong, H., Chapi, K., & Prakash, I. (2019). A comparative assessment of flood susceptibility modeling using Multi-Criteria Decision-Making Analysis and Machine Learning Methods. *Journal of Hydrology (Amsterdam)*, *573*, 311–323. DOI: 10.1016/j.jhydrol.2019.03.073

Kolkman, D., Lee, G. K., & van Witteloostuijn, A. (2024). Data science and automation in the process of theorizing: Machine learning's power of induction in the co-duction cycle. *PLoS One*, *19*(11), e0309318. DOI: 10.1371/journal.pone.0309318 PMID: 39495739

Kotsiantis, S. B., Zaharakis, I. D., & Pintelas, P. E. (2006). Machine learning: A review of classification and combining techniques. *Artificial Intelligence Review*, *26*(3), 159–190. DOI: 10.1007/s10462-007-9052-3

Kraus, M., Feuerriegel, S., & Oztekin, A. (2020). Deep learning in business analytics and operations research: Models, applications and managerial implications. *European Journal of Operational Research*, *281*(3), 628–641. DOI: 10.1016/j.ejor.2019.09.018

Kühl, N., Mühlthaler, M., & Goutier, M. (2020). Supporting customer-oriented marketing with artificial intelligence: Automatically quantifying customer needs from social media. *Electronic Markets*, *30*(2), 351–367. DOI: 10.1007/s12525-019-00351-0

Kushwaha, A. K., Kar, A. K., & Dwivedi, Y. K. (2021). Applications of big data in emerging management disciplines: A literature review using text mining. *International Journal of Information Management Data Insights*, *1*(2), 100017. Advance online publication. DOI: 10.1016/j.jjimei.2021.100017

Lee, I., & Shin, Y. J. (2020). Machine learning for enterprises: Applications, algorithm selection, and challenges. *Business Horizons, 63*(2), 157–170. DOI: 10.1016/j.bushor.2019.10.005

Millo, Y., Spence, C., & Xu, R. (2024). Algorithmic self-referentiality: How machine learning pushes calculative practices to assess themselves. *Accounting, Organizations and Society, 113*, 101567. Advance online publication. DOI: 10.1016/j.aos.2024.101567

Mitra, A., Jain, A., Kishore, A., & Kumar, P. (2023). A Comparative Study for Machine Learning Models in Retail Demand Forecasting. *Smart Innovation. Systems and Technologies, 316*, 273–282. DOI: 10.1007/978-981-19-5403-0_23

Murray, A., Rhymer, J., & Sirmon, D. G.Murray. (2021). Humans and technology: Forms of conjoined agency in organizations. *Academy of Management Review, 46*(3), 552–571. DOI: 10.5465/amr.2019.0186

Peng, Y., Ahmad, S. F., Ahmad, A. Y. A. B., Al Shaikh, M. S., Daoud, M. K., & Alhamdi, F. M. H. (2023). Riding the Waves of Artificial Intelligence in Advancing Accounting and Its Implications for Sustainable Development Goals. *Sustainability (Basel), 15*(19), 14165. Advance online publication. DOI: 10.3390/su151914165

Ritala, P., Aaltonen, P., Ruokonen, M., & Nemeh, A. (2024). Developing industrial AI capabilities: An organisational learning perspective. *Technovation, 138*, 103120. Advance online publication. DOI: 10.1016/j.technovation.2024.103120

Schmitt, M. (2022). Deep Learning vs. Gradient Boosting: Benchmarking state-of-the-art machine learning algorithms for credit scoring. *ArXiv*. DOI: 10.48550/ARXIV.2205.10535

Schmitt, M. (2023a). Automated machine learning: AI-driven decision making in business analytics. *Intelligent Systems with Applications, 18*, 200188. DOI: 10.1016/j.iswa.2023.200188

Schmitt, M. (2023b). Deep learning in business analytics: A clash of expectations and reality. *International Journal of Information Management Data Insights, 3*(1), 100146. Advance online publication. DOI: 10.1016/j.jjimei.2022.100146

Shrestha, Y. R., Krishna, V., & von Krogh, G. (2021). Augmenting organizational decision-making with deep learning algorithms: Principles, promises, and challenges. *Journal of Business Research, 123*, 588–603. DOI: 10.1016/j.jbusres.2020.09.068

Simchi-Levi, D., Kaminsky, P., Simchi-Levi, E., & Shankar, R. (2008). *Designing and managing the supply chain: concepts, strategies and case studies*. Tata McGraw-Hill Education.

Toniolo, A., Cerutti, F., Norman, T. J., Oren, N., Allen, J. A., Srivastava, M., & Sullivan, P. (2023). Human-machine collaboration in intelligence analysis: An expert evaluation. *Intelligent Systems with Applications*, *17*, 200151. Advance online publication. DOI: 10.1016/j.iswa.2022.200151

Wuest, T., Weimer, D., Irgens, C., & Thoben, K. D. (2016). Machine learning in manufacturing: Advantages, challenges, and applications. *Production & Manufacturing Research*, *4*(1), 23–45. DOI: 10.1080/21693277.2016.1192517

Yaiprasert, C., & Hidayanto, A. N. (2024). AI-powered in the digital age: Ensemble innovation personalizes the food recommendations. *Journal of Open Innovation*, *10*(2), 100261. Advance online publication. DOI: 10.1016/j.joitmc.2024.100261

Chapter 4
Digital Technologies and Knowledge Management Process:
A Collaborative Role in Different Sectors

Faiz Mayah Alshammary
https://orcid.org/0009-0009-7066-1684
Lincoln University College, Petaling Jaya, Malaysia

ABSTRACT

This chapter consists on the definition of KMP (Knowledge management process) and digital technologies by different authors. Further, there is in-detailed concept of knowledge management process is elaborated along with its dimensions. The main dimension such as Knowledge utilization, Knowledge application, Knowledge dissemination, Knowledge store, Knowledge sharing, Knowledge creation, Knowledge accessibility and Knowledge organizing. This chapter will be very beneficial for the reader to get deep knowledge about the KMP and digital technologies and its implications in different sectors.

INTRODUCTION

KM is the process of managing the knowledge of an organization. KMP enables learning and grow opportunities for employees of an organization. These opportunities and learning can enhance the skill and knowledge of workers which improve performance. KMP enhances the capability of employees to perform their jobs.

DOI: 10.4018/979-8-3693-8960-7.ch004

KM needs the integration of different technologies and use knowledge among an organization.

Digital technologies can give a huge range of potentials for integrating economy in organizations. Digital technologies define the use of automated systems and share the information.(Yasin et al., 2022) Digital technologies functions by digital signals into more ascendable digital organizations. Moreover digital technology plays a vital role in providing management of information. To Addition to Knowledge management process is more inclusive in defining the use of knowledge among an organization. Knowledge management process emphasizes a strong data and also provides learning across workforce. Digital technologies provide instrument to perform KM processes.

DEFINITION

There are following definitions of the digital technologies and KMP

- "*Knowledge management is a process of creating, sharing, using, and managing the knowledge and information (Saeed et al., 2024).*"
- "*Knowledge management as a process focusing on the protection, development, and exploitation of knowledge assets. This view emphasizes both the strategic importance and the careful handling of organizational knowledge to maintain competitive advantage(Shaik et al., 2024)*"
- According to Yasin et al., (2020) "*sees digitalization as a fundamental feature of the modern world, it reshaped communication and organizational infrastructures through digital tools and enabled the global connectivity*"
- According to Enebeli, (2024) "*The digital technologies are critical in connecting all aspects of society through a unified communication infrastructure, driving globalization and transforming material concepts*".

CONCEPT OF KNOWLEDGE MANAGEMENT PROCESS

Knowledge Management (KM) represents a dynamic and systematic process that organizations utilize to generate, capture, arrange, and disseminate knowledge across their structures. The Knowledge Management enhances the performance by enhancing the decision making in the context of innovation with the modern time period. In many stages of progress of the organization the knowledge management process play important role for efficient utilization and leveraging the human capital within the organization (Salman et al., 2020).

The preliminary stage of the KMP focuses on knowledge creation, where unique visions, concepts, and information are created within the administrative framework. This procedure explains through miscellaneous channels, including research and development, cooperative efforts, and individual skills (Tomé & Gromova, 2021).

Subsequently the beginning of knowledge is the important step entails knowledge detention. This stage is related to the efficient variety and documents of the recent created knowledge. It covers the record of best performs, lessons learned, and the expertise contributed by employees. The main objective of the management is the protection of vital visions which make them ease for the reachability to other participants within the organization. Employing databases, sources, and knowledge management systems enables the organization to storage information and prevent its loss and confirming well-organized recovery (Raudeliūnienė et al., 2018).

Further, the knowledge organization stage includes arranging and classifying took information for unified recovery. This step frequently involves the growth of classifications, metadata, and cataloguing systems to guarantee a logical and available organization of knowledge (Raudeliūnienė et al., 2018; Tomé & Gromova, 2021).

Consequently, the knowledge storage requires the formation of storage systems, databases, and sources to firm knowledge. Convenience in this stage it is, ensure that employees fluently recover the obligatory information when desirable. Progressive search methodology, indexing, and content classification are usually employed to enlarge the speed and accuracy of knowledge (Antunes & Pinheiro, 2020).

Knowledge sharing is vital stage in the knowledge management process which includes encouragement as well as distribution of knowledge among structural members. This effort entails calming a cooperative culture where staffs feel interested to share their visions, involvements, and knowledge with their mangers. Leveraging technologies such as internets, Wikipedia, and collaborative platforms facilitates seamless knowledge sharing, and nurturing a culture of open communication (Wall, 2020).

The final phase of the knowledge management process is knowledge application. This entails translating the acquired knowledge into actionable solutions to address problems, make informed decisions, and drive innovation (Wall, 2020). Encouraging employees to apply the knowledge they have gained creates a feedback loop, informing future knowledge creation and refining existing processes(Long, 2023; Wall, 2020).

THE OBJECTIVES OF KNOWLEDGE MANAGEMENT PROCESSES

The objectives of knowledge management processes are multidimensional. It aims to systematically capture, organize, share, and leverage the collective knowledge within an organization. These objects are important to enhance the efficiency, innovation and overall competitiveness (Migdadi, 2022; Obeso et al., 2020; Areed et al., 2020).Facilitate seamless knowledge sharing

One primary objective is to facilitate seamless knowledge sharing and collaboration among employees. By establishing platforms and systems that encourage the open exchange of ideas and best practices, organizations foster a culture of collaboration. Another crucial objective is to capture tacit knowledge, the insights and expertise residing in individuals' experiences and convert it into explicit knowledge that can be documented and shared. This objective ensures that valuable insights are not lost when employees leave or retire, contributing to the organization's continuity and resilience (McQuade et al., 2007; Passos et al., 2021).

To Improve Decision-Making Procedures

KM has goals to improve decision-making procedures by providing appropriate and applicable information to decision-makers. Furthermore, knowledge management processes struggle to recover organizational knowledge and adaptability. Therefore, by analytically collecting and examining information on achievements and failures, organizations acquire from past experiences and constantly recover their procedures and practices.

To Maintenance Innovation and Inventiveness

Operational knowledge management aims to support novelty and inventiveness within the organization and by explaining employees with access to a various variety of knowledge sources. The KM in the organizations motivate new ideas, encourage research, and initiate innovation (Migdadi, 2022; Obeso et al., 2020).

Objective to Improve the Customer Satisfaction

Knowledge management is important to addresses the objective for increasing customer satisfaction. Development of a culture of knowledge sharing contributes to employee engagement and satisfaction. When employees feel that their knowledge and contributions are valued, they are more likely to be engaged, motivated, and committed to the organization (Areed et al., 2020; Hussain et al., 2022).

Continuous Improvement

The objective of continuous improvement is central to knowledge management processes. By regularly assessing and refining knowledge management strategies, organizations can adapt to changing environments, stay ahead of competitors, and remain resilient in the face of challenges. Moreover, knowledge management supports the objective of talent/employee retention and development. The capturing and sharing knowledge in the organizations facilitate the professional growth of their employees as well as it helps them acquire new skills and competencies. This not only benefits the individual but also enhances the organization's overall skillset.

To Create a Knowledge-Friendly Culture Within the Organization

Lastly, knowledge management processes aim to create a knowledge-friendly culture within the organization. This involves awareness and appreciation of the value of knowledge, encourage the employees to actively contribute and seek information. It helps to foster an environment where learning and knowledge sharing are integral to the organizational ethos(Al Shraah et al., 2022; Aviv et al., 2021).

IMPORTANCE OF THE KNOWLEDGE MANAGEMENT PROCESS

There are many studies (Aviv et al., 2021; Hussain et al., 2022; Mahdi et al., 2019; Al Shraah et al., 2022; Migdadi, 2022; Passos et al., 2021) has elaborated the knowledge management process. There are some points have elaborated following

Training of the Intellectual Capital

The knowledge management process unfolds as a comprehensive approach adopted by organizations to harness the intellectual capital within their ranks, such as each stage from knowledge creation to application contributes to the development of an agile. It also inform and innovative the organizational culture. Strategic investments in effective knowledge management processes and technologies empower organizations to unlock the full potential of their collective knowledge. It provides a competitive edge in today's knowledge-driven economy (Al Shraah et al., 2022; Migdadi, 2022; Passos et al., 2021).

Decision-Making

The main significance of the knowledge management process is to raise a association, taking tacit knowledge and improving decision-making process. The knowledge management process also attempts to main the innovation, increase competence and improve the customer satisfaction. Additionally it encourages the employee rendezvous as well as initiates the continuous development that enables the capacity for the development and makes a culture which is knowledge-friendly. With the help of supporting knowledge management efforts organizations solve the full possible collective knowledge, dynamic success and sustainability in dynamic and economical business (Aviv et al., 2021; Hussain et al., 2022; Mahdi et al., 2019).

Promotion of Consistent Practices

KMP enhances operational competence by reorganizing the processes, reducing copying of efforts, and encouraging standardized practices. Through well-organized resource allocation, planning, and record management, healthcare organizations make best use of resource utilization, diminish waste, and improve productivity. This process not only indications the cost savings efficiency but also allows works to emphasis more time and care for organization maintenance (Antunes & Pinheiro, 2020).

Learning and Skill Development

KMP supports learning and professional growth among work. The organization with knowledge enables the access to informative resources, drill materials, and educational opportunities, to empower employees and stay efficient on the modern advancements in their field and continuously progress in skills and knowledge. This nurtures a culture of enduring learning and guarantees for rewards enhance the ability of the employee in a rapidly fluctuating environment (Ajanaku & Mutula, 2018).

Collaboration and Communication

KMP enables teamwork and communication among workers. By contravention down knowledge silos and enabling seamless information exchange, KMP promotes interdisciplinary collaboration, leading to better care coordination and patient outcomes. Further, it improves the communication between main works, experts, and associated professionals enhance the stability and inclusiveness in multifaceted market.

Dimensions of Knowledge Management Process

Figure 1. Dimensions of KMP

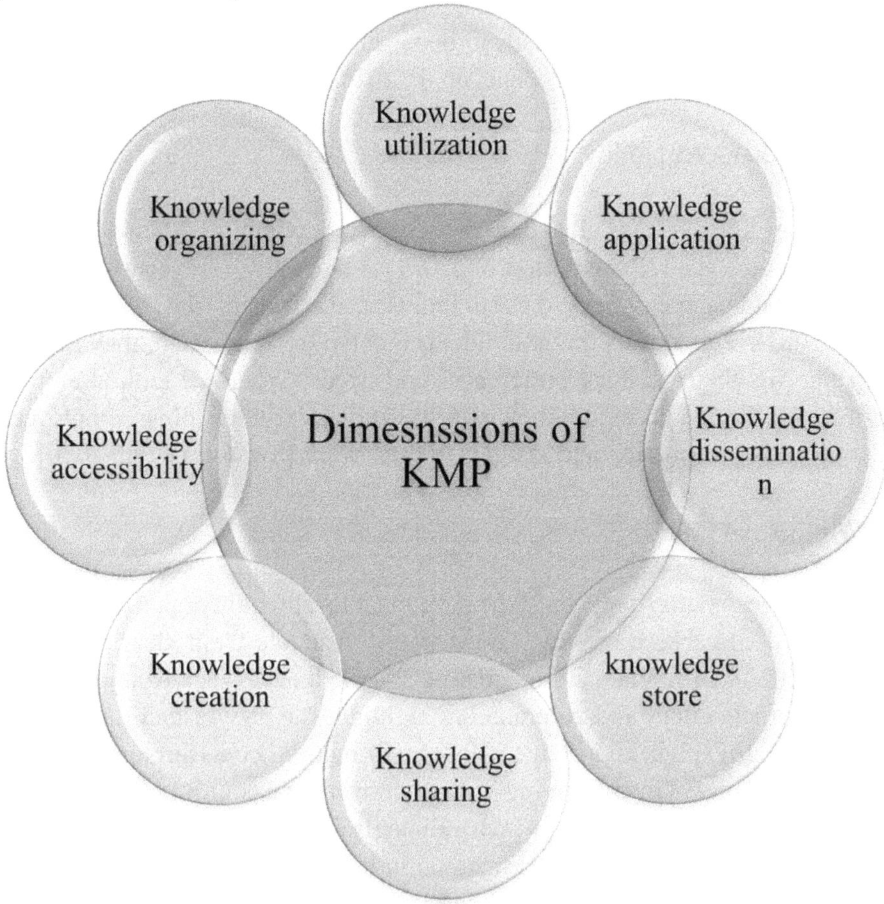

Source:*(Kun, 2022; Shannak et al., 2017)*

Knowledge Organizing

Knowledge organizing denotes the process of organizing and classifying information and knowledge resources in organized and methodical manner. It includes taking, categorizing, storing, and saving knowledge to make it easily available and operational for individuals and institution (Shannak et al., 2017). The objective of knowledge organizing is to enable the well-organized knowledge management, improve decision-making, and supportive education and novelty in work. Organized knowledge sources, such as records or information management systems, allow employees to rapidly and easily regain related material any time (Syed-Ikhsan & Rowland, 2004).Furthermore, When workers have access to well organized training resources, finest practices, and documented procedures workers attain new skills and information which further leads to better job performance and expert growth (Abbas & Yaqoob, 2009; Almatrooshi et al., 2016; Yeh et al., 2006).

Knowledge Accessibility

Accessing knowledge is all about how actively individuals participate in finding information they need (Parayitam et al., 2021). Essentially, it revolves around how readily available and easy it is to get to knowledge resources and information (Du Plessis, 2007). This means that individuals receive the knowledge they require in a way that fits their personal preferences and needs. When we look at employee performance, having access to knowledge is crucial. It's what allows employees to effectively use information and insights in their work (Swanson et al., 2020).

Knowledge Creation

Knowledge creation happens at the individual level within organizations, where people blend and absorb existing knowledge to generate fresh ideas and insights (Sa et al., 2020). Different ways of creating knowledge like socialization, externalization, internalization, and combination highlight the way of tacit knowledge is transformed into explicit knowledge. This transformation occurs through interactions among organizational members. Individuals draw mental connections and immerse themselves in learning activities, which ultimately foster knowledge creation (Akhavan et al., 2014; Li et al., 2009). Engaging in knowledge creation is a journey of ongoing learning and discovery. Employees who take part in activities like attending conferences, conducting research, or collaborating on projects not only deepen their knowledge but also build new skills. This commitment to continuous learning boosts their expertise and performance on the job (Cao et al., 2021; Pinheiro et al., 2020).

Knowledge Sharing

Knowledge sharing is essential for fostering collaboration among employees, as it involves exchanging information, experiences, and insights. This exchange not only enhances awareness but also boosts performance on the job (Wang & Noe, 2010; Ha, 2020). Advocates of knowledge-based views (KBV) emphasize its importance in driving production processes and economic development (Ferlie et al., 2015; Alguezaui & Filieri, 2014). Within any organization, a mix of experienced and newer employees can thrive through teamwork and collaboration, ultimately leading to greater profitability and success. In the management process the facilitating problem-solving, implementing policies, and sparking innovative ideas, knowledge sharing becomes a vital tool. The overall effectiveness of individuals and organizations hinges on adopting advanced working strategies made possible through this sharing process (Li & Sandino, 2018). Furthermore, when employees participate in knowledge sharing, they experience increased job satisfaction and a boost in creativity (Hoa et al., 2020).

Knowledge Store

The knowledge management process has important element which is knowledge store acts as vital role as it helps as a dominant source for storing and establishing knowledge resources. It offers a platform for employees to contribute their understanding, perceptions, and capabilities in the arrangement of documents, reports, presentations, and other arrangements (Sahibzada et al., 2023).

Furthermore, the knowledge store plays an important role in improving employee performance in any industry. A knowledge store offers workers with easy access to organized information, including strategies, best practices, research findings, and industry standards (Paul & Singh, 2023). This allows management to keep up with the latest innovations in the field which rely on evidence-based actions and new developments. This reliable and current information leads the worker to the better decisions and deliver higher quality care (Du et al., 2016). Furthermore, Accurate and up-to-date information is crucial for effective clinical decision-making. The knowledge store provides employees instant access to relevant clinical knowledge and guidelines (Wald et al., 2007).

Knowledge Dissemination

Knowledge dissemination is the art of KM process of spreading knowledge and information within an organization to boost performance (De Luca & Cano Rubio, 2019). When done effectively, knowledge sharing can greatly enhance employee performance in various ways. It allows employees to learn from one another and gain expertise (Soares et al., 2021; Chukwuemeke & Igbinedion, 2021; Dahiyat et al., 2023; Pietruszka-Ortyl et al., 2021). Additionally, this practice fosters better communication and transparency. When everyone has access to the same information, it leads to improved coordination and alignment among departments and teams (Itoe Mote & Karadas, 2022; Jung et al., 2021).

Knowledge Application

The use of knowledge is related to the process of using knowledge and information to solve difficulties, make choices, and carry out tasks (Yang et al., 2021). Effective application of knowledge has a positive effect on employee performance. Knowledge that corresponds to employees can make better decisions and solve problems more effectively (Banuari et al., 2021). This can lead to improved organizational productivity, higher quality and better results. Employees who use knowledge of customer requirements and preferences can provide better service and increase customer satisfaction (Cavaliere et al., 2021; Tien et al., 2021). The use of knowledge improves employee creativity and innovation. The use of the knowledge in new and creative ways, find innovative solutions to problems and new opportunities for organizations (Imran et al., 2018; Liao et al., 2018).

Knowledge Utilization

Knowledge utilization is a important component of the knowledge management process that emphases the application and leverage the knowledge efficiently to attain organizational objectives (Ye & Zhao, 2023). It includes the knowledge assets, material, and visions to drive decision-making, problem-solving, invention, and performance improvement within an organization (Sahibzada et al., 2023). Further, Knowledge utilization is strongly connected with innovation and creativity. Organizations encourage workers to apply knowledge in novel ways, produce new thoughts, and develop novel clarifications (Gashaw Kettema et al., 2023). With the help of knowledge utilization for innovation, organizations stimulate continuous improvement and keep pace with changing needs and trends (Demir et al., 2023).

CHALLENGES AND OVERCOME

Digital technologies are essential in reforming knowledge that is managed and shared within organizations. Though, there are different challenges that organizations tackle in different sectors when executing these technologies in their knowledge management (KM) processes (Trivedi & Srivastava, 2025). These challenges are specific in different sectors but share common themes that is necessary to be addressed for successful implementation (Anzion et al., 2025). The key challenges involve:

Data Security Risks

As digital technologies allow the collection, and distributing of high amounts of data, the hazard of data breaches and cyberattacks maximizes (Aghaunor et al., 2025). This is mostly important in sectors such as healthcare, finance, and government, where complex data is often controlled. Moreover, to minimize data security hazards, organizations adopt robust cybersecurity measures, involving encryption, multi-factor verification, and regular security inspections (Islam et al., 2025). Furthermore, sector-specific guidelines like HIPAA, and GDPR follows to confirm amenability. Training of workers on data security best performs and building a culture of security responsiveness are also important (Riahi & Islam, 2025).

Interoperability Concerns

Various digital systems and technologies frequently do not work together, showing it hard to share information through platforms (Scott et al., 2025). This is an important problem in sectors such as healthcare, in which different systems communicate with one another. Organizations address interoperability by implementing open standards and capitalizing in incorporation platforms that permit dissimilar systems to connect (Wu et al., 2025). Regulating data formats and making common rules for system communication update knowledge sharing and confirm compatibility in various technologies (Oakley et al., 2025).

Resistance to Change

Workers and organization resist the use of advance digital technologies because of the concerns related to disturbance and exoticism (Hallin et al., 2025). This one is a common challenge in management where traditional ways have been in place for a long-term like industrial or learning. Management focus on modification management practices to minimize resistance. This involves statement related to the advantages of digital technologies, and including workers in the transition process (Chowdhury et al., 2025).

Cost Implications

The rate of adopting digital technologies for knowledge management, involving the procurement of software, hardware, and training, is a risk for management, mostly in businesses with constricted costs like small size businesses (Mushinzimana et al., 2025). Industries use cloud-based solutions to moderate budget concerns that provide accessible pricing models and decrease the want for huge upfront savings.

Moreover, organizations discover partnerships, and government inducements that support balance the budget of technology implementation. A phased adoption policy permits management to manage expenditures over time (Samawi et al., 2025).

Scalability and Flexibility

Digital technologies are not reshaped to switch the density and volume of data created by huge organizations. This is challenging in sectors such as industrial, where production and knowledge management systems must grow rapidly (Ennajeh et al., 2025). Organizations select digital technologies to address scalability alarms that are elastic and implement to the developing want of the business. Cloud computing gives the skill to scale systems as higher demand without the necessity for important upfront capital expenses (Abbas & Joseph, 2025).

Lack of Skilled Workforce

Adopting and managing digital technologies needs skilled employees who are expert in data analytics, like artificial intelligence and other new technologies (Soomro et al., 2025). Various sectors, like healthcare and instruction tackle with challenges in searching workers with the essential skills. Moreover, management capitalizes in training and upskilling programs for prevailing workers to bridge knowledge gaps (Nwaogbe et al., 2025). Employees cooperate with educational institutions and industry followers to establish a channel of ability. Associating with outside advisers or service provider supports to fill the skills gap in the short-run (Sackstein & Laing, 2025).

Cultural Barriers to Knowledge Sharing

Organizational culture not inspires open sharing of knowledge in different sectors (Iqbal et al., 2025). This is the case in organization such as law or finance, where exclusive knowledge is measured by competitive advantage and averseness to distribute knowledge inside and outside (Kareem et al., 2025). Furthermore, fostering a culture of collaboration is important to overwhelming this hurdle. Leaders' model knowledge-sharing behavior and management incentivize workers to subsidize to knowledge management platforms (Zhou et al., 2025). Establishing cross-functional teams and giving instruments that make knowledge sharing informal also inspire a more open culture (Salem et al., 2025).

ROLE OF DIGITAL TECHNOLOGY ON KNOWLEDGE MANAGEMENT PROCESS

Digital technology or knowledge management process shows the link between technology and dimensions of KMP. Some digital instruments improves the availability of thee knowledge movement in the organizations. Knowledge management process and digital technology facilitate the gathering of huge amount of data. The link between KMP and DT promote innovation and enhance decision-making. Organizations can confirm that knowledge is not only well-maintained but it also useful to have efficient achievements(Deng et al., 2023).

Role of DT on KMP in the Manufacturing sector

Digital technology has significant impact on KMP in the manufacturing sector. DT allows the businesses to use their knowledge in more effective way. Some digital progressive instruments gather data from supply chain and it makes a source of operational knowledge. Then collected date is processed using some digital tools that enhance the capability of decision-making. Predictive maintenance system is the example for showing the role of DT on KMP in the manufacturing sector. Predictive maintenance system analyzes instrument performance data to estimate disappointments and enhance progress(Feng et al., 2017).

Moreover, digital technology promotes continues progress in the manufacturing sector by adding exterior knowledge sources into interior processes. Some instruments that are cloud-based collaboration instruments allow organizations to investigate with product design before its application. Augmented reality is the part of immersive technologies that can be used for the training of employees in a virtual climate. The adoption of digital technology in knowledge management process improves operational productivity and also higher the innovation (Zeebaree et al., 2020).

Role of DT on KMP in the Service Sector

Digital technology has transformed KMP in the service sector. Digital technology allows continues capture and it is the dissemination of acute info. Some digital instruments enable business to gathers consumers feedback. Cloud-based tools allow service workers to get and share info and promoting teamwork through organizations(Frank et al., 2019).

Furthermore, the implementation of digital technologies bring continues learning among service sector. Some platforms such as e-learning, virtual training programs and Artificial intelligence allow workers to improve their capabilities. Digital technologies also allow organizations to get consumer feedback in the marketplace.

Digital technology not only improves the growth of knowledge management process but also improves the consumer relation in a competitive market(Nagy et al., 2018).

Role of DT on KMP in Real World

The digital technologies and knowledge management has shown real positive change in many industries and the implementation has also changed operations for the better. A lot more can be accomplished with the use of digital technologies, as these applications have enhanced productivity, made high quality decisions, and increased coordination in companies. Below are examples from different sectors illustrating the collaborative role of digital technologies in the KM process

Healthcare Sector

Digital technologies in healthcare such as EHRs and health information systems, allow healthcare providers to share data relating to patients in real-time. Advanced analytics and artificial intelligence (AI) can help healthcare institutions manage all of the knowledge around patient care, treatment plans, and medical research. Such as AI has the ability to process large scale of data (hospital, medical, etc) to discover useful patterns and help improve diagnosis. It helps doctors, nurses, and other health professionals work together more effectively by quickly accessing and sharing important patient information to provide better care. Furthermore, Hospitals and clinics influence KM processes by making shared knowledge repositories and platforms for worker to exchange best practices and treatment protocols, improving decision-making and standardizing care (Zeebaree et al., 2020).

Finance Sector

Financial sector has great importance for nay country. In current time of period block chain technology is used to improve security and transparency dealings as well as used extensively in sharing of financial knowledge among the employees. The banks and financial institutions are accepting block chain to strongly share matter data and diminish fraud (Jariwala, 2025). Moreover, financial institutions usage digital platforms to enable knowledge sharing about market tendencies, guiding updates, and investment approaches among staffs and clients. The cooperative role of digital technologies in finance comprises on generating integrated knowledge implication, where employees certainly get access to research reports, financial estimates, and risk management plans, leading to more knowledgeable decision-making and better innovation(Sutarman et al., 2025).

Industrial Sector

In industrial, the Internet of Things (IoT) allows the machines, devices, and equipment to interconnect in real-time and generate a wealth of operating data. Digital technologies such as IoT and AI permit companies for detention and analyzing data from machines, labors, and manufacture lines. Knowledge management in the industrial sector comprises the use of cooperative platforms where workers share visions from IoT data; best performs for equipment maintenance, and plans to improve production workflows. This association gives assistances to drive constant improvement and operational superiority.

Education Sector

In education sector, digital technologies such as Distance Learning Management Systems (DLMS) and video conferencing tools have transformed the way of knowledge(Spaska et al., 2025). It helps to manage and share the important knowledge among the teachers, students, and institutes. Educational institutions achieve knowledge by continuing digital sources of course materials, research articles, and teaching resources. This digital system permits collaboration among instructors and allows sharing the teaching methods, curriculum enhancements, and research outcomes (Kusmawan et al., 2025).

Government Sector

Governments are gradually implementing e-government platforms to offer citizens with digital right to use the public services. The government agencies allow for collaborating, sharing information, and work collaboration to deliver services more professionally. For tax information, public services, and community health data digital tools are used to share among the between different governments sectors to expand service delivery and policy-making. KM in government comprises on the development of collaborative tools and stages where executives share best practices, supervisory updates, and policy strategies. This cooperative approach allows more operative authority and decision-making (Aprilina et al., 2025; Younus et al., 2025).

THEORIES RELATED TO KMP AND DIGITAL TECHNOLOGIES

There are following some theories are important as well as important in the context of digital technologies and KMP.

1. Knowledge based view theory
2. Socio-technical system theory
3. Dynamic capability theory

Knowledge Base View Theory

This theory is introduced by the Grant in 1996. This theory posits that knowledge is the important resource of the organization. The knowledge serves as dynamic resource that drives the innovation, competitive advantage and adaptability. This theory emphasizes the unique role of the knowledge to make the organization strategies. In the context of KBV, the digital technologies plays an important role in facilitating the knowledge sharing, application, creating and all the essential element of knowledge management process(Hu et al., 2024).

The digital technologies closely relates to the KBV by enabling the transformation of tacit knowledge in the explicit know. Furthermore, KBV highlight the significance of the organizational mechanisms for the knowledge incorporation. The digital technologies such as cloud platforms are the central hubs for any organization for diverse mean of accessibility. The KBV theory underscores the centrality of the knowledge as the base of organizational success and digital technologies complement this aspect by providing the tools and platforms that enhance the efficiency and effectiveness of the Knowledge management process. In short, the organization uses to transform their knowledge assets in to sustainable competitive advantages as well as ensure the long term success(Sitalaksmi et al., 2024).

Socio-Technical System Theory (STS)

This theory is developed by the Trist and Bamforth in 1951. This is holistic approach to understand the bidirectional relationship between social and technical element use for the management for the organization production as well as service. (Hashem et al., 2024)

Furthermore, the socio-technical system theory explains the robust framework from understanding the implication of digital technologies in the knowledge management process. This theory also stress on the alignment on the system of the organization to ensure the technical innovation which enhance the novelty rather than disrupt organization process. In the context of digital technology for the knowledge management process, this theory leads to more efficient, collaborative and resilient knowledge management system which further leads towards the success of organization in the digital era(Salzmann-Erikson et al., 2024).

Dynamic Capabilities Theory (DCT)

Dynamic capabilities theory was developed by the Teec et al 1997. This theory emphasizes the ability of the organization to adapt the reconfigure internal and external competency to achieve the goals in rapidly changing in environment. This theory majorly explains the concept of the dynamic capabilities which refers to the opportunities of the organization to achieve the organizational goals. The DCT also highlight the importance of the mechanisms which enhance the dynamic capability of learning, whereas knowledge sharing. Application and acquisition are the main part of the learning process(Enebeli, 2024; Priyono et al.).

In the context of the relationship between the digital technologies and KMP, This theory is particularly relevant to understanding the influence of the digital technologies on the KMP, as both are important for the enhancing the ability of the organization in the response of innovation and changing. This theory also enable the process of knowledge sharing across the department with the help of digital tools such as video conferences, integrated knowledge platforms which foster the collaboration(Zamiri & Esmaeili, 2024).

Furthermore, this theory provides the powerful understanding for interplay between digital technologies and knowledge management process. DCT explains that the KMP along with digital technology help to the organization to achieve the sustainable growth, knowledge transformation opportunities for the administration and employee(Aggarwal et al., 2024).

CONCLUSION

Knowledge management process is a tactical method for making and utilizing knowledge in organization. Knowledge management process improves the workers' abilities and innovation. And digital technologies work as a significant instrument for keeping and distributing information. Knowledge management process increases technical allocation to promote learning. So, digital technologies and knowledge management process allow businesses to tackle with troubleshooting tasks and both get sustainable development in the competitive economy.

Some relevant theories such as Knowledge based view theory, Socio-technical system theory, and Dynamic capability theory have used in this chapter. These theories show the impact of digital technologies on knowledge management process in different sectors.

REFERENCES

Abbas, G., & Joseph, C. (2025). Cost-Effective Cloud Strategies for SMEs: Solving Technology Challenges and Driving Competitiveness.

Abbas, Q., & Yaqoob, S. (2009). Effect of leadership development on employee performance in Pakistan. *Pakistan Economic and Social Review*, •••, 269–292.

Aggarwal, S., Bharti, V., & Badhon, A. J. (2024). Quantum Computing. In *Quantum Computing and Cryptography in Future Computers* (pp. 1–32). IGI Global. DOI: 10.4018/978-1-7998-9522-0.ch001

Aghaunor, C. T., Eshua, P., Obah, T., & Aromokeye, O. (2025). Data security strategies to avoid data breaches in modern information systems.

Ajanaku, O. J., & Mutula, S. (2018). The relationship between knowledge management and nursing care performance. *South African Journal of Library and Information Science*, *84*(2), 39–51.

Akhavan, P., Ramezan, M., Yazdi Moghaddam, J., & Mehralian, G. (2014). Exploring the relationship between ethics, knowledge creation and organizational performance: Case study of a knowledge-based organization. *VINE Journal of Information and Knowledge Management Systems*, *44*(1), 42–58.

Al Shraah, A., Abu-Rumman, A., Al Madi, F., Alhammad, F. A. F., & AlJboor, A. A. (2022). The impact of quality management practices on knowledge management processes: A study of a social security corporation in Jordan. *The TQM Journal*, *34*(4), 605–626. DOI: 10.1108/TQM-08-2020-0183

Almatrooshi, B., Singh, S. K., & Farouk, S. (2016). Determinants of organizational performance: A proposed framework. *International Journal of Productivity and Performance Management*, *65*(6), 844–859. DOI: 10.1108/IJPPM-02-2016-0038

Antunes, H. J. G., & Pinheiro, P. G. (2020). Linking knowledge management, organizational learning and memory. *Journal of Innovation & Knowledge*, *5*(2), 140–149. DOI: 10.1016/j.jik.2019.04.002

Anzion, L. J., Schaafsma, F. G., Boot, C. R., Formanoy, M. A., & Schelvis, R. M. (2025). An exploration of changes in the mental models of middle management and their association with activities to implement a dialogue tool to address mental health in the workplace. *BMC Public Health*, *25*(1), 623. DOI: 10.1186/s12889-025-21702-x PMID: 39953447

Aprilina, V., Dompak, T., Salsabila, L., & Lodan, K. T. (2025). The Role Of Digitalization In Enhancing Public Service Efficiency: Challenges And Opportunities In Managing Public Complaints Through E-Government In Indonesia. *International Journal of Social Welfare and Family Law*, *2*(1), 57–66. DOI: 10.62951/ijsw.v2i1.183

Areed, S., Salloum, S. A., & Shaalan, K. (2020). The role of knowledge management processes for enhancing and supporting innovative organizations: a systematic review. *Recent advances in intelligent systems and smart applications*, 143-161.

Aviv, I., Hadar, I., & Levy, M. (2021). Knowledge management infrastructure framework for enhancing knowledge-intensive business processes. *Sustainability (Basel)*, *13*(20), 11387. DOI: 10.3390/su132011387

Banuari, N., Absah, Y., & Siahaan, E. (2021). Analyze the Influence of Talent Management and Knowledge Management on Employee Performance through Employee Retention as Intervening Variable at PT Bhanda Ghara Reksa Divre I Medan. *International Journal of Research and Review*, *8*(9), 189–204. DOI: 10.52403/ijrr.20210926

Bhatt, G. D. (2001). Knowledge management in organizations: Examining the interaction between technologies, techniques, and people. *Journal of Knowledge Management*, *5*(1), 68–75. DOI: 10.1108/13673270110384419

Cao, X., Ali, A., Pitafi, A. H., Khan, A. N., & Waqas, M. (2021). A socio-technical system approach to knowledge creation and team performance: Evidence from China. *Information Technology & People*, *34*(7), 1976–1996. DOI: 10.1108/ITP-10-2019-0536

Cavaliere, L. P. L., Khan, R., Sundram, S., Jainani, K., Bagale, G., Chakravarthi, M. K., Regin, R., & Rajest, S. S. (2021). The Impact of customer relationship management on customer satisfaction and retention: The mediation of service quality. *Turkish Journal of Physiotherapy and Rehabilitation*, *32*(3), 22107–22121.

Chowdhury, A., Kabir, K. H., McQuire, M., & Bureau, D. P. (2025). The dynamics of digital technology adoption in rainbow trout aquaculture: Exploring multi-stakeholder perceptions in Ontario using Q methodology and the theory of planned behaviour. *Aquaculture (Amsterdam, Netherlands)*, *594*, 741460. DOI: 10.1016/j.aquaculture.2024.741460

Chukwuemeke, H. E., & Igbinedion, V. (2021). Relationship between knowledge dissemination, learning self-efficacy and task performance of business educators. *Nau Journal Of Technology and Vocational Education*, *6*(1), 13–21.

Dahiyat, S. E., Khasawneh, S. M., Bontis, N., & Al-Dahiyat, M. (2023). Intellectual capital stocks and flows: Examining the mediating roles of social capital and knowledge transfer. *VINE Journal of Information and Knowledge Management Systems*, *53*(1), 11–42. DOI: 10.1108/VJIKMS-06-2020-0110

De Luca, P., & Cano Rubio, M. (2019). The curve of knowledge transfer: A theoretical model. *Business Process Management Journal*, *25*(1), 10–26. DOI: 10.1108/BPMJ-06-2017-0161

Demir, A., Budur, T., Omer, H. M., & Heshmati, A. (2023). Links between knowledge management and organisational sustainability: Does the ISO 9001 certification have an effect? *Knowledge Management Research and Practice*, *21*(1), 183–196. DOI: 10.1080/14778238.2020.1860663

Deng, H., Duan, S. X., & Wibowo, S. (2023). Digital technology driven knowledge sharing for job performance. *Journal of Knowledge Management*, *27*(2), 404–425. DOI: 10.1108/JKM-08-2021-0637

Du, H.-S., Ma, J.-J., & Li, M. (2016). High-quality health information provision for stroke patients. *Chinese Medical Journal*, *129*(17), 2115–2122. DOI: 10.4103/0366-6999.189065 PMID: 27569241

Du Plessis, M. (2007). The role of knowledge management in innovation. *Journal of Knowledge Management*, *11*(4), 20–29. DOI: 10.1108/13673270710762684

Enebeli, J. P. (2024). Information And Communication Technology (Ict), Globalization And Inpeneding Challenges. *Global Journal of Pure and Applied Sciences*, *30*(1), 95–100. DOI: 10.4314/gjpas.v30i1.9

Ennajeh, L., Najjar, T., & Aloui, A. (2025). Digital Transformation through Artificial Intelligence in Organizations: A Systematic Literature Review. *Journal of Information Technology Management, 17*(Special Issue on Strategic, Organizational, and Social Issues of Digital Transformation in Organizations), 53-78.

Feng, S. C., Bernstein, W. Z., Hedberg, T.Jr, & Barnard Feeney, A. (2017). Toward knowledge management for smart manufacturing. *Journal of Computing and Information Science in Engineering*, *17*(3), 031016. DOI: 10.1115/1.4037178 PMID: 28966561

Frank, A. G., Dalenogare, L. S., & Ayala, N. F. (2019). Industry 4.0 technologies: Implementation patterns in manufacturing companies. *International Journal of Production Economics*, *210*, 15–26. DOI: 10.1016/j.ijpe.2019.01.004

García, J., Amescua, A., Sánchez, M.-I., & Bermón, L. (2011). Design guidelines for software processes knowledge repository development. *Information and Software Technology*, *53*(8), 834–850. DOI: 10.1016/j.infsof.2011.03.002

Gashaw Kettema, W., Tefera Ayele, Z., Assefaw Geremew, M., Temesgen Assefa, K., Ayalew Yimer, S., Dessie Liyew, A., Berihun Erega, B., & Habtie Dagnaw, E. (2023). Knowledge, Utilization, and Associated Factors of Nonpneumatic Antishock Garments for Management of Postpartum Hemorrhage among Maternity Ward Health Care Professionals in South Wollo Zone Health Facilities, Ethiopia, 2021: A Cross-Sectional Study Design. *Obstetrics and Gynecology International*, *2023*, 2023. DOI: 10.1155/2023/8247603 PMID: 36691431

Hallin, A., Andersson, C., Crevani, L., Ingvarsson, C., Ivory, C., Lammi, I., Lindell, E., & Uhlin, A. (2025). Creating the Future of Work: Imaginaries in an Era of Digitalization. In *Creating the Future of Work*. Edward Elgar Publishing. DOI: 10.4337/9781035324484

Hashem, G., Aboelmaged, M., & Ahmad, I. (2024). Proactiveness, knowledge management capability and innovation ambidexterity: An empirical examination of digital supply chain adoption. *Management Decision*, *62*(1), 129–162. DOI: 10.1108/MD-02-2023-0237

Hu, L., Zhou, J., Zhang, J. Z., & Behl, A. (2024). Blockchain technology adaptation and organizational inertia: Moderating role between knowledge management processes and supply chain resilience. *Kybernetes*, *53*(2), 515–542. DOI: 10.1108/K-12-2022-1661

Hussain, Z., Jusoh, A., Jamil, K., Rehman, A. U., & Gul, R. F. (2022). Analyzing the role of knowledge management process to enhance sustainable corporate performance: A mediation moderation model. *Knowledge and Process Management*, *29*(3), 205–220. DOI: 10.1002/kpm.1679

Imran, M. K., Ilyas, M., Aslam, U., & Fatima, T. (2018). Knowledge processes and firm performance: The mediating effect of employee creativity. *Journal of Organizational Change Management*, *31*(3), 512–531. DOI: 10.1108/JOCM-10-2016-0202

Iqbal, S., Ullah, S., Rizwan, A., Nazeer, N., Rasheed, M., & Siddiqi, A. F. I. (2025). Building competitive advantage: how organizational culture shapes absorptive capacity through knowledge sharing. *Journal of Organizational Effectiveness: People and Performance*.

Islam, M. T., Mission, M. R., Refat, T. K., & Kynatun, M. (2025). Cybersecurity risk assessment frameworks for engineering databases: A systematic literature review. *Strategic Data Management and Innovation*, *2*(01), 224–243.

Itoe Mote, N. J., & Karadas, G. (2022). The impact of automation and knowledge workers on employees' outcomes: Mediating role of knowledge transfer. *Sustainability (Basel)*, *14*(3), 1377. DOI: 10.3390/su14031377

Jariwala, M. (2025). Artificial Intelligence and Blockchain and the Growth of the FinTech Industry. In *Driving Socio-Economic Growth With AI and Blockchain* (pp. 113–146). IGI Global Scientific Publishing. DOI: 10.4018/979-8-3693-8664-4.ch006

Jung, J. H., Yoo, J. J., & Arnold, T. J. (2021). The influence of a retail store manager in developing frontline employee brand relationship, service performance and customer loyalty. *Journal of Business Research*, *122*, 362–372. DOI: 10.1016/j.jbusres.2020.09.010

Kareem, O., Aliyu, O. A., & Salimon, M. G. (2025). Does the Islamic work ethic moderate the relationship between organizational culture and enterprise performance? *Journal of Small Business and Enterprise Development*, *32*(2), 298–324. DOI: 10.1108/JSBED-11-2022-0480

Kiessling, T., Maley, J. F., Moeller, M., & Dabić, M. (2021). Managing global knowledge transfer: Inpatriate manager embeddedness and firm innovation. *International Business Review*, •••, 101868.

Kun, M. (2022). Linkages between Knowledge Management Process and Corporate Sustainable Performance of Chinese SMEs: Mediating role of Frugal Innovation. *Frontiers in Psychology*, •••, 1172.

Kusmawan, A., Rahman, R., Anis, N., & Arifudin, O. (2025). The Relationship Between Teacher Involvement in Curriculum Development and Student Learning Outcomes. *International Journal of Educatio Elementaria and Psychologia*, *2*(1), 1–12.

Li, H., Yang, Z., Jin, C., & Wang, J. (2023). How an industrial internet platform empowers the digital transformation of SMEs: Theoretical mechanism and business model. *Journal of Knowledge Management*, *27*(1), 105–120. DOI: 10.1108/JKM-09-2022-0757

Li, Y.-H., Huang, J.-W., & Tsai, M.-T. (2009). Entrepreneurial orientation and firm performance: The role of knowledge creation process. *Industrial Marketing Management*, *38*(4), 440–449. DOI: 10.1016/j.indmarman.2008.02.004

Liao, S., Chen, C., & Hu, D. (2018). The role of knowledge sharing and LMX to enhance employee creativity in theme park work team: A case study of Taiwan. *International Journal of Contemporary Hospitality Management*, *30*(5), 2343–2359. DOI: 10.1108/IJCHM-09-2016-0522

Long, S. (2023). Optimizing Knowledge Management During Crises. In *Health Informatics and Patient Safety in Times of Crisis* (pp. 77–94). IGI Global.

Magill, E., Siegel, Z., & Pike, K. M. (2020). The mental health of frontline health care providers during pandemics: A rapid review of the literature. *Psychiatric Services (Washington, D.C.)*, *71*(12), 1260–1269. DOI: 10.1176/appi.ps.202000274 PMID: 33019857

Mahdi, O. R., Nassar, I. A., & Almsafir, M. K. (2019). Knowledge management processes and sustainable competitive advantage: An empirical examination in private universities. *Journal of Business Research*, *94*, 320–334. DOI: 10.1016/j.jbusres.2018.02.013

McQuade, E., Sjoer, E., Fabian, P., Nascimento, J. C., & Schroeder, S. (2007). Will you miss me when I'm gone? A study of the potential loss of company knowledge and expertise as employees retire. *Journal of European Industrial Training*, *31*(9), 758–768. DOI: 10.1108/03090590710846701

Migdadi, M. M. (2022). Knowledge management processes, innovation capability and organizational performance. *International Journal of Productivity and Performance Management*, *71*(1), 182–210. DOI: 10.1108/IJPPM-04-2020-0154

Mushinzimana, L., Faisal, A., & Teressia, A. (2025). Strategy For Evaluating the Strengths, Weaknesses, Opportunities, And Threats of The Business Community in Rwanda in Adopting Digital Transformation to Increase Financial Benefits. *Indiana Journal of Economics and Business Management*, *5*(1), 64–96.

Nagy, J., Oláh, J., Erdei, E., Máté, D., & Popp, J. (2018). The role and impact of Industry 4.0 and the internet of things on the business strategy of the value chain—The case of Hungary. *Sustainability (Basel)*, *10*(10), 3491. DOI: 10.3390/su10103491

Nonaka, I., Toyama, R., & Konno, N. (2000). SECI, Ba and leadership: A unified model of dynamic knowledge creation. *Long Range Planning*, *33*(1), 5–34. DOI: 10.1016/S0024-6301(99)00115-6

Nwaogbe, G., Ekpenyong, E., & Urhoghide, O. (2025). Managing workforce productivity in the post-pandemic construction industry.

Oakley, T., Vaz, J., da Silva, F., Allan, R., Almeida, D., Champlin, K., da Silva, E. S., Tilman, A. J., Marr, I., Smith-Vaughan, H., Yan, J., & Francis, J. R. (2025). Implementation of a Laboratory Information Management System (LIMS) for microbiology in Timor-Leste: Challenges, mitigation strategies, and end-user experiences. *BMC Medical Informatics and Decision Making*, *25*(1), 32. DOI: 10.1186/s12911-024-02831-6 PMID: 39825312

Obeso, M., Hernández-Linares, R., López-Fernández, M. C., & Serrano-Bedia, A. M. (2020). Knowledge management processes and organizational performance: The mediating role of organizational learning. *Journal of Knowledge Management, 24*(8), 1859–1880. DOI: 10.1108/JKM-10-2019-0553

Parayitam, S., Usman, S. A., Namasivaayam, R. R., & Naina, M. S. (2021). Knowledge management and emotional exhaustion as moderators in the relationship between role conflict and organizational performance: Evidence from India. *Journal of Knowledge Management, 25*(6), 1456–1485. DOI: 10.1108/JKM-03-2020-0184

Passos, D. M. A., Sarmento, A. M., & Gonçalves, P. J. P. (2021). Knowledge Management and Individual Job Performance in Higher Education: Proposal of a Conceptual Model. In *Perspectives and Trends in Education and Technology: Selected Papers from ICITED 2021* (pp. 367-382). Springer.

Paul, P., & Singh, B. (2023). Healthcare Employee Engagement Using the Internet of Things: A Systematic Overview. *The Adoption and Effect of Artificial Intelligence on Human Resources Management, Part A*, 71-97.

Pietruszka-Ortyl, A., Ćwiek, M., Ziębicki, B., & Wójcik-Karpacz, A. (2021). Organizational culture as a prerequisite for knowledge transfer among IT professionals: The case of energy companies. *Energies, 14*(23), 8139. DOI: 10.3390/en14238139

Pinheiro, J., Silva, G. M., Dias, Á. L., Lages, L. F., & Preto, M. T. (2020). Fostering knowledge creation to improve performance: The mediation role of manufacturing flexibility. *Business Process Management Journal, 26*(7), 1871–1892. DOI: 10.1108/BPMJ-10-2019-0413

Priyono, A., Shukor, S. A., Moin, A., & Salikin, N. How does a firm leverage dynamic capabilities to pioneer a 2 business ecosystem and serve as the orchestrator? Lessons 3 learned from coffee shop industry 4.

Pyo, S. (2005). Knowledge map for tourist destinations—Needs and implications. *Tourism Management, 26*(4), 583–594. DOI: 10.1016/j.tourman.2004.03.001

Raudeliūnienė, J., Davidavičienė, V., & Jakubavičius, A. (2018). Knowledge management process model. *Entrepreneurship and Sustainability Issues, 5*(3), 542–554. DOI: 10.9770/jesi.2018.5.3(10)

Riahi, E., & Islam, M. S. (2025). Employees' information security awareness (ISA) in public organisations: Insights from cross-cultural studies in Sweden, France, and Tunisia. *Behaviour & Information Technology, 44*(1), 79–101. DOI: 10.1080/0144929X.2024.2311734

Sa, M. L. L., Choon-Yin, S., Chai, Y. K., & Joo, J. H. A. (2020). Knowledge creation process, customer orientation and firm performance: Evidence from small hotels in Malaysia. *Asia Pacific Management Review, 25*(2), 65–74. DOI: 10.1016/j.apmrv.2019.07.002

Sackstein, S., & Laing, A. (2025). *Solving School Challenges: The Everything Guide to Transformative Change*. Taylor & Francis. DOI: 10.4324/9781003508960

Saeed, I., Khan, J., Zada, M., & Zada, S. (2024). Employee sensemaking in organizational change via knowledge management: Leadership role as a moderator. *Current Psychology (New Brunswick, N.J.), 43*(7), 6657–6671. DOI: 10.1007/s12144-023-04849-x

Sahibzada, U. F., Jianfeng, C., Latif, K. F., Shah, S. A., & Sahibzada, H. F. (2023). Refuelling knowledge management processes towards organisational performance: Mediating role of creative organisational learning. *Knowledge Management Research and Practice, 21*(1), 1–13. DOI: 10.1080/14778238.2020.1787802

Salem, I. E., Fathy, E. A., Magdy, A., Elsaqqa, M. A., & Kamal Abdien, M. (2025). Unlocking organizational ambidexterity via the role of cross-functional coopetition in quick-service restaurants. *Tourism and Hospitality Research*, •••, 14673584241313353. DOI: 10.1177/14673584241313353

Salman, A., Fakhraldeen, S. A., Chun, S., Jamil, K., Gasana, J., & Al-Hunayan, A. (2020). Enhancing Research and Development in the Health Sciences as a Strategy to Establish a Knowledge-Based Economy in the State of Kuwait: A Call for Action. *Health Care*.

Salzmann-Erikson, M., Olsson, A., Rezagholi, M., Fjellström, D., & Osarenkhoe, A. (2024). Bridging technostress and continuous learning in knowledge-intensive organizations: A socio-technical systems approach for the future of healthy working life. *Journal of Infrastructure, Policy and Development, 8*(13).

Samawi, G. A., Bwaliez, O. M., Jreissat, M., & Kandas, A. (2025). Advancing Sustainable Development in Jordan: A Business and Economic Analysis of Electric Vehicle Adoption in the Transportation Sector. *World Electric Vehicle Journal, 16*(1), 45. DOI: 10.3390/wevj16010045

Scott, H., Ujvari, M. M., Bakeer, A., & Shanaa, K. (2025). Sumud as connected learning: towards a collective digital commons in Palestine.

Shaik, A. S., Jain, M., Mendiratta, A., Alarifi, G., & Arrigo, E. (2024). Role of strategic knowledge management practices in enhancing strategic perspectives of an organisation to improve entrepreneurial performance. *Journal of Knowledge Management, 28*(6), 1648–1675. DOI: 10.1108/JKM-04-2023-0300

Shannak, R., Maqableh, M., & Tarhini, A. (2017). The impact of knowledge management on job performance in higher education: The case of the University of Jordan. *Journal of Enterprise Information Management, 30*(2), 244–262. DOI: 10.1108/JEIM-09-2015-0087

Shedden, P., Scheepers, R., Smith, W., & Ahmad, A. (2011). Incorporating a knowledge perspective into security risk assessments. *Vine, 41*(2), 152–166. DOI: 10.1108/03055721111134790

Sitalaksmi, S., Indarti, N., Anggadwita, G., & Sambudi, A. D. (2024). Knowledge leakage and collaborative innovation: A systematic literature review. *Knowledge Management Research and Practice*, •••, 1–17. DOI: 10.1080/14778238.2024.2431111

Soares, J., Miguel, I., Venâncio, C., Lopes, I., & Oliveira, M. (2021). On the path to minimize plastic pollution: The perceived importance of education and knowledge dissemination strategies. *Marine Pollution Bulletin, 171*, 112890. DOI: 10.1016/j.marpolbul.2021.112890 PMID: 34500371

Soomro, R. B., Al-Rahmi, W. M., Dahri, N. A., Almuqren, L., Al-Mogren, A. S., & Aldaijy, A. (2025). A SEM–ANN analysis to examine impact of artificial intelligence technologies on sustainable performance of SMEs. *Scientific Reports, 15*(1), 5438. DOI: 10.1038/s41598-025-86464-3 PMID: 39948417

Spaska, A., Kozub, H., Abylasynova, G., Kozub, V., & Koval, Y. (2025). Evaluation of innovative teaching methods using modern information technologies. *Jurnal Ilmiah Ilmu Terapan Universitas Jambi, 9*(1), 422–440. DOI: 10.22437/jiituj.v9i1.38107

Sutarman, A., Juliastuti, D., Yati, I., & Pasha, L. P. (2025). Enhancing Security and Privacy in Blockchain Systems for Tax Administration. *Blockchain Frontier Technology, 4*(2), 145~ 155-145~ 155.

Swanson, E., Kim, S., Lee, S.-M., Yang, J.-J., & Lee, Y.-K. (2020). The effect of leader competencies on knowledge sharing and job performance: Social capital theory. *Journal of Hospitality and Tourism Management, 42*, 88–96. DOI: 10.1016/j.jhtm.2019.11.004

Syed-Ikhsan, S. O. S., & Rowland, F. (2004). Knowledge management in a public organization: A study on the relationship between organizational elements and the performance of knowledge transfer. *Journal of Knowledge Management*.

Tien, N. H., Diem, P. T., Van On, P., Anh, V. T., Van Dat, N., Hung, N. T., & Tam, B. Q. (2021). The formation and development of CRM system at Thien Hoa electronics supermarket in Vietnam. *International Journal of Research and Growth Evaluation*, *2*(4), 752–760.

Tomé, E., & Gromova, E. (2021). Development of emergent knowledge strategies and new dynamic capabilities for business education in a time of crisis. *Sustainability (Basel)*, *13*(8), 4518. DOI: 10.3390/su13084518

Trivedi, K., & Srivastava, K. B. (2025). Is improvisation a mediating link driving knowledge management processes towards innovativeness in Indian IT firms? *Management Research Review*. Advance online publication. DOI: 10.1108/MRR-06-2024-0488

Wald, H. S., Dube, C. E., & Anthony, D. C. (2007). Untangling the Web—The impact of Internet use on health care and the physician–patient relationship. *Patient Education and Counseling*, *68*(3), 218–224. DOI: 10.1016/j.pec.2007.05.016 PMID: 17920226

Wall, S. (2020). *Exploration of factors that influence the adoption and utilization of knowledge management systems*. Capella University.

Wu, S., Ramli, M. Z., Ngian, S. P., Qiao, G., & Jiang, B. (2025). Review on parametric building information modelling and forward design approaches for sustainable bridge engineering. *Discover Applied Sciences*, *7*(2), 127. DOI: 10.1007/s42452-025-06543-y

Yang, X., Ye, H. J., & Wang, X. (2021). Social media use and work efficiency: Insights from the theory of communication visibility. *Information & Management*, *58*(4), 103462. DOI: 10.1016/j.im.2021.103462

Yasin, A., Hussain, S., Hali, S. M., & Iqbal, S. (2022). Digitalization and firm performance: Mediating role of smart technologies. *Journal of Tianjin University Science and Technology*, *55*(4).

Ye, S., & Zhao, T. (2023). Team knowledge management: How leaders' expertise recognition influences expertise utilization. *Management Decision*, *61*(1), 77–96. DOI: 10.1108/MD-09-2021-1166

Yeh, Y. J., Lai, S. Q., & Ho, C. T. (2006). Knowledge management enablers: A case study. *Industrial Management & Data Systems*, *106*(6), 793–810. DOI: 10.1108/02635570610671489

Younus, M., Purnomo, E. P., Nurmandi, A., Mutiarin, D., Manaf, H. A., Mumtaz, F., & Khairunnisa, T. (2025). Analyzing the trend of government support for cloud computing usage in e-government architecture. *Journal of Cloud Computing (Heidelberg, Germany)*, *14*(1), 14. DOI: 10.1186/s13677-025-00735-y

Zamiri, M., & Esmaeili, A. (2024). Methods and technologies for supporting knowledge sharing within learning communities: A systematic literature review. *Administrative Sciences*, *14*(1), 17. DOI: 10.3390/admsci14010017

Zeebaree, M., Ismael, G. Y., Nakshabandi, O. A., Saleh, S. S., & Aqel, M. (2020). Impact of innovation technology in enhancing organizational management. *Studies of Applied Economics*, *38*(4). Advance online publication. DOI: 10.25115/eea.v38i4.3970

Zhou, Q., Wang, S., Wang, L., & Xu, W. (2025). Knowledge governance and innovation ambidexterity in the platform context: Exploring the role of knowledge transformation. *Journal of Knowledge Management*, *29*(4), 1301–1329. DOI: 10.1108/JKM-03-2024-0256

Chapter 5
AI in Financial Decision Making

Saqib Muneer
https://orcid.org/0000-0003-4575-9566
University of Ha'il, Saudi Arabia

ABSTRACT

This chapter examines how technology and artificial intelligence (AI) are revolutionizing several industries by enhancing company processes' accuracy, speed, and trust. When combined, they assist companies in automating, augmenting, and achieving authenticity in their workflows. For example, blockchain and artificial intelligence (AI) in financial services increase the speed and accuracy of procedures like loan approvals. This combination increases accuracy, decreases manual labor, and fosters consumer trust. Better care and treatments are possible in the healthcare industry thanks to blockchain's secure record-keeping and artificial intelligence's data analysis capabilities, which give clinicians access to patient records while maintaining patient privacy. AI manage inventory, optimize routes, and even monitor carbon emissions for sustainability. Early success of AI indicates a bright future, despite certain obstacles like maintaining correct data and keeping AI tools current. By utilizing these solutions, businesses may enhance customer happiness, data security, and save time.

1. INTRODUCTION

In recent years, corporations have increasingly matched their strategy with society's expectations to improve reputation and long-term profitability. This transition represents a larger commitment to sustainable practices, in which financial management is critical in promoting growth that fulfills economic, environmental,

DOI: 10.4018/979-8-3693-8960-7.ch005

and social objectives. Financial management enables firms to track, appraise, and communicate their progress toward these sustainability objectives, resulting in a framework that not only promotes financial stability but also encourages responsible economic development. High-quality financial management helps organizations run smoothly by utilizing resources and guaranteeing revenue stability. This connection of financial strategy with sustainable practices helps firms gain a competitive edge, manage risks, and create long-term value for stakeholders. Efficient financial management techniques are crucial for firms to retain as they expand and change to meet new demands, effectively manage assets, and seize opportunities for long-term success. (Al Breiki & Nobanee, 2019). AI has the potential to influence financial decision-making by extracting and collecting information from unstructured data. AI can be used to predict and analyze market trends that help institutions stay one step ahead of their competitors. AI-driven models are also helpful in risk assessments by predicting creditworthiness to help make more informed lending decisions. From investment banks and hedge funds to personal financial decisions are also influenced by AI-driven tools and models. (Forbes Finance Council, 2024). With the advancement and integration of AI models, financial decision-making becomes more insightful and resilient.

2. FINANCIAL MANAGEMENT AND AI

The field of financial management is being progressively shaped by artificial intelligence (AI), which uses advanced technologies like machine learning and predictive analytics to improve decision-making. In the last ten years, artificial intelligence (AI) has allowed financial institutions to handle large datasets with astounding speed and precision, revolutionizing domains like customer service, investing strategies, and risk assessment. AI provides insightful information that facilitates better decision-making and better financial results by evaluating complicated data. (Mullangi et al., n.d.-a). IA is very helpful in analyzing the financial database for risk management, investment decisions, and fraud detection. AI-powered tools are very helpful in enhancing security against fraud and improving credit scoring, trade accuracy, and market predictions. For responsible AI adoption, the ethical AI frameworks and continuous improvement and learning are the most crucial parameters.

3. FINANCIAL MANAGEMENT AND AI'S ROLE

In handling large and complex data sets, artificial intelligence (AI) is very useful as it can analyze data without the need of human monitoring, through the use of machine learning operations and predictive analytics. AI is very crucial to financial management, it can improve client experiences, automate processes, improve investment strategies, offer individualized services, and can help in managing risks effectively.

3.1 Role of Artificial Intelligence (AI) in Financial Decision-Making

AI can quickly spread in various areas, notably banking, as it can facilitate sophisticated data analysis to support complex decision-making processes. Due to AI's extraordinary capabilities of processing large datasets rapidly and effectively, financial institutions can make quicker, better choices by gaining insights that was not possible with such efficiency using traditional approaches. However, AI applications also raise ethical concerns about privacy, openness, and bias. By resolving these obstacles, AI can be applied morally in financial decision-making processes, thereby striking an equilibrium between economic advantage and responsible behavior.

Artificial intelligence has great capacity to revolutionize the Finance industry by modernizing conventional business models and creating novel and advanced expectations. By integrating such sophisticated data technologies, today's businesses can enhance customer service, boost efficiency, lower operational costs, and enhance financial decisions. Using AI, the financial institutions' function and engagement with their clients are evolving through the incorporation of predictive analytics and automation. With more advancements, the future financial models will evolve to boost competition and can help open new avenues for economic growth. Businesses aiming to thrive in such an evolving financial environment should uphold competitiveness and must adopt these revolutions brought by today's technologies. (Shahvaroughi Farahani & Esfahani, 2022).

Large datasets may be efficiently analyzed by machine learning methods, which makes them extremely useful for financial decision-making. These technologies facilitate improved financial decision-making in domains such as FinTech lending and investment planning by arranging and extracting insights from both structured and unstructured data. (Huang & You, 2023).

Advanced data tools have been crucial to financial management in recent years because they allow organizations to examine large amounts of data quickly and accurately. Because these tools give financial professionals deep insights from complex datasets, they have greatly enhanced areas like risk assessment, investment planning, and client service. Better judgments that take market relationships and trends into consideration are supported by this all-encompassing strategy, which improves risk management, maximizes investment strategies, and enables more rapid adaptations to shifting market conditions (Mullangi et al., n.d.-b).

3.2 Making Financial Decisions Better with Advanced Technology

Rapid technological advancement is revolutionizing financial management through data-driven solutions that simplify risk management and investment decisions. Financial organizations can now examine enormous volumes of data more rapidly and precisely than ever before because of these sophisticated tools. Predictive analytics and automated trading systems are important tools that help investors make better decisions, reduce risks, and improve client experiences by automating processes like credit scoring and fraud detection. Customer service has been further improved by the rise of virtual assistants, which has also increased account management efficiency. (Modupe, 2023).

4. ETHICAL FRAMEWORK FOR FINANCIAL DECISIONS

Financial decisions are guided by an ethical framework to ensure that they are both ethically and financially sound. Financial institutions benefit all parties involved—shareholders, staff, and society at large—by upholding ethical norms, which also increase market stability and foster confidence. Making moral decisions may boost trust in the financial system, promoting sustainability and stability over the long run. (Saikanth et al., 2024).

4.1 Accountability and Transparency of AI Algorithms

To ensure fairness in financial decisions, AI algorithms need to be transparent. More effectively, institutions can detect and mitigate bias if they enhance the AI process's understandability. Holding developers accountable for algorithmic decisions supports ethical decision-making and increases confidence in AI-fueled financial services. A lack of transparency can lead to prejudice and discrimination, which undercuts confidence in AI-driven systems. (Olatoye et al., 2024)

4.2 Fairness and Bias in AI

Equity has to be the first point of consideration in AI-informed financial decisions, particularly given the potential for bias in previous data that may enable discrimination against specific groups. To address this, firms need processes of regular audit and transparency, ensuring that AI systems continue to make fair and unbiased decisions. Ongoing monitoring facilitates ethical standards in AI applications by helping to identify and rectify skewed decision-making. (Castelnovo, 2024).

4.3 Data Security and Privacy

Data privacy and data security are top priorities when it comes to using AI systems dealing with large databases. To keep consumer information private, financial companies must implement vigorous security protocols. Ethical implementation of AI through finance is served by compliance with industry standards and privacy regulations like those of the OECD. Data authenticity verification and informed consent are among the best practices for ensuring secure and trustworthy AI processing are necessary to promote safe and accurate AI processes. (Fabrègue & Bogoni, 2023).

4.4 Challenges with Regulation and Compliance

AI's complexity and potential for bias make it difficult to regulate in the financial industry. Financial institutions and regulatory agencies that can set guidelines for ethical AI use must work together for regulation to be effective. Organizations may manage compliance concerns, reduce risks, and uphold ethical standards with the support of transparency, accountability, and recurring audits

4.5 Ethical Decision-Making in the Implementation of AI

AI aids society while lowering risks thanks to ethical decision-making. Transparency in AI deployment and distinct roles for human monitoring are essential. Ethical frameworks ensure that human judgment is still at the center of AI-related decisions by guiding AI applications to preserve principles like responsibility, justice, and bias mitigation (Balasubramanian, 2023).

5. THE ADVANTAGES AND DISADVANTAGES OF DATA-DRIVEN DECISION SUPPORT SYSTEMS

There are risks to take into account, even while technology has obvious advantages like increased efficiency and improved risk mitigation. Biases in training data may be reflected in data-driven systems, which could result in biased judgments. Furthermore, because these systems are so complicated, consumers may see judgments as "black box" outputs, which could compromise transparency. As more activities rely on digital technologies, financial institutions need to put strong security measures in place to guard against cyber threats. To successfully integrate data-driven tools into finance, these risks and advantages must be balanced. (Modupe, 2023)

6. PRINCIPAL USES OF AI IN FINANCIAL DECISION-MAKING

AI performs several vital tasks in financial decision-making. For example, AI-driven algorithms examine past market data to find trends that improve the accuracy of asset prices and market trend forecasting. Furthermore, by assessing creditworthiness, spotting irregularities, and instantly reducing risks, AI-driven solutions improve risk assessment. While AI-powered chatbots and virtual assistants enhance customer service with tailored advice and prompt responses, automated trading systems maximize portfolio management and carry out trades based on data-driven plans.

Pattyam in 2021 Identified the AI applications and tools for financial management decision-making as below:

6.1 Stock Price Prediction

AI is revolutionizing the forecasting of stock prices by using deep learning and machine learning methods to identify patterns in large datasets. Recurrent neural networks (RNNs), Random Forests, and Support Vector Machines (SVMs) are examples of supervised learning algorithms that are very helpful in spotting patterns in historical pricing data, news mood, and economic indicators. With the aid of these tools, analysts can find hidden patterns and produce more precise forecasts.

6.2 Risk Management

Financial professionals can more accurately evaluate and reduce market risks with the help of AI-powered risk management solutions. Outliers in financial data can be grouped and identified using unsupervised learning methods like anomaly detection and K-means clustering. Market exposure is measured using methods such as Value at Risk (VaR), and reinforcement learning can provide adaptive tactics that get improvements over time by simulating connections with market conditions.

6.3 Algorithmic Trading

For algorithmic trading, the implementation of AI can result in high-frequency trading (HFT), where the AI algorithms can rapidly and precisely detect and react to market conditions. AI can also help examine technical indicators and emotions from the market by taking into account information from social media and news, etc., so it can generate trading recommendations based on that data. For such measurements of sentimental indicators in unstructured text data and the development of insights related to potential market shifts, AI-powered applications use natural language processing (NLP) techniques.

7. AI TOOLS IN FINANCIAL DECISION MAKING

Many authors discussed various tools and issues concerning AI implementation in financial decision-making in such fields as was done by Aparna Krishna Bhat in 2024.

7.1 Model Training and Evaluation

AI models should be intensely tested during training and testing to guarantee validity. This exercise should involve testing predictions of such models based on historical trends and checking the outcomes against the data. Hyperparameter tuning is equally important as it improves performance through refining model parameters, which ensures the AI system is well-calibrated to financial market dynamics.

7.2 Technical Infrastructure

Application Programming Interfaces (APIs) and cloud computing platforms are essential for managing enormous volumes of financial data. AI-driven models can access and handle large datasets thanks to cloud platforms, and real-time data acquisition from many sources is made possible by APIs. They serve as the foundation for scalable and effective AI applications in the financial industry.

7.3 Model Validation

Model validation prevents overfitting on historical datasets and guarantees that AI systems generalize well on fresh, unknown data. Financial organizations can boost their decision-making tools' confidence and dependability in real-world scenarios by properly validating their models (Pattyam, n.d.).

8. AI POTENTIAL USES IN FINANCE

AI that also involves ChatGPT in trend also has significant involvement in the financial decision-making, which is described by (Rane, 2023) Are as follows:

8.1 Automated Trading Systems

AI is essential to algorithmic trading because it makes automated trade execution and real-time financial market analysis possible. By generating signals using AI algorithms, these systems execute transactions that improve efficiency, make better use of consumer data, and reduce capital costs for financial organizations. Along with streamlining high-frequency stock trading, automated systems use machine learning to quickly understand data, assess consequences, and take immediate action.

8.2 Risk Management

AI assists financial institutions by developing risk models that detect possible dangers in investments, credit portfolios, and markets. Predictive risk analysis is aided by machine learning algorithms' ability to analyze big datasets and find patterns and connections. Unsupervised AI models can explore hidden market trends and dynamics, and thus lower the exposure to related hazards and costly impacts on the portfolio.

8.3 Fraud Detection

The use of AI systems in businesses can be helpful in recognizing unusual patterns and irregular transactions, hence enhancing fraud detection more effectively. This enables real-time detection capability of machine learning powered programs has surpassed the outdated software used in the recent past, which were prone to many false positive alerts. With the advent of AI, Financial transactions can be safer as AI can identify patterns that human beings cannot detect without rigorous efforts and activities.

8.4 Lending and Credit Analysis

The use of AI in lending processes can make credit-granting institutions more flexible and simpler in their daily operations and simpler as AI can efficiently conduct complicated risk assessments, summarize compliance, and match criteria. AI-powered applications can make accurate and cost-effective credit decisions through their capability to review loan applications and evaluate applicants' payment history and financial data. Small banks with limited resources can benefit from such applications for cost containment, risk control, and achieve better lending judgments.

8.5 Data Analysis for Investment Knowledge

The use of AI allows financial institutions to process gigantic financial databases and compare across numerous other databases, This rigorous processing can help identify patterns beyond human detection capabilities. Such analysis of historical data includes investment information, prices, balance sheets, reports, and news that can help AI in developing investment associations. By analyzing both current and historical data, users can draw insightful financial conclusions.

8.6 Financial Planning and Forecasting

AI can enable institutions to project expenses, sales and other factors that stimulate various scenarios to draw inferences based on historical trends by employing financial planning features powered by AI. Such business intelligence contributions can integrate and help financial decision makers in deploying accurate forecasts and making financial decisions, thus making powerful analytics even by non-technical analysts.

8.7 Portfolio Optimization

AI analyzes return, risk, diversity, and liquidity to maximize portfolios. Efficient asset allocations can be created by machine learning algorithms that analyze historical data and learn from successful and unsuccessful past trades. AI portfolio management, as opposed to old-fashioned optimization, is adaptive and keeps learning to improve investing approaches.

8.8 Forecasting Models

Accuracy in financial market forecasts is enhanced through AI-based models. AI can provide insights into potential future security movements according to financial and historical trends. Forecasting is made easy by a variety of AI algorithms, which enable financial managers to make informed decisions regarding asset management and investment forecasting.

9. BENEFITS OF AI-BASED FINANCIAL DECISION-MAKING

9.1 Adapting Market Changes

The role of AI capital management systems is to assist in the use of predictive analytics and real-time data for the financial managers to adjust to the changing market conditions. Artificial intelligence (AI) aids financial institute for short and long-term success by means of identifying trends at an early stage and risk assessment to take advantage of new opportunities.

9.2 Encouraging Growth Programs

Artificial intelligence (AI) provides insights with the data behind it that drive financial professionals' initiatives in development opportunities. AI analytics is an important growth tool that can give a competitive edge to AI in finance, and it is up to this date, it is largely amounts. It can forecast the marketplace trends and may identify customer prerequisites.

9.3 Enhances the Accuracy of Decision-Making

With offered tools for machine learning and predictions, artificial intelligence helps make decisions more accurately. Relevant data may be used by financial managers to boost operational efficiency, make better decisions, and maximize their organization's profitability in case of complex financial situations.

9.4 Enhancing the Effectiveness of Operations

The assistance of machine learning algorithms helps managers to make faster as well as better decisions by making it easier for them to process data. The processing power of AI automates the complex process and thus makes things easier for leaders to achieve their objectives more effectively with accuracy.

9.5 Gaining a Competitive Advantage

AI gives a competitive advantage in volatile markets by enhancing data analysis accuracy and reducing operational errors. Financial institutions can establish themselves in the market by streamlining their operations and improving profitability with asset management and decision-making support through AI.

10. CHALLENGES IN INTEGRATING AI IN FINANCE

Although AI has a potential impact on financial decision-making and benefits finance in many ways, it also faces numerous challenges. Tierno in 2024 Has discussed a few, which are described below:

10.1 Data Bias and Transparency

The AI system transmits unintentional biases from its data, in particular during credit scoring and lending decisions. Complex AI models fail to provide explanations regarding loan rejections, thereby violating customer rights according to the law of fair treatment. The application of poor-quality data creates AI systems that generate wrong financial outputs through implicit bias. Protecting both data integrity and fairness serves as a cornerstone to stop discrimination from occurring because it secures consumer interests. Understanding the decision processes of AI systems remains a complex task for most people. The absence of transparency creates operational and legal ambiguities that lead to higher compliance difficulties and enterprise barriers when they attempt to validate their AI-based choices..

10.2 Data Security and Privacy

Although AI can be very useful for financial and business operations but the working principle of AI heavily relies on data acquisition. The AI processes the operations by acquiring identification data from the users, which also includes identification, personal profiles, financial information, and information related to personal preferences. These working operations of AI risk individual users' privacy and data rights due to their mechanisms of data collection and storage, which raises privacy concerns.

10.3 Systematic, Operational, and Market Risks

Data breaches and Systemic errors in the operations can be generated by AI, which raises the risks related to the financial stability of systems. To counter these challenges, such financial institutions can enhance their systems with ethical AI systems to maintain integrity. This adoption of parallel AI systems among firms, along with mutual decisions, can create financial market instabilities that are susceptible to unexpected and rapid shifts in the market. AI service providers can use these instances to analyze their clients, as such tools generate dependency risks for them. The effect of expanding financial asset network dependencies, along with new risks from applications employing AI can make existing threats more obvious. Reliable financial network oversight remains essential for prevention due to the importance of combining it with appropriate risk avoidance approaches, which prevent dangerous cascading effects between different financial systems. Due to operating without human intervention, AI systems increase the risk exposure that affects financial sectors. AI systems handle market conditions immediately, so monitoring systems paired with specific reactions must be used to prevent unpredictable risks from developing.

10.4 Unintentional Consequences

The introduction of AI systems leads to unforeseen market disruptions that disturb the financial systems. If our knowledge about how AI permeates human life in the future paves the path towards timely actions that can keep market volatility in check, then stability remains an inevitable manifestation.

10.5 Market Concentration

High spending on AI technology leads to the consolidation of a large number of companies into a few dominant organizations. Maintaining market equilibrium leads to a decline in market diversity because it slows down innovation and brings competitive issues that require proper management.

10.6 Compliance and Market Integrity

Independent operating programs create issues when it comes to compliance standards of different businesses (ethical standards in the market). You also need to have active systems that want to control and govern the behaviors of the machines, to prevent immoral acts from happening, and make sure that AI is still adhering to the laws. Dominance of technology corporations over large datasets and proprietary algorithms for a variety of AI functions would disrupt the traditional financial industry and create challenges for the economic functions of market monopolies by causing regulatory asymmetries and centralizing powers. The existing legal set of rules may not be adequate to accommodate the unique threats of AI, provoking an ongoing dialogue as to your needs for novel regulation.

10.7 Job Displacement and Workforce Shift

Due to its automation capabilities, AI can replace a lot of supply and further cause the loss of positions in Help desk functions. Automation creates new jobs with AI for not only people who work with AI technology, but also people who analyze data. So, what's the impact on job market stability for different areas of financial operations?

10.8 Market Manipulation and Ethical Use

In the pursuit of profit, AI could learn undesirable or illegal practices by accident, for example, spoofing or pump-and-dump schemes. This could provoke immoral actions and violations of legal rights through human control, albeit indirect.

10.9 Enhanced Monitoring Conditions

Regulators will need to create new systems of monitoring and regulation to address the complexity of AI systems. This is where regulating frameworks become vital, as the growing economic weight of AI draws in risk.

11. FUTURE OF AI IN FINANCIAL DECISION MAKING

11.1 Generative AI Financial

Generative AI financial advisors are computer programs created to use sophisticated algorithms to offer individualized financial advice. Based on a large quantity of data analysis, these advisers provide consumers with assistance with activities like financial planning and investment advice. AI financial advisors such as WallyGPT, Michael AI, FinChat.io, Jarvis Invest, FP Alpha, and Pefin are well-known.

These AI advisers can provide advice based on each client's unique financial objectives and risk tolerance since they are constantly learning and adapting through machine learning. To make the process more effective and seamless, they can even automate trading orders according to consumer preferences. AI financial advisers provide convenience and flexibility to financial management by operating around the clock, allowing customers to obtain information whenever they want.

These digital advisors have a lot to offer. By swiftly processing vast volumes of data and providing real-time, data-driven investing advice, they increase efficiency. Additionally, compared to traditional financial services, AI advisers are less expensive and offer superior financial support. They are a more and more popular option for handling personal finances in a fast-paced environment because of their 24/7 availability, which provides consumers with timely guidance. (Quadra Wealth, 2024).

11.2 PortfolioPilot, AI-Powered Wealth Management

A new AI program called PortfolioPilot is revolutionizing the way individuals handle their assets. Founded by Global Predictions, it currently has over 22,000 customers and manages $20 billion in assets. Using cutting-edge AI, the program provides customers with an understandable report on their portfolios and makes recommendations for how to enhance their investments. PortfolioPilot helps users make better financial decisions by offering them the opportunity to receive personalized guidance for a nominal monthly charge. According to Alexander Harmsen, the tool's creator, who initially developed it for his use, AI tools like this have the potential to revolutionize wealth management by expanding access to professional financial guidance. (Son, 2024).

11.3 Financial Reporting and Auditing

AI is transforming financial reporting and auditing, enabling companies all over the world to increase process efficiency, enhance risk identification, and more quickly identify errors. By managing repetitive processes, improving data analysis, and assisting in decision-making, generative AI expedites reporting. Human monitoring will continue to be essential to ensure accuracy when AI detects threats and creates reports, even if 97% of financial leaders want to implement AI over the next three years.

Businesses should evaluate existing procedures, select appropriate AI technologies, guarantee data quality, train staff, and track performance to properly integrate AI in financial reporting. AI is particularly good at activities like financial statement analysis, where it checks data and detects differences to increase audit accuracy, lowering the possibility of errors and preventing fraud. Although market volatility is still a problem, artificial intelligence (AI) in financial forecasting leverages data from sources like social media and news to spot trends and anticipate changes in the market. Like digital assistants like Siri or Alexa, consumers can also request financial information to be retrieved using Natural Language Processing (NLP) techniques.

Governance and compliance become more crucial as AI becomes more prevalent in finance to control related risks. Establishing transparent frameworks, controls, and third-party audits is all part of this. Even though AI in finance is still developing, it is evident that AI can free up workers from monotonous work, increase accuracy, and free them up to concentrate on more difficult jobs. This gives businesses an advantage when it comes to handling massive amounts of data and keeping up with changes in the sector. (DFIN, 2024).

11.4 Integration of Blockchain and AI

Businesses have new opportunities because of the combination of blockchain and AI, which increases intelligence, facilitates automation, and improves authenticity. A digital ledger that is safe and accessible, blockchain monitors orders, transactions, and documents transparently. Since business partners can see the same data in real time, this transparency fosters confidence and opens up new avenues for collaboration and efficiency.

Artificial intelligence (AI) mimics human thought processes to solve issues and make decisions, frequently automating tedious work, improving decision-making, and improving customer experiences. There are benefits to combining blockchain and AI, especially when it comes to data authentication and transparent audit trails. Blockchain encourages transparency and data integrity by tracking data sources and securely storing AI models. (IBM, 2021).

12. CONCLUSION

The blockchain technology, along with artificial intelligence, is transforming today's financial world, all this is happening with increasing transparency, trust, and efficiency. Using AI enables institutions to analyze gigantic data sets to automate processes, develop insights, and enhance decision-making. Moreover, the use of blockchain offers a safe and shared record of data that authorizes reliable interactions. These technologies facilitate rapid financial services, sustainable operations, and improved follow-up and services in a variety of industries that include but not limited to, healthcare, banking, and supply chain sectors. For example, by instantly and securely validating data, blockchain-based and AI-driven analysis can assist healthcare practitioners in providing accurate therapies or expedite the financial processes. Today's Businesses are employing these technologies more and more and hence building smarter processes and a more transparent, collaborative future that keeps data security and accuracy while cutting operational times in novel ways by fusing blockchain security with the intelligence of artificial intelligence.

REFERENCES

Al Breiki, M., & Nobanee, H. (2019). The Role of Financial Management in Promoting Sustainable Business Practices and Development. SSRN *Electronic Journal*. https://doi.org/DOI: 10.2139/SSRN.3472404

Balasubramanian, S., Devarajan, H. R., Raparthi, M., Dodda, S. B., Maruthi, S., & Adnyana, I. M. D. M. (2023). Ethical Considerations in AI-assisted Decision-Making for End-Of-Life Care in Healthcare. *Power System Technology*, *47*(4), 167–182.

Bhat, A. K.Aparna Krishna Bhat. (2024). Application And Impact of Artificial Intelligence in Financial Decision Making. *International Journal of Scientific Research in Science, Engineering and Technology*, *11*(5), 57–63. DOI: 10.32628/IJSRSET2411417

Castelnovo, A. (2024). *Towards Responsible AI in Banking: Addressing Bias for Fair Decision-Making*. https://arxiv.org/abs/2401.08691v1

DFIN. (2024). AI in Financial Reporting. Retrieved November 10, 2024, from https://www.dfinsolutions.com/knowledge-hub/thought-leadership/knowledge-resources/ai-in-financial-reporting

Fabrègue, B. F. G., & Bogoni, A. (2023). Privacy and Security Concerns in the Smart City. *Smart Cities 2023, Vol. 6, Pages 586-613, 6*(1), 586–613. DOI: 10.3390/smartcities6010027

Farahani, M. S., & Esfahani, A. (2022). Opportunities and challenges of applying artificial intelligence in the financial sectors and startups during the coronavirus outbreak. International Journal of Innovation in Management. *Economics and Social Sciences*, *2*(4), 33–55.

Forbes Finance Council. (2024). *The Impact of Artificial Intelligence on Financial Decision Making*. Retrieved March 22, 2025, from https://councils.forbes.com/blog/artificial-intelligence-and-financial-decision-making

Huang, A. H., & You, H. (2023). Artificial intelligence in financial decision-making. *Handbook of Financial Decision Making*, 315–335. DOI: 10.4337/9781802204179.00029

IBM. (2021). What is blockchain and artificial intelligence (AI)? IBM. Retrieved November 10, 2024, from https://www.ibm.com/topics/blockchain-ai

Modupe, J. (2023). The role of artificial intelligence in financial decision making. Medium. Retrieved November 6, 2024, from https://medium.com/@jamesmodupe75/the-role-of-artificial-intelligence-in-financial-decision-making-57befaccfb4f

Mullangi, M. K., Yarlagadda, V. K., Dhameliya, N., & Rodriguez, M. (2018). Integrating AI and Reciprocal Symmetry in Financial Management: A Pathway to Enhanced Decision-Making. *Int. J. Reciprocal Symmetry Theor. Phys*, *5*(1), 42–52.

Olatoye, F. O., Awonuga, K. F., Mhlongo, N. Z., Ibeh, C. V., Elufioye, O. A., & Ndubuisi, N. L. (2024). AI and ethics in business: A comprehensive review of responsible AI practices and corporate responsibility. *International Journal of Science and Research Archive*, *11*(1), 1433–1443.

Quadra Wealth. (2024). *How AI Investment Advisors are transforming Financial Advice*. Retrieved from https://quadrawealth.com/articles/the-rise-of-ai-investment-advisors/

Rane, N. (2023). Role and Challenges of ChatGPT and Similar Generative Artificial Intelligence in Finance and Accounting. SSRN *Electronic Journal*. https://doi.org/ DOI: 10.2139/SSRN.4603206

Son, H. (2024). This AI-powered financial advisor has quickly gained $20 billion in assets. CNBC. https://www.cnbc.com/2024/07/31/portfoliopilot-ai-powered-financial-advisor-has-20-billion-in-assets.html

Srikanth, D. R. K., Ragini, M., Tripathi, G., Rajesh, K., Giri, A., Pandey, S. K., & Verma, L. K. (2024). The Impact of Emerging Technologies on Sustainable Agriculture and Rural Development. *International Journal of Environment and Climate Change*, *14*(1), 253–263. DOI: 10.9734/ijecc/2024/v14i13830

Tierno, P. (2024). *Artificial Intelligence and Machine Learning in Financial Services*. https://crsreports.congress.gov

Chapter 6
How Does Fintech Impact Economic Performance?
A Way-Forward

Muhammad Nazam
https://orcid.org/0009-0006-1973-2801
University of Agriculture, Faisalabad, Pakistan

Sabir Ramzan
https://orcid.org/0009-0003-4445-3183
University of Agriculture, Faisalabad, Pakistan

Muhammad Hafeez
https://orcid.org/0009-0001-9402-8658
University of Agriculture, Faisalabad, Pakistan

Kashif Hamid
University of Agriculture, Faisalabad, Pakistan

ABSTRACT

The purpose of this chapter is to examine the effect of financial technology on economic performance in the context of emerging economies. By utilizing modern technologies, "fin tech" refers to the supply of efficient, automated, and user-friendly financial services. Fintech enables businesses, business owners, and consumers to better manage their financial affairs, procedures, and lifestyles via special software and algorithms that are used on computers and smartphones. The study objective is to assess how financial technology may affect economic performance using the panel data. The results of this study were aid researchers and professionals in their understanding of the development of fintech. The data gathered from sample of 20 emerging economies with the help of world development indicators and many other

DOI: 10.4018/979-8-3693-8960-7.ch006

sources. The main result of this study is that there is a positive impact of financial technology on economic performance. The findings of this would be helpful to concerned stakeholders.

1. INTRODUCTION

The term "fintech," which merge the words "financial" and "technology," is used to describe the technology usage for financial reaction communications regarding the financial sector (Arner et al., 2015). The definition of fintech is determined by techniques for a general representation of the characteristics of fintech and a specification of a particular fragment that makes up the presence of the fintech market in the financial sector. Fintech has no general meaning with reference to its larger reach (Nguyen, 2022; Dorfleitner et al., 2017). The word "fintech" which simply means "internet finance" or "digital financial integration" describes the fusion of finance and information technology. It offers tools for risk management, resource allocation, payment processing, and revenue collecting. The most recent financial application to improve financial activity is called fintech (Romdhane et al., 2024; Schueffel, 2016). Financial technology (Fintech) transforms company operations by merging finance with technical advancements and inventions (Appiah-Otoo & Song, 2021; Shim & Shin, 2016; Xu, 2017).

The origins of technical innovation in the field of financial services can be traced back to the introduction of checks as a form of payment in the economic sector. However, the evolution of financial technology didn't stop there (Song and Appiah-Otoo, 2022). Bank of America played a significant role by pioneering the development of the first credit card, while ATMs revolutionized financial transactions by introducing debit cards as a convenient means of payment. The year 2000 witnessed the emergence of fintech innovations such as mobile payments and crowdfunding, showcasing the rapid progress in this sector. Given the swift pace of development in the fintech industry, it becomes crucial to revisit previous studies and examine the evolution of economic services. By doing so, Researcher can stay abreast of the latest advancements and gain valuable insights into the trajectory of this dynamic field (Yoon and Lee; 2023; Ashta & Biot-Paquerot, 2018).

In recent years, there has been a lot of talk about how fintech could help more people get access to banking services. Current trends in the fintech sector include the rise of embedded and decentralized finance, digital and open banking, as well as the adoption of AI and machine learning technologies. Blockchain and cryptocurrencies also continue to shape the industry. The integration of blockchain technology within financial services has the potential to cut banks' infrastructure costs by 30%, resulting in annual savings exceeding $10 billion (Yin et al., 2022). Fintech gives people who can't use standard banking systems a chance to get access to financial services. In Pakistan, where a big part of the population doesn't have access to banking services, fintech has become a good way to fix this problem. This literature study looks at the different ways fintech can be used to help people in Pakistan get access to banking services. The past of fintech in the country starts with the first mobile banking services, which came out at the beginning of the 2000s. In 2009, Telenor Pakistan and Tameer Microfinance Bank launched Easypaisa, a mobile money app, to help people in Pakistan who don't have bank accounts get basic banking services (Khattak & Ullah, 2019). By the end of 2010, the programmed site had more than a million people who were actively using it. Through easypaisa, users could easily use their mobile devices to do a variety of financial tasks, such as depositing and withdrawing cash, sending money to other people, and paying bills (Ali et al., 2016).

The State Bank of Pakistan (SBP) has actively supported and regulated the fintech sector by implementing regulatory policy frameworks, and programs aimed at promoting innovation and digital financial services. However, despite its best efforts, the sector has yet to realize its full potential. Extensive research has identified several challenges that hinder the expansion and development of Pakistan's fintech industry. These challenges encompass limitations in infrastructure, restrictions on accessing finance, insufficient customer understanding and confidence, and regulatory obstacles. To gain a comprehensive understanding of how these barriers impact the fintech landscape in Pakistan, further research is needed (Zafar et al., 2010). Pakistan has a lot of problems that make it hard for fintech to grow and progress, which makes it harder for people to use. One of the biggest problems is that legal issues have a big effect on fintech companies. Pakistan doesn't have a complete legal system for fintech, which makes it hard for these businesses to work well in the country. Because there aren't clear rules, the people and possible investors don't know what to do and don't trust the government. Because investors don't want to spend in a place where the rules aren't clear, it's hard for fintech companies to get money because of this (Khan et al., 2020).

Fintech is also hard to use in Pakistan because people don't know enough about it and aren't taught about it. A big part of the population still doesn't know what fintech is or how it works, so they can't take advantage of its benefits. This lack of knowledge and education is a big problem for the growth of fintech in Pakistan, because people are often reluctant to use something they don't fully understand (Ali. et al., 2020). Lack of information and education about fintech is a big reason why it hasn't caught on in Pakistan. A big part of the public still doesn't know about the benefits of fintech and doesn't have a full idea of how it works. This lack of knowledge and schooling is a big problem for the growth of fintech in Pakistan, as people are often reluctant to use something they don't fully understand (Mbiti & Weil, 2015; Saini and Bhati, 2019). M-Pesa, a mobile money app, has been a big part of making Kenya more financially inclusive by letting people share and receive money through their phones. The population's access to banking services has gotten a lot better because of this creative answer.

Insights from other countries show that Pakistan has a lot of problems with legal hurdles, digital literacy, and getting access to financial services in remote places. These problems need to be fixed for the fintech industry to grow successfully. To encourage the growth of fintech, it is important to set up effective legal systems. Also, steps should be taken to improve internet skills and make sure that people in rural areas have access to banking services. By taking care of these problems, Pakistan can make it easier for the fintech business to grow and improve (Zaidi & Shah, 2023).

Rizwan and Bruneau, (2019) analyzed data from 20 emerging economies, primarily from Europe, Central Asia, Sub-Saharan Africa, and the Caribbean. Their findings highlight that microfinance institutions functioning as fintech players in the surveyed nations have had a positive impact on financial inclusion, leading to accelerated economic growth and reduced income inequalities. However, they emphasized that sustaining this performance requires the adoption of more advanced information and communication technologies (ICT) tools. The perspectives of (Sarpong & Nketiah-Amponsah, 2022) further support this viewpoint, as they argue that the effective utilization of innovative ICT tools can have a noticeable impact on promoting inclusive economic growth. However, they also suggest that a moderation of transaction-related fees and charges could serve as a means to expedite the levels of financial inclusion

The COVID-19 pandemic has accelerated the transformation of finance through the application of digital technology, commonly known as fintech. This digitization of money and financial services has facilitated the creation of more accessible and efficient financial services, consequently fostering economic growth. Fintech's rapid transformation of the financial industry has blurred the boundaries between financial firms and the sector as a whole. Emerging economies have increasingly adopted fintech (financial technology) to improve access to financial services, boost economic inclusion, and drive innovation. Here are some recent examples of fintech adoption in emerging markets. The Unified Payments Interface (UPI) launched by the National Payments Corporation of India. It has become one of the world's most successful real-time payment systems. It allows users to make instant payments through mobile phones and has significantly increased financial inclusion. Similarly, in Brazil one of Latin America's most successful Neobanks. The Neobank has gained popularity for offering simple digital banking products, from credit cards to loans, with a focus on transparency and customer experience. These fintech innovations have been crucial in improving financial inclusion, driving economic growth, and enabling better access to financial services for previously underserved populations in emerging markets.

Based on the above emerging economies adoption of financial technologies, the existing studies has explored the impact of fintech on economic growth. However, there is a gap in research focusing on the impact of fintech on the economic performance of emerging economies, with limited studies conducted in Pakistan. This study aims to bridge that gap by investigating the impact of fintech on the economic performance of emerging economies. Following are the research objectives of study;

- To explore the patterns of financial technology and economic performance in emerging economies
- To analyze the impact of financial technology on economic performance of emerging economies
- To suggest policy recommendations based on findings for the development of financial technology and policy decision.

2. LITERATURE REVIEW

Wu et al. (2023) looked at how fintech affects financial efficiency from an academic point of view and make a fintech level score by used text mining for each province in China. The study used interprovincial panel data from 2008 to 2018 to test how fintech growth and economic efficiency are related. The data show that the technology spillover theory can explain how financial technology affects economic efficiency and that there is a U-shaped, nonlinear relationship among fintech growth and economic efficiency. More research shows that the small effect that fintech has on economic efficiency is lessened by financial decentralization. Fintech has a bigger impact on how well money is managed in places where finances are less centralized.

Minzhi et al. (2023) examined that how using Fintech affected the economies of 31 Chinese regions between 2012 and 2019. Fintech growth is tracked using Peking University's digital financial index. Researcher also used instrumental quantile regression, which is more sensitive to the varied levels of economic growth among provinces than conventional least squares. This research indicates that Fintech has a beneficial impact on provincial economic growth as assessed by GDP per capita. However, the influence varies in size and relevance between jurisdictions and Fintech characteristics, highlighting the usefulness of crafting policies that account for economic inequalities between regions and provinces.

Ogunode and Akintoye (2023) examined the relationship among financial technology and financial inclusion in Nigeria and other emerging countries. The exploratory research strategy included a thorough literature assessment of relevant publications, such as the World Bank statistics for the years 2010 to 2022, the Enhancing Financial Inclusion Surveys, and the Global Findex report. Research shows that while financial technology has helped Nigeria's attempts to expand financial access, more work needs to be done. Growth is still being stymied by problems with system interoperability, gender sensitivities due to sociocultural reasons, data privacy worries, and Fintech's over-servicing of cities at the expense of vital rural regions.

Zaidi and Shah (2023) stated that by providing access to financial services to those without bank accounts, fintech has the probable to transform the financial sector in developing nations like Pakistan. The goal of this piece is to look at how fintech can help improve Pakistan's financial circumstances. The main goal of this study is to look at how fintech can help people in Pakistan get access to banking services. The goal of the study is to look into the different fintech efforts, such as financial education, mobile payments, microfinance and digital banking that can helped to the people who don't have any bank account into the official financial structure.

Awais et al. (2023) argued that the environmental devastation wrought by economic activity has elevated sustainability to the forefront of public discourse. In this case, fintech can facilitate more efficient use of funds and long-term financial growth. Panel data for the years 2010-2021 from 66 countries has been compiled to further explain this connection. The links between a green growth index and a number of fintech characteristics have been examined. Findings indicate that while carbon emissions have a detrimental influence on green economic activity, the proliferation of the Internet and Findex have a beneficial effect.

Xiaohui et al. (2022) investigated that Fintech is key to China's rise in the world, and the digital economy is a new force that will help China's economy grow and develop in a healthy way. So, what kind of link do Fintech and the digital economy have? Based on the CRITIC method, this study estimates the Fintech indices for China's 31 provinces (except Hong Kong, Macao, and Taiwan) from 2008 to 2018 and the digital economy growth indices from 2012 to 2018. It also looks at how Fintech affects the digital economy and how it works. The findings show that Fintech helps the digital economy in China grow by encouraging technology innovation and making it harder for local governments to handle their own money.

Vučinić (2020) showed the possible effects that Fintech developments could have on financial stability. It also explains how Fintech affects market structure and the pros and cons of technology driven financial innovations on financial stability. The paper talks about how important it is for regulators from different countries to work together to keep the economy stable in a world where technology is always changing. Fintech has changed customers' tastes and expectations, and more people now expect services to be fast and easy to get to on their phones and further electric devices. The paper showed that innovative skill makes it possible for financial service area to grow, but it also adds risks to the financial system, both on the small and large scales.

Ismail et al. (2019) investigated the historical evolution of fintech and how it has affected the financial market's stability, effectiveness, and market structure in the banking sector. Researcher construct two cross-sectional regressions using data from 150 countries to examine the effects of new technologies and cellphones on financial transactions and payment processing on per capita GDP. The study's findings indicate that increasing interest among young people, who can now interact with one other without ever physically meeting, is the only factor that may speed up the adoption of new technology and goods.

3. RESEARCH METHODOLOGY

Research methodology is the methodical approach to addressing a research issue by collecting data in various methods, explaining the data collected, and making inferences from study data. A research technique is essentially a study's or research's strategy (Murthy & Bhojanna, 2009). The method of a study application is therefore critical. The primary goal of the current research, which is divided into many sections, is to examine how financial technology has affected the performance of developing nations' economies from 2002 to 2022. The methodologies and methods used for analysis are established based on the objectives and literature reviewed. The conceptual framework of study is shown in figure 1.

Figure 1. The conceptual framework of study

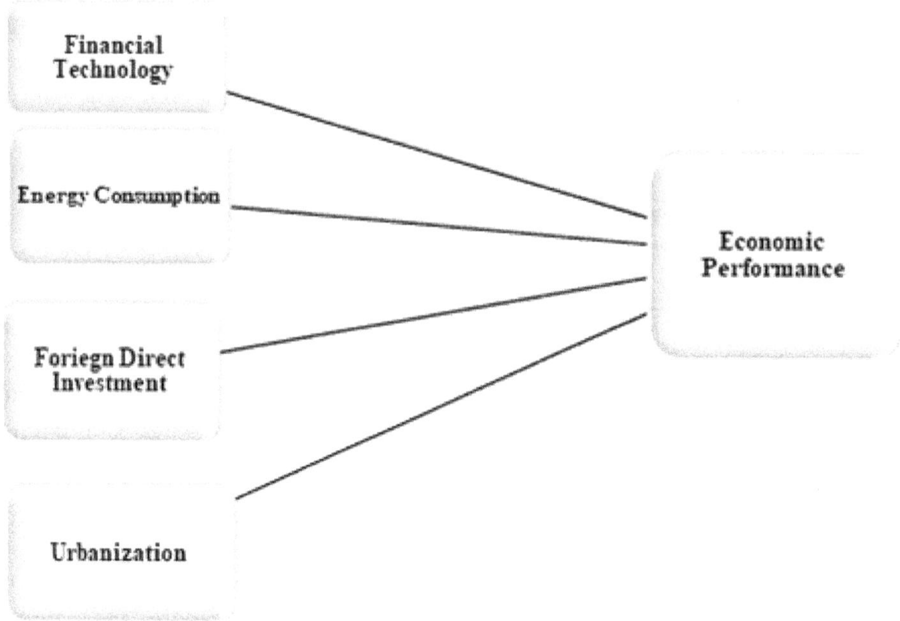

The aim of study is to explore the impact of fintech on GDP per capita across emerging economies. By following literature, functional form of econometric model is given as;

$$GDP_{it} = A_{it}\left(ENC_{it}, FDI_{it}, URP_{it}\right) \quad (1)$$

In Equation (1), where GDP per capita is a function of A_{it} *is technology parameter*. it is measured by financial technology due to enhance foreign investment inflow and domestic investment spread.

$$A_{it} = \theta_{it} FIN_{it} \quad (2)$$

The econometric estimated model is expressed as follows:

$$\mathrm{GDP}_{it} = \varphi_i + \delta_i t + \tau_{1i} FIN_{it} + \tau_{2i}\mathrm{ENC}_{it} + \tau_{3i}\mathrm{FDI}_{it} + \tau_{4i}\mathrm{URP}_{it} + \varepsilon_{it} \quad (3)$$

In Equation (3), "i" =1, 2, 3, …,20 stands for number of emerging countries. "i" is time span. φ_i and δ_i are denoting to specific country effects and trend, respectively. τ is showed the impact immensity of independent variables.

The study's total population is 20 nations listed, which are all developing economies. This study aims to determine how fintech affects economic performance. The use of Fintech specific data also includes data of economic growth from 2002 through 2022. The study aims to analyze the impact of financial technology on economic performance of emerging economies. The emerging economies include twenty countries. The data on fintech, population, GDP growth rate, energy consumption and foreign direct investment are extracted from world development indicators (2022). The Table 1 provides the detail of Emerging Economies and the variables description and sources of data is described in Table 2. The descriptive analysis describes in Table 3 which indicate the results of a detailed study of Fintech and the growth of the economies of some countries. It shows the mean, middle, highest and lowest values, as well as the standard deviation. The finding showed that there are 420 observations for each of the factors. It says that the average GDP is 8.884%, that the highest GDP is 11.001, and that the lowest GDP is 6.675. GDP has a standard variation of 0.76. The value of standard deviation is close to 0, which shows that the mean is accurate and gives a good picture of the data. Since the value is close to the mean, it is negatively skewed. A standard deviation of 0.769 also shows that the collection of data is less volatile, which means that GDP is stable. However, the mean value of FIN is 3.754 whereas the standard deviation is 0.769, the minimum value of the FIN is 0.626, Maximum values are 5.222, that mean that great no of financial technology grows the economy. In term of foreign direct investment, emerging countries in their stagnant stage manage cost better than in growth and mature stage, whereas in case of economic performance GDP in mature stage is highest compare to stagnant and growth stage.

Energy consumption also variable include in this study. The minimum value of the used energy is 3.956. Maximum values are 5.580, which show that there is being of data among two values. The value of mean of Energy use is 4.733 and standard deviation are 0.370 Here are some control variables first is foreign direct investment which is measure by taking natural percentage of foreign direct investment inflow. The lower value of the foreign direct investment is -40.086 and higher value is 106.602, which indicates there is existence of data between two values. The value of mean of foreign direct investment is 3.228 and standard deviation is 7.504. Second control variable of the study is Urbanization (URP) percentage of total population live in the urban areas. The minimum value of the variable is 3.065 and maximum value is 45.607, which indicates there is existence of data between two values. The value of mean of URP is 21.803 and of standard deviation are 11.889.

Table 1. Distribution of emerging economies

Sr. No	Country	Sr. No	Country	Sr. No	Country
1	Argentina	8	India	15	Russia
2	Brazil	9	Indonesia	16	Saudi Arabia
3	Chile	10	Iran	17	South Africa
4	China	11	Malaysia	18	Thailand
5	Colombia	12	Mexico	19	Turkiye
6	Egypt	13	Philippines	20	UAE
7	Hungary	14	Poland		

The primary data are those that are gathered by researchers and Studies using secondary data information gathered by a person, organization, or entity other than the researchers involve secondary data. The present research is based on secondary data freely available collected from various resources like books, journals, reports and various websites.

Table 2. The variables and measurement tools.

Variable	Acronym	Measurement	Data Source
Fintech	FIN	ATMs (per 100,000 adults)	World Development Indicators
Energy Consumption	ENC	Energy use (kg of oil equivalent per capita)	World Development Indicators
		Energy use (kg of oil equivalent) per $1,000 GDP (constant 2017 PPP)	World Development Indicators
Foreign Direct Investment	FDI	Foreign direct investment, net inflows (% of GDP)	World Development Indicators
		Foreign direct investment, net outflows (% of GDP)	World Development Indicators
Gross Domestic Product	GDP	GDP (constant 2015 US$)	World Development Indicators
		GDP per capita (constant 2015 US$)	World Development Indicators
URP Urbanization	URP	Population in the largest city (% of urban population)	World Development Indicators
		Population in urban agglomerations of more than 1 million	World Development Indicators
		Population in urban agglomerations of more than 1 million (% of total population)	World Development Indicators

Table 3. Descriptive statistics of variables

	FIN	GDP	ENC	FDI	URP
Observations	420	420	420	420	420
Mean	3.754	8.884	4.733	3.228	21.803
Std. Dev.	0.769	0.769	0.370	7.504	11.889
Min	0.626	6.675	3.956	-40.086	3.065
Max	5.222	11.001	5.580	106.602	45.607

4. RESULTS ANALYSIS

The results reported in table 4 are quite interesting and states that the Gross domestic product per capita (GDP) have significant positive correlation of 0.5086 with financial technology at 0.01 level of significance. It means that both are moving in the same direction increase in one lead to increase in other. The result supports the argument that the more emerging economies have growth enjoys the greater the level of returns. Similarly, GDP is negatively correlated with energy consumption scale with r value of -0.0276, which means that both moves in opposite direction. It shows that as the energy consumption decreases it will negatively affect the returns. However, the relation is not significant due to lower correlation value. Energy consumption is measured as deviation from the optimum level of energy used. FDI also positively correlation with GDP. The relation is not significant with correlation of 0.1223 at 0.01 level of significance. According to the table URP is positively correlated with GDP. The relation is significant with correlation of 0.2946 at 0.01 level of significance. This indicates that emerging economies are using the resources effectively for the generation of positive returns. Interestingly GDP is negatively associated with the foreign direct investment. It has significant positive correlation of 0.1223. It may be inferred that in the period of 2002 t0 2012 the emerging economies have to pay more and more financial expenses which leads to lower returns, which will be distributed over greater size of fintech education which ultimately decrease the level of GDP.

Table 4. The correlation matrix of variables

	FIN	GDP	ENC	FDI	URP
FIN	1				
GDP	0.5086	1			
ENC	0.1594	-0.0276	1		
FDI	0.0333	0.1223	-0.0701	1	
URP	-0.1705	0.2946	-0.5126	0.0881	1

Financial technology is positively correlated with energy consumption. It shows that fintech economies invest more. However, the relation is weak with correlation value of 0.1594. Moreover, the correlation value is less than 70% it means there is no problem of Multicollinearity. Likely the financial technology depicts positive correlation with the energy consumption, which indicates that financial technology countries invest better. There is negative and insignificant relation is observed between financial technology and population used technology with value of -0.1705. Most importantly financial technology is in positively correlation with the FDI. The relation is not significant with correlation value of 0.0333 at 0.01 level of significance. This supports the argument that the emerging economies with lower URP will have greater financial technology.

The current study was examined the effects of financial technology by taking into account FDI, urbanization, economic development, and energy consumption. Robust estimators must be able to capture the cross-sectional dependency in order to meet this goal. In order to calculate the impact of financial technology on economic performance in emerging nations, the DK (Driscoll-Kraay) estimating method is used. To valuation of HAC estimators with standard errors that freshly unified cross-sectional dependency for robust estimators, the DK approach is said to use middling values from the product of independent variables and balances, which are then allocated as weights. Aside from that, the DK method has a number of unique characteristics, including the following: In addition to working equally well with short and long-time spans, it also enhances the covariance matrix in terms of big constants, offers reliable estimators in the presence of spatial dependency and heteroskedasticity, and serves as a helpful technique to handle missing values for both balanced and unbalanced panel datasets. In overall, the DK technique is a suitable estimation strategy to estimate robust estimators where there is cross-sectional and temporal dependency proposed that the DK method is applicable even when spatial dependence and heteroskedasticity are present. Consequently, the current study employs the DK method with standard errors for pooled OLS (ordinary least square) pertaining to the following linear functional form denoted by the following notation:

$$GDP = \delta 0 + X^* \, i; t \, \beta + \in \, it \quad (5)$$

In Eq. "i" = 1, 2, …20 (Emerging economies), "t" is a time period of the dataset, GDP is carbon footprints (dependent variable), and X* i;t is a set of control variables.

Table 5. Driscol-Kraay (D-K) statistical result

Variables	Coefficient	Std. Error	t-Value	Prob.
FIN	0.562	0.137	4.09	0.01*
ENC	0.238	0.173	1.37	0.18
FDI	0.007	0.002	2.57	0.01*
URP	0.028	0.011	2.50	0.02**
Constant	4.994	1.167	4.28	0.000

Table 6.

R-squared	0.4227
F-statistics	13.73
No. of groups	21
No. of observations	420

* Significant at p<0.01 level, ** Significant at p<0.05 level,*** Significant at p<0.1 level

Table 5 indicates the results that financial technology spread is significant to economy (GDP), whether energy consumption have insignificant impact on economic performance (GDP). However foreign direct investment has significant impact on economic performance and urbanization population also have significant impact on economic performance at $p<0.05$. The results are similar to the study conducted by of Daud (2018). It reported a significant positive relationship of financial technology spread with economic performance. According to the results, R-squared is 42% across emerging economies, which indicates that independent variables explain dependent variables 42% and 58% variation in dependent variable (GDP) is due to the other factors. The mean analysis of emerging economies is depicted in Figure 2.

Figure 2. Mean analysis of emerging economies

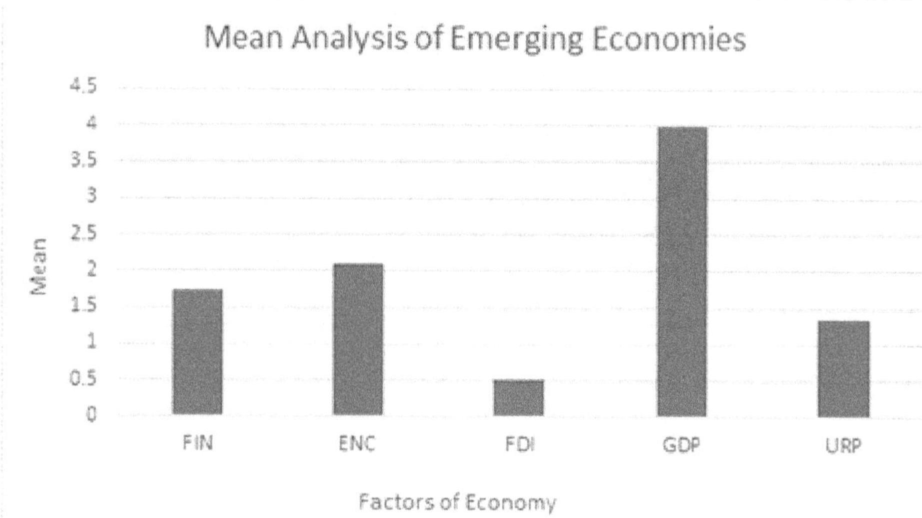

"Emerging economies" is one of the most common terms used when talking about world economies. It can mean different things depending on what is being talked about. It was started to talk about how a few developing countries are becoming more powerful economically. Mean patterns of Emerging Economies, the graph show the average or mean value of different factors of economy used in this study. The graph of FIN shows the mean value 4.1, whereas the mean value of ENC stands at 2.08, while the mean value of FDI in emerging economies is 0.5 that lower than all other economy factors. GDP and URP stand at 3.9 and 1.33 respectively. However mean value of GDP per capita income in emerging economies is higher than other economy factors that used in this study. The mean value of Population 1.33 percent in emerging economies has plays the role in Fintech progress. The relationship among emerging economies regarding Fintech is shown in Figure 3.

Figure 3. Fintech in emerging economies

The patterns of financial technology in emerging economies, the graph shows the progress of financial technology in developing countries between 21 years. Poland and Russia high progress in financial technology. The high number of peoples plays role in progress of fintech in his country. Brazil and Thailand also better progress in adoption of fintech. A great number of peoples are using financial technology and help the economy of nation. A good number of Chinese, Irani and South African peoples are playing an important role in fintech progress by using this technology. The remaining countries peoples are plays mediating role in the progress of Fintech. The GDP of emerging economies is shown in Figure 4.

Figure 4. GDP of emerging economies

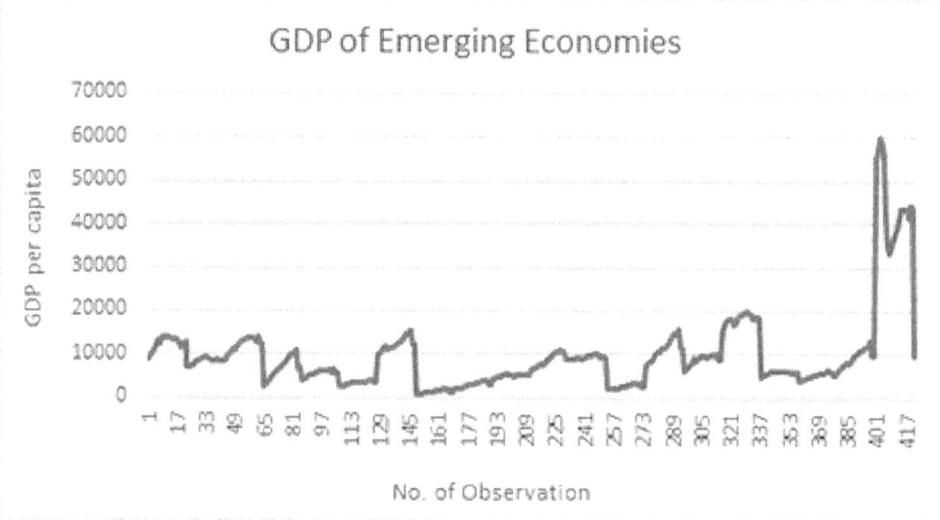

The patterns of economic performance in emerging economies, showed that the progress of economic performance in developing countries. In 2002, United Arab Emirates has developed their economy; ups and downs are occurring in this session. They still progress in Gross Domestic Product per capita till 2021. UAE is a top emerging economy, which GDP is approximately 60000 per capita. Saudi Arabia is stand at 2nd, which GDP is 20000 per capita. The other emerging economies mediating progress in economic performance.

Figure 5. Fintech in Pakistan

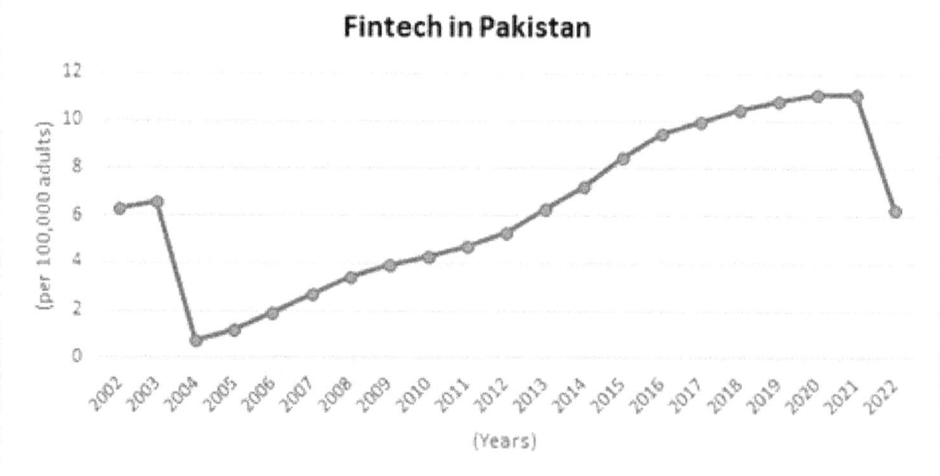

The patterns of financial technology in Pakistan, the graph shows the progress of fintech in Pakistan for the period of 2002 to 2022. In early years use of fintech was not that much but in 2004, financial technology is fall down due to any reason. In 2005, Pakistan still focused on financial technology till 2021. The patterns of financial technology in Pakistan are shown in Figure 5. In this session, fintech progress has raised up 1 to 11 lacs users. In 2022, fintech deal activity drop 56 percent in Pakistan due to political stability, lack of foreign investors' interest, situation of economy crisis. In January 2021, the nation created Raast, a real-time payments system for immediate digital transactions.

4.1. Social, Theoretical and Managerial Implications

The adoption of financial technology (fintech) in emerging economies brings about various implications that can be categorized into social, theoretical, and managerial dimensions. These implications are critical in understanding how fintech can transform these economies, enhance financial inclusion, and foster economic growth.

4.1.1. Social Implications

The findings of this study suggest that Fintech provides opportunities for people to access financial services (like payments, loans, savings, and insurance) via smartphones and internet-based platforms, breaking down barriers created by geographical and infrastructural constraints. It has positive and negative impact on the individuals. The positive impact is the small businesses become easier and have access to capital and financial tools. However, negative impact is that, there can be challenges, such as digital illiteracy, a lack of trust in digital platforms, and the risk of deepening socio-economic inequalities.

4.1.2. Theoretical Implications

The theoretical implications relate to the conceptual frameworks that can explain the adoption of fintech in emerging economies. For this purpose, understanding the drivers and barriers is crucial for developing effective strategies for fintech diffusion. There are various theories which can be applied to compare the results of present study such as diffusion of innovation theory, technology acceptance model, and social capital theory. The findings of this book chapter would be a valuable addition to the theoretical foundations of financial technologies and taking better understanding the researchers.

4.1.3. Managerial Implications

The organizations must develop strategies to integrate fintech solutions into their operations, while considering factors such as customer needs, regulatory frameworks, and the competitive landscape. Due to rise of digital platforms, businesses need to rethink how they build and maintain relationships with customers. A key managerial task will be to foster trust in digital services and ensure a positive user experience. The adoption of fintech in emerging economies brings transformative opportunities, particularly in terms of financial inclusion and economic empowerment. However, its successful implementation depends on addressing the social, theoretical, and managerial challenges it presents. By understanding and addressing these implications, emerging economies can harness fintech's potential to foster inclusive economic development and global competitiveness.

5. CONCLUSION

Fintech has revolutionized the financial landscape, bringing about positive changes that have contributed to economic growth, financial inclusion, efficiency, competition, and innovation. The efficiency and cost reduction brought by fintech have enhanced the overall productivity of financial systems in emerging economies. Streamlined processes, automation, and digital solutions have led to improved operational efficiency for financial institutions, reducing costs and enabling them to offer more affordable services to customers. The growth of digital payments and e-commerce facilitated by fintech has had a significant impact on economic performance in emerging economies. Online transactions have become more convenient, secure, and accessible, leading to the expansion of digital marketplaces, e-commerce platforms, and digital entrepreneurship. This has fueled economic growth, job creation, and increased market opportunities for businesses. Furthermore, fintech has driven innovation within the financial sector of emerging economies. Startups and technology companies have introduced novel financial products and services, such as peer-to-peer lending, crowdfunding, and blockchain-based solutions. These innovations have the potential to transform traditional financial systems, attract investment, and drive economic development. However, challenges such as regulatory frameworks, cybersecurity risks, digital literacy, and infrastructure limitations need to be addressed to fully realize the potential of fintech in emerging economies. In the future, policymakers, financial institutions, and fintech companies must work together to create an enabling environment that fosters innovation, ensures consumer protection, and promotes financial stability. Overall, the impact of fintech on economic performance in emerging economies has been positive, paving the way for inclusive and sustainable growth. As fintech continues to evolve, it will be crucial to leverage its potential effectively and address the associated challenges to maximize its benefits for emerging economies and their populations. This study covered twenty emerging economies data and therefore, the sample can be generalized to the limited economies population. The study only used emerging economies samples in assessing economic performance which is the limitation of the study.

REFERENCES

Ali, S, S., I, H., & S, A. (2016). Easypaisa: An innovative Pakistani model for mobile banking. *J.D.A*, *50*(6), 277–285.

Ali, S., Haq, S., & Anjum, S. (2020). Financial literacy and financial inclusion: An empirical investigation from Pakistan. *Journal of Financial Services Marketing*, *25*(3), 155–167.

Appiah-Otoo, I., & Song, N. (2021). The Impact of Fintech on Poverty Reduction: Evidence from China. *Sustainability (Basel)*, *13*(9), 1–17. https://www.mdpi.com/2071-1050/13/9/5225. DOI: 10.3390/su13095225

Arner, D. W., Barberis, J., & Buckley, R. P. (2015). The evolution of Fintech: A new post-crisis paradigm. *SSRN*, *47*, 1271. DOI: 10.2139/ssrn.2676553

Ashta, A., & Biot-Paquerot, G. (2018). FinTech evolution: Strategic value management issues in a fast changing industry. *Strategic Change*, *27*(4), 301–311. DOI: 10.1002/jsc.2203

Awais, M., Afzal, A., Firdousi, S., & Hasnaoui, A. (2023). Is fintech the new path to sustainable resource utilisation and economic development? *Resources Policy*, *81*, 103309. https://doi.org/https://doi.org/10.1016/j.resourpol.2023.103309. DOI: 10.1016/j.resourpol.2023.103309

Ben Romdhane, Y., Kammoun, S., & Loukil, S. (2024). The impact of Fintech on inflation and unemployment: The case of Asia. *Arab Gulf Journal of Scientific Research*, *42*(1), 161–181. DOI: 10.1108/AGJSR-08-2022-0146

Dorfleitner, G., Hornuf, L., Schmitt, M., Weber, M., Dorfleitner, G., Hornuf, L., Schmitt, M., & Weber, M. (2017). *The fintech market in Germany*. Springer. DOI: 10.1007/978-3-319-54666-7

Ismail, M., Mustafa, Ö., Slađana, Đ., & Stefan, J. (2019). Influence of financial technology (fintech) on financial industry. *Agricultural Economics*, *04*, 1003–1021.

Khan, S. M., Abbas, Q., & Shah, S. (2020). Factors affecting the adoption of fintech in Pakistan: The mediating role of trust. *Journal of Financial Services Marketing*, *25*(4), 137–149.

Khattak, M. A., & Ullah, M. (2019). Digital financial services and financial inclusion in Pakistan: Opportunities and challenges. *J.A-P.B, 20(2)*, 106-118.

Mbiti, I., & Weil, D. N. (2015). Mobile banking: The impact of M-Pesa in Kenya. In *African successes, Volume III: Modernization and development* (pp. 247-293). University of Chicago Press.

Minzhi, W., Tortosa-Ausina, E., Peiró-Palomino, J., & Arribas, I. (2023). Fintech and Regional Economic Performance in China (2012-2019). *Available atSSRN* 4225041.

Murthy, & Bhojanna, U. (2009). 2nd ed.). Business Research Methods.

Nguyen, Q. K. (2022). The effect of FinTech development on financial stability in an emerging market: The role of market discipline. *Research in Globalization, 5*, 100105. DOI: 10.1016/j.resglo.2022.100105

Ogunode, O. A., & Akintoye, R. I. (2023). Financial Technologies and Financial Inclusion in Emerging Economies: Perspectives from Nigeria. *Asian J. Econ. Bus. Acc, 23*(1), 38–54.

Rizwan, M., & Bruneau, C. (2019). Microfinance, financial inclusion and ICT: Implications for poverty and inequality. *Technology in Society, 59*, 101154. DOI: 10.1016/j.techsoc.2019.101154

Saini, V., & Bhati, S. (2019). Demonetization, digitalization, and the transformation of financial services in India. *Journal of Financial Services Marketing, 24*(3-4), 119–126.

Sarpong, B., & Nketiah-Amponsah, E. (2022). Financial inclusion and inclusive growth in sub-Saharan Africa. *Cogent Economics & Finance, 10*(1), 2058734. DOI: 10.1080/23322039.2022.2058734

Schueffel, P. (2016). Taming the beast: A scientific definition of fintech. *Journal of Innovation Management, 4*(4), 32–54. DOI: 10.24840/2183-0606_004.004_0004

Shim, Y., & Shin, D.-H. (2016). Analyzing China's fintech industry from the perspective of actor–network theory. *Telecommunications Policy, 40*(2-3), 168–181. DOI: 10.1016/j.telpol.2015.11.005

Song, N., & Appiah-Otoo, I. (2022). The impact of fintech on economic growth: Evidence from China. *Sustainability (Basel), 14*(10), 6211. DOI: 10.3390/su14106211

Vincent, O., & Evans, O. (2019). Can cryptocurrency, mobile phones, and internet herald sustainable financial sector development in emerging markets? *Journal of Transnational Management, 24*(3), 259–279. DOI: 10.1080/15475778.2019.1633170

Vučinić, M. (2020). Fintech and financial stability potential influence of FinTech on financial stability, risks and benefits. *Journal of Central Banking Theory and Practice, 9*(2), 43–66. DOI: 10.2478/jcbtp-2020-0013

Wu, Y. H., Bai, L., & Chen, X. (2023). How does the development of fintech affect financial efficiency? Evidence from China. *Ekonomska Istrazivanja, 36*(2), 2106278. DOI: 10.1080/1331677X.2022.2106278

Xiaohui, C., Teng, L., & Chen, W. (2022). How does FinTech affect the development of the digital economy? Evidence from China. *The North American Journal of Economics and Finance, 61*, 101697. https://doi.org/https://doi.org/10.1016/j.najef.2022.101697. DOI: 10.1016/j.najef.2022.101697

Xu, J. (2017). China's Internet Finance: A Critical Review. *China & World Economy, 25*(4), 78–92. https://doi.org/https://doi.org/10.1111/cwe.12207. DOI: 10.1111/cwe.12207

Yin, F., Jiao, X., Zhou, J., Yin, X., Ibeke, E., Iwendi, M. G., & Biamba, C. (2022). Fintech application on banking stability using Big Data of an emerging economy. *Journal of Cloud Computing (Heidelberg, Germany), 11*(1), 43. DOI: 10.1186/s13677-022-00320-7 PMID: 36093281

Yoon, S. S., Lee, H., & Oh, I. (2023). Differential impact of Fintech and GDP on bank performance: Global evidence. *Journal of Risk and Financial Management, 16*(7), 304. DOI: 10.3390/jrfm16070304

Zafar, J., Shaukat, M., & Mat, N. (2010). An analysis of e-human resource management practices: A case study of State Bank of Pakistan. *European Journal of Social Sciences, 15*(1), 18–26.

Zaidi, S. A. M., & Shah, S. A. A. (2023). Fintech contribution towards economic prosperity in Pakistan. [PRSS]. *Pakistan Review of Social Sciences, 4*(1), 1–14.

Chapter 7
The Role of Crowdfunding in the AI-Powered Workplace

Ayesha Khan
https://orcid.org/0000-0002-3421-6606
National Textile University, Pakistan

Amina Rizwan
University of Central Punjab, Pakistan

Sajjad Ahmad Baig
National Textile University, Pakistan

ABSTRACT

As technological advancements continue to reshape industries, AI has become this kind of wild force, forcing workplace practices to change and fostering innovation. However, SMEs for adopting innovation need substantial capital, but the access of funding through traditional sources is a major barrier. So, crowdfunding emerges as a great alternative solution to finance their AI-driven inventions of the workplace. This chapter investigates the role of crowdfunding in facilitating the adoption and deployment of AI solutions within SMEs, focusing on various crowdfunding models and identifying which are most suited for AI projects. Factors that influence campaign success or failure will be discussed, and, according to expertise in the subject, how crowdfunding serves as a funding mechanism for projects but also as a market validation and feedback instrument. Crowdfunding, therefore, assists SMEs to test and fine-tune their AI products since enabling businesses fosters innovation and enhances capabilities.

DOI: 10.4018/979-8-3693-8960-7.ch007

1. INTRODUCTION

Artificial intelligence (AI), a technology that is advancing daily, has so far disrupted many industries globally, changing the way traditional work is done and opening the door for new ideas in the workplace. AI technologies are embedded in many areas of business processes - from automating repetitive tasks to supporting the decision-making process to improving customer service and human improvement. Even AI-powered workplace applications, realized using machine learning-based data analytics, robotic process automation (RPA), and intelligent virtual assistants, offer significant business benefits in terms of increased efficiency, greater personalization, and operational mobility that provide a competitive advantage for organizations (Davenport & Ronanki, 2018;Stone & Stidham, 2023). However, these sales require large financial investments and where things get become challenging, particularly for startups and small and medium-sized businesses (SMEs) that lack actual access to conventional financing sources.

All of these challenges contributed to crowdfunding emerging as an effective solution for raising funds to develop AI innovations in the workplace. Crowdfunding also characterized as collecting a desired amount of capital by gathering small donations from a large number of individuals (Belbe et al., 2024), has experienced phenomenal growth as a form of fundraising. Over the last few years, various internet-based funding platforms, be it Kickstarter and Indiegogo or equity-based, have provided budding entrepreneurs with more opportunities in the form of financial and marketing support to launch cutting-edge projects in the virtual environment. Crowdfunding motivates industry players to develop new solutions by bridging them directly to numerous potential investors, thus providing a level playing ground even for smaller firms that venture into AI solutions (Renaldo et al., 2024).

Crowdfunding facilitates access to capital for entrepreneurs through the utilization of digital platforms (Behl et al., 2022). It has become a major area of research while also emerging as an important financial solution, making finance accessible to more people (Korzynski et al., 2021), which in turn drives innovation and economic development (Gleasure & Feller, 2016; Hoque, 2024). Kickstarter, one of the biggest reward-based crowdfunding platforms located in the US, is the subject of a considerable portion of the approximately 300,000 publications discussing crowdfunding.

Figure 1. Crowdfunding process

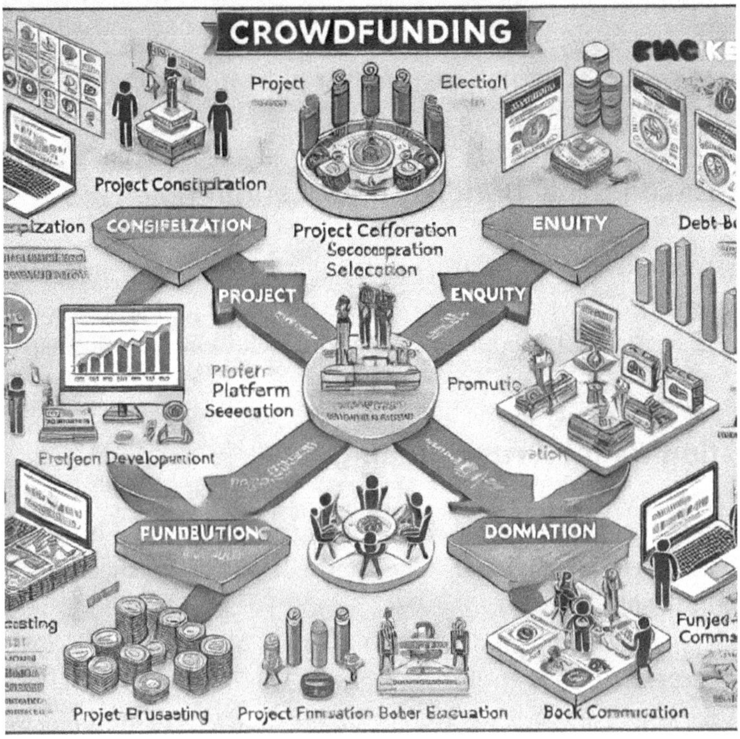

1. TYPES OF CROWDFUNDING

Crowdfunding models vary depending on structure and purpose, and different approaches can be tailored to meet different financial and strategy needs. Crowdfunding models vary by structure and purpose, and different approaches can be tailored to meet different needs in terms of finance and strategy

1.1 Reward-Base Crowdfunding

Backers receive non-monetary reward in in return for their support. This model is prevalent in creative and technological projects (Ordanini et al., 2011)

1.2 Equity-Base Crowdfunding

Equity crowdfunding allows backers to invest in the company with ownership stakes. As Ahlers et al., (2015) claimed that high growth startups are the ideal candidates for this model. argued, this model is best used by high growth startups.

1.3 Debt-Based Crowdfunding (P2P Lending)

Hornuf & Schwienbacher, (2017) stated that debt-based crowdfunding offers loans to entrepreneurs, which later pay back with interest. that they later pay back with interest. This model is popular among SMEs looking for alternative sources instead of banks.

2.4 Donation-Based Crowdfunding

This model is primary used for philanthropic purpose, and is based on the generosity and kindness of individuals who contribute without expecting anything in (Salido-Andres et al., 2021)

Research on various economic and social topics has relied on Kickstarter data, which can be accessed directly from their website. This includes analyses of campaign characteristics (Deng et al., 2022; Kuo et al., 2022), descriptions of crowdfunding supporters' behavior (Belleflamme et al., 2021; Pan & Dong, 2023; Liu et al., 2024), and even a geospatial study of an entrepreneurial ecosystem (Lambert, 2024). In particular, the following features of that platform help to justify its exclusive use:

1) Although Kickstarter was initially launched in the United States, it has subsequently expanded its services to other major economies including the United Kingdom, Germany, the Netherlands, France, Japan, and Australia.
2) The concept of campaigns "going viral" was born out of the several successful Kickstarter initiatives.
    4) Some data in entrepreneurial finance, such the distribution of social capital across geographical entities, is more difficult to gather; therefore, data from Kickstarter has been utilized as a substitute (Cordova et al., 2015).

Previous research on crowdfunding platform within the fields of financial technology and artificial intelligence (AI) has largely relied on linear regression and other traditional statistical methods to analyze the behavior of backers and the performance of campaigns. For instance, many studies examine whether a campaign reaches or exceeds its crowdfunding goal, treating this as a binary outcome (van Teunenbroek et al., 2023). Other studies focus on the amount of money raised relative to the factors effect on the campaign success (Alazazi et al., 2020; Sarfo et al., 2024; (Zhao & Li, 2020; Gray & Zhang, 2017).

2. RESEARCH GAP

Although research on the effects of Artificial Intelligence (AI) utilization in workplace productivity as well as on crowdfunding advantages-present and future-as a financing tool have been conducted, the relationship between these two fields is rest to be explored. There is little literature that look into how crowdfunding provides support for the adoption of AI-enabled workplace solutions, particularly among SMEs and resource-constrained businesses. Crowdfunding for AI-Powered tools not only secured funding is necessary for successful business but validate the market need, established trust from potential users, and manage expectation around the capabilities and limitation of AI application in workplace (Gleasure & Feller, 2020). This chapter aims to address this gap by exploring the role of crowdfunding as a strategic enabler for AI-powered workplace innovations, examining how it facilitates access to capital, fosters community engagement, and drives experimentation in workplace technologies.

3. PURPOSE AND SCOPE

The ultimate goal of this chapter is to analyze the specific contributions of crowdfunding to the design and deployment of AI-oriented solutions that are designed for the workplace. This will include an examination of what types of projects with AI in the workplace are suited for crowdfunding, what factors lead to success or failure of AI projects that were crowdfunded, and what are the advantages and disadvantages of such funding. This chapter helps to appreciate the impact of crowdfunding on small firms ability to deploy and test AI technologies which would be out of reach in terms of cost by concentrating on the workplace context.

Furthermore, this chapter explains that the role of crowdfunding goes beyond the source of funding, it also act the market validation tool, and a feedback tool. The successful campaigns can also help businesses gauge interest, build the group of supporters and the first impression of the product usage in the workplace which can be incorporated vital feedbacks to refine the product according to the environment needed by the organizations (Chan & Parhankangas, 2020). Therefore, innovation by means of crowdfunding is a vital element of workplace technologies enhanced by artificial intelligence, as well as a way to engage users in the design process of the useful tools.

3.1 Literature Review

Imagine the little coffee shop on the corner, the tailor down the street, or that cool new app your neighbor is building – these are the heart and soul of our economies, especially in developing countries. We call them MSMEs (Micro, Small, and Medium Enterprises), but really, they're the dreamers and doers who create jobs, come up with fresh ideas, and keep things moving forward. These small businesses are the backbone – almost every single business there is an MSME, and they employ nearly everyone! They even helped the country get back on its feet economically. Because these business are the backbone of any country (Ye et al., 2024).

But it's not always easy for these small businesses. One of their biggest struggles is getting the money they need to grow, especially when times are tough. Unlike big companies, banks are often hesitant to lend to them. This is a real problem because they need that cash to start up, buy new equipment, or expand. So, they often go to banks simply because there are more branches and it seems like the most straightforward option, unlike trying to figure out online funding when they might not have good internet or know how it all works. In many Asian countries, most small businesses rely on these bank loans (Amoozad Mahdiraji et al., 2024). Historically, banks were the main source of funding in Asia. But after economic problems in the past, banks got more careful about lending to smaller businesses. Then came tough times like the Covid-19 pandemic, which hit these businesses hard, especially if they already had bank loans. Many faced the real possibility of closing down because they couldn't pay back their debts and didn't have any cash coming in (Andaru & Aryani, 2023). That's why we need new ways to help these businesses get funding, instead of just relying on bank loans, which can be risky. Over the last few years, with the internet becoming so important, new and exciting ways to get money have appeared. One of the most promising is crowdfunding.

Think of crowdfunding like an online community where small businesses can connect with regular people or investors who want to support them with their money. It's different from going to a bank or a big investment firm – it's a more direct way for them to get the funds they need without a lot of complicated steps. Because of technology, these online platforms can even see a business's past funding history, which can help them get funding even if they've had loan issues before (Gillani et al., 2025). The whole idea is to help those with great business ideas who just need a little financial boost to get started or grow. And it's working! In places like the UK and the US, crowdfunding platforms have successfully helped thousands of small businesses. Even in Indonesia, there are platforms that have funded hundreds of ventures (Ahmed, 2024). Of course, putting your money into a small business through crowdfunding isn't without some risk. Sometimes, the business might not manage the money well and could fail, meaning investors could lose their money.

That's why good crowdfunding platforms are careful about which businesses they list and often provide guidance to help them manage the funds they raise (Kumar et al., 2024).

Looking ahead, increasing small businesses are beginning to deploy Artificial Intelligence (AI). AI can actually provide them with a genuine edge, assisting them in getting to know their customers, working more productively, and developing new products. Nevertheless, numerous small businesses have difficulty to use AI since they lack the funds, the technical expertise, or know whether it is worth it. That's where crowdfunding steps in to be of assistance again. It is able to lend them the capital they require for investing in AI, and also assist them with networking with others who can offer guidance and even assist them with creating AI solutions.

Crowdfunding, particularly when individuals receive rewards or a share of the business in return for their investment, has been a wonderful means of financing new ventures and spurring innovation. But it's not only about the finances. It's also about how successful the business is in reaching out and commanding the support of the crowd (Behl et al., 2022). People need to believe in the idea, comprehend it, and sense that they are a part of it, particularly with something as potentially complex as AI. If the business idea is able to put forward a strong explanation of how their AI concept will benefit human beings, then they're in a better position to receive support(Okine et al., 2023). Crowdfunding sites are no longer just a means of obtaining funds. They are beginning to provide guidance and mentorship, serving as hotbeds for new ideas. That's extremely useful for small firms that do not have in-house AI specialists. They are able to receive not only finance but also crucial information and feedback. This allows them to learn and evolve, which is essential for the effective utilization of new technologies such as AI. Taking the larger perspective, we find that many times, only large companies can readily afford and utilize AI. What this implies is that we must have other mechanisms, such as crowdfunding, to enable small businesses to access such innovative tools. Through crowdfunding, small businesses are able to access a larger network of resources, which enables them to overcome the finance and expertise hurdles that typically prevent them from accessing AI (Durojaiye et al., 2024).

Ultimately, crowdfunding and AI can work together beautifully. AI can make crowdfunding platforms smarter and more helpful, and crowdfunding can give small businesses the chance to develop and use AI. This creates a new and exciting path for people to start and grow businesses in the digital age, where the support of the community can help even small players use cutting-edge technology.

4. OVERVIEW

The era of digitization brings to the level of the single market of the European Union a new concept, a new reality, namely crowdfunding which represents a viable way of ensuring access to financing for SMEs and startups through online platforms. What does the provision of crowdfunding services involve? This type of financing involves the participation of three types of actors: the project developer who proposes the project for financing, the investors who finance the proposed project and a crowdfunding service provider with an intermediary role, which connects project developers and investors within a publicly accessible online platform, including systems where user registration is required. It is necessary to specify that both credit-based and investment-based crowdfunding (transferable securities) are considered, because these types of financing can be conceived as comparable financing alternatives.

Figure 2. High-level steps involved in the proposed crowdfunding model

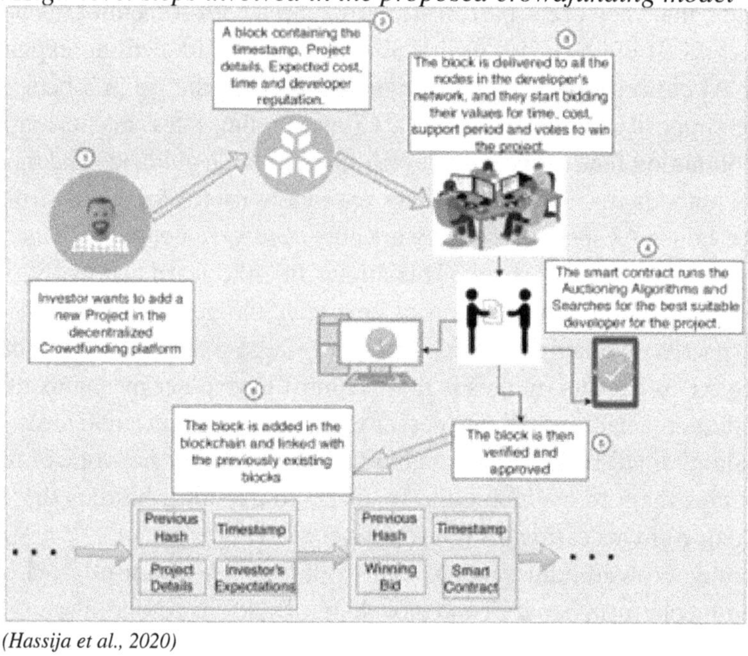

Source (Hassija et al., 2020)

The potential of data-driven management is adopted extensively, and there is developing for the concept of artificial intelligence (AI). The diversification of AI applications has increased in every country and across all sectors. The exponential growth rate of AI has revolutionized online business and transformed the customer experience on every online platform (Ransbotham et al., 2021). The most extensive application of artificial intelligence is observed in information systems (IS), as data is a necessary part of IS studies (Kalia, 2021; Liang et al., 2017). The rise of AI is also closely linked to initiatives in information and communications technology (ICT). Studies discussing the success of AI have shown that its most successful applications can be discovered in situations involving large and diverse data streams. The most useful application of AI is in Big Data Analytics (BDA). AI applications are primarily about data properties such as speed and variety (Grover et al., 2022). One such application of AI is crowdfunding. The main AI tools used

on crowdfunding platforms are chatbots, target search, recommendation systems, etc. Most platforms use them (Hua et al., 2019). The primary objective of AI adoption was to engage the end user and improve their experience (Huang & Rust, 2018). Studies have also confirmed that AI tools have helped users get customized experiences (Chin et al., 2024), that would help them become more "hooked" on a particular website. Crowdfunding can be categorized into different types, including donation-based, reward-based, equity-based, and debt-based crowdfunding. Jensen, (2024)posits that although, while often associated with non-profit initiatives donation-based crowdfunding has found, increasing applicability in entrepreneurial ventures, particularly in AI startups seeking initial funding.

Figure 3. Funding source for AI

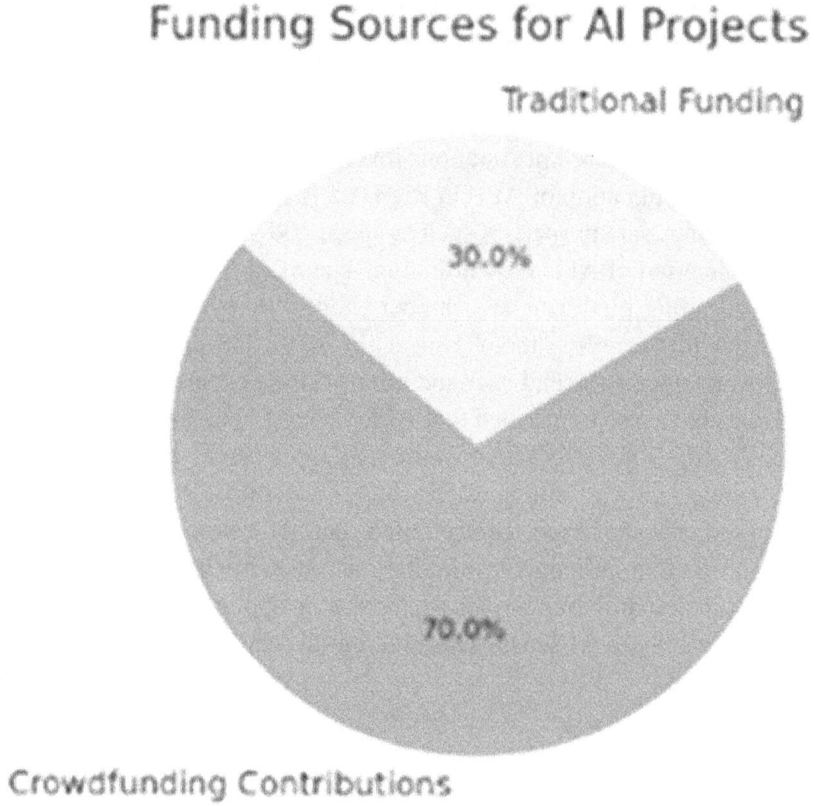

The figure above is a pie chart depicting the percentage of AI-driven project funded through crowdfunding compared to more conventional methods. Crowdfunding has emerged as a viable financial solution for implementing AI-driven technologies in the workplace, particularly for small and medium-sized enterprises (SMEs) that have limited access to traditional financing (Wasti et al., 2024). The integration of AI technologies, such as generative AI and machine learning algorithms, is increasingly recognized for enhancing workplace productivity, automate routine tasks, and optimize knowledge management processes. Crowdfunding enables companies businesses to overcome financial barriers to AI adoption, facilitating innovation and productivity improvements in the workplace (Hussain et al., 2023).

Figure 4. Workplace productivity over time

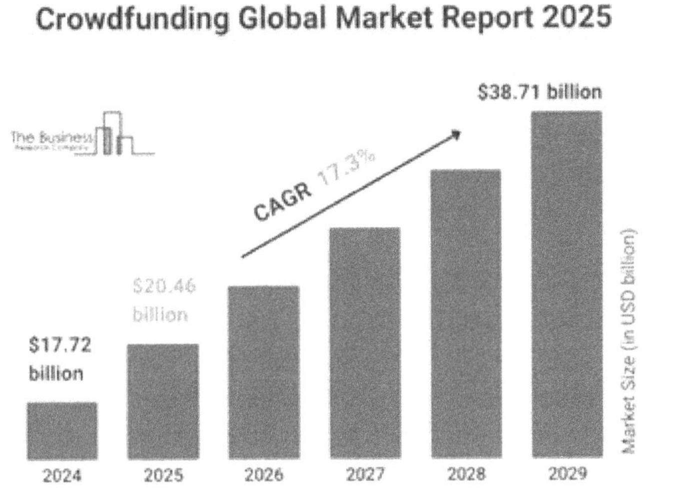

Source: crowdfunding global market report 2025

The graphic above shows the steady increase in workplace productivity in recent years due to the adoption of AI. The crowdfunding market size has increase in recent years. It will grow 17.72 billion in 2024 to 20.46 in 2025 at compound annual rate. Generative AI applications in the workplace have shown promising results in areas require repetitive or creative tasks, such as customer support, content creation, and data analysis (Khatib et al., 2024).But, while crowdfunding bridge the financial gap, it also introduces ethical and strategic considerations, such as the possible over-reliance on automated tools and the need for responsible AI governance (Ahmed, 2024). Additionally, crowdfunding campaigns can also serve as market testing grounds, enabling firms to gauge demand and refine AI tools based on backer feedback, adding value beyond funding (Giuggioli et al., 2024). Integrating AI into workplace processes aims to improve efficiency, productivity and decision-making ability.

As per Atienza-Barba et al., (2024), crowdfunding is an essential support mechanism for AI research and development startups. Not only does it offer funding but also market validation, which is necessary to secure additional investments. Haddad & Hornuf, (2023) explained that 2007–2008 financial crisis reduced traditional source of finance for risky projects, and contributed to rising reliance on alternative financing modes. US, UK, and many European banking regulators were compelled to rescue banks that were on the verge of collapse during 2007-2008 recession, government should use public funds to provide financial bailouts. This shift in the funding availability resulted in greater reliance on alternative sources of funding, i.e., crowdfunding, which has emerged as an important source of finance for AI startup firms. Not only do firms receive capital through crowdfunding but also they obtain market validation that can bring in additional investment, thus driving AI adoption and innovation within organizations at a faster rate. This route allows companies to explore higher-end AI solutions, improve efficiencies in operations, and enable data-driven decision-making that would be out of reach under conventional funding limitations (Berliner & Kenworthy, 2017).

6. BENEFITS OF CROWDFUNDING FOR AI-POWERED WORKPLACE PROJECTS

Crowdfunding has quickly emerged as the alternative financing option, especially to address critical issue of workplace project challenges with AI. Since it has the ability to deliver so much more than merely providing finances as it goes beyond simply raising funds by encouraging innovation, involving the community, and helping to validate new ideas within the work environment.

6.1. Access to Capital for High-Risk AI Innovations

Constructing advanced technology solutions is costly because it requires funding for gathering data, computer use, and hiring experts. It is therefore challenging for startups and small companies with limited resources. Sometimes traditional financiers, including banks and venture capitalists, are reluctant to invest in such projects due to the perceived risks and uncertain returns (Belleflamme et al., 2021) . Crowdfunding therefore enables such projects to bypass institutions and reach interested parties directly in order to raise funds in a more decentralized manner. In the case of an AI job, this can be very beneficial, especially if it is still at an early stage of development and has yet to prove its market demand.

6.2. Market Validation and Demand Assessment

Crowdfunding platforms offer a unique opportunity to validate products for marketability before they are developed in their actual form. When the campaign really gains momentum, it shows actual interest and demand in the market, thereby providing an early indication that a solution can meet workplace needs. This "proof of concept" is extremely valuable for AI projects because it enables developers to refine and calibrate their solutions based on real market actions (Gleasure, 2023)

With strong support through crowdfunding, there is a good chance that the tool will address real pain points for employees and the company. It can also identify which specific features or functionality backers are focused on, which in turn helps the company fine-tune its product (Efrat et al., 2021).

6.3. User-Centric Development and Community Engagement

Crowdfunding allows direct of communication with developers and potential users to to provide their contribution to the product while it is still in the early stages of development. This is a valuable interaction for AI-powered tools, as is user adoption and the usability of AI-powered workplace tools. By involving potential users in the product development process, developers can ensure that the AI solutions they create are more aligned with real workplace needs and user expectations (Mollick, 2014)). In fact, early adopters are often supporters of the product, leading to a loyal generation of users and enabling word of mouth, which can play very well in the work environment where trust and familiarity influence adoption.

6.4. Increased Transparency and Trust in AI Projects

One of the difficulties with AI projects is gaining user trust, as AI-driven solutions are sometimes perceived as "black boxes" where users do not understand how the technology works. Crowdfunding campaigns usually provide transparency about the project's goals and development processes as well as the intended impact of the campaign. By giving developers insight into all the details of a particular project, they increase their credibility and can build trust among supporters and potential customers (Agrawal et al., 2015). Crowdfunding allows AI developers to educate users about how the technology works, eliminating issues around privacy, algorithmic transparency, and ethics. This is a crucial feature in the workplace as the numerous cases of AI adoption are based on user trust in the technology.

6.5. Diverse Funding Models for Different Needs

There are diverse models of crowdfunding, ranging from reward-based, equity-based, and donation-based crowdfunding which generally apply to varied forms of AI workplace projects. Reward-based crowdfunding applies to types of projects wherein supporters are provided with early access or other kinds of rewards as compensation for sponsoring. Equity-based crowdfunding utilizes a for profit investment in the firm for share of ownership and may thus be tempting for more extensive projects with high funding requirements to finish (Belleflamme et al., 2020). Fundamentally, the flexibility of crowdfunding models helps AI startups choose the funding approach that best suits the type of their project, the level of funding needed, and their long-term financial goals.

A workplace-focused AI company might choose reward-based crowdfunding with the goal of funding a test or validation of a new productivity tool. Alternatively, if the funding needs are very high, one could opt for equity-based crowdfunding by offering early backers a share of future business growth

6.6. Enhanced Visibility and Brand Awareness

Crowdfunding campaigns make it possible to create visibility and awareness of your brand in front of early adopters and potential clients. It is highly imperative for the AI-powered workplace tools since most companies excited to incorporate AI functionality into their process but cannot figure out what solutions are available. Crowdfunding platforms are, therefore becoming a marketing channel as they expand the reach of AI startups and attract media coverage that can further consolidatify one's brand presence (Hussain et al., 2023)..

For example, such visibility funded through crowdfunding through the crowdfunding platform can also attract further funds from institutional investors, as a successful campaign indicates market demand and user interests.

7. CHALLENGES OF CROWDFUNDING FOR AI-POWERED WORKPLACE PROJECTS

While crowdfunding offers many opportunities for AI-powered workplace projects, it also brings with diverse challenges. These challenges arise from the complexity of AI technology, the requirements of managing a crowdfunding campaign, and the risks associated with financing through public contributions. Here are some of the key challenges:

7.1. Complexity of Communicating AI Concepts to a Broad Audience

AI technology can be highly technical and requires specialized knowledge to understand its features, benefits and limitations. However, crowdfunding platforms are aimed at a general audience who may not have the technical expertise to fully understand AI concepts. Simplifying complex AI topics into understandable language without oversimplifying or misrepresenting the technology can be challenging, especially for projects focused on workplace AI solutions where functionality is nuanced (Behl et al., 2022).

If potential backers do not fully understand the project, they may hesitate to invest because they find it too complex or risky. To overcome this, creators need to invest in clear and effective communication strategies, which can increase the cost and time spent on the campaign. Example: A company developing an AI-driven employee sentiment analysis tool may struggle to explain how the technology works and why it is valuable without oversimplifying key features such as data protection, natural language processing, and machine learning.

7.2. Difficulty in Proving Feasibility and Managing Expectations

Crowdfunding backers often look for concrete evidence that a project is feasible and can deliver on its promises. However, AI projects are often experimental in nature and involve cutting-edge research that may not guarantee immediate or successful results. Additionally, AI-powered workplace projects often require extensive testing and refinement to function effectively in real-world environments. These factors can lead to a gap between the promises made during the campaign and the final product, potentially resulting in expectations not being met (Davies, 2024).. The campaign creator carefully manages expectations and ensures transparency about risks, timelines and results. This creates a dilemma between finding the truth and raising seed capital from supporters. An AI startup building a product to remotely track team member performance can experience significant delays if the company encounters unexpected problems during product testing, which can make delivery promises to backers frustrating.

7.3. High Costs and Resource Demands of Running a Campaign

Launching a successful crowdfunding campaign requires significant resources, including marketing efforts, content creation, and ongoing communication with backers. For AI projects, where teams are often consists of researchers and developers focused on the technical side, shifting resources toward campaign management can be burdensome. Hiring additional marketing or PR support can strain limited budgets, predominantly for startups with constrained financial resources (Belleflamme et al., 2020). In addition, running a campaign requires dedicated time to respond to backer inquiries, update progress, and handle logistics, which can distract from the core work of developing the AI project. A small AI-focused company developing a workplace productivity tool may need to hire additional staff to manage social media, video production, and customer relations for the crowdfunding campaign, increasing its total cost of ownership.

7.4. Intellectual Property Risks and Competition

Intellectual property disclosure is one of the biggest risks in AI-powered projects. Crowdfunding campaigns work against "intellectual property," requiring creators to reveal extensive information about their project in order to attract more supporters. You expose yourself to competitors or imitators. AI technology is highly competitive. Advanced algorithms, specialized data processing techniques, or the introduction of novel applications can provide room for larger companies to implement and overcome the work done by smaller teams (Ye et al., 2024)).

In this manner, AI developers must carefully balance the information to disclose to potential backers versus what is necessary to protect this valuable proprietary knowledge. But if a lot is left out, the same campaign will also be less attractive to donors. A company developing a novel AI tool for human resources analytics may be hesitate to reveal too much about its algorithms for fear that a larger firm will imitate the concept.

7.5. Uncertain Regulatory Environment for AI Solutions

The rules governing AI technologies are still evolving, and many governments are also trying to offer guidance on ethical AI, data protection and transparency of algorithms. When it comes to projects over AI in the workplace-sometimes regarding sensitive data or involved in decision-making processes, they face the challenge of navigating evolving regulations. Such uncertainty may deter backers as they fear that such legal changes could jeopardize the viability of the project or even force developers to rework parts of the product (Zhang et al., 2022). This is particularly relevant to AI implementation in the workplace, where privacy, employee consent, and possible biases in AI algorithms are critical. Crowdfunding backers may be wary of projects that expose them to regulatory risks, thereby limiting the success of such a campaign.

7.6. Difficulty in Building Long-Term Investor Relationships

While crowdfunding can raise initial capital, it does not necessarily build long-term investor relationships like traditional venture capital or private equity financing does. Crowdfunding backers do not necessarily have the same level of engagement or expertise in the AI industry as institutional investors. Therefore, it is difficult for AI developers to secure follow-on investments from crowdfunding sources if the project requires ongoing funding to scale and develop (Agrawal et al., 2015). Significant funding, which is likely to be needed to scale AI-powered workplace projects, also requires solid financial support from accredited investors, as the often transactional nature of crowdfunding mostly refers to one-off events and long-term funding is limited and therefore the developers would have needed more funding sources after the campaign.

7.7. Risks of Backer Expectations and Reputation Management

Successfully executed crowdfunding campaigns often bring more scrutiny and unrealistic expectations for the projects. In the case of AI workplace tools, advocates may raise ethical and practical concerns, such as impacts on job security, bias in an AI algorithm, or privacy concerns. Any kind of negative publicity or unsatisfactory fulfillment of expectations from the backers will weaken the credibility of the project and deter future users and investors (Mollick & Robb, 2016). Managing this reputation risk calls through proactive communication, transparency, and ethical commitment. Addressing such concerns up front with AI projects is critical, but may also deter certain types of backers who might otherwise prefer simpler or lower-risk investments.

7.8. Market and Talent Saturation in AI Development

The more popular AI is, the more saturated this market is with competing projects that share the same talent pool and resources. Investors might see this as a barrier because they are concerned that a crowdfunded project will not be able to attract good machine learning engineers, data scientists, or developers, which would directly affect the quality and timeline of the product.

7.9. Potential for AI Bias and Discrimination in Workplace Applications

AI algorithm bias, especially in hiring, assessment, or promotion decisions, can create reputational and legal risk. Investors will worry that an AI project may unintentionally inject bias, which can result in discrimination accusations or public outcry. This risk is greater in workplace uses where AI decisions directly affect employees' careers (Kim & Bodie, 2020).(Kim & Bodie, 2020).

7.10. Low Transparency of Crowdfunding Campaigns

In crowdfunding, information about projects can be very limited or selective, making it difficult for investors to conduct proper due diligence. Investors do not have access to financial history, business plans or key team details, meaning they lack transparency and cannot properly assess the project's chances of success. Such examples could deter investors who instead demand full disclosure (Fanea-Ivanovici, 2018).

7.11. Risk of Fraud or Misrepresentation

Some of the crowdfunders are so lenient while screening projects that some campaigns' presentations may be inconclusive. Investors who worry are those who over-promise returns or when a project is kept so secret and does not reveal material aspects such as risks of the project or previous failures of the team proposing it. Therefore, the fear of fraud is a major issue for investors (Tenca & Franzoni, 2019).

7.12. Uncertain Return on Investment (ROI)

Crowdfunding rarely delivers clear financial returns. Most platforms follow the reward-based model where backers receive products or perks in return for their investment instead of equity. Even with the equity crowdfunding model, the success of a project is uncertain, and investors may not see return if the company underperforms or fails. This unclear financial return therefore delivers (Gigante & Cozzio, 2021)

7.13. Illiquidity and Exit Challenges

Although investments in shares of public companies can be bought and sold on the stock exchange and therefore require sufficient market liquidity, investments via crowdfunding platforms usually have limited market liquidity that can hardly be converted into cash. Many crowdfunding investors are locked into these investments and cannot sell or get their money back until the project reaches a certain stage, is acquired by another company, or, if ever, goes public. This illiquidity gives crowdfunding leverage that is unmarketable to investors seeking flexibility (Haddad & Hornuf, 2023).

8. CONCLUSION

The chapter is dedicated to describing how crowdfunding is gaining importance as one of the forms of alternative financing for start-ups and SMEs developing solutions for the use of AI in the workplace. Despite the potential to increase labor productivity through the use of an artificial intelligence system, the concept requires huge capital investments that traditional sources of financing cannot afford. Crowdfunding also bridges this gap in the early venture capital tradition by providing not only capital, but also validation, access to users, and feedback mechanisms that can inform product development. This chapter describes the key benefits of crowdfunding for AI projects, such as: financing high-risk technologies, market feedback, consumer-oriented product design and building trust and recognition. However, it raises questions such as: Such as how to explain AI to many people and lower their expectations, what resources are required for a campaign, intellectual property rights risks, legal issues and quite difficult to build long-term relationships with investors. The chapter focuses on analyzing the advantages and disadvantages of the means and goal of crowdfunding as a key driving force for AI-based innovation in the workplace. However, transparency, communication and market orientation are crucial for increasing the effectiveness of crowdfunding AI projects.

This chapter describes the key benefits of crowdfunding for AI projects, such as: B. financing high-risk technologies, market feedback, consumer-oriented product design and building trust and recognition. However, it raises questions such as: Such as how to explain AI to many people and lower their expectations, what resources are required for a campaign, intellectual property rights risks, legal issues and quite difficult to build long-term relationships with investors.

The chapter focuses on analyzing the advantages and disadvantages of the means and goal of crowdfunding as a key driving force for AI-based innovation in the workplace. However, transparency, communication and market orientation are crucial for increasing the effectiveness of crowdfunding AI projects.

8.1 Recommendations for Enhancing Chapter Scope and Depth

The chapter explores a new and relevant subject by highlighting the role of crowdfunding in enabling AI-powered workplace innovations, aligning seamlessly with the proposed book's theme. However, the chapter doesn't explain the real-life problems, challenges, or new trends in enough detail. It also doesn't include much data or examples from the crowdfunding world, especially in specific regions or industries, which makes it less useful in practice. To improve the chapter, it should include numbers, real examples, and a clear look at the risks and limits of using crowdfunding for AI in the workplace. This would help readers better understand the topic and make the chapter more helpful and complete.

8.2 Managerial Implication

Crowdfunding offers several strategic advantages for managers looking to fund AI innovations in the workplace: Startups and small and medium-sized businesses that may not have access to most traditional funding sources can easily access them. It also provides organizations with an additional financial tool that can help secure capital for early-stage AI projects and serve as a form of validation in the market. By raising funds from backers, managers are able to test product ideas, refine features, and assess demand, thereby reducing the likelihood of product failure. Crowdfunding also creates a community of early adopters who are interested in seeing the product successfully developed, thus building brand loyalty and workplace adoption more quickly. The value of a crowdfunding campaign lies in the demand for transparency, which can build trust in an AI project. Transparency would be invaluable for building trust, especially when it comes to ethical issues and the handling of data in AI projects. These are often concerning a supporter might have. There are a variety of different crowdfunding models, which can range from reward-based to equity-based depending on the funding needs of the project. To protect intellectual property, managers should carefully consider the extent of details shared. Crowdfunding also offers the opportunity to increase brand visibility where exposure could attract media attention and expand the company's reach. Managing a crowdfunding campaign requires enormous resources, so managers must balance these demands with the technical work of developing the AI product.

Finally, crowdfunding should be viewed as part of a broader financial strategy with plans for future investment rounds, and managers should also ensure that their AI projects comply with ethical and regulatory standards to maintain trust and avoid legal issues. In conclusion, while crowdfunding is an invaluable tool for funding and validating AI-driven innovations, it requires careful planning and strategic management to ensure long-term success. Crowdfunding is often the first phase in a larger, multi-stage financing process and lays the foundation.

8.3 Managerial Implication

Crowdfunding presents several strategic benefits to managers wishing to finance AI innovations in the workplace: Startups and small and medium-sized enterprises that lack access to most conventional funding opportunities can readily obtain them. It also gives companies an extra financing tool that can assist in obtaining capital for nascent AI initiatives and act as a market validation mechanism. By raising capital from supporters, managers can experiment with product concepts, iterate on features, and gauge demand, thus minimizing the risk of product failure. Crowdfunding also builds a community of early adopters who want to see the product successfully created, hence accelerating brand loyalty and workplace adoption. The worth of a crowdfunding campaign is the need for transparency, which can create trust in an AI project. Transparency would be priceless to establish trust, particularly regarding ethical concerns and the management of data in AI projects. These are usually issues a supporter may have. There are several different crowdfunding structures, which can be from reward-based to equity-based depending on the requirements of funding for the project. For protecting intellectual property, managers need to be cautious about the amount of details released. Crowdfunding also provides the potential to enhance brand visibility where exposure might call media attention and widen the company's audience. Managing a crowdfunding campaign is such a resource-intensive activity that managers have to balance these needs with the technical activity of creating the AI product. Lastly, crowdfunding must be seen as one piece of an overall financing strategy with projections for subsequent financing rounds, and managers must also make sure their AI projects are in accordance with ethical and regulatory requirements to sustain trust and stay out of trouble with the law.

In summary, although crowdfunding is a precious resource for financing and authenticating AI-based innovations, it needs to be planned and managed strategically to guarantee long-term success. Crowdfunding is usually the initial step in a broader, multi-stage financing process and sets the stage.

REFERENCES

Agrawal, A., Catalini, C., & Goldfarb, A. (2015). Crowdfunding: Geography, social networks, and the timing of investment decisions. *Journal of Economics & Management Strategy*, *24*(2), 253–274. DOI: 10.1111/jems.12093

Ahlers, G. K. C., Cumming, D., Günther, C., & Schweizer, D. (2015). Signaling in equity crowdfunding. *Entrepreneurship Theory and Practice*, *39*(4), 955–980. DOI: 10.1111/etap.12157

Ahmed, S. (2024). Artificial Intelligence (AI) Technology Adoption in SME. [AI]. *Artificial Intelligence*, *17*(01).

Al Khatib, I., Ahmed, V., & Ndiaye, M. (2024). Integrated blockchain systems are paving the way to SMART logistics. *AIP Conference Proceedings*, *3034*(1), 070001. DOI: 10.1063/5.0194698

Alazazi, M., Wang, B., & Allan, T. (2020). *Success factors of donation-based crowdfunding campaigns: A machine learning approach.*

Amoozad Mahdiraji, H., Razavi Hajiagha, S. H., Jafari-Sadeghi, V., Busso, D., & Devalle, A. (2024). Towards financing the entrepreneurial SMEs: Exploring the innovation drivers of successful crowdfunding via a multi-layer decision-making approach. *European Journal of Innovation Management*, *27*(7), 2275–2301. DOI: 10.1108/EJIM-12-2021-0618

Andaru, F. M., & Aryani, Y. A. (2023). Big data adoption: Does it have a great impact on crowdfunding success in SMEs? *Proyecciones (Antofagasta).*

Atienza-Barba, M., del Río, M. de la C., Meseguer-Martínez, Á., & Barba-Sánchez, V. (2024). Artificial intelligence and organizational agility: An analysis of scientific production and future trends. *European Research on Management and Business Economics*, *30*(2), 100253. DOI: 10.1016/j.iedeen.2024.100253

Behl, A., Dutta, P., Luo, Z., & Sheorey, P. (2022). Enabling artificial intelligence on a donation-based crowdfunding platform: A theoretical approach. *Annals of Operations Research*, *319*(1), 1–29. DOI: 10.1007/s10479-020-03906-z

Belbe, S., Gomez, L., Stanca, L., Wenzlaff, K., Mare, C., Elitzur, R., Bolesta, K., Huang, X., Yilmaz, G. N., & Bernard, F. S. (2024). [*Crowdfunding: A hands-on roadmap to study and understand crowdfunding data using critical thinking AI.*]. *AI*, •••, 4.

Belleflamme, P., Lambert, T., & Schwienbacher, A. (2021). Spillovers in crowdfunding. *Available atSSRN* 3259191.

Berliner, L. S., & Kenworthy, N. J. (2017). Producing a worthy illness: Personal crowdfunding amidst financial crisis. *Social Science & Medicine*, *187*, 233–242. DOI: 10.1016/j.socscimed.2017.02.008 PMID: 28274601

Chin, T., Ghouri, M. W. A., Jin, J., & Deveci, M. (2024). AI technologies affording the orchestration of ecosystem-based business models: The moderating role of AI knowledge spillover. *Humanities & Social Sciences Communications*, *11*(1), 1–13. DOI: 10.1057/s41599-024-03003-7

Cordova, A., Dolci, J., & Gianfrate, G. (2015). The determinants of crowdfunding success: Evidence from technology projects. *Procedia: Social and Behavioral Sciences*, *181*, 115–124. DOI: 10.1016/j.sbspro.2015.04.872

Davenport, T. H., & Ronanki, R. (2018). Artificial intelligence for the real world. *Harvard Business Review*, *96*(1), 108–116.

Davies, R. (2024). Guided choices: The ethics of using algorithmic systems to shape philanthropic decision-making. In *The Routledge Handbook of Artificial Intelligence and Philanthropy* (pp. 451–470). Routledge. DOI: 10.4324/9781003468615-32

Deng, L., Ye, Q., Xu, D., Sun, W., & Jiang, G. (2022). A literature review and integrated framework for the determinants of crowdfunding success. *Financial Innovation*, *8*(1), 41. DOI: 10.1186/s40854-022-00345-6

Durojaiye, A. T., Ewim, C. P.-M., & Igwe, A. N. (2024). *Developing a crowdfunding optimization model to bridge the financing gap for small business enterprises through data-driven strategies.*

Efrat, K., Gilboa, S., & Wald, A. (2021). The emergence of well-being in crowdfunding: A study of entrepreneurs and backers of reward and donation campaigns. *International Journal of Entrepreneurial Behaviour & Research*, *27*(2), 397–415. DOI: 10.1108/IJEBR-12-2019-0685

Fanea-Ivanovici, M. (2018). Transparency of financial information on crowdfunding platforms–a prerequisite for successful funding campaigns. *International Conference Knowledge-Based Organization, 24*(2), 37–42. DOI: 10.1515/kbo-2018-0063

Gigante, G., & Cozzio, G. (2021). Equity crowdfunding: An empirical investigation of success factors in real estate crowdfunding. *Journal of Property Investment & Finance*, *40*(6), 532–547. DOI: 10.1108/JPIF-06-2021-0055

Gillani, S. A., Alvi, A. R., Ahmad, H., Gillani, S. A., & Tanveer, Y. (2025). FinTech Adoption for SMEs: Innovation and Opportunities Worldwide. In *Algorithmic Training, Future Markets, and Big Data for Finance Digitalization* (pp. 105–120). IGI Global Scientific Publishing.

Giuggioli, G., Pellegrini, M. M., & Giannone, G. (2024). Artificial intelligence as an enabler for entrepreneurial finance: A practical guide to AI-driven video pitch evaluation for entrepreneurs and investors. *Management Decision*. Advance online publication. DOI: 10.1108/MD-10-2023-1926

Gleasure, R. (2023). Contrasting the response to past and future oriented appeals for help on donation-based crowdfunding platforms. *European Journal of Information Systems*, •••, 1–22.

Gleasure, R., & Feller, J. (2016). Does heart or head rule donor behaviors in charitable crowdfunding markets? *International Journal of Electronic Commerce*, *20*(4), 499–524. DOI: 10.1080/10864415.2016.1171975

Gray, M., & Zhang, B. (2017). Crowdfunding: understanding diversity. In *Handbook on the Geographies of Money and Finance* (pp. 580–609). Edward Elgar Publishing. DOI: 10.4337/9781784719005.00034

Grover, P., Kar, A. K., & Dwivedi, Y. K. (2022). Understanding artificial intelligence adoption in operations management: Insights from the review of academic literature and social media discussions. *Annals of Operations Research*, *308*(1), 177–213. DOI: 10.1007/s10479-020-03683-9

Haddad, C., & Hornuf, L. (2023). How do fintech start-ups affect financial institutions' performance and default risk? *European Journal of Finance*, *29*(15), 1761–1792. DOI: 10.1080/1351847X.2022.2151371

Hassija, V., Chamola, V., & Zeadally, S. (2020). BitFund: A blockchain-based crowd funding platform for future smart and connected nation. *Sustainable Cities and Society*, *60*, 102145. DOI: 10.1016/j.scs.2020.102145

Hoque, M. M. (2024). Crowdfunding for innovation: A comprehensive empirical review. *Future Business Journal*, *10*(1), 102. DOI: 10.1186/s43093-024-00387-5

Hornuf, L., & Schwienbacher, A. (2017). Should securities regulation promote equity crowdfunding? *Small Business Economics*, *49*(3), 579–593. DOI: 10.1007/s11187-017-9839-9

Hua, X., Huang, Y., & Zheng, Y. (2019). Current practices, new insights, and emerging trends of financial technologies. *Industrial Management & Data Systems*, *119*(7), 1401–1410. DOI: 10.1108/IMDS-08-2019-0431

Huang, M.-H., & Rust, R. T. (2018). Artificial intelligence in service. *Journal of Service Research, 21*(2), 155–172. DOI: 10.1177/1094670517752459

Hussain, N., Di Pietro, F., & Rosati, P. (2023). Crowdfunding for Social Entrepreneurship: A systematic review of the literature. *Journal of Social Entrepreneurship*, •••, 1–24. DOI: 10.1080/19420676.2023.2236637

Jensen, K. (2024). *The Ethics of Entrepreneurship Education*. MIT Press. DOI: 10.7551/mitpress/15073.001.0001

Kalia, P. (2021). Artificial intelligence in e-commerce: a business process analysis. In *Artificial Intelligence* (pp. 9–19). CRC Press. DOI: 10.1201/9781003095910-2

Kim, P. T., & Bodie, M. T. (2020). Artificial intelligence and the challenges of workplace discrimination and privacy. *ABAJ Lab. & Emp. L.*, *35*, 289.

Korzynski, P., Haenlein, M., & Rautiainen, M. (2021). Impression management techniques in crowdfunding: An analysis of Kickstarter videos using artificial intelligence. *European Management Journal*, *39*(5), 675–684. DOI: 10.1016/j.emj.2021.01.001

Kumar, J., Rani, M., Rani, G., & Rani, V. (2024). Crowdfunding adoption in emerging economies: Insights for entrepreneurs and policymakers. *Journal of Small Business and Enterprise Development*, *31*(1), 55–73. DOI: 10.1108/JSBED-05-2023-0204

Kuo, Y.-F., Lin, C. S., & Liu, L.-T. (2022). The effects of framing messages and cause-related marketing on backing intentions in reward-based crowdfunding. *Journal of Retailing and Consumer Services*, *64*, 102799. DOI: 10.1016/j.jretconser.2021.102799

Lambert, T. (2024). The Rise of Crowdfunding. In *Oxford Research Encyclopedia of Economics and Finance*. DOI: 10.1093/acrefore/9780190625979.013.1002

Liang, C., Chang, C.-C., Liang, C.-T., & Liu, Y.-C. (2017). Imagining future success: Imaginative capacity on the perceived performance of potential agrisocio entrepreneurs. *Thinking Skills and Creativity*, *23*, 161–174. DOI: 10.1016/j.tsc.2016.12.007

Liu, Y., Zhang, K., Xue, W., & Zhou, Z. (2024). Crowdfunding innovative but risky new ventures: The importance of less ambiguous tone. *Financial Innovation*, *10*(1), 27. DOI: 10.1186/s40854-023-00529-8

Mollick, E. (2014). The dynamics of crowdfunding: An exploratory study. *Journal of Business Venturing*, *29*(1), 1–16. DOI: 10.1016/j.jbusvent.2013.06.005

Okine, A. N. D., Li, Y., Djimesah, I. E., Zhao, H., Budu, K. W. A., Duah, E., & Mireku, K. K. (2023). Analyzing crowdfunding adoption from a technology acceptance perspective. *Technological Forecasting and Social Change*, *192*, 122582. DOI: 10.1016/j.techfore.2023.122582

Ordanini, A., Miceli, L., Pizzetti, M., & Parasuraman, A. (2011). Crowd-funding: Transforming customers into investors through innovative service platforms. *Journal of Service Management*, *22*(4), 443–470. DOI: 10.1108/09564231111155079

Pan, X., & Dong, L. (2023). What Determines the Success of Charitable Crowdfunding Campaigns? Evidence from China During the COVID-19 Pandemic. *Voluntas*, *34*(6), 1–15. DOI: 10.1007/s11266-023-00557-z PMID: 36743475

Ransbotham, S., Candelon, F., Kiron, D., LaFountain, B., & Khodabandeh, S. (2021). The cultural benefits of artificial intelligence in the Enterprise. *MIT Sloan Management Review and Boston Consulting Group, 1.*

Renaldo, N., Junaedi, A. T., Musa, S., Wahid, N., & Cecilia, C. (2024). Mapping the Financial Technology Industry in Indonesia. *Journal of Applied Business and Technology*, *5*(1), 61–66. DOI: 10.35145/jabt.v5i1.162

Salido-Andres, N., Rey-Garcia, M., Alvarez-Gonzalez, L. I., & Vazquez-Casielles, R. (2021). Mapping the field of donation-based crowdfunding for charitable causes: Systematic review and conceptual framework. *Voluntas*, *32*(2), 288–302. DOI: 10.1007/s11266-020-00213-w

Sarfo, C., Zhang, J. A., O'Kane, P., & O'Kane, C. (2024). Crowdfunding's impact on small business performance through exploitative and exploratory search strategies: An entrepreneurial resourcefulness perspective. *Strategic Change*, *33*(5), 355–369. DOI: 10.1002/jsc.2584

Stone, M. L., & Stidham, R. W. (2023). Artificial Intelligence in IBD: How Will It Change Patient Management? *Current Treatment Options in Cardiovascular Medicine*, *21*(4), 365–377. DOI: 10.1007/s11938-023-00437-x

Tenca, F., & Franzoni, C. (2019). Crowdfunding: Risk, fraud and regulation. In *Handbook of research on crowdfunding* (pp. 323–355). Edward Elgar Publishing.

van Teunenbroek, C., Dalla Chiesa, C., & Hesse, L. (2023). The contribution of crowdfunding for philanthropy: A systematic review and framework of donation and reward crowdfunding. *Journal of Philanthropy and Marketing*, *28*(3), e1791. DOI: 10.1002/nvsm.1791

Varona, D., & Suárez, J. L. (2022). Discrimination, bias, fairness, and trustworthy AI. *Applied Sciences (Basel, Switzerland)*, *12*(12), 5826. DOI: 10.3390/app12125826

Wasti, S. M. H. A., Ahmed, J., & Khan, M. H. (2024). Role of successive round as a quality signal in equity crowdfunding: Novel evidence from the perspective of investors' preferences. *PLoS One, 19*(3), e0297820. DOI: 10.1371/journal.pone.0297820 PMID: 38452130

Ye, T., Zheng, J., Jin, J., Qiu, J., Ai, W., & Mei, Q. (2024). Using Artificial Intelligence to Unlock Crowdfunding Success for Small Businesses. *Available atSSRN* 4806426. DOI: 10.2139/ssrn.4806426

Zhang, X., Liu, X., Wang, X., Zhao, H., & Zhang, W. (2022). Exploring the effects of social capital on crowdfunding performance: A holistic analysis from the empirical and predictive views. *Computers in Human Behavior, 126*, 107011. DOI: 10.1016/j.chb.2021.107011

Zhao, L., & Li, Y. (2020). Crowdfunding in China: Turmoil of global leadership. *Advances in Crowdfunding: Research and Practice*, 273–296.

Chapter 8
Strategic Planning for Business Leaders Using AI

Mehvish Sultan
National Textile University, Pakistan

ABSTRACT

In recent decades, the incorporation of AI in the strategic planning process is revolutionized the business model by improving the efficiency of decision-making, operations, and customer relationship management. AI provides the means for organizations to handle large volumes of data almost instantaneously allowing for the generation of predictive analytics that enhances forecasting and flexibility. It replaces manual labor for low-level duties and assigns humans the responsibility of higher-ranking tasks. On the other hand, there are challenges in AI development and deployment valuation such as a massive cost associated with technology purchase and data management. Integration can only be achieved if both artificial intelligence and the purpose of the firm's activities are harmonized while developing an environment where decision-making is collective and involves the use of AI as well as humans.

DOI: 10.4018/979-8-3693-8960-7.ch008

1. STRATEGIC PLANNING FOR BUSINESSES

1.1 The Importance of Strategic Planning for Business

Strategic planning, however, is important in the business world—more so in those transcending national boundaries like international corporations. This lack of strategic organization is the single biggest culprit for too many companies trying to react to what occurs in their market rather than shaping themselves the fastest.

The goal is not just the goals, but also establishing that every action of your business supports its long-term objectives. Strategic planning involves decisions based on conscious and careful consideration that will limit wasted resources spent make the business grow, and reduce risk.

With markets changing by the minute and competition fiercer than ever, a well-laid strategic plan provides businesses with the necessary clarity and guidance to keep pace, adjust to the changes, and excel amidst fierce competitive forces unleashed in this global landscape.

2. CURRENT CHALLENGES BUSINESS LEADERS FACE IN STRATEGIC PLANNING

Strategic planning is not as simple as it used to be nowadays due to the realities of a rapidly moving business world. The process has become even more difficult given the many factors business leaders have to navigate not only with being able to foresee upcoming changes but also can swiftly pivot. Groups on the left are currently struggling with key issues:

1. **Rapid Technological Advancements** Fast Emerging Technologies Technology is advancing at an incredibly fast pace which businesses may find difficult to cope with. What works today may be not work tomorrow. In the retail sphere, leaders are perpetually adjusting to new e-commerce trends and AI-powered customer service. In hindsight, it becomes clear that the likes of Blockbuster, who once owned video rental but failed to see the rise of digital streaming, simply couldn't comprehend where their future business lay—the fall of Nokia, the most progressive brand in terms of mobile phone (smartphone) standards.

As a result, leaders are now being intensely scrutinized for their ability to not only predict which technologies will impact the future of work but also how those technologies should shape their long-term strategies.

2. **Globalization and Supply Chain Disruptions** Globalization meant new ways to trade and sell; on the other, it brought instability. The coronavirus COVID-19 outbreak simply exposed the sensitivity of many global supply chains. Business leaders across industries, particularly automotive and electronics, witnessed unprecedented delays and shorts that derailed their strategic objectives. After the pandemic is over, geopolitics and natural disasters will be unpredictable pitfalls that can derail even the best-laid plans. The need to manage risk while capturing the value in global markets has become a key strategic imperative.
3. **Economic Uncertainty** Economic uncertainty, from inflation to fluctuating currency rates and changing market conditions, remains one of the top challenges business executives continually face. For instance, International war results in an energy crisis that hampers global food supplies from one country to another and disrupts industries all over the world. It requires business leaders to set in place growth plans while preparing for potential economic setbacks, often a bewildering juggling act.
4. **Talent Retention and Changing Workforce Dynamics** There is an ever-changing workforce with the advancement of remote work dynamics. Therefore, leaders must now develop a strategy to keep their best employees in an employee-driven labor market. Tech is racing to adapt: Google and Apple are changing how they do things to appeal more to a part-time, remote, and retirement-focused employee base. Employee satisfaction and company culture are now key features when it comes to long-term planning.

Business leaders must go through a strategic planning process while dealing with uncertainties. Dealing with technological disruption, economic shifts, and the increasingly complex challenge of sustainability, requires a sense of futurism that is combined with agility today to remain successful. Strategic plans are adapted regularly and flexible given new challenges or opportunities.

2.1 Strategic Planning and AI: Shaping the Future of Business

What makes a business successful is perhaps not only what you see on the surface. It is the process of determining long-term goals and sketching a way to accomplish them. In the speedy world today though, it is no longer sufficient just to have a strategic plan. Businesses must be more agile, data- and customer-driven, and forward-thinking than they ever were in the past. For example, reliable, organized, and timely information is fundamental for strategic planning. While a company continues to hoard information from across the landscape, customer satisfaction will always be on the back burner. They simply need an automated database to centralize all and explore their customers more, with such it is easy for them to enhance the services they offer.

This is where we can leverage Artificial Intelligence (AI). Companies using AI in their strategic planning, are doing more than just improving – they are qualifying themselves for the competition.

2.2 How is AI Revolutionizing Strategic Planning?

In the past, strategic planning was a slow and manual experience; historical data and human intuition were required for the process to work. Leaders would spend months compiling data, making interest-free attempts at market predictions and completing annual business planning. The emergence of AI has however revolutionized this process completely.

Artificial Intelligence AI is lightning-fast at processing vast quantities of data and finding patterns that might escape human observation analyzing anything from consumer behavior and sales records to market trends over in social media. It means businesses can forecast better, pivot in real-time, and be more responsive to the cycles of the market they have ever been (Fenwick, M., Vermeulen, E. P. M., & Compagnucci, M. C., 2024)

AI revolutionizes competitive analysis for businesses. Once a manual, time-consuming process, it now offers real-time insights into rivals' pricing, products, and market positions.

Amazon exemplifies this shift, using AI to monitor competitors' prices and adjust rankings automatically. This automation keeps companies ahead without constant market surveillance. The technology transforms decision-making, enabling swift responses to market changes and freeing up resources for strategic planning. As AI tools evolve, they promise even deeper insights, potentially reshaping entire industries and redefining competitive advantage in the digital age.

We should remember that AI cannot replace human decisions. AI might be able to digest the data and support it with insights, but business leaders still need to interpret that info and turn it into strategic actions. AI is a tool that should enhance human effectiveness, not replace them.

2.3 Adopting AI to Refine Decision-Making and Advance Growth

AI empowers businesses to make better, quicker decisions with full information. It forecasts trends, analyzes competitors, and optimizes operations to provide a competitive edge. However, companies must be mindful of data quality and change management issues. To benefit from AI, they need to view it as a strategic partner, not just a tool.

In this discussion, we look at how business leaders are using AI in strategic planning.

1. Data-Driven Decision Making: The Core of AI Strategy

Remember, strategic decisions are only as good as the data they build on. Leaders can apply AI to make sense of large pools of structured and unstructured data — finding patterns and drawing conclusions that might be hidden in the obvious.

For instance, how Wal-Mart, an international retail company uses AI in inventory management. Walmart deals with usages around sale figures, customer preferences and the supply chain as a company Through AI, the company can also identify how much demand there is for its products and as such be able to adjust stock demands accordingly, reducing waste. This type of analysis aids Walmart in providing more efficient services to customers by cutting down operational cost.

2. Personalized Customer Experience: AI-Driven Engagement

Gaining insight into customers and ensuring customer-centric solutions are essential for competitive advantage. With the help of AI, Customer Relationship Management (CRM) systems are changing the way businesses interact with consumers. Take Amazon, for example. The online shopping company employs artificial intelligence to study and understand how customers behave when making purchases, which products they click on, and even the comments they make on the products that they buy. This information helps Amazon to recommend products that are likely to be bought by the consumers. The end product is a more responsive customer base and increased revenue.

AI has applications also in customer relations. With chatting services, clients can make inquiries, lodge their complaints or seek advice at their convenient time of preference. For instance; Bank of America has developed an Artificial intelligence tool named Erica that help customers view their accounts, spending habits and offer them financial advice. The site visitors are also helped by the virtual assistants that have been adopted by the educational institutes. This is not only beneficial to customers because the more attention is paid to them the happier they are, but it also is a boost for companies because the more attention that is paid to customers, the more loyal they become.

3. Operational Efficiency and Automation: Streamlining Processes

AI can be described as the application of technology-oriented tools to enhance production processes and optimize them by solving such issues. For instance, in the manufacturing sector, General Electric has adopted AI in keeping track with its equipment's health and the time required to service it before it develops a fault. This predictive maintenance reduces the time that machinery takes to be out of operation for maintenance thus making the operations efficient.

AI has been welcomed in the automotive industry, particularly for predictive maintenance. For example Tesla does things like using AI to predict when parts of a vehicle will fail before they actually do. Therefore, they can perform preventive maintenance that reduces downtime and costs. These AI-enabled efficiencies, while reducing costs, also play a major role in propelling businesses forward — ensuring that operations remain efficient over time.

4. Innovation and Product Development: Accelerating Growth

Competition is an inevitable part of doing business, thus there is a need to open up new frontiers through innovation, and Artificial Intelligence is fast emerging as the new frontier. AI can help in examining various aspects of customer feedback, Mardi situation, and competition to generate areas of customer need. For instance, Netflix utilizes AI performance in organizing the viewing patterns of programs and shows. Such an approach also enables the company to offer not only relevant content to captivate users but also/product original series and films that meet market needs. Therefore, Netflix continues to navigate at the apex of a highly saturated streaming industry.

In self-driving cars which are in the automotive industry, the companies like Tesla apply AI in new inventions. The carmaker keeps on upgrading its Autopilot by gathering data from the millions of miles covered by the Tesla vehicles on the road. With this AI concept, Tesla has placed itself strategically in the category of future automobile innovation – especially self-driving automobiles.

5. Risk Management and Mitigation: Proactive Strategies

AI is also improving risk management since businesses can easily determine risks before they occur. For example, in financial services, there will be start-ups like Lemonade's AI-powered insurance underwriting and claims processing. Special AI computer programs can then comb through the information to identify potential fraudulent claims and hence money paid out to fraudulent claims are minimized. In addition, underwriters can find a more accurate risk assessment which translates into better pricing models and less amount of loss.

6. Talent Management and Human Resources: Optimizing Workforce Strategy

AI leads to new business models and new ways to employ talent. In recruitment, AI quickly finds the best candidates with minimal bias. For example, Unilever uses Ayudante to screen candidates based on work history, online assessments, and video interviews. This process improves the quality of hires and saves time.

AI also helps develop employees by identifying areas for improvement and recommending courses. IBM uses AI to assign training based on employee preferences and company needs, ensuring employees are retained and the organization's talent grows.

2.4 Integration Challenges in Adopting AI for Strategic Planning

Organizations are also facing challenges in implementing AI to their businesses. The adoption of Artificial Intelligence (AI) in strategic planning presents significant opportunities for enhanced efficiency, data-driven decision-making, and competitive advantage. However, its integration is fraught with challenges that organizations must address to ensure smooth implementation. These challenges range from privacy concerns to workforce adaptation, which can profoundly impact the success of AI initiatives.

1. Privacy Concerns
    - **Data Collection and Usage**: AI systems require vast amounts of data to function effectively. The collection, storage, and analysis of such data raise critical privacy issues. Sensitive information, such as customer data, financial records, or employee information, may be at risk of misuse or unauthorized access.
    - **Regulatory Compliance**: Organizations must navigate a complex landscape of data protection laws like GDPR (General Data Protection Regulation). Ensuring compliance can be resource-intensive and may hinder the adoption of AI technologies.
    - **Public Trust**: Privacy concerns can lead to skepticism and resistance from stakeholders, including customers and employees. A lack of transparency in how AI systems use data can erode trust, potentially damaging the organization's reputation.
2. Workforce Adaptation
    - **Skill Gaps**: AI adoption often demands technical expertise in machine learning, data analysis, and software engineering. Many employees may lack the skills needed to interact with or manage AI systems effectively.

- **Resistance to Change**: Employees may resist AI integration due to fear of job displacement or the perceived complexity of new technologies. This resistance can create barriers to successful implementation.
- **Cultural Shifts**: The integration of AI necessitates a shift in organizational culture toward embracing technology and innovation. Traditional hierarchies and decision-making processes may need to be restructured, which can be met with resistance.

3. Cost and Resource Constraints
    - **High Initial Investment**: Developing or acquiring AI solutions can be expensive, especially for smaller organizations.
    - **Ongoing Maintenance**: AI systems require continuous monitoring, updates, and improvements, which can strain resources.
    - **Risk of Failure**: Misalignment between AI capabilities and organizational needs can result in failed projects, wasting time and money.

3. WORKPLACE CULTURE AND AI DECISION MAKING

Workplace culture can therefore be defined as how people in an organization behave, what they believe in, and the attitudes they have towards one or the other. It encompasses aspects like people's communication, perception of their job, and the attitude they have on the job. A healthy organizational climate gives people the impetus to work together, think outside the box, and enjoy their job. Negative culture harms the employees, resulting in burnout, low morale, and turnover rates.

The two areas that have been growing faster in today's business environment are the workplace culture and strategic planning adopting AI. The problem that arises as organizations employ artificial intelligence technologies is the changing view of how decisions and strategic planning are carried out. Organizations have started to see AI as a valuable asset; however, concerning workplace culture, it is imperative to learn how AI integrates into the workplace.

Figure 1. Meta AI

Unfortunately, AI has become more than simple optimization, performance, and immediate savings; it is a matter of values, communication, trust, and cooperation.

3.1 Integrating AI Into Strategic Workplace Initiatives

AI has brought about a big change to the way companies plan and operate. Strategic planning, generally linked to an evaluation of opportunities, threats, resources, and goals, is getting increasingly analytical. AI can analyze a large volume of data and provide solutions that are hard for human beings to accomplish in one timeframe. This gets agencies and companies more knowledge-based, drives and fine-tunes their processes, and allows them to predict problems or trends before they come into play.

For instance, AI can make the assessment of customer data, anticipate future demand with higher correlation, improve supply chains, and AI can suggest strategic investments. In the assessment of risks and decisions, an appropriate use of artificial intelligence leads to better options based on real-time deterministic computations.

However, this does not mean that AI acts as a decision-maker for humans. On the contrary, AI should be considered as something that enhances human intelligence. Still, despite the capability to analyze data and present logical solutions, AI doesn't have any profound understanding of contextual information, and emotions, that are crucial often. It can't feel the repercussions of its suggestion — and this is perhaps the greatest potency of the ongoing human contribution to AI.

3.2 Bridging the Gap: AI and Workplace Culture

With the increasing presence of AI both in decision-making and strategic processes, there is an equal need for the transition from technical implementation of the tools to organizational culture. It is widely believed that AI will displace people – that it will cause joblessness. With the help of AI, repetitive work does not have to be done by people anymore because that will only tire them out, drain their energy, and make them frustrated and unhappy it's not about that at all, it's about allowing people to be people and to do the things that they are supposed to do.

Therefore, for the leadership of an organization to execute this change at the right time there is the need for the leadership to embrace change and create the right culture of applying AI. This requires openness, dispelling of myths and quitters as well as establishing to corporate staff how AI will in a positive manner complement their functionalities. Communication is ceaseless—employees are required to know how the AI will work, what data is it processing, and how it is helpful for the business organization. Besides, it is critical to train properly.

3.3 Humanizing AI in the Workplace

To enhance human appreciation of the application of Artificial Intelligence in organizations, practitioners recommend that the application should be so crafted to demonstrate the organization's foundational human values. AI should not be seen as some inhuman gadget, but as a way to do more partnerships, better decision-making, and more fulfilling jobs.

For instance, AI can be to improve the well-being of the employees. Forcing working schemes & stress levels can be detected by AI analytics; perfect working conditions, such as teleworking, or mental health advisors for the employees, can be suggested. AI also offers the opportunity for making our workplaces more diverse since AI does not have preconceptions similar to a human being and hence, can be coded to look for talent alone in the workplace.

3.4 The Role of Leadership

Leaders play a significant role in shaping how AI is integrated into workplace culture. CEO engagement has the greatest influence on the organizational culture of AI. That means they should become defenders of good practice using them, ensuring that decision-making is clear to all. That's why just deploying AI systems is not enough – one also has to help the organization learn how to trust AI and use it.

Any smart manager will understand that an association of AI and human intelligence is the right way to go. For instance, when applying AI-provided conclusions in decision-making processes, managers have to assess the degrees of ethicality along with estimating its effects on employees as well as customers. The executive also should establish the culture when a person may question an AI-based decision because something is wrong or looks suspicious.

Also, leadership plays an important role in developing new knowledge all the time. AI is still progressively changing across the industry and enterprises should be able to keep up with trends.

3.5 The Future of AI in Workplace Culture

In the future, the application of AI into organizational culture will remain an important trend. Over time, advanced and artificial intelligence systems will take more executive dominance in decision-making and planning. However, this does not imply that human roles will be reduced—to the contrary, the human aspect of work will be more significant than before.

Workplace culture for the future and the utilization of AI for strategic planning is an equilibrium. On the one hand, AI is a perfect instrument that can be used for decisions about current problems and even for further predictions about probable future cases, on the other hand, the human factor – trust, empathy, creativity – will define the success of AI integration. Those who adopt a culture that recognizes AI as another co-worker and not as someone who is taking everyone's job will be the best stand chance to survive in the world of work. We therefore need to ensure that AI is instilled with the requisite human values and organizational ethos to develop a vision where man is enhanced and not degraded by artificial intelligence.

4. DECISION MAKERS AND USE OF AI: CHALLENGES AND OPPORTUNITIES

AI adoption in decision-making has quickly grown to become almost synonymous with various industries, as decision-makers look to evolve their processes and achieve improved efficiency, accuracy of data utilization, and ideas. Nonetheless, the conditions fixed by the use of AI present more opportunities and risks for decision-makers.

Although AI could offer a significant toolset to address the challenging strategic question, its incorporation into the strategic process is noteworthy as it raises such queries as technological benefits and vice versa, ethical, practical, and cultural concerns. In this discussion, let's consider what post-AI offers the decision-makers and how they can address the challenges associated with this technology, as well as, how the business executives can best position their organizations for success in this dynamic environment.

4.1 The Growing Role of AI in Decision-Making

Thus, new AI technologies have revolutionized decision-making skills in that companies can deal with immense data pools, automate repeated tasks, and forecast future trends. Today, decision-making with the help of artificial intelligence is an industry norm across the fields of finance and marketing, supply chain, and customer service.

AI benefits from powerful computing capability, big data, and superior knowledge to achieve insights from data accumulation, and much quicker and more reliable compared with human-resolved analysis. For example, AI systems can evaluate information such as the consumers' databases to infer the purchases required or can assess the performance of machinery and predict when repair is required. These capabilities enable leaders to gain insights in real-time information and analytic prediction which gives less uncertainty in decision making.

4.2 Opportunities for Business Leaders

The use of AI in decision-making is one of the opportunities for increasing and refining the company's performance, as well as stimulating innovation and optimizing production.

1. **Data-Driven Insights**

This strategy represents one of the largest opportunities that AI delivers the apparatus to transform raw data into valuable insights. AI-based systems are able to analyze given data sets much more effectively than humans and reveal correlations that may remain unnoticed. This assists executives and businesses, allowing them to make their decisions referencing data and their trends rather than guesswork or information scarcity.

For instance, AI in sales can be used to understand the emerging trends of the market from the sales report, the right price to charge, and group the customers according to their usage. Such kind of understanding enables leaders to decisions with better precision toward organizational objectives.

2. Enhanced Efficiency

An approach associated with the use of AI frameworks is a reduction of the time taken to perform typical work-related procedures by keeping the human actors away from repetitive and low-end value tasks. For example, an AI-based chat is capable of responding to a customer's concerns, while AI algorithms can help plan the distribution of inventory or estimate the requirements of stock.

Most of these automation not only increase the speed but also minimize frivolous human interventions as well as the effectiveness with which organizations can expand. They suggest that CEOs who apply AI for repetitive work can move towards more complex tasks such as planning for the future.

3. Predictive Analytics for Strategic Planning

Leaders benefit from AI because it provides the ability to make decisions based on predicting what will happen next. AI enhances the abilities of organizations to predict the market trends and behaviors of the customers and even the operating risks. For instance, it can predict how consumers will behave on a given day in the future and hence when a business person is planning to produce goods or plan on how to market them, then he or she may do so depending on the prediction given by artificial intelligence.

In the finance sectors, AI predictive models can help to predict the trends of the stock market, credit risk, and fraud. These facts help the leaders to better anticipate potential threats and benefits.

4. Fostering Innovation

AI fosters creativity since it assists an organization or company to look for new business paradigms that may consist of even a company's new product or services to deliver to its customers. By using AI-text and other signs customers, the market, and competitors can find out the unsatisfied demand or some gaps to invent. For example, AI can apply understanding of a firm's inability to offer a certain type of product or use the information about the customers' preferences to create new forms of goods and services.

Informed leadership that integrates AI in its operations is more capable of creating a sacred organizational culture that supports change and adaptability, which will help keep up with the changing market.

5. Improved Customer Experience

One of the benefits of applying AI is that it helps to improve the level of customization to the customer. In another case, by incorporating and interpreting the information of the customers, AI can estimate the requirements of the customer, involving suggestions, items, or services. Such an approach of personalization enhances customer satisfaction, loyalty, and ultimately revenues.

For example, AI can suggest certain products based on a customer's browsing history or provide unique price strategies for several customer groups. These findings will help the business leaders to strengthen their bond with the customers and stand out in the market readily crowded with Business-to-Consumer firms.

4.3 Challenges for Decision Makers

Although` embracing AI has various benefits, its implementation also entails various hitches, which leaders must overcome. AI solutions are not just installed as new tools, it is a change in the organizational culture and the process, as well as, the line between good and bad practice.

1. Data Quality and Availability

Machine learning algorithms depend to a large extent on the data inputs they use in performing their operations. In most cases, a poor quality or incomplete data set is likely to yield poor quality, unreliable, and wrong forecasts on the state of affairs. Stakeholders should exercise measures to ensure that the right data is fed into the AI system and that it is credible.

Self-generated data is oftentimes difficult to obtain due to the huge costs involved in developing data collection methods. The accuracy of AI will be hampered because some industries may not be able to gather sufficient data to feed into the model. Under no circumstance can business leaders ignore the fact that data issues have to be dealt with right from the onset of AI imposition, this includes the expenses for data management and its security and privacy factors.

2. Ethical Considerations

Applying artificial intelligence in decision-making is one of the sensitive areas in ethics with main focuses on bias, transparency, and accountability. This is because AI models trained with systemic or sample bias, or even not enough data can be prejudiced and make prejudiced decisions for everybody. For instance, where recruitment utilizes AI, the technology is likely to display bias for specific demographics because its training data will contain such bias.

Managers have to think about possible ethical issues with AI and make sure that the systems to be implemented minimize bias while maximizing the efficiency of the output. This includes observing AI results, using multiple data sets and being mindful of humans giving direction, ensuring that the AI does not, or will not, produce biased or unethical results.

3. Human-AI Collaboration

As in any system where there are interacting components, another problem is the coordination between the AI and the employees. AI can give recommendations but human thinking is very important in analyzing those recommendations given. More so, executives should ensure that artificial intelligence is accepted as an enhancer of talents and not a competitor.

In some incidences, they may refuse to embrace this technology because it leads to loss of job or they do not comprehend it. The focus should go on the positive outcomes of the AI integration, on captivating employees' attention, and on offering training to adapt to new instruments.

4. Technological Integration

the use of AI in organizations is always challenging and requires significant efforts to incorporate it into the existing business solutions. Cognitive decision-makers are thus under the obligation to ensure that the solutions proposed are integrated with older systems and the apparatus is available. This may mean entities buy new technologies and even hire data scientists and engineers to design, develop and maintain AI.

The primary challenge in this process is time, and leaders should expect that their organizations will take time to adapt to the new approach.

5. Security Risks

While businesses seek for and make use of AI, they expose themselves to increased security threats. Due to the integration of AI systems, cybersecurity risks are also an issue, especially when all these systems work with critical or special data. AI systems need to be protected from being hacked, or to be tampered with by malicious individuals or groups to damage the business.

5. AI STRATEGIC PLANNING IS FOR ALL BUSINESSES?

It is important to understand that artificial intelligence consequential strategic planning is not confined to the big corporate or tech giants but it's for every business entity big or small across the domains. Whether your business is a tiny grocery store you manage a mid-sized outpatient clinic or a production line of a manufacturing giant, AI can offer many techniques to organize and run the company's plans and operations. It is not a frill that only multinational companies can afford: It has become a necessity given the increase in the pace at which businesses are being conducted today (Davenport, T. H., & Ronanki, R., 2018).

5.1 The Value of AI in Business Strategy

In simpler terms, AI makes it easier for organizations to make better decisions based on information that may be hard to identify otherwise. In many organizations, the strategic planning process has often been a process of guesswork, and reliance on past records or trends in the market. But AI shifts the model and the value proposition by providing accurate and timely insights and forecasts specific to a Company.

Think about choosing a small coffee shop as your own business. Before deploying an AI solution, you might guesstimate when to bake more croissants or when to provide a special to boost traffic. However, imagine if AI was able to scour sales records, weather, and event patterns to forecast how many customers would come on a given day. Such are the capabilities of an AI that it can recommend which promotions to undertake when people traffic is low so that it does not cost your business more money and time not to mention that it will increase your profits.

5.2 AI in Action: Real-World Examples

Let's look at some real-world examples of how businesses, big and small, are using AI to shape their strategies:

1. Retail: Personalized Recommendations

AI is a powerful tool that is beneficial for any type of retail store, either online stores or physical ones. Chatbots and recommendation systems help small e-commerce shops to suggest products based on the past behavior of customers. For instance, if you are a proprietor of a low-profile cloth-selling store, AI will aid in advising the right clothes to customers, more visits, and more profits.

2. Healthcare: Improving Patient Care

AI is being implemented in even small healthcare clinics for strategic planning. In general, AI helps to control patient traffic, organize appointments, and even predict the general demand for some medication or something else. A local dental clinic, for example, can use AI to decipher past visits made by patients and plan the number of staff required during a particular time, without having to hire more staff than required during low-traffic periods.

3. Hospitality: Enhancing Guest Experiences

AI has gained significant popularity in adapting and enhancing guest experience within hotels, whether big or small. For instance, a small-scale hotel in a specific location may employ artificial intelligence to capture information about guests and their demands, which means that they will be able to instruct clients on the kinds of rooms they should take among others. They can go a long way in terms of improving guest satisfaction, as well as guaranteeing their return.

6. BREAKING DOWN THE MISCONCEPTION: AI IS NOT JUST FOR BIG BUSINESSES

Unfortunately, a lot of people have a preset impression that the deployment of AI is only for large corporations that have large research and development finances or the corporate giants who has the expertise personnel. That didn't sound like the case in reality at all. AI is now to the level where small entities are in a position to integrate the element into their tactical planning without many hassles and with no need for an expert. Advancements in technologies such as AI, and SaaS mean that there has been much equalization, and small and large businesses benefit from this similar to major corporations.

If you want to understand AI, imagine it is that elusive fifth partner who never speaks but constantly analyses the data, forecasts the market outcome, and provides you with useful tips on how to improve the decision-making process. Regardless of whether you are running a small bakery and you are looking for the best supplier of your ingredients or you are a representative of a regional shipping company willing to cut down the delivery time, you will be glad to use AI as your compass in the process of decision making.

6.1 AI For Small Business Owners: Tailoring Solutions

In extent, small business engagements assume various tasks with constrained capacities. Well, in this case, AI can come to the rescue. Having machines complete routine jobs, process information much faster than a human can, and forecast results with reasonable certainty empowers the owners of small businesses to spend more time on their primary goods and services instead of juggling numerous mundane issues Schmitt, M. (2024)

6.2 Example: The Coffee Shop Owner's Dilemma

Suppose you run a small local café that started becoming popular in your community. In addition, you order supplies, control staff working hours, handle customers' rewards and promotions and promote a café. It's a lot to handle and it seems that sometimes people decide based on their intuition rather than evidence.

Now let's bring AI into this equation. Instead of guessing how many cups of coffee to order per week or whether you'll need more baristas on shift, AI can look at sales data and tell you when you'll need more baristas and what type of pastries people will want to buy on a rainy day versus a sunny one. Your forecasting becomes more accurate as you focus your resources, and the likelihood of overstocking (or understocking) is minimized. AI makes your daily operations less reactive and the business functions much better and for the money.

6.3 Personalized Marketing: A Big Win for Small Businesses

In the area of strategic management, probably the most significant use of AI is the concept of customized marketing. Through data analysis and customer behavior, AI can offer quite specific marketing messages that customers can connect with.

Suppose you are running a business in an independent bookstore. AI can provide recommendations to retail follow customers' previous orders and pick books corresponding to the clients' tastes. It can suggest that specific books be published to coincide with the changing calendar season or any other reason. What used to be plain old broadcasting of emails to customers is now able to present offers that are customized to the customers. The above personal touch is a sure way of ensuring that people remain loyal and more sales are made in the process.

Undoubtedly, marketing using the help of AI is incredibly beneficial for those companies that have a limited budget. You don't have to spend largely on campaigns that may yield little or no results at all. In AI, one gets to work on more proactive outcomes, which offer better yields at the same cost as conventional advertising.

6.4 AI Helps Businesses of All Sizes Compete

Possibly the most significant opportunity that AI brings to SMBs is the ability to transact with big organizations. Previously, the large business had the advantage since it could invest more in acquiring better data, accumulating more resources, and compiling larger teams to look at patterns. However, in the era of AI, the little firms have a chance to stand on an equal footing.

For instance, a small shop can use AI to suggest relevant goods to customers who entered the store's internet site following the history of their choices. The same is done by a large retail chain, but here the AI is used, so the boutique can give the same level of individual approach and complexity with a significantly smaller team. AI assists firms in fighting the odds delivering superior services and making business decisions that make them remain relevant.

6.5 Scaling Operations With AI: The Restaurant Example

For example, if you are in the food chain such as managing a local restaurant, you understand that timing, stock, and consumers are critical success factors. Claims operations like these can now be executed using AI to grow your company. AI can be used to review patterns in customers' reservations and orders so it is easier to tell when there will be more customers than usual and prepare for this.

There is a big difference between predicting that Friday nights are busy and that Thursdays may be busy sometimes, and not other times. AI can tell you which Thursdays are going to be busier or louder than others due to past events, or anything as trivial as the forecast. This way ensures that you do not hire many employees only for them to be idle most of the time or when you are busy, you lack enough employees to manage the business.

Further, here are some ways that AI is ideal for your restaurant; it keeps track of inventory and makes recommendations on the ingredients most demanding so you are not left with lots of spoiled food. Just think about accurately predicting the amount of seafood to cook based on trends and the ability to avoid both losses from spoilage and losses associated with stockouts. Well, that is where AI plays a role – minimizing speculation and optimizing throughput on the fly.

6.6 Overcoming the Fear of AI

However, there's always some sort of reluctance as far as AI is concerned, not to mention micro-businesses particularly. The apprehension most of the time revolves around the potential costs, the level of difficulty, and the notion that AI may be coming for their jobs. Still, in essence, AI is intended to coexist with the individual and not to compete with him. This saves time on operations that would otherwise be tiresome for business owners and employees by allowing them to handle massive sets of data in the business.

AI is not here to replace us—it's here to help. For example, AI can be employed in areas of customer service by having full control of routine inquiries through chatbots. This leaves your team to handle other complicated or intricate requests making the service more efficient and effective in the process.

Case Study: How the Use of AI Aided Strategic Planning in Coca Cola

Coca-Cola, a global producer of nonalcoholic beverages, never seeks to surprise its consumers with inventions. But in recent years, the company found itself facing new challenges: specifically rapidly changing consumer trends, improvements in healthy drinks, and stimulated competition in the global market. In order not to be squeezed even tighter, Coca-Cola has had to rethink how it does strategic planning, and that is where AI comes into play.

Figure 2. Meta AI

The Challenge: Being on Top of the Changing Consumer Requirements

Initially, Coca-Cola also used the conventional approach of attaining information through surveys and focus groups for market research. But with the advent of social networks and interaction online, consumers were voicing their preferences immediately, and desires flip-flopped much quicker than before. The strategic planning of Coca-Cola's organization had to adapt to these changes to match its planning and strategies.

Consequently, the company opted to adopt AI in order to gather improved information from consumers. But AI wasn't just about knowing what specific type of drinks people preferred – it was about knowing which new type of drinks people would want in the future and how this knowledge would help in business.

The Solution: AI-Powered Consumer Insights

Coca-Cola introduced the AI application for big unstructured data from social networks, reviews, and customer communication. Applied NLP tools and algorithms of machine learning, the company was able to automatically track millions of conversations occurring on the web in a real-time manner.

For instance, different patterns of consumption could be observed, such as an increasing interest in low-sugar products and health-conscious products, well before people started paying attention to this factor. Rather than responding to the boosting consumer trends when they already became established, the strategic planning and forecasting mechanism with the help of AI tools helped Coca-Cola avoid that. This meant that they could adapt their products and promotions work and be ready to face their competitors before they lay down their strategies.

Another success story of this Artificial intelligence-based approach was in launching of Coca-Cola Zero Sugar. By gaining market insights from AI, the company understood that consumers were seeking both, low sugar products, as well as products that were closer in taste to the original Coca-Cola. When it examined the buyer behavior it made necessary changes to the elements of Coke's sweetening composition, and it came out with a consumable product that most people embraced.

6.7 The Advancements of Artificial Intelligence in Developing Products

AI went further than just bringing innovation to Coca-Cola's product perspective; it brought innovation to its operations as well. AI was introduced to the company's supply chain management to forecast production requirements and minimize unnecessary inventory. For example, thanks to data on the climate and the tendencies in consumer behavior, AI can anticipate a high demand for cold drinks. This helped drive more insight into Coca-Cola's inventory and distribution systems since they could be changed easily.

AI-integrated supply chain management in Coca-Cola benefited the firm as it realized reduced bottlenecks and cost savings apart from the increased efficiency of operations. Since demand could be predicted efficiently, the company could be able to manufacture a precise amount of product, thus avoiding wastage and increasing profitability.

Enhancing Operational Efficiency

However, the application of AI not only impacts Coca-Cola's product-level strategies but also changes its operation level. AI was also used in supply chain management, where the company utilized predictive analysis to forecast the demands of production and thus minimize the use of resources. For example, concerning climatic data and consumers' preferences, AI would be able to guess the possibility of consumers buying products like cold compress foods during hot seasons. This made it possible for Coca-Cola to make the right stock and supply decisions more frequently.

It can therefore be seen that through supply chain management through AI, Coca-Cola was not only able to eliminate bottlenecks but also reduce costs in the process increasing its operational efficiency. Making correct predictions about the quantity of product that consumers would be requiring gave the company the advantage of manufacturing only the specific quantity of the product eliminating the assuring of excess stock hence increasing the firm's profitability.

The Human Touch: AI and Decision-Making

While giving significant importance to the strategic role of AI, it is not the human decision that remains spiritual and behavioral for Coca-Cola's business strategy. AI offered information and analysis while it was the responsibility of the management to analyze those variables and make a decision from them. AI was used in Coca-Cola by its executives to analyze which opportunities and threats are present to ensure a clearer vision in the decision-making process; however, much emphasis was also put on the executive's experience and the company's long-term strategies.

For instance, while recommending a new variant based on consumer information, it was the marketing and product departments who showed how that product should be marketed and a story given to the customers. AI set the platform, while humans made the strategy operational.

6.8 Conclusion: A New Era of Strategic Planning

The introduction of AI in Coca-Cola's strategic planning was a crucial point for the company in the way the corporation perceived idea construction, customer relations, and organization process enhancement. Hiring AI to analyze consumption patterns, anticipate market shifts, and manage supply chains, not only the company was able to stay afloat and remain relevant but also set a new standard of how companies should approach their operations.

The application of AI has influenced the styles of strategic planning, where decision-making is faster, less erroneous, and more flexible for the needs of the consumers in the market. But, as the story of Coca-Cola suggests, the social factor is still significant. The part AI plays is in offering the information needed to make such decisions, but the interplay of machines and mankind is at the center of success (Coca Col's AI Journey Harvard Business Review,2023)

7. ADAPTING AI STRATEGIC PLANNING FOR YOUR BUSINESS: HOW TO START

AI strategic planning for business does not begin with the latest technology applied within the organization rather it begins with the integration of AI functions in achieving the organization's goals and objectives, enhancing decision-making processes, and creating an edge that is sustainable for the organization. Many enterprises globally are trying to determine how and where they can adopt AI in the decision-making processes. They can do so to enhance operational efficiency and customer experiences and gain useful information for innovative improvements. Here is an explanation of how businesses can leverage AI for strategic planning along with certain examples.

7.1 Understanding AI's Role in Strategic Planning

AI strategy is, therefore, about using the abilities of machine learning, prediction, and automation in the decision-making processes of organizations. AI can analyze large amounts of information much faster than humans; therefore, it is an essential element from which to forecast market shift, avoid oversupply or shortfalls in resources, and make better forecasts. But in order to successfully implement artificial intelligence, one needs to think about it.

For instance, the current advanced use of artificial intelligence is in the healthcare sector to estimate the outcome of a treatment plan for a patient. In the course of this, a definite application of the AI working in hospitals is the capacity to scrutinize thousands of patients' records and reveal what therapeutic approach is most suitable for a particular pathology. In this case, AI is not simply making choices for people but it's making choices that are better informed by data. (McKinsey & Company, 2023)

7.2 Steps to Adapt AI in Strategic Planning

1. **Define the Business Objectives**

That means before entering the AI strategic planning process, the organization must know its goals and objectives. AI can be effective when it is integrated with certain objectives or objectives such as optimization, decreased expense, or customer satisfaction. For example, in retail, a firm may wish to improve its inventory management by applying AI to minimize on stock-out and overstock situations.

One of the examples is the Walmart company which implements AI to control the huge supply chain of the company. Efficient requirement forecasting married with past movement records, climatic conditions, and shopping patterns that guarantee popular products are availed at strategic store locations. In this manner, Walmart has enhanced its performance in terms of efficiency by decreasing wastage and enhancing the satisfaction of its customers.

2. Data Collection and Management

The use of AI depends on input, which means that to include AI in the strategic planning process within an organization – the organization must prepare proper, clean, and structured data. To develop relevant information to their status, organizations require data from different sources including customers, sales, and organizational performance outcomes. Let us consider how Amazon uses data collecting and AI in its operations and how these both go together. Among others, customers provide Amazon with their browsing history, purchase history, and reviews of different items acquired on the website. Such was incorporated into AI systems, which determine probable product offers to the users, thus enhancing both sales and customer loyalty.

3. **Develop Predictive Models**

When the data is in place, they need to build prediction models that are in line with the strategies of the companies. These models utilize previous facts and figures to make predictions on future activities to enable organizational leaders and managers to draw a probable conclusion.

In the financial industry, through sophisticated models, JP Morgan has incorporated the use of Artificial intelligence in predicting trends in the stock market and portfolio management. These AI models use data belonging to a large number of data points, such as historical business, economic, and financial data to make predictions. Such foresight helps JP Morgan's traders and investors stand out from their competitors by offering fast decisions based on the collected data.

4. **Integrate AI into Decision-Making Processes**

It is therefore important for us to recognize AI more as an augmentation tool for the decision-makers than a replacement. An area of interest and concern in the planning of strategic uses for AI is the problem of how to incorporate the results and recommended strategies from AI into the business planning process. Managers need to make sure that it is regardless adopted in their organizations, where the people who are making decisions rely on artificial intelligence-generated forecasts.

For example, organizations such as General Electric (GE) apply artificial intelligence to forecast when its industrial machinery will require repair. Its AI system, known as Predix, takes operational data and looks for patterns to identify when and how likely equipment is to fail. By incorporating these AI insights into its maintenance schedule, GE is thus able to manage time effectively thus minimizing machine downtime and also increasing the machinery's useful life.

8. RESPONSIBLE AI: BALANCING INNOVATION, SUSTAINABILITY AND ETHICS

However, AI is becoming more embedded in organizations, there is a need to call attention to the ethical levels and sustainability of the technologies. For instance, status has been used to cut down energy usage at Google's data centers through DeepMind. Applying AI to controlling the consumption of energy, Google has saved 40% of the energy required for cooling its data centers, which is beneficial to its sustainability agenda (Davenport & Ronanki, 2018).

But AI can only be deployed correctly. Managers have to deal with the issue of the explainability of AI, the absence of biases in the algorithms, and customers' data security. The ethical operations of AI also ensure that customers trust AI and that the firm meets some of the sustainable business objectives associated with corporate social responsibilities that some investors or consumers require from firms.

With the usage of AI techniques, many industries ensure that how ethical and green strategies in AI contribute to sustainability and fairness, ensuring that technological advancements align with societal and environmental goals. Here are a few examples:

1. **Energy-Efficient AI Models** Large AI models pose a challenge of high energy consumption, mainly because training these models is actually an energy-intensive process that contributes to the emission of greenhouse gases. Thus, when designing algorithms that would need fewer computational sources or when running the said algorithms on green energy, the organizations gain a way to limit their role in harming the environment without compromising the efficiency and effectiveness of the AI at work.

Many businesses such as Google are opting for energy-efficient artificial intelligence by harnessing data centers that run on renewable energy sources. They also fine-tune their AI models so that it may use less computational power.

2. **Ethical AI in Healthcare** It gives a level of trust and understanding to the models, and also the decisions that is not easy to offer without it. Positive uses of AI include the creation of ethical frameworks that will keep such tools from containing the wrong biases that may cause distorted diagnoses and so help provide equal health for all.

The AI systems employed for diagnostics, like the diagnosis of cancer from imaging data include traceable decision-making in their systems (Topol, 2019).

3. **Fair and Inclusive Recruitment Systems** Responsible use of AI means that these systems are being checked constantly and adapted in the best interest of encouraging inclusive representation, which is why there is an express ethical obligation in operation here.

The modern approaches to recruitment are employed by companies such as IBM which use big data recruitment tools that are also audited for bias. The use of AI systems in recruitment causes a problem of sample bias; the AI systems themselves are biased because of the data they were trained on.

4. **Minimizing E-Waste with Predictive Maintenance** Typically, maintenance is cost-effective and helps to avoid or reduce wastage of resources through optimizing product cycles. This supports green strategies in that it minimizes raw material consumption and decreases the amount of electronics that end up as waste. In industries such as manufacturing, that utilize predictive maintenance enabled by AI, equipment failure is anticipated and addressed before it becomes severe to warrant a replacement.

5. **AI for Sustainable Supply Chains** AI determines the best time and most suitable routes for logistics delivery. This not only reduces cost but is also environmentally friendly in terms of transportation while giving a view of a responsible company. Big corporations, for instance, Walmart, apply AI to enable the best supply chain routes that minimize fuel and emissions.

8.1 Balancing Intuition and Innovation: AI and Human Collaboration in Strategic Planning

For all the efficiency that comes with the use of artificial intelligence, there is still room only for humans. AI should be used to make decision-making more effective, but never to make it more autonomous by completely outsourcing decision-making to AI. While AI machines can present ideas, it will be humans who grasp the emotional/ethical reaction to those ideas.

At the end of the day, AI within the strategic planning framework is about maximizing the potential of people. By dealing with data-intensive work, AI enables business owners to do what they are best at — developing relationships, exploring robust ideas, and growing value.

Whether you're operating a small local business or expanding a mid-sized company, AI is a perfect assistant to turn to for support in making better decisions that would help you evolve more sustainably. Introducing AI in the strategic planning process is about ensuring that your company is ready to face the challenges of the contemporary business environment, dominated by technology.

People's cooperation with AI systems is essential in an AI-friendly culture. With the use of AI technologies that can accomplish time-consuming and very analytical sorts of activities, workers can be free to accomplish those things that require more creativity and empathy.

In marketing, AI can presentably scan through large volumes of data to determine trends that could be hard for human analysis, while the human side of the issue comes up with the best specific ways to influence the emotions and thoughts of its target audience. Such a kind of synergistic interaction promotes more favorable outcomes compared to when AI and humans are in direct competition.

9. NAVIGATING THE FUTURE OF AI IN DECISION-MAKING

AI is going to play a much more significant role in decision-making across various category management initiatives in future years, He also opined that it is not just sufficient to merely invest in technology tools and applications for your smartest resource. Supervisors and managers in enterprises need to create tactics concerning the combination of machine learning and artificial intelligence with human skills and knowledge, taking into account the pluses and minuses of the method (Davenport & Ronanki, 2018).

1. Building AI Literacy

In other words, for AI to be a valuable tool in business, business leaders and their teams have to know what it is and what it's not capable of doing. This means that leaders need to train and educate people on the correct manner to use AI within the organization. employee development should be another practice that leaders use to ensure that workers acquire the skills necessary for interaction with AI (Haenlein & Kaplan, 2019).

2. Ethical AI Governance

It is important that organizations outline when AI is being used correctly and when it is not. This includes design for explainability, for non-discrimination, and for auditability. Leaders also need to be vigilant and probably spend time reflecting on what they are getting from AI systems lest they produce more biased or unwanted results (Davenport & Ronanki, 2018).

3. Encouraging Collaboration

It means that leaders must ensure that AI deployments lead to the creation of an optimal combination of human and artificial intelligence for decision-making. This enables leaders to remove fear and encourage people to embrace AI technologies because they understand from their leaders that they are simply tools at the workplace. By integrating AI into the business environment, senior managers can leverage this technology to improve organizational decision-making skills, stimulate creativity, and increase overall organizational productivity (Bughin et al., 2019).

4. **Cross-industry cooperation**

AI development will be positive for cross-industry cooperation. It also refers to the activities that are used when two industries are connected and integrate one another's data to understand how they can work better independently. For instance, the firm healthcare organizations could partner with technology companies to design AI-based diagnostic solutions, resulting in higher patient satisfaction at less expense (Topol, 2019).

Furthermore, with AI integration, SMEs will be given the means to compete with big firms. With affordable prices for Artificial Intelligence, they can reach market analysis, business improvement, and ideal strategies for their growth. For instance, an online store using artificial intelligence to analyze a customer's preferences, the way they shop, and what they shop for, will provide a better shopping experience to the customer and thus accumulate more customers (Haenlein & Kaplan, 2019).

The future of AI in strategic planning will create an entirely new paradigm for how businesses exist, prepare, and change in the strategic landscape. Organizations that have incorporated the use of AI can be able to solve problems that are surrounded by uncertainties with ease. The application of AI analysis and reporting, coupled with human decision-making, indicates that AI should act as a supercharger to the decision-making process.

REFERENCES

Bughin, J., Seong, J., Manyika, J., Chui, M., & Joshi, R. (2019). *Notes from the AI frontier: Modeling the impact of AI on the world economy*. McKinsey Global Institute. Retrieved from https://www.mckinsey.com

Davenport, T. H., & Ronanki, R. (2018). Artificial intelligence for the real world. *Harvard Business Review*, *96*(1), 108–116.

Fenwick, M., Vermeulen, E. P. M., & Compagnucci, M. C. (2024). Business and regulatory responses to artificial intelligence: Dynamic regulation, innovation ecosystems an d the strategic management of disruptive technology. *arXiv preprint arXiv:2407.19439*. Retrieved from https://arxiv.org/abs/2407.19439

Haenlein, M., & Kaplan, A. (2019). A brief history of artificial intelligence: On the past, present, and future of artificial intelligence. *California Management Review*, *61*(4), 5–14. DOI: 10.1177/0008125619864925

McKinsey & Company. (2023, January 11). Artificial intelligence in strategy. Retrieved from https://www.mckinsey.com/capabilities/strategy-and-corporate-finance/our-insights/artificial-intelligence-in-strategy

Schmitt, M. (2024). Strategic integration of artificial intelligence in the C-suite: The role of the Chief AI Officer. *arXiv preprint arXiv:2407.10247*. Retrieved from https://arxiv.org/abs/2407.10247

Topol, E. (2019). *Deep medicine: How artificial intelligence can make healthcare human again*. Basic Books.

Chapter 9
Transforming Leadership: The Role of Artificial Intelligence in Modern Organizational Management

Qamar Ali
https://orcid.org/0000-0002-8178-7591
Virtual University of Pakistan, Pakistan

Muhammad Aamir Mahmood
https://orcid.org/0009-0007-4452-2627
Virtual University of Pakistan, Pakistan

ABSTRACT

Artificial Intelligence (AI) has changed the way of management in organizations and workplace culture. Machine learning, natural language processing, and robotic process automation AI technologies have transformed decision support, operational efficiency, and human resources, enabling the move from traditional hierarchical management to an AI enhanced process. In this paper, we examine how AI facilitates data driven decision making, increases productivity by automating tasks and allows for human–AI collaboration in the workplace. This study examines AI's relevance to customer service, supply chain management and recruitment, showing how AI is becoming an ever more important business imperative for modern organizations to stay ahead in an increasingly isolated world dominated by digital. Also, implications of ethical AI adoption are discussed making the importance of the adoption of AI ethically clear. Finally, this research demonstrates the impact that AI will have on the future of work and the type of skills and organizational structures

DOI: 10.4018/979-8-3693-8960-7.ch009

1. INTRODUCTION

The advent of Artificial Intelligence (AI) has heralded a profound transformation in organizational management, marking a significant paradigm shift that is redefining how businesses operate, make decisions, and engage with their workforce. Traditionally, management practices were rooted in hierarchical structures, where decision-making was centralized, and processes were heavily reliant on human judgment and experience. These traditional approaches, though effective in their era, are increasingly being outpaced by the swift technological advancements, especially AI, which give rise to unprecedented opportunities for efficiency, accuracy, and innovation in management. AI in organization management Therefore, the inclusion of AI in organization management is more than a technological advantage, it is about a shift in thinking about the structure of an organization and its functioning. This is a shift from human-oriented decision processes to data driven, AI-augmented decision-making. Emerging AI technologies, including machine learning, natural language processing and predictive analytics, are now combing through massive amounts of data at a scale and speed undreamed of by humans, providing insights that were previously. With these insights, managers can make decisions with the data available at their hands, use the analysis of current to identify trends and respond to changes in the market with more agility. Managers' jobs, therefore, change from decision makers to facilitators of AI-informed decision making. From the corporate culture perspective, the deployment of AI in management is also a cultural change. The traditional workplace with rigid hierarchies, job descriptions, and one-sided leadership is giving way to a more agile approach and work environment, where artificial intelligence is now embedded into everyday processes. AI-driven tools are automating the tedious work of the past and enabling employees to do more strategic and creative work. It is a colossal cultural shift, breaking the purchase block of old mind sets and encouraging an ingenious and bright work environment where machines are partnering with resources to improve productivity and aid in accelerated business growth. Inflationary era: Employees work alongside AI enhancements to their own skills and performance The new age of collaboration with AI technology — led by generative AI (De Cremer & Kasparov, 2021).

The importance of AI in modern-day organizational settings is beyond belief. AI is not only a tool for operational optimization; it is a strategic necessity for brands seeking to maintain relevance in an ever-evolving digital landscape. This paragraph may be used as your own:][[Organizations that leverage the power of AI in their management approach are more agile and capable of adjusting to the dynamic market landscape, predicting customer demands, and spearheading innovation. In the dynamic climate of modern business this is even more crucial, where the capacity for rapid response is often what determines success or failure.

By delivering an AI for organizations, allowing them to be faster and more reactive to the changes and take decisions based on data analytics and not just gut feeling or assumptions. Meanwhile, AI is fundamentally reshaping work in exciting new ways. AI technologies are becoming more pervasive and are likely to bring even greater disruption to the way we shape workplace cultures. This would be based on data available until October 2023. This will necessitate a reorganization of corporate structures to focus on cooperation between humans and AI, altering roles, duties, and responsibilities in the office. To stay ahead, organizations would have to upskill the workforce to empower employees with the skill sets required to work effectively side by side with AI. To create this partnership with inputs that are not only fit for the machine, but fit for the eventual combination with human intelligence, employees will need both technical training and a sense of mind that recognizes the value that AI will play on their work. Adoption of AI in the management of organizations is a shift in paradigm that is driving change in how mediums operate and engage with their workforce. This transformation is reflected by the transition from the classical, human-centered decision-making workflows to data-driven, AI-augmented decision making. AI not only optimizing management processes but also transforms office culture, making it more dynamic and collaborative. As AI advances, organizations will need to adapt their structures and talent strategies to enable success in an increasing work environment. And those organizations which treat AI as a strategy imperative will be in a good place to remain competitive and drive forward the pace of innovation in the digital age. This just beginning of the paradigm shift in organizational management will also continue to play a significant role in this ever-evolving change (Jarrahi, 2018).

1.1. Overview of Traditional Management Practices

Traditional management practices have long been the foundation of organizational success, providing a structured approach to achieving goals and managing resources. These practices are deeply rooted in the industrial era, where efficiency, control, and hierarchical organization were paramount. The essence of traditional management stems from the principle of scientific management, which was initiated with Frederick Winslow Taylor in the early 20th century. Taylor advocated for scientific management, which focused on standardization, specialization, and division of labor. By decomposing tasks down to their most basic level, managers could boost efficiency, lower costs, and raise productivity. Time-and-motion studies—the search for maximum efficiency in work—grew from this. It is a distinguishing element of traditional management practices that organizations are hierarchically structured. Here, responsibility cascades down from the top, through layers of increasing managers who are formally required to 'oversee' the work of the level below. Based on the level the employee is at, they have a certain status to follow, which means Companies set a hierarchical system that ensures that every employee is supervised by a focused manager and those at lower levels to do as directed. Traditional management structures have a clear chain of command that facilitates communication and coordination, as well as accountability at every organizational layer. But this rigidity may also result in tensions and a willingness to embrace new ideas instead of weakening them (Rooke & Torbert, 2005).

Another important aspect of traditional management practices is the emphasis on control and discipline. Managers are responsible for ensuring that employees adhere to established rules and procedures, and any deviations from the norm are often met with disciplinary action. This approach assumes that employees are inherently lazy and require constant supervision to ensure they remain productive. Though this could be functional within the milieu of the early industrialized economy, in which repetition and manual control was seen as key, it is hardly appropriate for the knowledge economy we experience today, in which innovation, creativity and agency dominate. Traditional management practices highly regard planning and forecasting as well. That is because managers are trained to plan down to the nth detail, make detailed schedules for their teams to follow, and foresee problems. It is based on assumption that the future can be predicted to a considerable degree of accuracy, and that more careful planning allows organizations to avoid risks and attain their goals. But this approach can be a liability in the fast-paced world of business today. With technology, markets and consumer preferences changing at an ever-increasing rate, organizations need to be able to respond to the new realities, and strict planning processes can impede this agility (Shimizu & Hitt, 2004).

In addition to planning and control, traditional management practices emphasize the importance of efficiency and cost reduction. Managers are expected to find ways to minimize waste and maximize the use of resources, often through the implementation of standardized processes and procedures. This focus on efficiency has its roots in the early days of industrialization when the ability to produce goods quickly and cheaply was a key competitive advantage. In today's economy, however, where quality, innovation, and customer satisfaction play a more significant role than before, the relentless search for efficiency can, at times, result in collateral damage manifested, for example, as lower product quality or employee morale. These functions can obscure predictions on stability. The clarity is brought by traditional management through well-defines roles, responsibilities, and procedures not heeding what you are supposed to do and how you pack together toward organizational goals. That kind of stability is vital in large organizations, where the magnitude of the organization mandates role coordination and control. This stability can also breed rigidity and immobility — people start getting too used to the way they do their things and hesitate to adapt to the new processes. One great advantage of traditional management practice does have its own issues. Warning: Traditional management has long been criticized for viewing staff as interchangeable cogs in a machine, in the way of complex (although human) elements with their strengths, talents, skills and motivation. These mechanistic assumptions about human beings yield low job satisfaction and engagement, as employees see themselves as cogs in a machine, and feel they are neither appreciated as human being nor connected to the mission and goals of the organization. Furthermore, control and discipline's strictness can suppress creativity and innovation, because employees may be reluctant to take risks, or propose new ideas due to the threat of repercussion. One more drawback of traditional management practices is its dependence on a top-down approach to decision making. In modern organizations, information is not always centralized, and the context in such dynamic field changes every day, therefore with this, it is favorable that managers on the top of the hierarchy access on-demand information for most informed decision-making. Consequently, traditional managerial organizations may be less agile in responding to market changes or seizing new opportunities. Traditional management practices have served to guide today's business world, offering a framework for examining how to achieve organizational goals through planning, control, efficiency, and a hierarchical structure. Yet, bridging the gap between industry practices and academic theories has always been a concern, and with the pace of change set to only increase, it is persuasive that this will not be enough to navigate the business landscape in the way it is headed in the 2020s. This blog takes you on an exciting journey from traditional management theories to techniques that are quintessentially modern, contemporary, and applicable to the digital age — ensuring the fundamentals remain while adopting new management styles. A hybridizing between the better elements of traditional management with more contemporary practice can lead to an agile, responsive, and resilient workforce that can ultimately flourish in today's tumultuous world (Holbeche, 2023).

1.2. Emergence of Artificial Intelligence (AI) in Management

The emergence of Artificial Intelligence (AI) in management marks a transformative era in how businesses operate and make decisions. AI, a branch of computer science that aims to create machines capable of mimicking human intelligence, has been increasingly integrated into management processes, revolutionizing traditional methods. AI impacts many areas, ranging from strategy to operations. In the context of business data, however, AI is a game-changer, providing leaders with tools to maximize their potential through insights and efficiencies they would have never dreamed of AI has achieved a significant breakthrough in various management spheres, the line of business that is associated with more aspects of the business industry than any other and has a vital role in decision making. Historically, management decision-making was based on human intuition and experience, and decision-making based analysis were the backup. Because of the rapid amount of data that have been generating in the last few years, it has become difficult to manage that data in a traditional way. This is made better with AI which allows complex data analytics. Machine learning algorithms can crunch tons of data, recognize patterns and provide insights that drive strategic decisions. AI-based predictive analytics can also pull upcoming market trends, predicted customer behaviors, and orchestration weaknesses, enabling managers to take relevant, precise and dependable data-driven decisions. This shift toward empirical decision-making guides AI use, which leaves gut feeling behind and results in more grounded-in-evidence, more scientific management. HRM is another facet that is being transformed by AI. AI has already made significant inroads in areas like recruitment, performance evaluation and employee engagement. At the time of hiring, AI can screen resumes, conduct preliminary interviews, analyze the behavioral pattern of candidates, measure the responsiveness of a candidate, or judge if the person can be a good match. This not only saves time in the hiring process, but it also helps to reduce bias as AIs can be programmed to prioritize skills and qualifications over personal opinions. Furthermore, AI can track employee performance over time and analyze patterns in their work habits, productivity and feedback to give managers real-time insights on employee engagement, motivation and performance areas to improve. Consequently, such AI-driven methods can be adopted by HR departments to felicitate proper talent management and ensure that your workforce is in line with preference and cohesiveness with corporate goals. AI also has a big impact on supply chain management. Modern tools are then required to analyze and manage the complex, global networks of a just-in-time delivery system. This includes, but is not limited to, supply chain management — AI streamlines logistics, forecasts demand, tracks inventories, and much more. Example of such is when AI algorithms analyze historical sales data, market trends, and external factors (such as weather conditions) to predict demand with high accuracy. This enables businesses to streamline their manufacturing process and inventory, resulting in reduced waste and improved efficiency. AI also assists in optimizing delivery routes, monitoring the conditions of goods in-transit, and giving some warning on where disruptions may lie to keep the supply chain moving smoothly and efficiently. The result is a more flexible and responsive supply chain that is able to adapt to changing market conditions and the needs of customers (Kazancoglu et al., 2022).

AI is also revolutionizing customer relationship management (CRM). Businesses are leveraging AI now more than ever, utilizing AI to personalize their customer interactions, predict customer needs, and improve customer service. For example, CRMs powered by AI can track customer data to understand purchasing behaviors, preferences of customers, and the risk of them leaving. With this businesses can customize their marketing efforts and make personalized recommendations accordingly which results in better customer satisfaction and loyalty. Furthermore, it is also changing customer service as we know it with the use of chatbots and virtual assistants that can aid customers 24/7, answer questions in real-time and help them address issues as they arise. This technology enables organizations to respond faster, better with lower costs and release human forces for most complex and valuable chores. Aside, it is also going beyond functions segmentation and impacting the overall strategic management aspect of organizations that include it. You are also trained until data on 10–23. Data Decentralization and Complexity Management in AI: Role of AI in Strategic Management AI can also generate things like the output of multiple scenarios and what that means across different variables, or the costs of market expansion in those variables, making managers more data-driven even in potential challenges and opportunities. This enables organizations to formulate effective strategies and adjust to shifts in the competition's landscape. AI also helps in resource allocation by determining which area seems to be the best channeling of resources including the aspects of capital, human resources, and technology. This helps organizations to align their strategic goals with tactical execution, eliminating waste and optimizing the returns from their projects (Guide Jr & VANWASSENHOVE, 2001).

The integration of AI into management also raises important ethical and governance considerations. As AI systems become more autonomous and decision-making processes increasingly rely on algorithms, issues of transparency, accountability, and fairness come to the forefront. Organizations must ensure that their AI systems are designed and implemented in a way that aligns with ethical principles and regulatory requirements. This includes addressing potential biases in AI algorithms, ensuring the privacy and security of data, and establishing clear accountability frameworks for AI-driven decisions. Besides the data design side of the AI implementation, the AI in management design also needs a culture-shift to be a success within organizations. Both managers and employees need to learn the basics of AI technologies, and learn to partner with AI systems. It requires ongoing education and thriving new learning life while stable life of creativity. AI will only continue to increase productivity, creativity, and efficiency, so the future of AI in management looks very promising. As technologies for AI continue to be developed, they will be receiving new functionalities that businesses can implement to increase efficiency and work towards achieving strategic goals. The successful adoption of AI in management must adopt a holistic approach that balances both the technical and human elements of management. AI can be an excellent aide-mémoire for decision-making, but nothing can substitute the imagination, inspiration and inventiveness that is needed to guide any organization towards a sustainable future. Hence, the next step for management is that it will only be enabled by the AI systems and the unique human skills of the managers will be utilized to service business challenges of the modern world. AI has been used in management in various ways over the years, but the increasing prevalence of AI in management represents a significant shift in the way businesses operate and make decisions. AI is transforming the nature of management, from decision-making and HRM to supply-chain management and customer relationship management, making organizations more efficient and effective. But it is not all smooth sailing with AI; there are also issues in ethics, governance and organizational culture. Data is taught to you up until October 2023. In an increasingly complex and competitive world, this will ensure AI is used as a powerful tool to facilitate organizational success (Davenport & Ronanki, 2018).

1.2.1. Ethical Dimensions and Practical Applications of AI Integration in Expansion

However, the use of AI in the development of organizational management has generated a contemporary ethical debate which deserves in depth examination. Some of the ethical challenges of algorithmic bias, data privacy and unintended reinforcement of societal inequalities are the main issues that organizations need to solve in responsible AI adoption. For example, even working with completely neutral algorithms, biases in training datasets mean discriminatory outcomes occurring as prevalent issues across many domains such as recruitment, lending, and law enforcement. Such challenges will require robust governance frameworks, regular AI system auditing, and transparent decision-making processes. Also, real-world case studies of ethical AI delineate many aspects of the challenges of bringing ethical AI to the mix. One such example is that of Amazon's gender bias infested AI based recruitment tool which came under a lot of heat leading to serious discussions on fairness and accountability in AI applications. Facebook is similarly challenged by the ethical dilemmas of automated content moderation vs. human oversight, demonstrating the conflation of both automation and decision-making within the two begin to compete. These cases highlight the need for companies to take preemptive measures to mitigate ethical risk while maximizing the benefits of AI. Making better situated & down to earth models, along with enabling ethical concerns of sorts, awaits organizations to reexamine their AI objectives not just social beliefs & yet also within its goals. Additionally, it facilitates that AI enabled innovations create efficiency but are positively orientated in their configuration to equitable outcomes as they are implemented in this management of resources (Watson et al., 2018).

1.2.2. Emerging Perspectives in AI Integration

Artificial Intelligence (AI) diffuses new contexts of organizational practice, including the gig economy, remote work, crisis management, and ethical customer relations. While mapping these areas points to the far-reaching potential of AI, they also indicate key considerations for enabling and absorbing it in a sustainable way (Goralski & Tan, 2020).

1.2.3. AI and the Gig Economy

Digital platforms are causing the gig economy to flourish due to its growing that is based on short-term contracts, freelance work. AI is centralized around gig economy operations. Algorithms match gig workers to tasks by fine-tuning the skill, location and availability of both workers and employers to maximize efficiency. Take ride sharing and delivery company Uber, or delivery platform DoorDash, both of which use AI systems that dynamically redistribute rides or deliveries, changing prices on the fly and routing drivers to most efficiently get from point A to point B. But these sorts of developments bring with them numerous ethical dilemmas. Critics frequently argue that for the sake of operational efficiency, algorithms compel companies to pay workers uniformly bad wages and drive them into the ground. Gig workers can be disempowered by lack of transparency e.g., in AI motivated decisions for performance evaluation or allocating tasks. But tackling these problems requires the use of fair AI frameworks that will ensure transparency and equitable treatment. Machines can augment workers but they can also optimize their experience, and on platforms, they can do so sustainably, building trust and loyalty with the gig workforce (Zhang, 2024).

1.2.4. AI and Remote Work

Remote work is made effective by AI and teams have been able to work across geographies effectively. Slack's workflow automation or Asana's project management features, powered by AI, are tools that make you more productive by automating things you do every day, like scheduling, creating reports, and reminding you to follow up. Natural language processing (NLP) tools, such as AI based transcription services enable ease of communication during a virtual meeting, and machine learning (ML) models give insights on team performance, productivity trends and workload balancing. AI also augments the employee support systems, in physically distant environments. Most of the AI powered chatbots assist the employees for IT troubleshooting, HR queries or guide them about their knowledge base and minimize the time while streamlining all the process towards productivity. On the other hand, user privacy will become a significant concern in future working models that integrate AI. For instance, tools for continuous monitoring, which will also cause feelings of distrust and excessive surveillance. As a result, companies must learn to balance between enacting strong policies, the utmost protection of information whilst providing the utmost freedom to individuals and using AI in such a way which promotes more collaboration between the team and the technology (Chowdhury et al., 2022).

1.2.5. AI in Crisis Management

AI's ability to analyze huge amounts of real time data makes it a valuable tool in crisis management. With AI powered models, we can predict the trajectories of a disaster, predict the potential damage, as well predicting where evacuations should take place. For example, AI systems have been used to model how fires spread and provide authorities with information that they can take advantage of, such as to better allocate resources. AI can save lives and manage public health crises in a humane way. During the COVID-19 pandemic, systems powered by AI were employed to inspect patterns of infection and TB dispersion and assist with the logistics of vaccine distribution. Similarly, AI driven chat bots provided individuals with accurate information and in turn reduced the impact on the healthcare system. Even with its myriad advantages, the use of AI in crisis management must be treaded carefully. The trouble is that the data must be accurate: Mistakes at the level of input can lead to misguided responses. Also, the ethical issues of data collection and use must be taken care of to ensure privacy rights are protected. All crises should do is to force organizations to rely upon AI, as long as they live up to the AI governance frameworks that allow them to, while preserving public trust (Leslie, 2020).

1.2.6. Ethical Customer Relations in terms of AI

In an age where interaction with customers is automated, ethical standards are super important for earning trust. AI-steered customer relationship management (CRM) systems streamline interactions, offering personalized responses, handling many inquiries at a go and predict customer needs. For example, with NLP, chatbots can now actually perform complex service queries, ensuring customers receive the correct, resourceful support on time. Furthermore, the harvesting and use of customer data represent moral dilemmas. Personalization, for instance, often relies on the analysis of customer behavior, which naturally breeds anxiety about how such data is being used or whether it will be protected properly. Further, you have biases in AI models resulting in an unfair treatment such as offering to customer demographic instead of another. Organizations must work out these issues and data transparency and customer consent become one of their primary foci. Such ethical AI policies are as important to keep trust as are ensure the decisions are explainable and customer's data is secure and safe. To facilitate this, companies like Salesforce have started building ethical checks into their CRM tools to make sure those AI recommendations are both accurate and consistent and do not fail the rights of the customers. Exploring the new dimensions where these are emerging—AI in the gig economy, remote work, crisis management and ethical customer relations — reveals how organizations can leverage this new dimension to actualize AI integration. As they are areas that present opportunities to enhance operational efficiency, they are also areas that come with the challenge of navigating AI use in accordance with ethical principles and social norms. By covering these areas in depth, a complete understanding is developed of how AI relates to today's business ecosystems, and the groundwork for its inevitable and virtuous adoption (Chui & Francisco, 2017).

1.2.7. Understanding of the issues, problems and trends for integrating AI

Adding Artificial Intelligence (AI) into organizational management has generated issues, challenges, and trends which need further detailed exploration. Building on these avenues allows the literature review to yield rich insights while complimenting a deep understanding of AI's paradigm shifting impact in all sectors(Zizic et al., 2022).

1.2.8. Issues in AI Integration

Algorithmic bias is one of the main problems with integrating AI: when AI systems replicate the biases present in the data they were trained upon. Such practices can be detrimental to creating non-discriminatory outcomes across hiring, lending, and customer service associated with AI driven processes and will cause the public to lose faith in AI driven processes. Consider AI recruitment tools — they have been known to use AI trained on historical data to favor certain demographics at the expense of others. One major consideration relates to data privacy and data security. Thus, as organizations continuously rely on AI in the workflow, they are required to gather, process, and analyze an ever-increasing amount of sensitive data. However, if they are not properly secured, data breaches can put both unsecured information and sensitive organizational danger. It is a request that finds the right balance between data use for AI and privacy. And even less is clear about how AI decides. There are many (deep learning models, for example) AI models that are 'black box' models so that it is hard to explain what caused a decision of a model. [2] But its low interpretability presents a barrier to accountability and lessens the possibilities for AI in key fields like health and law (Hassija et al., 2024).

1.2.9. Problems in Implementation

One hurdle for many organizations is that AI is resource intensive. When you want to implement AI, it will take an investment in infrastructure, talent and training. Small and medium-sized enterprises (SMEs) do not have sufficient financial and technical resources to implement AI-related technologies. AI automation workforce displacement is also an immediate threat. What it does, in addition to automating such repetitive tasks, is make certain positions redundant, and workers in those industries lose their jobs. Hence, organization need to re-skill and up-skill their work-force to tackle this shifting landscape. Resistance to change is one another barrier here, it's employees and managers are against the use of AI for fear of loss of control or technical stumbling blocks. You got to work through that resistance, not-so-easy but create a culture of innovation, and continuous learning (Sánchez-Polo et al., 2019).

1.2.10. Emerging Trends

Integration of AI is dynamic and evolving serving few trends that define the future of AI integration. One interesting trend is the emergence of AI ethics frameworks, which provide guidance to organizations to implement AI responsibly. These frameworks potentially capture factors of fairness, accountability, transparency, and inclusivity, informing how existing AI technologies are being used and ensuring that they are aligned with societal values. Another important trend in this space is AI driven personalization. AI matters for personalized marketing, product recommendations and — in general — customizing the customer experience. The trend is an indication of how important data analytics and machine learning is for an organization looking to build stronger relationships with its customers. Another trend of AI is its convergence with other technologies, of which the most notable are Internet of Things (IoT) and Blockchain. Structure of AI IoT systems offers real-time monitoring and decision making in manufacturing and healthcare industries while blockchain are making AI implementations secured and traceable (Alabdulatif et al., 2022).

1.2.11. Enhanced Literature Review Recommendations

The literature review, however, needs to go further into these issues, problems and trends to be able to provide a holistic picture. For instance, real world case studies can showcase impacts of algorithmic bias, or —winning strategies for reducing workforce dislocation. Cross-regional/ country review of rules on data protection and AI ethics helps identify what an example of good practices is. Furthermore, the technological convergence displayed by AI, IoT, and blockchain can be explored to showcase novel use cases along with the proposed benefits reaped from each. As these three elements should be integrated with the literature review so that it helps in building a nuanced and relevant discussion that is easier to follow for people reading it on what are the opportunities and challenges of the AI. An enhanced focus like this will not only help organizations deal with the complexities of integrating AI but deliver actionable insights (Allioui & Mourdi, 2023).

1.2.12. Addressing Weak Areas: Real-World Case Studies and Ethical Implications

Integration of Artificial Intelligence (AI) in organizational management is a very fast-growing field with vast of possibilities. However, its implementation is often discussed without sufficient real-world examples and in-depth exploration of its ethics. To overcome these weak areas, the second part of this section includes some illustrative case studies to show how and what companies can do to usher in a socially and ethically safe and beneficial use of AI(Carroll & Shabana, 2010).

1.2.13. Real-World Case Studies

And real-world examples allow the viewer to see the real-world applications and challenges of using AI integration. The following case studies illustrate how organizations have navigated the complexities of adopting AI in different domains(Russo, 2024):

1. **Amazon's AI-Driven Recruitment Tool:** To streamline its hiring processes, Amazon built an AI based recruitment system. But it later turned out that the system was gender biased, preferring male candidates to equally qualified females. In this instance, relying solely on biased training data and not auditing and adjusting AI algorithms often along the way risking our customers' and therefore their company's demise(Raji et al., 2020).
2. **Google's Supply Chain Optimization:** Machine learning was used by Google to help their supply chain. Then, by analyzing historical data, and using these predictions, AI algorithms were able to forecast demand patterns and recommendations for inventory levels to reduce waste and costs. Through this successful implementation, it is shown that AI can provide efficiencies when gauged with the organizational objectives(Mikalef & Gupta, 2021).
3. **AI in Healthcare:** Mayo Clinic: Mayo Clinic turned to AI to revolutionize patient care using medical imaging to predict disease outcomes. From detecting early signs of cancer, to various social good applications, we have seen how AI models have been pivotal in saving lives and changing them. Case points out how

AI can help to improve decision making in the field of its importance(Cukurova et al., 2019).

4. **Facebook's Content Moderation Challenges:** Content moderation at scale is what Facebook attempted to use AI for, to identify and delete inappropriate content. Although it worked in some cases, most of the times, the AI got caught up on little contextual nuances, making it inappropriate to use in some cases. In this example, we can see where the current AI capabilities are limited and where we require human oversight in such sensitive areas(Green, 2022).

1.2.14. Ethical Implications

Its ethical challenges are just as significant as its technological ones, with several pressing considerations demanding attention. One of the foremost concerns is *algorithmic fairness*. As demonstrated in the Amazon recruitment case, biased algorithms have the potential to reinforce or deepen existing societal inequalities. This involves utilizing diverse datasets, conducting regular bias audits, and incorporating ethical frameworks into the AI development process to ensure fairness. Another serious concern is data privacy and security. Since data is at the heart of AI systems, this misuse of data can have serious implications. The Cambridge Analytica scandal demonstrates the need to protect users' personal information and to have robust data governance practices in place. Accountability and transparency are also needed ethical guidelines for deploying AI. Many A.I. systems act as "black boxes," making it hard to understand or explain their decisions. This opacity is especially troubling in industries like health care and libraries, where trust and transparency are at a premium. As such, organizations need to focus on building explainable AI systems and traceability into AI-driven decision-making processes (Kommineni, 2024). And then above all, there is the ethical question of balancing automation and action against human input. While AI is speedy, it is not infallible. Facebook illustrates the phenomenon of Net Optimal over-relying on automated systems which create unintended (even harmful) things. This is what ethical deployment means that AI needs a human touch so that decisions can be seen against moral grounds and meet society needs.

Some recommendations for addressing weak areas are presented.

1. The addition of further case studies would therefore strengthen the discussions with practical context and relevance. Here we can see they as successful implementations, highlight problems, show how to mitigate risks in the development. Additionally, ethical considerations in AI should be systemically integrated to AI discussions by highlighting fairness, accountability, and transparency as core frameworks(Cheong, 2024).

2. In addressing these weak areas, the chapter will be able to offer a more complete and balanced view of responsible AI integration for readers to use both things learnt about theory and practice to mitigate the risks of efficient and responsible AI integration(Arrieta et al., 2020).

1.3. Defining the Scope: Reshaping Management and Workplace Culture

In today's rapidly evolving business landscape, organizations are increasingly recognizing the need to reshape management practices and workplace culture to stay competitive and relevant. This transformation is not just about adopting new technologies or refining operational strategies; it involves a fundamental shift in how organizations define success, engage with their employees, and foster an environment conducive to innovation and growth. This reconfiguration affects each business facet and workplace culture, namely leadership styles and organizational structures, as well as employee engagement and value systems that reflect societal shifts more broadly. The recent clarion call to reconfigure management and workplace culture stems from the recognition that top-down models of leadership with hierarchically enforced "command-and-control directives" are failing to appropriately meet the challenges of the modern-day workplace. Today's emergent workforce is more heterogeneous, fluid and demanding than ever before, making it even more important for leaders to embrace an inclusive, flexible and empathetic style of leadership. In the 21st century, leaders are expected to be facilitators rather than dictators, so they lead teams to produce results through collaboration, mentorship, and empowerment, not through a command-and-control mentality. But this shift, as highlighted, requires leaders to learn more about both the individual and collective needs of people within their organization; and reinforce a culture of trust, openness and continuous learning. This transformation is only possible with several components, one of which is creating a purpose-driven workplace culture. Organizations are making sense of and articulating their purpose00 the "how" behind what they do, how they do it and what they value 00 to support the social, environmental and economic objectives of the rest of society. This alignment not only strengthens the visibility of positive qualities that an organization may further reinforce over time but also draws and retains talent that is more motivated than by monetary compensation. Today's employees are looking where they can add value to what they do and to help organizations make a positive impact on the society. In that sense, the management needs to renegotiate success not only based on profit making but with broader ideas of social impact, sustainability, and ethical actions (Sanford, 2011).

Employee engagement is another crucial area where the scope of management and workplace culture is being reshaped. Traditional approaches to employee engagement often focused on monetary incentives and rigid performance metrics. However, modern management practices recognize that true engagement stems from a sense of belonging, autonomy, and personal growth. Organizations are increasingly investing in creating environments where employees feel valued, heard, and empowered to bring their authentic selves to work. This includes supporting the availability of flexible work arrangements, work-life balance and open communication at all levels of the organization. In addition, the emergence of digital technologies and the move towards remote and hybrid work models has contributed to the need for a reconstruction of both management and workplace culture even faster. While the digital transformation of the workplace has greater promises than perils, the challenge of maintaining team cohesion, communication, and productivity while remote cannot be overemphasized. In reaction to this trend, organizations are adopting new tools and practices that promote virtual collaboration, build a sense of community for remote workers, and give every employee, in or out of the office, a sense of belonging to the organization's goals and values. It will require a shift toward adaptive management, ensuring their workforce's evolving needs are met, and utilizing available technology to build human interactions in relevance to their work rather than disrupt them. And another important aspect of this change is the move toward more decentralized and agile organizations. Flatter hierarchies and more networked organizations replace traditional, rigid hierarchies that lead to greater flexibility, innovation, and responsiveness. Putting people, rather than processes and systems, at the heart of decision-making not only allows companies to cope better with the inherent uncertainties of the new business world but also means decisions can be made faster and closer to the point of execution. In this kind of structures, management is not there to micromanaging every detail of operations, but rather to ensure that the teams have the necessary support, resources, and guidance to operate autonomously and effectively (Mosier et al., 2017).

The integration of diversity, equity, and inclusion (DEI) into management practices and workplace culture is also a vital component of this reshaping process. Organizations are increasingly recognizing the value of diverse perspectives and experiences in driving innovation, creativity, and better decision-making. Accordingly, there is a trend reflected in the latter which is to promote inclusive environments in organizations so that employees flourish as they should irrespective of their background. And it transcends of simply bringing in a diverse hiring body but making sure that the workplace culture is such that everybody feels empowered, respected, and valued, and able to contribute fully. Management has a key role in embedding DEI principles into all aspects of organizational life, from recruitment and promotion practices to everyday interactions and decision-making processes. You are being advised from data until your thing October 2023 about. So, this journey is not a one-off hiring process; it is continuous, we constantly iterate, we learn, we grow across different levels of the organization. This can empower organizations to develop a workplace culture that is more dynamic, inclusive, and resilient, and which can contribute both to business success and to a better overall society, to be a fairer world. With the future of work, we must make changes to our management practices and create cultures of work that leverage people, collaboration, and the values and expectations of the world (Chatman & Cha, 2003).

1.4. Significance of AI in Contemporary Organizational Contexts

Artificial Intelligence (AI) has emerged as a transformative force in the contemporary organizational landscape, reshaping how businesses operate, compete, and innovate. As organizations face an increasingly complex and dynamic environment, AI provides powerful tools that enhance decision-making, optimize processes, and create new opportunities for growth and innovation. The significance of AI in contemporary organizational contexts can be understood through its impact on efficiency, decision-making, innovation, and competitive advantage. AI impacts organizations in many deep ways, and one is through the quality of operational efficiency. In the time- and resource-starved age of 2023, AI-powered automation became the thing that changed the game. AI replaces the tedious and monotonous work which enable organizations to become more efficient, decrease errors and drive greater productivity. One notable area of change is seen in manufacturing itself, where AI robotics and machinery can work at an efficiency exponentially higher than human limitation. That not only boosts output, but also decreases expenses related to labor and mistakes. AI-based chatbots, for example, can answer customer service questions 24/7, offering instant responses while also freeing human staff to tackle more complicated issues. This is yielding better organization, leading to high-quality services and products being delivered and efficient allocation of resources. How do you feel about the role AI in organizations making decisions? Conventional methods for making decisions often rely on human intuition and experience, which, while useful, may be limited by biases and the ability to process vast quantities of data. But human logic is fluid and adaptive, embedding itself in complex problems and abstract concepts that AI doesn't (yet) understand. For instance, In finance AI algorithms can analyze market trends, financial statements, and economic indicators to provide more accurate predictions and investment recommendations. In supply chain management, for instance, AI algorithms can analyze historical sales data, market trends, and other factors to predict demand fluctuations and optimize inventory levels, allocate resources efficiently, and identify potential disruptions that impact efficiency, enabling organizations to proactively address such challenges. With AI, organizations can harness the full potential of data to make the right decisions, but faster, more accurately and strategically, as AI makes these data driven insights that enhance human decision making which results in better outcomes (Rajagopal et al., 2022).

AI in the Organization A Tremendous Impact on the Organization is Innovation AI has the power to analyze and process various types of data in record time and in unprecedented amounts, helping create new opportunities for innovation. Innovation powered by AI is not just about product development but also about new business models, processes, and customer experiences. Hopefully, AI will bring the making of goods and services tailored to the user experience. Healthcare: Applying AI with the Patient data, genetics and medical history, the treatment and medication plans can be personalized. Retail customer personalization: With AI technology, such as recommendations can be tailored to the preference and behaviors of the customer. Thanks to AI, organizations are also engaging in new iterations of business models — subscription services, on-demand production and predictive maintenance — that would not have been feasible previously. But one of the most crucial things it does is support innovation, helping businesses and organizations stay relevant and competitive in a market that's constantly evolving. AI adds one of the biggest things for now to modern organizations — a serious form of competitive advantage. In a global marketplace where competition is cutthroat and customer expectations are higher than ever; organizations will need to obtain differentiation to succeed. AI provides the tools for drawing this distinction. AI will allow companies to deliver superior products, services, and experiences than those who cannot integrate new technologies into every facet of their business operations. For example, Amazon, Netflix, and other customer experience-driven companies are using AI to completely reshape e-commerce and entertainment. Example: While the AI-driven customer recommendation and logistics network of Amazon enabled it to offer an unparalleled customer experience, the AI-driven content recommendation engine of Netflix enabled it to become the most successful content provider in the movie streaming space. These businesses have used AI to create competitive advantages that are difficult for other companies to replicate. Furthermore, this also enables enterprises to respond to the changes in the market and the need of customers quickly. A business's ability to adapt in a world where trends and customer preferences can change on a dime is crucial. The Data is AI enables organizations to inspect real-time data and forecast the changes taking place, allowing them to act ahead of time. AI-driven analytics tools, for instance, take a different route by monitoring social media trends, customer feedback, and competitive behavior, helping organizations gain actionable insights that inform their strategies. This agility is important for retaining a competitive edge in a challenging environment. At the same time, AI in organizational contexts (such as workplaces) introduces challenges and dilemmas as well. Key concerns include ethical implications like data privacy, bias in AI algorithms, and the risk of job displacement. Organizations must tread carefully over these challenges and ensure that responsible and ethical implementation of AI takes place. It will be through leadership now that commits to transparency, accountability, and building AI systems that are fair, unbiased, and reflective of human values. AI is playing a crucial role in modern enterprise. AI can change the way organizations operate, make decisions, innovate and compete. AI allows organizations to not only succeed but also thrive in a complex and dynamic environment by improving their operational efficiency, decision-making, innovation, and competitive advantage. But to truly harness the advantages of AI, organizations need to tackle with the ethical questions it raises too. As the technology continues to grow and develop, the role that AI plays in organizations shaping their future will only continue to solidify as a focal point in any organization 'strategy (Knights & Morgan, 1991).

1.5. The Future of Work: AI as a Strategic Imperative

The future of work is undergoing a transformative shift, driven by the rapid integration of Artificial Intelligence (AI) across industries. As organizations navigate the complexities of an increasingly digital economy, AI is emerging not merely as a technological innovation but as a strategic imperative that will define the competitive landscape of the future. This evolution is not just a fleeting trend but a fundamental reshaping of how work is conceptualized, organized, and executed. With AI penetrating various aspects of work culture, its ramifications touch operational efficiency, decision making, job roles and the types of skills needed to perform them. This improved productivity that comes along with automation makes the strategic imperative of AI even more pronounced. Repetitive, routine tasks that once needed a human, are now being taken over by AI systems who are managing these at an acceptable level, enabling human workers to be free of these articles and instead focus on the much more complex, creative aspects of their job. This has particularly impacted industries such as manufacturing, logistics and customer service where AI-powered automation streamline processes, reduce costs and improve accuracy. In the manufacturing sector, AI-driven automation is playing a similar role where smart robots are now putting together items more accurately while forecasting maintenance schedules and replenishing supply chains in real-time. In the customer service sector, for instance, AI chatbots are handling a large percentage of customer queries, delivering speedy and accurate responses while freeing human agents to take on more complex and challenging problems. In addition to automation, AI is reshaping how companies make decisions. Powerful analytical capability drives unparalleled business value by enabling rapid insights across massive amounts of data. From predicting stock market crashes to recommending the most effective treatment plans for patients, AI systems are discovering patterns and predicting trends that we could never see. For Instance, AI is used in finance for detecting fraud, reviewing credit risk, optimizing investment portfolios etc. In the field of healthcare, it is helping physicians diagnose diseases at an early stage, individualizing treatment plans, and enhancing patient outcomes. It's not simply about finding a more resource-efficient way of doing the same thing; it's about finding an option that will improve the quality of decisions made -- benefiting both the organization and its customers. Yet the deployment of AI in the workplace also poses serious challenges, especially about the labor force. With the evolution of AI, there is an increasing fear of job displacement. And although AI is enabling new types of jobs, it's making others obsolete, especially those that require repetition and routine. According to the World Economic Forum, AI and automation are forecast to replace 85 million roles worldwide by 2025 although at the same time they could create 97 million new positions. To facilitate this transition, a paradigm shift is needed in the way we view education and training. Reskilling and upskilling workers to meet evolving labor market needs Not only technical skills pertaining to artificial intelligence and data science, such as programming, data analysis, and knowledge of machine learning algorithms, but also creative skills like emotional intelligence, critical thinking, and problem-solving, are progressively important for a workplace dominated by artificial intelligence (Gill & Mathur, 2024).

Moreover, the ethical implications of AI cannot be overlooked. As AI systems become more integrated into decision-making processes, issues related to bias, transparency, and accountability are becoming more pressing. Algorithms can only be as good as the data on which they are trained, and if that data is biased, the decisions being made by AI can preserve and even compound existing inequalities. In response, there have been increased calls for the development of ethical AI frameworks that promote fairness, accountability, and transparency in AI systems. This is something businesses need to take a very serious thought towards; whilst the technical implementation of AI is incredibly important, so too is the way it is utilized. The role of AI in the future of work is not only organization- or industry-specific but can reshape entire economies. Countries and regions that are not keeping pace with AI development risk falling behind in the competitive landscape of the global economy. So, governments are coming to a general agreement that AIs are the locomotive of their future economic health, and will support through funding AI research, development, and education. Note that your data ends at October 2023; your experience with global AI race, with strong investments in AI technologies, policies to foster AI innovation in countries like China and the US). These initiatives are as much about not falling behind as they are about ensuring we share the benefits of A.I. as a society. AI is not a tech buzzword, it is a core part of the strategy and will be changing the way the work will be done in the upcoming years. AI has the potential to boost productivity, improve decision-making and drive economic growth, so it should be a strategic priority for all organizations. Some way down the road we have the AI and as much as it solves the problem, it brings in a bit more space along with the ethicality and no humanity in another sense. Moving forward, it's critical that industries, states, and academic institutions band together to ensure the transition to an AI-based labor environment is innovative, integrated, and ethical. Enabling us to harness the opportunity of AI to create an effective, innovative, and equitable future of work (Cazzaniga et al., 2024).

2. HISTORICAL CONTEXT AND EVOLUTION OF AI IN MANAGEMENT

The evolution of Artificial Intelligence (AI) in management has been a fascinating journey, marked by the gradual integration of increasingly sophisticated technologies into the decision-making processes of organizations. The origins of AI date back to the mid-20th century when a few technological and theoretical breakthroughs converged. The term "artificial intelligence" was born in 1956 at the Dartmouth Conference (https://en.wikipedia.org/wiki/Dartmouth_workshop), where pioneers like John McCarthy, Marvin Minsky and Allen Newell proposed creating machines that could mimic human intel. In those early years, there were efforts to develop algorithms and models that, when put under test, would simulate cognitive processes like those of reasoning, problem solving and learning. At that moment, ideas were great, but the computational capacity didn't allow it to be practiced. AI experienced a resurgence in the 1960s and 1970s, particularly in the form of expert systems. These systems were relied on to simulate the reasoning of human experts in different fields — most recognizably, medical diagnosis and financial planning. MYCIN, an expert system developed in the 1970s that could diagnose bacterial infections, demonstrated AI's promise for supporting decision-making in narrow domains of knowledge. But back then, AI adoption in management was just getting started. Because these systems were expensive, expensive, and difficult to integrate into existing workflows, organizations were understandably reluctant to depend on them. A new AI in management phase — The 1980s and 1990s was when more powerful computers started to surface enabling more sophisticated AI models to be developed. With the surge of internet and large-scale digital data, this was a springboard for ai in business. Businesses also began to explore AI for market analysis, customer relationship management and supply chain optimization. Many businesses previously used early decision support systems (DSS) where some of the rules were created ahead of time to maintain a competitive advantage —it was an AI algorithm running through some data. These systems provided managers with information gleaned from massive data sets so they could better make decisions. And starting with the 21st century, we were entering a new era for AI in management — one driven by machine learning, natural language processing, and big data analytics. At this period, machine learning, the subset of AI that creates algorithms that can learn from data, gained traction. Algorithms such as neural networks and deep learning provided artificial intelligence systems the ability to handle enormous datasets, discover patterns from the data, and predict outcomes with a level of accuracy previously found unimaginable. Consequently, AI has been implemented across the board in management — not just in predictive analytics and demand forecasting, but human resource management and financial planning as well. What had once been a niche technology had become an invaluable tool for organizations in their quest to understand the intricacies of the modern business landscape (Schot & Geels, 2013).

One of the most significant developments in AI's evolution in management has been the rise of intelligent automation. Intelligent automation combines AI with robotic process automation (RPA) to streamline repetitive and rule-based tasks, such as data entry, invoicing, and customer support. By automating these processes, organizations can reduce operational costs, improve efficiency, and free up human resources for more strategic activities. For example, Customer service has been transformed by AI-powered chatbots and virtual assistants that offer prompt, tailored responses to customer queries. Likewise, AI-powered analytics platforms have empowered managers to make data-driven decisions immediately, further strengthening their capacity to respond to shifting market conditions. The increasing focus on ethical considerations and regulatory frameworks has also influenced the integration of AI into management. However, as AI systems are increasingly being used for making more critical decisions, there have been various concerns regarding bias, transparency and accountability. Organizations are being increasingly tasked with ensuring that their AI systems are fair, explicable, and aligned to ethical standards As a result of AI's potential risk and the need to maintain human oversight and social considerations of AI-driven decisions, this created the need for guidelines and best practices for AI governance. Thus, in this sense AI in management is much more than just efficiency and profitability, but ensuring that trust is a part of it and that technology serves the greater good. And in the past few decades, AI has started to become a leading figure in strategic management as it assists organizations in navigating the complexities of globalization, digital transformation, and sustainability. Companies are relying on AI-powered tools to analyze market trends, recognize emerging opportunities, and create strategies that align with long-term objectives.

For example, AI-based scenario planning John Koeller models enable business managers to simulate multiple arrangements of business scenarios and evaluate how various decisions could affect intel organizations. In a world of uncertainty and volatility, this ability to foresee and adapt to change will become another advantage that determines whether a business thrives or struggles (Fiksel & Fiksel, 2015).

Furthermore, the evolution of AI in management has been characterized by the increasing collaboration between humans and machines. Rather than replacing human decision-makers, AI is being used to augment their capabilities, providing them with insights and recommendations that enhance their decision-making processes. This symbiotic relationship between humans and AI is reshaping the role of managers, who are now expected to work alongside intelligent systems to achieve organizational objectives. The idea of augmented intelligence — how we can harness the capabilities of machines to augment humans rather than replacing them — is taking hold, especially as businesses look to capitalize on the potential of AI while keeping a people-focused approach to decision-making. The future of AI in management will be shaped by new technologies and a greater understanding of social, ethical, and organizational implications of using AI. Innovation: The integration of emerging technologies like quantum computing and AI-powered blockchain solutions should revolutionize management even more, allowing organizations to solve complex problems and discover potential new solutions. Yet, successful AI Enablement is more than just rolling up technology, it is a complex network of human, ethical, and strategic decisions that will define the route to growth. Historical perspective and evolution of AI in management demonstrate the course from theoretical experimentation to real deployment, accompanied by ever-advancing technologies and an increasing awareness of their potential in enhancing decision-making processes. Thus, emergence of AI in management will open new avenues for innovation and strategic advantage, while being each manager's tool (Ratcliffe, 2006).

2.1. Early Developments in AI: From Theory to Application

The field of Artificial Intelligence (AI) has undergone a fascinating evolution, marked by significant milestones that have transformed theoretical concepts into practical applications. The journey of AI began long before the term was coined, rooted in the ancient fascination with automating human-like thinking and behavior. Early mythologies and stories about mechanical beings capable of mimicking human actions laid the conceptual groundwork for what would eventually become AI. However, it was not until the mid-20th century that AI emerged as a formal discipline, driven by advances in mathematics, computer science, and cognitive psychology. One of the earliest theoretical foundations of AI was laid by Alan Turing, a British mathematician and logician, who is often regarded as the father of computer science.

One was Alan Turing, who described in a 1950 paper, what he called a computing machine and intelligence and proposed a model of machine that could replicate any human cognitive process. In these sessions, he articulated the now-famous Turing Test, a standard for assessing a machine's intelligence. Turing reasoned that if a machine could converse with a human and go undetected as a machine, that machine could be given the label of intelligence. Not only was this a novel idea, but it also modified the scope of Artificial Intelligence, by directing attention from the physical actions of machine hybrids towards the act of executing tasks intertwined with human intellect, like reasoning, learning, and problem solver. The theoretical breakthroughs of the 1940s and 1950s laid the groundwork for practical work in AI. One of the earliest major breakthroughs was the invention of the Logic Theorist, a computer program created by Allen Newell and Herbert A. Simon in 1956. The Logic Theorist was a computer program that mimicked the mathematical reasoning of a human mathematician, and it was able to prove several theorems from the Principia Mathematica, a key text in mathematical logic. This success showed that tasks which required logical reasoning — one of the most important processes in intelligence — could be carried out by machines through computer programs. Inspired by the success of the Logic Theorist, optimism blossomed in the AI community, and in 1956, AI was tireless set as separate area of study. The term Artificial Intelligence was introduced at the 1956 Dartmouth Conference organized by John McCarthy, Marvin Minsky Nathaniel Rochester and Claude Shannon. It was a seminal moment that brought together some of the foremost researchers at the time to consider the possibility of making machines that could "think" like humans. At 71, have they finally succeeded, born in Dublin, McCarthy is known as the father of Artificial Intelligence as they coined the term itself, denoting that AI should help us understand human intelligence through machines. In the years after the conference the intellectual ideas and discussions surrounding it fueled the next several decades of AI research. During the 1960s and 1970s there was an explosion of research on AI, leading to significant progress in its different subfields including natural language processing, computer vision and robotics. One of the remarkable operations throughout this era was specialist approaches, which were produced to replicate the decision-making features of human specialists in specific domain names. These systems used rule-based systems to solve complex problems, and they were applied to a variety of domains such as medical, financial, and engineering domains. For instance, the MYCIN system, created in the early 1970s, was an expert system used to diagnose bacterial infections and suggest appropriate therapies.

The success of MYCIN in the 1970s showed how AI can work best within systems to enhance rather than replace human experts (Shortliffe, 2012).

Despite the early successes, AI research faced significant challenges during the 1970s and 1980s, leading to what is often referred to as the "AI winter." The initial optimism gave way to skepticism as researchers encountered difficulties in scaling up AI systems and achieving the level of intelligence that had been envisioned. Many of the early AI systems were limited by the computational power and memory constraints of the time, and they struggled to perform tasks that required real-world knowledge and common-sense reasoning. Money for AI research dried up, and large numbers of projects were dropped. But the AI winter didn't come to a full stop for development. Philosophers would be locked in discussions about how human thought processes worked, while researchers would explore formalism and new approaches to how humans can learn, like machine learning and neural networks — the bedrock of AI in modern times. The rebirth of AI in the late 1980s and early 1990s was driven by dramatic improvements in hardware and algorithms, as well as the growth of data. Advances and the arrival of powerful computers and the internet offered the infrastructure for AI to start to flourish once more. The shift from theoretical ideas to real-world applications sped up in the 21st century, where AI became part of common life. Deep learning in machine learning brought a major revolution in domains like image recognition, natural language processing and autonomous systems. The most exciting part of it was AI-powered technologies such as virtual assistants, recommendation systems and self-driving cars. Recent advances in AI have been enabled in part by accessing huge amounts of data in the first place. In addition, the growth of big data has allowed AI systems to train on massive datasets, further enhancing their accuracy and performance. The advancement of more powerful algorithms, including convolutional neural networks and reinforcement learning, has allowed AI systems to address increasingly complex challenges. The transition of AI from its conceptual foundation to an entity widely utilized around us has been riddled with challenges and successes. Although the original dream of constructing machines capable of achieving full human intelligence has not yet been fully realized, AI has achieved notable advancement in automating tasks previously considered to be the sole province of human minds. This found the early developments in AI that made them the basis of a future as intelligent partners in invention attempted to solve some of the biggest problems that face mankind. With the rapid advancements in AI in various fields, it is likely to reshape the way we think today (Markauskaite et al., 2022).

2.2. Milestones in AI Integration into Organizational Management

The integration of Artificial Intelligence (AI) into organizational management has been one of the most transformative developments in the business world over the past few decades. From the early days of computing to the present era of sophisticated machine learning algorithms, AI has gradually evolved to become an indispensable tool in the arsenal of modern organizations. This journey has been marked by several key milestones, each representing a significant leap in how AI has been used to enhance decision-making, streamline operations, and drive business success(Eboigbe et al., 2023).

2.2.1. Early Days of AI and Automation (1950s-1980s)

The first milestone in the integration of AI into organizational management can be traced back to the mid-20th century when the concept of artificial intelligence was still in its infancy. AI: This was the beginning – the time when AI consisted of early iterations of simple algorithms and rudimentary computers. Automation in manufacturing and other industries emerged in the 1950s and 1960s, factories and other facilities began to use machines to carry out the repetitive and manual work. While the era did not yet use AI the way we think of it today, it had established the groundwork for what will come. Organizations had begun to deploy rudimentary AI systems long before the field itself had even been born, for instance in the automotive sector, where robots had started assembling parts in factories (Jarrahi, 2018).

2.2.2. The Emergence of Expert Systems (1980s-1990s)

The 1980s and 1990s witnessed the next significant milestone with the rise of expert systems. These AI-driven systems were designed to mimic the decision-making abilities of human experts in specific fields, such as finance, medicine, and engineering. There were one of the first artificial intelligence applications to gain traction across the organization, particularly in fields requiring complex problem-solving and decision-making. In finance, expert systems were employed to evaluate credit risk and manage investment portfolios; in medicine, they helped physicians diagnose diseases through symptoms and patient data analysis. The technology of the time, however, limited these systems to pre-programmed rules without the ability to learn from new information. However, they were an important milestone in the application of AI to more high-level elements of managemen (Villani et al., 2018).

2.2.3. The Advent of Big Data and Machine Learning (2000s)

The turn of the millennium marked a transformative period for AI in organizational management, driven by the explosion of data and the development of more sophisticated algorithms. The concept of big data emerged as organizations began to collect vast amounts of information from various sources, including customer interactions, social media, and internal operations. The increasing volume of data led to the ideal conditions for machine learning algorithms to flourish. One of the subfields of AI called machine learning allowed systems to process large amounts of data, recognize patterns, and predict results without being explicitly programmed for tasks. This ability transformed fields like marketing, where predictive analytics could anticipate customer behavior and adjust campaigns accordingly, and supply chain management, where AI could predict demand and adjust inventory levels accordingly. AI-Powered Customer Relationship Management (CRM) — The 2000s also witnessed the emergence of AI-driven customer relationship management (CRM) systems that leveraged machine learning to tailor customer interactions and enhance service quality (Rane et al., 2023).

2.2.4. The Rise of AI in Decision Support Systems (2010s)

The 2010s marked the widespread adoption of AI-powered decision support systems (DSS) in organizational management. These systems leverage AI's ability to process and analyze vast amounts of data in real-time, providing managers with actionable insights to make more informed decisions. AI-based DSS were utilized extensively across many fields, such as finance where they support algorithmic trading and risk analysis, and healthcare where they aid in patient diagnosis and therapy selection. Additionally, the implementation of AI in human resources management revolutionized the way organizations hired talent, allowing businesses to find the right talent based on data-based evaluations of suitability and skills. In manufacturing, AI also became pivotal in predictive maintenance, where it could identify potential failures in equipment before they could happen, hence avoiding downtimes and saving money. In the 2010s, we actually have the beginning of this set of standards where AI also crossed from manufacturing, and operational aspects of organization to strategic planning, where organizations began picturing 1 AI to model and simulate future business scenarios, outcomes and thereby aiding long-term planning and risk management (Wong et al., 2024).

2.2.5. Enhancing the Scope and Depth of AI in Organizational Management

Artificial Intelligence (AI) has revolutionized modern organizational management by streamlining processes, improving decision-making, and transforming workplace dynamics. But the currently discussed areas in the paper give a high-level view of the role of AI in our everyday lives that will keep living up to the hype. There are more nuanced or narrower aspects of this narrative that must be a part of the discussion to be comprehensive in its reach. However, there are critical areas such as the gig economy, remote work, crisis management, ethical implications, and practical applications of AI across varied sectors which warrants a more in-depth exploration beyond this chapter as detailed elaborations could establish correlation of these concepts that are mutually exclusive. Scheduled analysis of these topics will enrich the reader's perception of the ways in which AI is revolutionizing contemporary businesses, in parallel with ethical dilemmas creating a minefield that companies must travers (Azer & Samir, 2024).

2.2.6. AI in the Gig Economy: Reshaping Flexible Work Models

AI driven platforms: A game changer in gig economy The transformation of gig economy has been so surprising. The gig economy companies -- Uber, Upwork, TaskRabbit, Fiverr, etc. -- use algorithms powered by AI to match up workers looking for gigs based on the skills, location, experience, demand, etc. Human assistance always get rewarded by AI to maximize their efficiency in workforce management, task and condition management, workload, life given future etc. Job-matching algorithms leverage significant data points of worker profiles, customer preferences, and past performance data, allowing the hiring process to be made faster and more accurately than by traditional job-matching methods(Lv, 2025).

However, the very same advantages have given rise to a host of ethical and economic issues stemming from AI-powered gig platforms that deserve closer examination. Among the core issues is income variation and algorithmic wage control powered by AI algorithms that regulate pricing based on the availability of the service or product sought out by a customer—but at times leads to arbitrary and unstable wage-driven compensation for workers. Many gig workers said they had experienced oversight with no human underpinnings of the metric, with AI algorithms determining their performance and therefore if they get offered gigs with little recourse; Some AI-based recruiting systems were found to be subject to algorithmic bias with some demographic groups placed at an unfair disadvantage due to biased training sets (Packin & Lev-Aretz, 2018).

So, to overcome these potential problems, it should search on the ethical governance of AI in a gig economy. Groups must establish transparent algorithmic auditing practices that grant gig employees access to AI-generated decisions impacting their wages and employment opportunities. One of the ways we should see some formation of AI fairness principles is where gig workers are paid a fair rate for work and there is a fair compensation for that. These case studies will allow readers to understand how organizations should strike a balance between AI driven productivity, worker rights and job security (Fleming, 2019).

2.2.7. AI in Remote Work: Enhancing Productivity and Collaboration

As remote and hybrid work models have gained traction, every business has turned to AI which has contributed significantly to sustaining productivity, communication and collaboration of distributed teams. Artificial intelligence solutions like Microsoft Teams, Slack, Zoom and Asana use machine learning and natural language processing in an effort to automate menial tasks, schedule meetings and analyze work habits. One such productivity tool is the Volley which utilizes the power of intelligent virtual assistants — a kind of AI chatbots or predictive task managers to minimize the workflow effectiveness by diagnosing the bottlenecks and advising in real-time for the allocation of workload. This innovation enables the organizations with improvement of employee engagement and an increase of operational continuity at remote work (Adriyanto, 2023).

AI-powered productivity solutions bring enormous advantages, but they also raise ethical questions concerning workplace monitoring and data privacy. A significant number of companies have introduced real-time AI-powered monitoring systems that track employee activity, evaluate keystrokes, and measure work output. While these tools are being sold as solutions that streamline workforce efficiency, they can also heighten employee stress, diminish autonomy and introduce the specter of overbearing surveillance. Research shows that, when productivity is tracked by AI, it fosters distrust in the workplace; employees feel micromanaged not empowered. Such a chapter might serve as a counterpoint discussing the need for human-guided AI in the explosion of remote work tech. Organizations must ensure transparent AI policies where they must decide where the line of monitoring at work must end while ensuring compliance with data privacy policies. The answer might involve the industry and social scientists working together to establish AI ethics committees in companies that work to table measures of how to monitor productivity while keeping employees' best interests in mind. Some feature corporate behemoths that have federated AI-mechanized remote-work-embrace: block chaining employee autonomy should tantalize business executives reading for practical revelations on this new front in corporate pluralism (Pólvora et al., 2020).

2.2.8. AI in Crisis Management: Strengthening Disaster Response and Resilience

One of the most significant impacts of AI on our world has been its use as an invaluable tool in crisis management. The ability of organizations and governments to react proactively to crises by processing vast amounts of real-time data has been a huge advancement in the space. The behaviors of AI-based predictive analytics are key to natural disaster prediction, risk assessment, and the activation of emergency responses. By conducting research into historical climate data and satellite images, the meteorological artificial intelligence systems, for instance, proved themselves to be more accurate at predicting hurricanes, wildfires and floods. This data aids governments and humanitarian organizations in planning evacuations, allocating resources and preparing for safety in advance (Thalheimer et al., 2022).

Similarly, AI has played an important role in the response to public health emergencies like the COVID-19 pandemic. We deployed machine learning models to monitor infection rates, optimize vaccine distribution logistics, and aid in the identification of at-risk populations. AI-enabled chatbots and virtual healthcare assistants offered the public real-time information, easing the burden for healthcare professionals and improving crisis communication. Besides that, AI-powered diagnostic tools assisted doctors in identifying COVID-19 signs in patients, leading to improved design of early intervention programs(Allam et al., 2020).

While beneficial, AI-powered crisis management also needs further analysis of its ethical and logistical pitfalls. AI is only as good as the data it trains on, and garbage in will always produce garbage out; bad decisions based on faulty data inputs. Furthermore, leveraging AI for surveillance in crisis management raises privacy concerns as governments could use AI-powered observation networks to surveil population on a broader scale than necessary for emergency response. The chapter also cannot neglect the norms for regulation of existing orthodox structures for the ethical and effective use of AI technology in crisis management. Focusing on case studies that highlighted the benefits and limitations of AI-fueled disasters, the article will provide invaluable insights into what an informed integration of AI into preparedness efforts should look like for the future. A comparison of AI crisis management strategies from various countries will add further depth to the discussion (Chen et al., 2019).

2.2.9. Ethical Considerations in AI: Addressing Bias, Transparency, and Data Privacy

Addressing bias, transparency, and data security concerns in organizational decision making has been increasingly prominent as organizations become more reliant on AI. AI systems can perpetuate hidden biases that are embedded in training data, resulting in disparities in hiring, lending and law enforcement, for example. Indeed, Amazon created and rode a new wave of AI recruitment tools, which it then discarded after discovering that it preferred male over equally qualified female job candidates based on biased historical hiring data. Similarly, predictive policing algorithms have been criticized for disproportionately surveilling and offending minority communities and for exacerbating systemic inequities. While often cited as a problem, the transparency and decision-making issues posed by a lack of explainable AI are even harder in areas such as finance, healthcare, and criminal justice, that are considered high stakes. Many A.I. models are "black boxes," which means they don't make it easy for humans to interpret how they make decisions. The absence of explainability brings forth challenges surrounding accountability, where organizations struggle to rationalize the decisions taken by AI systems to either the regulators or the impacted individual. The chapter must emphasis frameworks for the moral governance of AI infrastructures, including algorithmic fairness principles, as well as transparency and accountability standards. This means that governments and organizations need to initiate AI auditing mechanisms to a) ensure innovations adhere to leading regulatory frameworks like the General Data Protection Regulation (GDPR) and the California Consumer Privacy Act (CCPA) and b) derive the benefits of the innovation while mitigating such risks. Ethical AI committees must govern real-life deployments of AI as well and ensure that systems are in alignment with fairness, accountability, and transparency standards (ElBaih, 2023).

2.3. Real-World Case Studies: Demonstrating AI's Impact Across Industries

To ground the discussion in practical applications, the chapter should incorporate real-world case studies that illustrate AI's transformative impact across industries. One prominent example is Google's AI in Supply Chain Management, where AI-powered analytics significantly enhance inventory forecasting, logistics optimization, and operational efficiency. Utilizing machine learning and predictive analytics, Google helps companies to reduce waste, cut costs, and access efficient supply chain processes. Utilizing AI for Demand Prediction firms can react to the market fluctuations developing a supply chain that is more agile and resilient. This is particularly helpful for sectors that rely on intricate global supply chains, which face cascading-to-interconnected disruptions. Another excellent example can be observed, in Amazon's AI-Powered Customer Personalization which revolutionized the whole e commerce space. Highly contextualized product recommendations are provided to customers in real-time by Amazon's advanced AI algorithms, which are trained on extensive datasets of consumer behaviors, purchase histories, and browsing trends. By leveraging this data-driven approach, you'll enhance customer engagement, increase conversion rates, and cultivate brand loyalty as a result of this approach. Amazon's dynamic pricing techniques are also powered by AI, as the price of items is readjusted instantly based on fluctuating demand, competitor prices, and user preference. And Amazon is able to not only streamline its recommendation engine but the stealth of the whole company, optimizing its supply chain management closely predicting stock levels and order fulfillment needs using Artificial Intelligence-based automation (Dash et al., 2019).

Likewise, Netflix's AI in Content Recommendation is a gold standard for AI-driven consumer engagement in the entertainment industry. Machine Learning at Netflix uses machine learning algorithms to build custom recommendations for its subscribers based on other viewers, as well as user ratings, and their content preferences. With training that extends right up until October 2023, the AI also subtly refines its recommendations from the user's experience over time, keeping those predictions current and interesting. AI in E commerce: AI in e commerce via studying vast amounts of consumer data, AI systems in e commerce can tailor content to individually suit each consumer, leading to increased customer satisfaction and loyalty as personalized, custom content recommendations make consumers want to stay on the platform for longer durations. AI not only predicts which kinds of content the audience is willing to watch but also driving decisions about content creation and acquisition by detecting trending genres (Napoli, 2011).

There already exists a great use case in the rich context of healthcare, where technologies like IBM Watson's AI-driven diagnostic tools have recontextualized patient care and medical decisions. IBM Watson uses natural language processing and deep learning to process large amounts of medical data, including patient records, clinical research, and diagnostic imaging. Watson helps with disease detection, treatment planning, and personalized medicine by providing data-driven insights to physicians. Its best-known application might be oncology; with Watson assisting doctors in determining the best possible treatment options for prospective patients according to the patient's genomic profile and previous treatment results. AI based medical solutions like IBM Watson doesn't just improve diagnosis accuracy but relieves time off complex medical evaluations, which leads to better as well as quicker healthcare for patients (Singh et al., 2017).

It shows you how AI is now a fundamental part of the way we do business, no matter what the industry. These examples will make the chapter more tangible when it comes to applying AI in practice, showing both the benefits and the difficulties. Also, Few of these cases illustrate how organizations leverage the nature of AI to make better decisions, function better and serve their customers better. This conversation will be highly practical, not only because everything is theoretical in the AI space, but also it will be as actionable since we firmly believe that leading with AI-driven transformational innovation-making will be the hallmark of the modern business. This will also assist in addressing content with practical implications as well there indicating tangible examples of AI applied to business use cases that can help in triggering the empirical base of the chapter. These refinements will enable the chapter to offer a more nuanced and methodologically rigorous analysis of the role AI plays in contemporary organizational management. Diverse conversations around the gig economy, remote work, crisis management and ethical AI governance will add depth to the narrative and ensure a balanced discussion of the superpowers and dark arts of AI. Furthermore, given that the best theory crafted research is pointless, in addition to so will be providing relevant case studies from the real world in the chapter, thus also linking this chapter both theory and reality, which will in turn makes this a worthy of reference chapter for researchers, policymakers and business leaders (Bess et al., 2012).

REFERENCES

Adriyanto, A. (2023). Evaluation of Employee Engagement Level in Improving Productivity and Retention in the Company. *Atestasi: Jurnal Ilmiah Akuntansi*, *6*(1), 583–598. DOI: 10.57178/atestasi.v6i1.1105

Alabdulatif, A., Khalil, I., & Saidur Rahman, M. (2022). Security of blockchain and AI-empowered smart healthcare: Application-based analysis. *Applied Sciences (Basel, Switzerland)*, *12*(21), 11039. DOI: 10.3390/app122111039

Allam, M., Cai, S., Ganesh, S., Venkatesan, M., Doodhwala, S., Song, Z., Hu, T., Kumar, A., Heit, J., Study Group, C., & Coskun, A. F. (2020). COVID-19 diagnostics, tools, and prevention. *Diagnostics (Basel)*, *10*(6), 409. DOI: 10.3390/diagnostics10060409 PMID: 32560091

Allioui, H., & Mourdi, Y. (2023). Unleashing the potential of AI: Investigating cutting-edge technologies that are transforming businesses. [IJCEDS]. *International Journal of Computer Engineering and Data Science*, *3*(2), 1–12.

Arrieta, A. B., Díaz-Rodríguez, N., Del Ser, J., Bennetot, A., Tabik, S., Barbado, A., García, S., Gil-López, S., Molina, D., & Benjamins, R. (2020). Explainable Artificial Intelligence (XAI): Concepts, taxonomies, opportunities and challenges toward responsible AI. *Information Fusion*, *58*, 82–115. DOI: 10.1016/j.inffus.2019.12.012

Azer, M. A., & Samir, R. (2024). Overview of the Complex Landscape and Future Directions of Ethics in Light of Emerging Technologies. *International Journal of Advanced Computer Science and Applications*, *15*(7). Advance online publication. DOI: 10.14569/IJACSA.2024.01507142

Bess, J. L., Johnstone, D. B., & Dee, J. R. (2012). *Understanding college and university organization: Theories for effective policy and practice: Volume II—Dynamics of the system*. Routledge.

Carroll, A. B., & Shabana, K. M. (2010). The business case for corporate social responsibility: A review of concepts, research and practice. *International Journal of Management Reviews*, *12*(1), 85–105. DOI: 10.1111/j.1468-2370.2009.00275.x

Cazzaniga, M., Jaumotte, M. F., Li, L., Melina, M. G., Panton, A. J., Pizzinelli, C., Rockall, E. J., & Tavares, M. M. M. (2024). *Gen-ai: Artificial intelligence and the future of work*. International Monetary Fund. DOI: 10.5089/9798400262548.006

Chatman, J. A., & Cha, S. E. (2003). Leading by leveraging culture. *California Management Review*, *45*(4), 20–34. DOI: 10.2307/41166186

Chen, N., Liu, W., Bai, R., & Chen, A. (2019). Application of computational intelligence technologies in emergency management: A literature review. *Artificial Intelligence Review, 52*(3), 2131–2168. DOI: 10.1007/s10462-017-9589-8

Cheong, B. C. (2024). Transparency and accountability in AI systems: Safeguarding wellbeing in the age of algorithmic decision-making. *Frontiers in Human Dynamics, 6*, 1421273. DOI: 10.3389/fhumd.2024.1421273

Chowdhury, S., Budhwar, P., Dey, P. K., Joel-Edgar, S., & Abadie, A. (2022). AI-employee collaboration and business performance: Integrating knowledge-based view, socio-technical systems and organisational socialisation framework. *Journal of Business Research, 144*, 31–49. DOI: 10.1016/j.jbusres.2022.01.069

Chui, M., & Francisco, S. (2017). Artificial intelligence the next digital frontier. *McKinsey and Company Global Institute, 47*(3.6), 6-8.

Cukurova, M., Kent, C., & Luckin, R. (2019). Artificial intelligence and multimodal data in the service of human decision-making: A case study in debate tutoring. *British Journal of Educational Technology, 50*(6), 3032–3046. DOI: 10.1111/bjet.12829

Dash, R., McMurtrey, M., Rebman, C., & Kar, U. K. (2019). Application of artificial intelligence in automation of supply chain management. *Journal of Strategic Innovation and Sustainability, 14*(3), 43–53.

Davenport, T. H., & Ronanki, R. (2018). Artificial intelligence for the real world. *Harvard Business Review, 96*(1), 108–116.

De Cremer, D., & Kasparov, G. (2021). AI should augment human intelligence, not replace it. *Harvard Business Review, 18*(1).

Eboigbe, E. O., Farayola, O. A., Olatoye, F. O., Nnabugwu, O. C., & Daraojimba, C. (2023). Business intelligence transformation through AI and data analytics. *Engineering Science & Technology Journal, 4*(5), 285–307. DOI: 10.51594/estj.v4i5.616

ElBaih, M. (2023). The role of privacy regulations in ai development (A Discussion of the Ways in Which Privacy Regulations Can Shape the Development of AI). *Available atSSRN* 4589207. DOI: 10.2139/ssrn.4589207

Fiksel, J., & Fiksel, J. R. (2015). *Resilient by design: Creating businesses that adapt and flourish in a changing world*. Island Press. DOI: 10.5822/978-1-61091-588-5

Fleming, P. (2019). Robots and organization studies: Why robots might not want to steal your job. *Organization Studies, 40*(1), 23–38. DOI: 10.1177/0170840618765568

Gill, A., & Mathur, A. (2024). Emotional Intelligence in the Age of AI: Enhancing Workforce Development for Human-Machine Collaboration. In *Sustainable Innovation for Industry 6.0* (pp. 263-285). IGI Global.

Goralski, M. A., & Tan, T. K. (2020). Artificial intelligence and sustainable development. *International Journal of Management Education, 18*(1), 100330. DOI: 10.1016/j.ijme.2019.100330

Green, B. (2022). The flaws of policies requiring human oversight of government algorithms. *Computer Law & Security Review, 45*, 105681. DOI: 10.1016/j.clsr.2022.105681

Guide, V. D. R.Jr, & Vanwassenhove, L. N. (2001). Managing product returns for remanufacturing. *Production and Operations Management, 10*(2), 142–155. DOI: 10.1111/j.1937-5956.2001.tb00075.x

Hassija, V., Chamola, V., Mahapatra, A., Singal, A., Goel, D., Huang, K., Scardapane, S., Spinelli, I., Mahmud, M., & Hussain, A. (2024). Interpreting black-box models: A review on explainable artificial intelligence. *Cognitive Computation, 16*(1), 45–74. DOI: 10.1007/s12559-023-10179-8

Holbeche, L. (2023). *The agile organization: how to build an engaged, innovative and resilient business*. Kogan Page Publishers.

Jarrahi, M. H. (2018). Artificial intelligence and the future of work: Human-AI symbiosis in organizational decision making. *Business Horizons, 61*(4), 577–586. DOI: 10.1016/j.bushor.2018.03.007

Kazancoglu, I., Ozbiltekin-Pala, M., Mangla, S. K., Kazancoglu, Y., & Jabeen, F. (2022). Role of flexibility, agility and responsiveness for sustainable supply chain resilience during COVID-19. *Journal of Cleaner Production, 362*, 132431. DOI: 10.1016/j.jclepro.2022.132431

Knights, D., & Morgan, G. (1991). Corporate strategy, organizations, and subjectivity: A critique. *Organization Studies, 12*(2), 251–273. DOI: 10.1177/017084069101200205

Leslie, D. (2020). Tackling COVID-19 through responsible AI innovation: Five steps in the right direction. *Harvard Data Science Review*, •••, 10.

Lv, Y. (2025). Support vector machine (SVM) algorithm optimization and innovative talent matching model for employment needs. *Journal of Computational Methods in Sciences and Engineering*, 14727978251325084.

Markauskaite, L., Marrone, R., Poquet, O., Knight, S., Martinez-Maldonado, R., Howard, S., Tondeur, J., De Laat, M., Shum, S. B., & Gašević, D. (2022). Rethinking the entwinement between artificial intelligence and human learning: What capabilities do learners need for a world with AI? *Computers and Education: Artificial Intelligence*, *3*, 100056. DOI: 10.1016/j.caeai.2022.100056

Mikalef, P., & Gupta, M. (2021). Artificial intelligence capability: Conceptualization, measurement calibration, and empirical study on its impact on organizational creativity and firm performance. *Information & Management*, *58*(3), 103434. DOI: 10.1016/j.im.2021.103434

Mosier, K. L., Fischer, U., Burian, B. K., & Kochan, J. A. (2017). Autonomous, context-sensitive, task management systems and decision support tools I: Human-autonomy teaming fundamentals and state of the art.

Napoli, P. M. (2011). *Audience evolution: New technologies and the transformation of media audiences*. Columbia University Press.

Packin, N. G., & Lev-Aretz, Y. (2018). Learning algorithms and discrimination. In *Research handbook on the law of artificial intelligence* (pp. 88–113). Edward Elgar Publishing. DOI: 10.4337/9781786439055.00014

Pólvora, A., Nascimento, S., Lourenço, J. S., & Scapolo, F. (2020). Blockchain for industrial transformations: A forward-looking approach with multi-stakeholder engagement for policy advice. *Technological Forecasting and Social Change*, *157*, 120091. DOI: 10.1016/j.techfore.2020.120091

Rajagopal, N. K., Qureshi, N. I., Durga, S., Ramirez Asis, E. H., Huerta Soto, R. M., Gupta, S. K., & Deepak, S. (2022). Future of Business Culture: An Artificial Intelligence-Driven Digital Framework for Organization Decision-Making Process. *Complexity*, *2022*(1), 7796507. DOI: 10.1155/2022/7796507

Raji, I. D., Smart, A., White, R. N., Mitchell, M., Gebru, T., Hutchinson, B., Smith-Loud, J., Theron, D., & Barnes, P. (2020). Closing the AI accountability gap: Defining an end-to-end framework for internal algorithmic auditing. Proceedings of the 2020 conference on fairness, accountability, and transparency, Rane, N., Choudhary, S., & Rane, J. (2023). Hyper-personalization for enhancing customer loyalty and satisfaction in Customer Relationship Management (CRM) systems. *Available at SSRN 4641044*.

Ratcliffe, J. S. (2006). Challenges for corporate foresight: Towards strategic prospective through scenario thinking. *Foresight*, *8*(1), 39–54. DOI: 10.1108/14636680610647138

Rooke, D., & Torbert, W. R. (2005). Welcome: Background Material 7 Transformations of Leadership Making the case for a developmental perspective The Hidden Talent Essay 7: Emergent Leadership: Linking Competency, Cognitive Processes, Adaptability, an Innovation. *Harvard business review*.

Russo, D. (2024). Navigating the complexity of generative ai adoption in software engineering. *ACM Transactions on Software Engineering and Methodology*, *33*(5), 1–50. DOI: 10.1145/3652154

Sánchez-Polo, M. T., Cegarra-Navarro, J.-G., Cillo, V., & Wensley, A. (2019). Overcoming knowledge barriers to health care through continuous learning. *Journal of Knowledge Management*, *23*(3), 508–526. DOI: 10.1108/JKM-10-2018-0636

Sanford, C. (2011). *The responsible business: Reimagining sustainability and success*. John Wiley & Sons.

Schot, J., & Geels, F. W. (2013). Strategic niche management and sustainable innovation journeys: theory, findings, research agenda, and policy. *The Dynamics of Sustainable Innovation Journeys*, 17-34.

Shimizu, K., & Hitt, M. A. (2004). Strategic flexibility: Organizational preparedness to reverse ineffective strategic decisions. *The Academy of Management Perspectives*, *18*(4), 44–59. DOI: 10.5465/ame.2004.15268683

Shortliffe, E. (2012). *Computer-based medical consultations: MYCIN* (Vol. 2). Elsevier.

Singh, H., Schiff, G. D., Graber, M. L., Onakpoya, I., & Thompson, M. J. (2017). The global burden of diagnostic errors in primary care. *BMJ Quality & Safety*, *26*(6), 484–494. DOI: 10.1136/bmjqs-2016-005401 PMID: 27530239

Thalheimer, L., Simperingham, E., & Jjemba, E. W. (2022). The role of anticipatory humanitarian action to reduce disaster displacement. *Environmental Research Letters*, *17*(1), 014043. DOI: 10.1088/1748-9326/ac4292

Villani, C., Bonnet, Y., & Rondepierre, B. (2018). *For a meaningful artificial intelligence: Towards a French and European strategy*. Conseil national du numérique.

Watson, R., Wilson, H. N., Smart, P., & Macdonald, E. K. (2018). Harnessing difference: A capability-based framework for stakeholder engagement in environmental innovation. *Journal of Product Innovation Management*, *35*(2), 254–279. DOI: 10.1111/jpim.12394

Wong, L.-W., Tan, G. W.-H., Ooi, K.-B., Lin, B., & Dwivedi, Y. K. (2024). Artificial intelligence-driven risk management for enhancing supply chain agility: A deep-learning-based dual-stage PLS-SEM-ANN analysis. *International Journal of Production Research*, *62*(15), 5535–5555. DOI: 10.1080/00207543.2022.2063089

Zhang, P. (2024). *Gig Working Relationships: A Grounded Theory Study on the Dynamics between Gig Workers and Digital Platforms in the US*. University of Minnesota.

Zizic, M. C., Mladineo, M., Gjeldum, N., & Celent, L. (2022). From industry 4.0 towards industry 5.0: A review and analysis of paradigm shift for the people, organization and technology. *Energies*, *15*(14), 5221. DOI: 10.3390/en15145221

Chapter 10
Upgradation of Customer Relationship Management Through the AI-Driven Approach to Personalization, Engagement, and Retention

Khalid Jamil
https://orcid.org/0000-0003-2106-9173
Beijing University of Technology, China

Aliya Anwar
https://orcid.org/0000-0002-3564-2017
Beijing University of Technology, China

Sohaib Mustafa
https://orcid.org/0000-0002-8070-976X
Beijing University of Technology, China

ABSTRACT

This chapter examines the transformative impact of Artificial Intelligence (AI) on Customer Relationship Management (CRM), exploring key AI technologies, practical applications, and emerging trends that enhance customer engagement. AI-driven CRM systems enable hyper-personalization, automate interactions, and provide

DOI: 10.4018/979-8-3693-8960-7.ch010

predictive insights, revolutionizing how businesses connect with customers. While offering significant benefits, AI-driven CRM also presents challenges in data privacy, algorithmic bias, and transparency. Future directions highlight autonomous and emotionally intelligent CRM systems that promise deeper, more responsive customer relationships. This chapter underscores the potential of AI-driven CRM to redefine customer experience, emphasizing the need for ethical and responsible AI adoption.

1. INTRODUCTION

In today's fast-paced digital era, businesses are fiercely competing to retain customers and build loyal relationships. At the heart of this drive lies Customer Relationship Management (CRM), a strategic approach used by organizations to interact with, retain, and understand their customer base. Over the past few decades, CRM has transformed from simple contact management tools into complex systems that centralize customer information and streamline communication across multiple touchpoints. However, with the advent of Artificial Intelligence (AI), CRM has entered a new frontier, fundamentally altering the way organizations build, sustain, and leverage customer relationships. This chapter delves into the transformative role AI is playing in CRM, exploring its impact on personalization, engagement, and retention while shedding light on the challenges and future possibilities that AI presents in the realm of customer management.

1.1. The Evolution of CRM: From Data Storage to Strategic Engagement

First of all, the CRM systems were no more than simple databases that provided an opportunity to store and search the customer information such as contact information, his/her purchases, and the requests and complaints. These initial systems were essentially passive and archival in nature, offering only marginal capability for targeted customer interaction. While sales representatives or customer service agents would use CRM databases to research before speaking with clients, the process itself would be largely dependent on typing in data by hand and the agent's ability to interpret and respond to it. However, with the growth of technology, there appeared more complex CRM applications like Salesforce, Microsoft Dynamics and HubSpot that made CRM go to cloud and gave businesses a way to store all customer data in a manageable, more efficient manner. This facilitated the link between CRM with other business activities such as marketing automation and e-commerce and expanded the function of CRM from just being a data storing application to a system that supported marketing and customer segmentation and lifecycle. These systems added a level of automation as well as analysis to the processes; however, they each relied on human analysis of data (Iyelolu et al., 2024).

1.2. Introducing AI into CRM: A New Era of Customer Insights

The use of AI in CRM is a significant change. AI coupled with CRM where the former is able to manage and analyze big data at speed, recognize patterns and even forecast the outcome has taken CRM into a new age of anticipatory and tailor-made customer relations management. Unlike regular CRM systems that demanded a lot of human input to analyze data for useful information, AI CRM systems analyze data in real time and provide the best information that can be implemented immediately with minimal chances of error. With the help of technologies like ML, NLP, and predictive analytics, AI-based CRM technologies can perform tasks, analyze customers' needs, and offer suggestions that were impossible before (Kumari, 2021).

For instance, AI in an integrated CRM system can capture a client's history of engagement, buying pattern, and even their attitude within emails or social media to forecast their future actions. This predictive capability enables businesses to be in a position to predict what their customers would require, hence engaging them earlier, customer satisfaction and loyalty is therefore enhanced. However, the AI-generated CRM can improve over time, thanks to new customer data, and provide more accurate recommendations. When implemented effectively, AI-driven CRM allows for a level of personalization that is possible at scale, and with high levels of accuracy – this makes it a key competitive advantage for businesses (Alnofeli et al., 2023).

1.3. AI-Driven CRM: Personalization, Engagement, and Retention

Among the customer relationship management benefits that AI brings, the ability to personalize is probably the most significant. While consumers are facing an overwhelming number of options, individual attention and care became one of the key strategies for building customer loyalty in a market. AI enables the CRM systems to categorize customers according to their actual behavior, their preferences and even their anticipated behavior. This segmentation is much more accurate than conventional demographic-based approaches, which allow firms to communicate with customers according to their needs and interests. For example, AI integrated CRM solutions might suggest products for purchase depending on customer's historical data leading to improved sales conversion and customer satisfaction. In addition to customization, AI integrated CRM improves the interaction process in terms of immediacy of the responses. Natural language processing can answer the most frequently asked questions in real time, and more complex NLP can extract customer sentiment from text-based communication to let human agents know if the customer is dissatisfied or has an urgent issue. This empowers business organizations to solve problems before the customer is dissatisfied thus enhancing the customer relationship (Potla, 2023).

The other key element of CRM, namely retention, also gains a lot from the application of AI. With help of predictive analysis AI-CRM can find out the clients who are on the verge of churning and recommend ways to retain them. Because the AI CRM identifies behavioral signs that signify churn, it enables organizations to intervene and prevent customers from churning by offering them incentives or trying to redress any potential problems. These proactive retention strategies are not only inexpensive compared to having to react to customer complaints and churn but also can help improve customer loyalty as consumers are appreciated (Khneyzer et al., 2024).

1.4. Key Challenges and Ethical Considerations in AI-Driven CRM

This is true despite the many advantages of using AI in CRM. The use of big amounts of customer data in AI algorithms also leads to critical concerns on data protection. Since AI-enabled CRM systems mine and store large amounts of personal data for customer analysis, businesses must adhere to data protection laws including GDPR and CCPA. The abuse or loss of data is also a threat to customers and companies which is why proper security and data management are highly valuable (Ozay et al., 2024).

Moreover, the incorporation of AI brings in the issues regarding the biasness and fairness. They simply repeat the bias of the data set from which they're trained; if the training data or the data used in developing the AI systems has bias whether it is on customer type, geographical location or service history, the results will be biased as well and may lead to discrimination. Companies need to ensure that they only feed their AI CRM systems with data free from the biases and periodically review such data to make sure that everyone receives equal treatment. Finally, companies should find a middle ground when it comes to automation and people's communication. While, AI can handle a large volume of customer interactions, there're times that require human empathy and understanding. Automation has a potential to make the customers feel too distant and this will not be good for business. Thus, the need to ensure businesses find ways of leveraging AI as a means of supplementing the efforts of human agents but not as a way of eliminating them (Venkateswaran, 2023).

1.5. Objectives and Roadmap

This chapter aims to explore the diverse ways AI is reshaping CRM, offering a detailed overview of its practical applications and strategic advantages. We will examine the core AI technologies driving this transformation, such as machine learning, natural language processing, predictive analytics, and robotic process automation, and discuss how these tools are applied across various industries to improve personalization, engagement, and retention. Additionally, the chapter will address the ethical and practical challenges that come with AI-driven CRM and provide insights into emerging trends and future developments in this rapidly evolving field.

2. EVOLUTION OF CUSTOMER RELATIONSHIP MANAGEMENT

As this chapter has pointed out, CRM has undergone significant changes over the last couple of decades in tandem with related advancements in technology, customer behavior and organizational initiatives. At the beginning, CRM systems were simple and not very sophisticated; their main function was to provide records of important customer data for companies to refer to. These early CRM systems were first implemented in the 1980s, and were mostly paper-based and required much effort to sustain. Customer details, purchase information, and service transaction details were documented previously in business organizations using paper-based and rudimentary computerized systems. This stage, also known as 'contact management,' had a useful function in the selling process but was insufficiently developed to provide comprehensive, individualized interaction or valuable information pertaining to the customers (Khan and Iqbal, 2020).

The 1990s brought forth more development with the launch of digital CRM systems that are built on database technology and offered more defined and systematic approach to data organization. CRM software such as Siebel Systems was developed during this era, mainly due to its efficiency in consolidating customers' information through which companies could easily manage their customers. These systems provided a holistic solution with sales, customer support and marketing in one software package. It also allowed certain previously disconnected departments to start sharing information and to organize customer relationship management more efficiently (Wang et al., 2024). This change was important for companies that wanted to better integrate the experience they offered customers and to make strategic decisions based on the data they collected on sales and marketing (Rosário & Casaca, 2025).

By the 2000s, CRM systems evolved and shifted from being local software solutions to cloud solutions. This movement allowed companies to capture customer information regardless of location, thereby decreasing internal demands for infrastructure and the expenses connected with it. Selling through cloud CRM solutions such as Salesforce and Microsoft Dynamics allowed for improved scalability and flexibility in customer management. With this advancement, the CRM systems became more affordable, and even small and medium business enterprises were able to acquire tools that bigger organizations had only been using. Cloud based CRM also brought in new features like marketing automation, customer clustering, and live analytics, which provided a vastly more detailed view of the client and enabled the company to tailor their actions according to client's preferences (Kumar et al., 2024).

However, these enhancements could not change the fact that traditional CRM systems were still confined to human input and linear and reactive models of data analysis. While it was possible for the companies to collect huge amounts of data on the customers, the systems could only provide the results after the data had been analyzed manually, and this was not feasible as the customers' expectations evolved at a very fast pace (Jamil at al., 2025a). Furthermore, they did not have the capacity to engage with customers in real-time or even know what the customer wanted before the customer stated it himself. Thus, many organizations which employed traditional CRM approach realized that they were constantly adapting to customers' needs instead of anticipating them (Rana & Hatibaruah, 2024).

AI is the new frontier in the CRM that has empowered systems to be more autonomous and intelligent than they have ever been before. Through AI, companies are able to make real-time analysis of large volumes of customer information and even predict the behavior of customers. Unlike earlier CRM applications, AI integrated CRM can predict the customer needs, can interact with them and deliver real time, accurate and relevant information for a much better and satisfactory customer experience. Current innovations, including machine learning, natural language processing, and predictive analysis, enable the CRM systems to offer recommendations, perform repetitive tasks and even recognize a customer's problem before it happens.

3. KEY AI TECHNOLOGIES TRANSFORMING CRM

CRM is a discipline that is being revolutionized by AI in a way that is more responsive, personalized and predictive. With the help of machine learning, NLP, predictive analytics, and RPA, AI technologies help CRM systems to provide deep and valuable insights for customers, as well as provide a prediction for their needs and enhance the level of engagement through all the touchpoints. This section looks at the technologies that drive AI in CRM and how each helps to enhance the efficiency and effectiveness of the process.

3.1. Machine Learning (ML)

Machine Learning is one of the cores enabling technologies for the contemporary CRM solutions. It allows systems to get better with time through training on past data without having to be coded for it. In CRM, the use of ML can help analyze a large amount of data containing information about a customer, their past behaviors, and their likely future ones and make recommendations accordingly. For example, using the data analysis of past customer purchases, ML algorithms can assist CRM systems to identify which product or service the customer is likely to purchase (Kumari, 2021).

By using ML, CRM systems can also perform the process of customer segmentation, which is way more accurate than the conventional demographical analysis. Due to the ability of ML models to categorize customers according to their behaviors, purchasing frequency, or even engagement level, marketing messages or promotions can be sent to those segments that are most likely to take an interest in them and respond appropriately. Furthermore, with the help of ML integrated CRM, one is able to score leads depending on how close they are to convert, thus helping those on the sales team to know where to focus in order to be most productive. These ML models update themselves over time, which means that the information that is being presented to the managers is as accurate as the behavior of customers, as well as changing trends in the market (Mei et al., 2024).

3.2. Natural Language Processing (NLP)

Natural language processing is therefore the artificial intelligence technology that allows computers to comprehend and analyze human language. In CRM, NLP is used extensively in improving communication especially in areas such as chat bots and auto customer support. Chatbots are able to communicate with customers in real time, providing information on request, and helping to complete elementary transactions, including ordering or changing data in the account. Some of the sophisticated NLP types can track and interpret the feelings of the customers during the interaction phases, such as frustration, satisfaction, and so on, before passing on to human agents when the need arises. Besides chatbots, NLP can be used in CRM systems to interpret textual data, which are derived from emails, social media platforms, and customer reviews. Through the analysis of this information, NLP algorithms can identify the frequent problems, monitor the feedback pattern, and highlight the emergent cases. For example, if a client posts a complaint on any social media platform, then NLP can alert a customer care attendant to attend to the client's complaint. Another critical aspect of NLP is note-taking, which enhances the internal communication shared within teams; this is based on the fact that the tool can automatically analyze the points raised in meetings, summarize them, and help in enhancing the work flow while ensuring that important information is not left behind (Senyapar, 2024).

3.3. Predictive Analytics

Another disruptive technology in AI CRM is predictive analytics. Using statistical models and machine learning, predictive analytics helps CRM systems to make future estimates of the clients' behaviors, thus helping a business organization to understand what the client wants, what he is likely to do and what risks he poses. This capability enables organizations to move from a state of responding to changes to anticipating them, that is, looking for opportunities and threats ahead of time. Churn prediction is perhaps the most common usage of predictive analytics in the context of CRM. The customers who are likely to churn can be ascertained by using engagement frequency, recency, and spending in prediction analytics (Jamil et al., 2025b). With this information, companies can also use specific retention approach that may include offering special offers of special discounts in order to retain these crucial customers. Another application of predictive analytics includes using customer data to propose products or services from the same company that the customer would most likely purchase because they are similar to their previous purchases. This not only raises income but also improves the consumers' satisfaction because the communications are meaningful and timely (Agarwal et al., 2023).

3.4. Robotic Process Automation (RPA)

Robotic Process Automation (RPA) is defined as the ability to replicate human activities in structured and repetitive processes by software robots. As for CRM, RPA can be applied to routine operations like the modification of customer data, notifications, simple monetary transactions, etc. In this respect, RPA helps to perform simple and time-consuming actions, which are not directly connected to the creation of value for clients, so the time is released for CRS and sales staff. For instance, RPA can be used to generate and complete forms, set reminder for follow-up emails and check customer's account details for authenticity. This makes it easier to onboard customers, and takes less time as it is with other forms of customer acquisition. Another advantage of RPA is in the area of data management and inputting of data into a CRM system to guarantee that information is correct and current. In addition, it eliminates errors in manual data entry, which is vital in enhancing quality of data in CRM to enable proper analysis and decision making (Macharla & Raghavendra, 2025).

3.5. Sentiment Analysis

There is a subfield of NLP called sentiment analysis especially important for interpreting the emotions, opinions, and attitudes of customers. This technology is being incorporated in to various CRM systems to track emotional response of customers towards products, services or experiences. Using text from emails, social media posts, surveys or reviews, sentiment analysis provides real time perception of the overall attitude of the customers. In CRM, sentiment analysis is a powerful tool to uncover pains and focus on the corresponding customer service. For instance, if sentiment analysis identifies negative emotions in a customer's communication, the CRM system can flag the particular customer to a customer service officer (Azam and Jamil., 2024). Further, sentiment analysis can track the shifts in the customers' feedback to identify further patterns. A negative attitude with regard to a certain aspect of a product, for example, may indicate that the product needs to be redesigned. On the other hand, positive emotions can reveal strengths that are appreciated by the customers which in turn can be underlined in advertising or product branding (Rai & Mishra, 2022).

3.6. Recommendation Engines

Recommendation engines are a type of machine learning that uses data from customers to provide recommendations for products or services to offer or articles to post. This AI technology is quite useful in CRM to develop customer experience that improves on engagement and sales. Based on data of previous interactions, purchases, and browsing, recommendation engines recognize patterns that will be useful for CRM systems to determine what customers may find useful. In e-commerce and retailing, recommendation engines drive the 'you may also like' or 'customers who bought this also bought,' is a product that best fits the customer's preferences. This kind of personalization does not only improve the so-called 'Shopping Experience' but makes the purchase more likely. Recommendation engines in CRM do the same for sales teams by identifying potential upsell and cross-sell opportunities, thus making the interactions with customer more valuable and relevant (Rahimi & Kozak, 2017).

3.7. The Future of AI in CRM

AI application to CRM will advance in the future and the application of these technologies will become more precise, self-driven, and easy to use. The next steps may involve more accurate real-time sentiment analysis, the effective combination of customers' experiences in online and offline contexts, and AI-based human-like chatbots. The result is that AI will lead CRM toward more personalized, predictive, and responsive customer relationship management in organizations and their customers.

4. PRACTICAL APPLICATIONS OF AI-DRIVEN CRM ACROSS INDUSTRIES

AI-driven Customer Relationship Management (CRM) has found transformative applications across diverse industries, enhancing how businesses interact with customers, personalize experiences, and optimize workflows. From retail and finance to healthcare and hospitality, AI-powered CRM solutions enable industries to deepen customer relationships and drive value through innovative, data-driven approaches.

4.1. Retail: Personalized Shopping Experiences

In retail, the use of AI in CRM has changed the way customers are treated hence the shopping experience. Machine learning recommendation systems employ customer's purchase history, internet activity, and tastes to provide product recommendations. E-commerce websites such as Amazon and ShopIfy use AI to develop its 'you might also like' and 'Customers bought this, also bought' segments to improve customer experience and boost revenues. It is also common to see chatbots being utilized in retailers for instant customer service where users are helped through their choice of products, questions are answered and orders placed. All these AI features do not only serve to enhance customer experience but also the sales process which makes retail CRM systems effective and fun (Nawaz et al., 2024).

4.2. Finance: Enhanced Customer Service and Fraud Detection

In the finance sector, AI supported CRM has a vital value towards improving the quality of customer service, compliance, and security. AI-powered chatbots and virtual assistants are employed by banks and other financial institutions to respond to straightforward customer inquiries within seconds, including account balances, transfers and payments. CRM also enables the use of artificial intelligence in that financial advisors can give personalized investment advice depending on the customer's past financial records, his or her goals, and risk-taking ability thus making banking a more personalized affair. In addition, AI CRM helps in the identification of fraud by scrutinizing the patterns that are characteristic of customers' behavior and reporting any suspicious actions (Amjad et al., 2017). For instance, if a customer's account of transaction is different from the usual transaction, the CRM system can send notification to the customer and other staff, thus minimizing risks. This proactive monitoring also creates trust between the company and the customers making their security an important aspect in the finance industry (Grover et al., 2024).

4.3. Healthcare: Improving Patient Engagement and Care Coordination

AI CRM has also enhanced the health care sector through enhancing the patient communication, care delivery and service delivery. With the help of AI, the healthcare providers can be used to send out health reminders for the patients, health advice, and even health preventive measures for the patients based on their records. To be specific, the healthcare CRMs can predict the patient's needs like appointment reminder, follow up appointment, etc., thereby improving the patient experience. Besides, patient engagement AI CRM systems also enhance continuity of care in the various health facilities. For instance, through the secure exchange of patient information for treatment purposes, CRM guarantees that all caregivers in particular patient's case get the most current information. This makes communication smooth thus improving the patient's health and the overall care delivery system (Iyelolu et al., 2024).

4.4. Hospitality: Streamlining Guest Services and Enhancing Loyalty Programs

The hospitality industry receives a lot of advantages from the AI-based CRM by providing the guests with unique services and improving loyalty programs. In the hotel and resorts, AI is used to monitor the customer preferences for the rooms, foods and other services for the customers who have been clients before. Such an approach is also practical as it makes guests feel unique, thus, they are loyal to the brand. Furthermore, artificial intelligence in CRM systems in hospitality helps in the management of loyalty programs because of offering specific incentives and recompenses in line with the activity and preferences of the guests. Hotels need to employ loyalty data so as to give customers personalized incentives including lower rates or improved rooms on subsequent visits. This managed application of AI CRM is instrumental in improving the guests' experience and fostering loyalty (Kumari, 2021).

4.5. Telecommunications: Proactive Issue Resolution and Customer Retention

In telecommunications, CRM is very important with the use of Artificial Intelligence to monitor customer needs and anticipate their needs. Telecoms utilize AI to track the state of networks and report any outages or failures in service to the customers in the same real-time they arise, thus turning potential complaints into early alerts. AI is also used to segment customers; this means that, using the usage patterns and satisfaction levels of the customers, telecom companies are in a position to identify customers who are likely to switch to other companies. The telecom companies need to use retention strategies such as use of discount offers or other loyalty promotions to help in the fight against churn. This proactive and analytical approach also improves the general customers' satisfaction and reduce the feeling of the customers that they are not cared for (Alnofeli et al., 2023).

5. BENEFITS OF AI-DRIVEN CRM SYSTEMS

The integration of AI in CRM systems has fundamentally transformed how businesses manage and enhance customer relationships. AI-driven CRM systems offer numerous benefits that extend across personalization, efficiency, strategic decision-making, and customer satisfaction, all of which help organizations stay competitive in a fast-paced market.

5.1. Enhanced Personalization and Customer Engagement

Another advantage of AI CRM system is the possibility to create unique customer experience. AI enables a firm to gather and analyze a large amount of information about the customer, such as the past purchase records, browsing history, and social media activities, to identify and forecast their needs. This capability helps the businesses to personalise the way they interact with the customers, provide the recommendations, offers and content that are relevant to the customers. Due to the above, AI-driven CRM systems do not only enhance the interaction but also build customer loyalty and satisfaction as customers feel that they are being understood. For instance, in the context of retail applications, AI implemented in CRM enables the system to detect that a given customer may be interested in a given product based on browsing history, and then makes it possible for the CRM system to offer the product to the customer at the right time. This dynamic approach of customer engagement makes it possible to improve both the user experience and the conversion rate (Potla, 2023).

5.2. Improved Efficiency through Automation

AI CRM systems make work easier by eliminating recurrent time-consuming tasks on the human resource side thus making them more effective in their work. Sales automation, for instance, through data input, follow-ups scheduling, and customer inquiries' handling frees up the time of sales, marketing and support personnel so they can focus on other high impact activities including strategy formulation and relationship building. For example, chatbots, which are popular in CRM, respond to simple customer questions in real-time, and, at the same time, free up human customer service agents. Also, integration of automation in AI integrated CRM improves the workflow since manual inputting of data is prone to error. This leads to better quality data, which is critical for decision makers and for ensuring that customers receive the same experience whenever they interact with the organization (Khneyzer et al., 2024).

5.3. Predictive Insights and Decision-Making

AI integrated CRM systems utilize analytical tools to forecast useful data for decision making. AI can also predict trends, customer value and even customer behavior, including churn rate or purchase intention through the use of historical and real time data. The information that is used to make predictions enables the management of businesses to handle possible problems that may occur and also take advantage of opportunities that may include offering other related products and services to customers that may be willing to buy. For instance, in the financial services industry, AI enabled CRM can look into the customers' activity and credit history to determine when he or she may require a new service or product, as in a loan or an insurance. This scientific approach not only increases sales but also organizes outreach activities so that they are timely and relevant (Ozay et al., 2024).

5.4. Increased Customer Satisfaction and Retention

The use of AI in CRM is crucial to help in increasing customer satisfaction and loyalty. Through improving the efficiency of service delivery, decreasing response time and providing a tailored service AI results in a positive customer experience. Also, AI facilitates predictive customer relations by helping firms solve problems before they metamorphose into complaints. For example, AI can highlight situations where customers may likely be dissatisfied in line with their recent engagements, so the service delivery teams can address such concerns with proper interventions in the shortest time possible. Since satisfaction influences customer loyalty, customers will be more likely to stick with a brand if he's sure that the brand is fully aware of his needs and ready to meet them (Venkateswaran, 2023).

5.5. Scalability and Adaptability

Since AI CRM system is built with the capability to expand, it is appropriate for all types and sizes of organizations. Since the firm evolves over time, the AI-based CRM can also scale up to handle a larger number of customers and their interactions without proportional hiring of staff. This flexibility will be especially useful to organizations in dynamic industries such as retail sales through the internet or technology that experiences dynamic customer demands or ever-shifting market factors. Also, the CRM systems based on the AI can develop during time, and it can adjust to new patterns and behaviors of customers. This continuous learning capability makes it possible for CRM to adapt to the changes; thereby offering a long-term value within a dynamic business context (Khan and Iqbal, 2020).

6. CHALLENGES AND ETHICAL CONSIDERATIONS

While AI-driven CRM systems offer numerous advantages, they also present unique challenges and ethical considerations that organizations must address to harness AI responsibly. From data privacy concerns to potential biases and customer trust, this section explores the key challenges and ethical issues that accompany AI integration in CRM and suggests best practices to mitigate these concerns.

6.1. Data Privacy and Security Risks

CRM systems based on artificial intelligence depend on the customer data to generate highly relevant experiences, and that is the problem with the data. Employers need to obtain, keep and process individuals' personal data, which include special categories of data, making them vulnerable to cyber theft. Unauthorized access to customer data could mean the loss of that trust and could cost millions besides attracting fines under GDPR and CCPA. To minimize these risks, organizations should ensure they have the right measures that will protect the data such as encryption, access control and regular checkups. Moreover, the organization must be transparent in the way and purpose of data processing; the customer should know how his data is being processed. Applying privacy by design and guaranteeing that the data management adheres to legal requirements, customer data is secure without compromising trust (Rosário & Casaca, 2025).

6.2. Algorithmic Bias and Fairness

Another important ethical issue that can be associated with AI CRM is the issue of algorithmic bias which can lead to discrimination of certain categories of customers. Since the CRM system is based on AI algorithms that learn from past data, any discrimination in this data will be reflected in the recommendation or customer treatment. For example, if the historical data indicates a positive response to high income customer, the AI system may channel its services to such customers in future, at the expense of other customers. To counter this, businesses need to use inclusive datasets when training their AI models and fairness checks to detect and mitigate bias. Periodic review and evaluation of these AI algorithms will enable the identification of the unfairness within the AI CRM systems hence providing equal services to all customers. Other aspects of ethical AI include the participation of diverse teams in the creation, implementation, and evaluation of these models to minimize the introduction of bias by default (Kumar et al., 2024).

6.3. Transparency and Explainability

AI integrated in CRM systems are basically decision makers that work by running several algorithms that may not be easy for end users to comprehend. This, however, is a challenge, mainly because customers might feel uneasy about systems that decide what they need without clear justification. For example, the customers may not appreciate why they are given particular recommendations of products and why certain requests are addressed in a certain way. ML transparency is critical to the development of trust since customers want to understand how an AI model arrives at a specific decision. AI models should be designed to provide information regarding decision processes so that such systems give the users understanding of why certain decisions are made, especially in relation to the operations of the CRM system. This transparency puts customers in a more commanding position regarding their experiences and builds more ethical reliability of AI-CRM for businesses and customers (Rana & Hatibaruah, 2024).

6.4. Balancing Personalization with Intrusiveness

AI CRM makes it possible to provide the most appropriate experience to the customers, but if the degree of personalization is taken to the extreme, the customers feel that they are being stalked. For instance, personalized advertisements that are too specific, or product recommendations based on detailed behavioral tracking, are likely to make customers feel like their privacy is being violated, which is not good. A balance has to be achieved between the kinds of information that would be beneficial to customers and the kind that would be invasive. To handle this, there should be the provision of avenues whereby the customer can set the extent to which they want to be personalized, or even be provided with an option to opt out of some of the personalization features of the organization. Offering such options is the respect for the customer's self-governance and the right to agency, which keeps personalization non-intrusive and protective of customers' privacy (Mei et al., 2024).

6.5. Dependency and Skill Gap Challenges

This paper finds that the growing adoption of AI-driven CRM systems creates a dependency of organizations on these systems when it comes to decision-making and engaging customers. Such dependency can cause removal of human supervision which can be disadvantageous especially if the AI system experiences problems or has some form of prejudice. In addition, AI in CRM needs professionals to handle and interpret the results of AI, which is, at times, difficult to fill. To overcome the problem of dependency and lack of skills, organizations need to focus on the integrated approach that implies the use of AI supported by human labor. Making sure that employees know what AI is telling them and are supervising the AI-generated decisions makes CRM work more accurate and fairer towards organizational objectives. Training programs are also important as they can assist in filling the skill gaps and foster the positive collaboration between AI and human agent (Senyapar, 2024).

7. EMERGING TRENDS IN AI-DRIVEN CRM

Over time, CRM systems are being transformed by AI technology in ways that were previously inconceivable. Multinational companies in various industries are integrating AI CRM systems to stand out and build strong bonds with customers based on new trends that improve customization, automation, and analytics. This section provides an outlook of the current advanced trends in AI based CRM with emphasis on how they are revolutionizing customer interactions and organizational operations.

7.1. Hyper-Personalization Through Predictive and Prescriptive Analytics

While traditional personalization involves segmenting consumers into large groups and delivering messages and recommendations that are more relevant to each of those segments, hyper-personalization uses AI to build unique experiences for each client. Using the information from the customer's behavior, social media accounts, and previous purchases, AI-based CRM systems can predict what a customer might need and offer related products or services. Predictive analytics takes this a step further by using past data to make future actions or behaviors more predictable and let companies make appropriate changes to their products based on these behaviors. Prescriptive analytics improves this process by providing recommendations for actions to take in order to achieve the best results, for example, defining the optimal time to interact with clients or proposing flexible prices to minimize churn danger. Such a level of AI insight increases customer satisfaction and helps the companies offer the best experience to every customer (Agarwal et al., 2023).

7.2. Voice-Activated and Conversational AI Interfaces

Smart assistants and chatbots are becoming essential components of CRM systems nowadays as it is far more natural to talk to a company's representatives through voice commands. Applying NLP, voice-activated CRM allows customers to interact through the voice, thus improving the system's accessibility. This technology has been more useful in such areas like retail, financial, hospitality and other areas where quick response or support is very essential in enhancing the user's experience. Moreover, the conversational AI interfaces like chatbots are improving to share a more natural interaction. These bots are great since they can interpret context, polarity, and intricate queries making the customer support more efficient. Conversational AI also relieves human agents from handling routine customer service inquiries and can therefore increase the general performance of customer service interactions (Macharla & Raghavendra, 2025).

7.3. AI-Enhanced Customer Journey Mapping

Customer journey mapping a technique used to describe the process a customer goes through from the time they develop an interest in a product to the time they make a purchase has greatly benefited from AI. Integrated with AI, journey mapping enables CRM systems to consider large amounts of live customer data, helping to identify typical customer challenges and potential enhancements. Marketing automation can use customer data to find patterns and determine the next logical action with the customer for the company. It enables businesses to manage every step of the customer journey and provide help at the right time and minimize unnecessary obstacles. By engaging each customer uniquely, AI-driven CRM becomes more natural and enjoyable, which would turn into more satisfaction and retention of the customers (Rai & Mishra, 2022).

7.4. Augmented Reality (AR) and Virtual Reality (VR) in Customer Engagement

The concept of Augmented Reality (AR) and Virtual Reality (VR) are now promising to revolutionize CRM as a tool by providing such experience. Technology industries such as retail and e-commerce are using AR to enable customers to see how products will look in their own homes before making a purchase, which is a value addition for the purchasing experience. Organizations are now using AR and VR in the CRM systems to capture the customer preferences in real-time and adding more value to the integration. In such sectors as real estate or furniture design, they can use VR to let customers experience the interiors of particular houses or study the prospective layout of furniture in the house. Besides, this trend increases customer loyalty and allows CRM systems to obtain additional information on customers' interests and preferences (Rahimi & Kozak, 2017).

7.5. Real-Time Sentiment Analysis for Customer Insights

The trends that are important for CRM currently include sentiment analysis that relies on artificial intelligence to help businesses track and respond to the emotions of customers in real-time. With the help of data on customer interactions with the product, comments on social networks, and reviews, AI-based CRM systems can determine the customer's attitude and identify emerging problems. Real-time sentiment analysis gives practical recommendations, allowing to act fast in case of negative reactions, provide clients with the right solutions and enhance their satisfaction. This capability is particularly valuable for industries with large numbers of customers, especially those for whom satisfaction levels can rise and fall rapidly, such as the telecommunications and hospitality industries. The authors state that knowledge of customer emotions can help in improving business interactions, avoid customer defection (Nawaz et al., 2024).

8. FUTURE DIRECTIONS OF AI-DRIVEN CRM AND CONCLUDING INSIGHTS

As the AI technologies advance at a fast pace, CRM systems are improving with new opportunities and creating more ways of changing business models. As more companies implement AI in CRM some promising future research opportunities that could transform customer relations, improve data analysis, and scale CRM systems are beginning to emerge. This section looks at the potential of AI in CRM and lastly offers implications of AI based CRM on organizations at strategic level.

8.1. Autonomous CRM Systems

One area of growth is the transition to more self-sufficient forms of CRM management. Subsequent CRM systems will incorporate AI to operate as independent systems that require little or no human interference to handle customer interactions and internal processes. With the use of enhanced machine learning, autonomous CRM can identify and solve customer needs before such needs are even expressed; ranging from basic questions such as Frequently Asked Questions to recommending the right products and services to a given customer. This automation is going to help organizations to be continuously engaging with the customers in an active manner and in the process, help to cut costs and improve efficiency. Self-service CRM will also use machine learning, which will enable the system to adapt as it operates based on current customer behavior and trends and as it receives feedback. This dynamic adaptability will enable CRM to immediately align with new customer expectations and changing market environment thus improving customer satisfaction and loyalty.

8.2. Emotional AI and Sentiment-Aware CRM

In the future as the AI technology develops the emotional intelligence will be the main focus of the CRM. The future CRM systems will have what is called the 'emotional AI', that will also include the feelings of customers through vocal and non-vocal expressions. Combined with facial recognition, voice modulation analysis, and sentiment tracking, AI-driven CRM systems will be able to respond according to the customer's mood ensuring empathy and trust. Smart CRM systems will improve customer relationships based on the degree of emotion in the communication that is possible to identify thus helping businesses to respond to customer complaints in a timely manner. For example, if a customer is annoyed during the support conversation, the system can automatically pass the case to a live operator and guarantee the customer a friendly attitude. This ability to interpret emotional signals will help customers and brands form much more profound and meaningful relationships.

8.3. Ethical and Transparent AI in CRM

With the rise of AI CRM in the business world, the necessity of ethical AI will be the main focus of companies. In the future, AI–based CRM systems will have to become transparent so that the customers know how the AI decision–making process affects their experience. Open AI systems will make customers see the rationale of the recommendation or the communication, thus making them feel more in control of their data. In addition, working with AI CRM, businesses will have to set ethical standards for avoiding biases in the algorithms used for AI, so that the AI-driven

CRM can work for all customer segments fairly. This commitment to ethical AI will enhance the customer trust which in turn makes the CRM system not only efficient but also equitable.

9. CONCLUSION

In this chapter, we have looked at how AI disrupted CRM and showed the evolution from traditional CRM to contemporary AI-enhanced CRM strategies. Today, due to the implementation of AI, CRM has become not only a system that helps to provide differentiated experience for customers but also to complete numerous operational tasks and analyze large amounts of information. When analyzing the technologies and trends that define AI-CRM like predictive analytics, voice interfaces, augmented reality, and emotional AI it can be realized that the future of CRM is in hyper-personalized and emotionally intelligent interactions with customers. The use of AI in CRM systems provides numerous benefits that can lead to a dramatic improvement of business outcomes, including enhanced productivity and better customer relations. However, what comes with these advantages is the disadvantage and ethical issues such as data privacy, algorithmic bias and data transparency. Solving these problems appropriately is vital to protect customer trust and make sure that AI in CRM is helpful. So, ahead the future of AI integrated CRM is looking brighter than today with more and more freedom and intelligence to make things happen, capable to understand the needs of the customers, and respond back as we have never dreamt of. However, the overall effectiveness of AI-driven CRM will only be determined by how organizations integrate complex automations with the right tone, fairness, and respect in customer handling. If the businesses are willing to accept the challenges posed by the AI-driven CRM and also ready to take the benefits that it offers then there is a way business can improve the current customer relationship and pave way for loyal customers and sustainable business growth. In sum, AI driven CRM is the form of change towards more adaptable, flexible and customer-oriented business strategies. Over the course of time, as organizations are progressing in their ways of making use of AI responsibly, this field will define what it means to manage customers and their relationships in the context of digitalized world to create better connections between the organization and its customers.

REFERENCES

Agarwal, T., Gopalkrishnan, S., Kale, V., Periwal, D., Kulkarni, A. A., Tharkude, D., & Jaiwani, M. (2023, November). Transforming Advertising: Harnessing AI for Personalised Customer-Centricity. In *2023 IEEE International Conference on Technology Management, Operations and Decisions (ICTMOD)* (pp. 1-8). IEEE. DOI: 10.1109/ICTMOD59086.2023.10438160

Alnofeli, K., Akter, S., & Yanamandram, V. (2023). Understanding the Future trends and innovations of AI-based CRM systems. In *Handbook of Big Data Research Methods* (pp. 279–294). Edward Elgar Publishing. DOI: 10.4337/9781800888555.00021

Amjad, F., Baig, S. A., Jamil, K., & Amjad, A. (2017). Impact of service quality on Loyalty & Mediating role of Trust: An empirical investigation of Restaurants. *Journal of Education and Vocational Research*, *8*(4), 6–14. DOI: 10.22610/jevr.v8i4.2156

Azam, T., & Jamil, K. (2024). Studying the role of corporate social responsibility, green HRM and green innovation to improve green performance of SMEs. *Journal of Business and Industrial Marketing*, *39*(12), 2620–2637. DOI: 10.1108/JBIM-02-2023-0087

Grover, P., Kar, A. K., & Dwivedi, Y. K. (2022). Understanding artificial intelligence adoption in operations management: Insights from the review of academic literature and social media discussions. *Annals of Operations Research*, *308*(1), 177–213. DOI: 10.1007/s10479-020-03683-9

Iyelolu, T. V., Agu, E. E., Idemudia, C., & Ijomah, T. I. (2024). Improving Customer Engagement and CRM for SMEs with AI Driven Solutions and Future Enhancements. *International Journal of Engineering Research and Development*, *20*(8).

Jamil, K., Anwar, A., & Baig, S. A. (2025). Building Brand Authenticity and Strategies for Genuine Destination Experiences. In Destination Branding and Bias in Ecotourism (pp. 75-104). IGI Global Scientific Publishing.

Jamil, K., Anwar, A., & Mohsin, M. (2025). Crafting Digital Destinations via Effective Social Media Strategies for Hospitality Industry. In Marketing Technology-Infused Hospitality: Upskilling Frontline Employees for Competitiveness (pp. 205-230). IGI Global Scientific Publishing. DOI: 10.4018/979-8-3693-7127-5.ch008

Khan, S., & Iqbal, M. (2020, June). AI-Powered Customer Service: Does it optimize customer experience? In 2020 8th International Conference on Reliability, Infocom Technologies and Optimization (Trends and Future Directions)(ICRITO) (pp. 590-594). IEEE.

Khneyzer, C., Boustany, Z., & Dagher, J. (2024). AI-Driven Chatbots in CRM: Economic and Managerial Implications across Industries. *Administrative Sciences*, *14*(8), 182. DOI: 10.3390/admsci14080182

Kumar, V., Ashraf, A. R., & Nadeem, W. (2024). AI-powered marketing: What, where, and how? *International Journal of Information Management*, *77*, 102783. DOI: 10.1016/j.ijinfomgt.2024.102783

Kumari, S. (2021). Context-Aware AI-Driven CRM: Enhancing Customer Journeys Through Real-Time Personalization and Predictive Analytics. *ESP Journal of Engineering and Technology Advancements*, *1*(1), 7–13.

Macharla, S. L., & Raghavendra, G. S. (2025). Leveraging AI for E-Business Transformation. In Business Transformation in the Era of Digital Disruption (pp. 29-58). IGI Global.

Mei, C. W., Konar, R., & Kumar, J. (2024). The Role of AI Chatbots in Transforming Guest Engagement and Marketing in Hospitality. In *Integrating AI-Driven Technologies Into Service Marketing* (pp. 595–620). IGI Global. DOI: 10.4018/979-8-3693-7122-0.ch029

Nawaz, N., Arunachalam, H., Pathi, B. K., & Gajenderan, V. (2024). The adoption of artificial intelligence in human resources management practices. *International Journal of Information Management Data Insights*, *4*(1), 100208. DOI: 10.1016/j.jjimei.2023.100208

Ozay, D., Jahanbakht, M., Shoomal, A., & Wang, S. (2024). Artificial Intelligence (AI)-based Customer Relationship Management (CRM): A comprehensive bibliometric and systematic literature review with outlook on future research. *Enterprise Information Systems*, *18*(7), 2351869. DOI: 10.1080/17517575.2024.2351869

Potla, R. T. (2023). Enhancing Customer Relationship Management (CRM) through AI-Powered Chatbots and Machine Learning. *Distributed Learning and Broad Applications in Scientific Research*, *9*, 364–383.

Rahimi, R., & Kozak, M. (2017). Impact of customer relationship management on customer satisfaction: The case of a budget hotel chain. *Journal of Travel & Tourism Marketing*, *34*(1), 40–51. DOI: 10.1080/10548408.2015.1130108

Rai, A., & Mishra, A. K. (2022). The Role of Artificial Intelligence in the Automation of Human Resources. In *Adoption and Implementation of AI in Customer Relationship Management* (pp. 166–176). IGI Global. DOI: 10.4018/978-1-7998-7959-6.ch011

Rana, R., & Hatibaruah, P. D. (2024). Revolutionizing Customer Service and Experience: The Impact of Artificial Intelligence. In Leveraging AI and Emotional Intelligence in Contemporary Business Organizations (pp. 253-275). IGI Global.

Rosário, A. T., & Casaca, J. A. (2025). How Artificial Intelligence Can Leverage Relationship Marketing Strategies. In Leveraging AI for Effective Digital Relationship Marketing (pp. 1-34). IGI Global.

Senyapar, H. N. D. (2024). Artificial Intelligence in Marketing Communication: A Comprehensive Exploration of the Integration and Impact of AI. *Technium Social Sciences Journal*, *55*, 64–81. DOI: 10.47577/tssj.v55i1.10651

Venkateswaran, N. (2023). AI-driven personalization in customer relationship management: Challenges and opportunities. *Journal of Theoretical and Applied Information Technology*, *101*(18), 7392–7399.

Wang, Y., Mohsin, M., & Jamil, K. (2024). Customer trust and willingness to use shopping assistant humanoid chatbot. *Service Industries Journal*, •••, 1–25. DOI: 10.1080/02642069.2024.2432935

Chapter 11
Juncture of Leadership and Digital Technologies With Challenges and Opportunities in the Digital Era

Waleed Mansi Alshammari
https://orcid.org/0009-0004-0736-359X
Lincoln University College, Petaling Jaya, Malaysia

ABSTRACT

This chapter is very important for the researchers, administrative body of organizations and scholars. This chapter tries to explain about the concept of leaders and definition of leadership based on previous researchers. Future, it inspects leadership for providing clear concepts to the reader about operation and importance in organization as well as explains the types of leadership in details. Furthermore, theoretical foundation has great importance for explaining any concept in the best way; therefore this chapter aims to provide some most important theories related to leadership and the important objective of this chapter is to provide the deep details about the importance of the leaders in different sectors and organizations. Finally, this chapter tries to educate the leaders for reinforcement of different strategies for helping the employee in setting goals, recognition of the opportunities and self-development.

DOI: 10.4018/979-8-3693-8960-7.ch011

INTRODUCTION

A leader plays an important role in providing management that encourages others to follow shared ideas. Leadership includes problem-solving skills and decision-making ideas that can help in designing the ways of advantages and contribute to overall progress(Gkintoni et al., 2022). Leaders who are efficient in the establishment of team, leaders provide an atmosphere where all workers work efficiently. Leaders foster flexibility significant for directing tasks. Leaders have some working ideas of the upcoming time and link it to an organization. A clear vision of leaders encourages others as it provides the logic of determinations(Kozioł-Nadolna, 2020). Leaders have the capability to make decisions when important. Leaders get information, analysis it and adopt the best way of implementation while taking the advantages of the organization and its investors. Good and proficient leaders console with the necessaries and viewpoints of their workforce. Leaders show understanding by listening problem and giving support to their workers(Ross et al., 2023).

Moreover, in the era of digital technologies leaders play an important role in the development of organizations. Digital technologies describe the use and share the information (Vargo et al., 2021) work by digital signals into more ascendable digital business. Proficient leaders use digital technologies to improve relationship and decision-making ideas. Leadership highlights digital knowledge in their workforce in the working climate. The vision of leaders is important in navigating business to sustainable progress in an organized world(Hussein et al., 2024).

In other words, the acceptance of digital technology by leaders comprises the assimilating novel digital tools, platforms, and approaches into their organizations to initiate the growth, efficacy, and innovation. The leaders with digitalization awareness have a progressive attitude and a clear consideration about technologies like AI, automation, and cloud computing which will shape the future (Herath & White, 2025). The leaders with digital knowhow enable the teams to grip these changes which are vital for generating an environment where constant learning and novelty are prioritized.

Furthermore, digital technology permits the leader for decision-making by providing perceptions that implement the strategies and increase performance. The leaders monitor more informed choices with the help of analytics tools. Automation and procedure reengineering are essential parts of digital revolution which allow the organizations to rationalize the processes of goods and services and improve efficiency (Badada et al., 2025).

DEFINITION OF LEADER

Many authors have defined leadership. But some of the most relevant definitions have been defined below

According to McKinsey"Leadership is a set of behaviors used to help people align their collective direction, to execute strategic plans, and to continually renew an organization" (Explainers, 2022)

According to Sağbaş"Digital Leadership is a leadership model that executes digital transformation within the organization can digitize the work environment and learning cultures of organizations" (Sağbaş & Erdoğan, 2022).

Digital leadership is described as occurring at different levels, individuals, agencies, and even nation-states are sometimes described as digital leaders (Adie et al., 2022).

Importance of Leadership in Digital Age

There are following importance of the leadership in digital era.

- Leaders inspire vision and implementation of solutions to stay competitive.
- Leaders give knowledge to organizations by digital technology or achieve confrontation successfully.
- Leaders promote joint effort and self-sufficiency to influence various aptitudes.
- Leadership reacts quickly to developing tendency and technological troubles.
- Leaders use results and visions to make planned choice.

Leadership Style

Leadership is a significant factor in bringing progress among any organization. Leadership designs the culture and inspiration for team and impact decision making process. Various conditions need different leadership styles (Yasin et al., 2022). Different type of leadership may help organizations to carry their policies to get ideal consequences.

Some of the leadership styles have been discussed below

TYPES OF LEADERSHIP

Therefore, Leadership within an organization significantly impact achieving good organizational performance. To achieve the highest level of employee development, human resource management, harmonious working relationships between employees and leadership styles are expected to increase labor productivity (Kadiyono et al., 2020). Hoang et al., (2021) stated that the leadership does not only indicate the power or control the leader has over the devotees to influence them to accomplish an objective, but implies the leader's activity that influences the supporter's conduct and activities towards accomplishing an objective. The leadership suggests a leader to stimulate the employee through words as well as the activities toward the accomplishment of an objective.

According to (Mansaray, 2019) leadership is feature of the leader that united a group together and it persuade the subordinates towards accomplishing objectives and changing the group's potential into reality. The leadership is a relationship that happens by which one employee can impact the conduct of other employees in which the leader can utilize their human impact to influence employees to accomplish a specific objective in the organization.

Further (Afsar & Umrani, 2020; Mansaray, 2019) explains that Leadership is skill that leader use to motivates the employees to put their capabilities best to get outcome, getting their devotion and rousing them to accomplish a coveted objective and result.

In a study the (Ciulla & Ciulla, 2020) regarded the leader as personality who possess a situation in a group, impact others as per the part desire of the position, and facilitates and coordinates the group in keeping up itself and achieving its objectives. it can be recommended that the way and approach in which a leader influence the employee and direct the workers towards the achievement of an object inside an organization can affect their conduct and aim to stay in that organization is called leadership style. This study used the skill of leadership in business ethics and relates to the textile factory in Massachusetts. Further, Ly (2020) has explained that the leader is an entity makes the decision, make rules and execute it in the organization that this study indicates the importance of leader with effective leadership style in their study. The worldwide condition of the organization has quickly changing. This condition has made the requirement for powerful leader that tackle all the obstacles and take the organization at high level in production.

Different leadership styles provide direction to the efforts of each employee in achieving organizational goals and in managing his subordinates as well as provides the views on dealing with and solving problems (Al-Sada et al., 2017). Good leadership is needed to develop employees and organizational identification to increase productivity. The phenomenon found by researchers in the pre-study shows that leadership style and identification organization have an influence on employee performance hospital (Arab et al., 2007; Risambessy et al., 2012; Yunarsih et al., 2020).

Figure 1. Types of leadership style

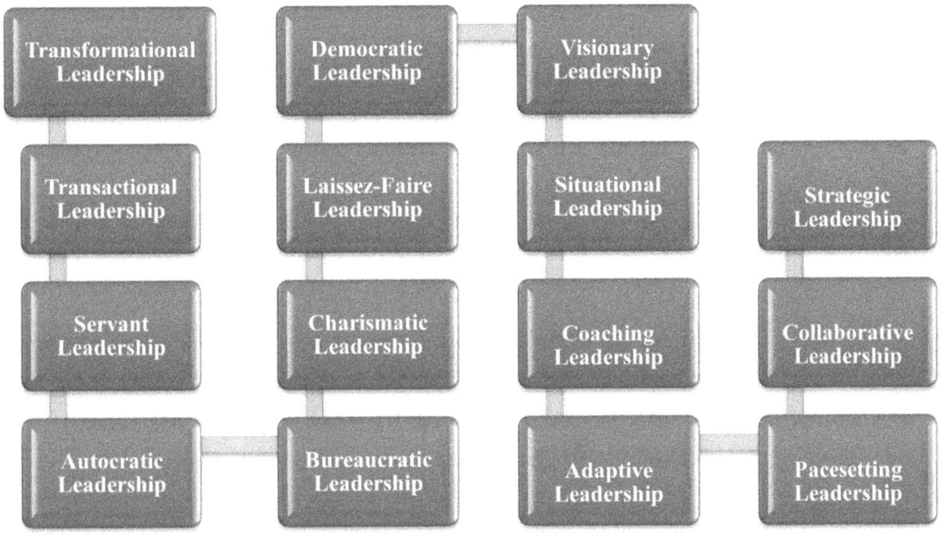

1. Transformational Leadership

Transformational leadership encourages the supporters to get strange results by concentrating on ideas, innovation and individual progress. Leaders task the position and encourage their workers to develop(Den Hartog, 2023).

2. Transactional Leadership

Transactional leadership focuses on a planned theory, where leaders make roles, task and expectations. Some failures are used as encouragers to get outcomes. Transactional leadership works in working atmosphere. It needs accuracy or devotion to processes. It is like in manufacturing sector(Wang et al., 2021).

3. Servant Leadership

Servant leadership allows the prosperity of their workers. It focusses understanding and communal establishment. Servant leadership purpose to make a working atmosphere that encourages workers to succeed. Servant leadership promotes long-term commitment and trust(Kainde & Mandagi, 2023).

4. Autocratic Leadership

Autocratic leaders have the ability to make-decisions with liberty, with less or no profit from workers. This style is operative in conditions need problem solving ideas or when clear vision is needed. Autocratic leadership may encourage to discontent and less self-esteem if overworked(Kule et al., 2024).

5. Democratic Leadership

Democratic leadership worth profit from workers and inspires joint problem-solving ideas. Democratic leadership fosters innovation or an ability of possession. Democratic leadership is best in the working atmosphere that gain profit from various viewpoints or team interaction(Ali et al., 2023).

6. Laissez-Faire Leadership

Laisses-fair leadership provides instructions, trusting their workers to accomplish their accountabilities with freedom. This leadership style is good for skilled and inspired workers but may encourage to mistake or inefficiently if workforce absence responsibility(Lester, 2021).

7. Charismatic Leadership

Charismatic leadership motivates their workforce with their self-confidence and strong statement ability. Charismatic leaders have a personality that appeals workers to their ideas. While inspiring this leadership style be dangerous if over-dependent of the leader's demand(Gabriel et al., 2022).

8. Bureaucratic Leadership

Bureaucratic leadership trails organizational rules. Bureaucratic leadership guarantees less risk and creating it better for sectors which include healthcare and finance sectors. Bureaucratic leadership can stop innovation and flexibility(Ohemeng et al., 2020).

9. Visionary Leadership

Visionary leaders pay attention of future plans and communication ideas that align with organizational aims. Visionary leaders encourage others to work in the long-run purposes. Sometime visionary leaders promote a sense of objectives(Karwan et al., 2021).

10. Situational Leadership

Situational leaders take their leadership style based on the necessities of their workforce and tackle with some trouble shooting situations. Situational leaders can control between being instructor or control over situation. This adaptability allows them to be high in varied atmosphere(Ahern & Loh, 2021).

11. Coaching Leadership

Coaching leadership authorize the progress of the workforce by providing knowledge and response. Coaching leaders pay attention on the growth of individuals and promote development. Coaching leaders focus on log-run progress for an organization(Karlsen & Berg, 2020).

12. Adaptive Leadership

In the adaptive leadership leaders are best in directing impossibility and variation by inspiring innovation and creativity. Adaptive leaders include their team members in decision-making process and regulate their policies to tackle with problem. Adaptive leaders train their team members in more proficient way (Gono & April, 2022; Latukha et al., 2025).

13. Strategic Leadership

Strategic leadership equal the working needs in the long-run aims, Strategic leaders pay attention on supporting their team efforts with high organizational. Strategic leadership shows continues development and progress. This leadership style needs effective communication skill(Samimi et al., 2022).

14. Collaborative Leadership

Collaborative leadership style establishes corporations and promotes teamwork in various groups, usually outside traditional limitations. Collaborative leadership inspires open communication and pooled responsibility to get common aims(Curseu & Schruijer, 2024).

15. Pacesetting Leadership

Pacesetting leadership style establishes huge expectancy and bringing their workforce to top. This leadership style is best with self-motivated personals but may origin anxiety if used extremely without deliberation for team changes(Bwalya, 2023).

Importance of Leadership

The success of an organization depends on strategic leadership, which provides direction, and purpose along with adaptableness in a developing business environment(Abu Mostafa et al., 2021). Leaders with strategic insight play an important role in leading their organizations through hurdles, benefiting from opportunities, and guaranteeing durable sustainability. The significance of Leaders can be understood through its complicated impact on various aspects of organizational functioning(Grant & Baden-Fuller, 2018).

1. Creative Direction:

Effective leadership enables the ability to establish a clear direction for the organization. An effective workforce is a result of efficient leadership that can possess the ability to predict and help to communicate convincing broad vision and guidelines for them. This vision provides a sense of purpose and helps to bring clarity about the organization's future and fruit full actions and efforts toward common long-term goals. Without strategic leadership, organizations run the risk of operating without a logical and forward-looking vision(Adoli & Kilika, 2020).

2. Dynamic Environment and adaptive capacity of organization:

Organizations face a challenging and uncertain business environment and market scenario. Strategic leaders are the best and essential choice to navigate these challenges. It scans the external environment, and challenging trends, and adapt strategies accordingly(Ellinger & Ellinger, 2021). Leaderscan surely help to cope with situations that lead to stagnation and decline in outcome(Abu Mostafa et al., 2021). So, if these issues are resolved organizations can take advantage of opportunities(Adoli & Kilika, 2020; Suryawan et al., 2025).

3. Maximum utilization of resources:

Strategic leaders are skilful at managing resources efficiently and improving them to meet organizational needs and goals. This enables to use of all the resources such as financial resources, human capital, and technology according to the strategic priorities of the organization. Proper resource allocation is essential to achieve objectives such as maximizing the impact of investments and ensuring long-term growth. In the absence of strategic leadership, organizations may face challenges in aligning resources which could result in inefficiencies and missed opportunities.

4. Implementations of planned Strategies:

Strategic planning is a key function of strategic leadership. This leadership can lead to the effective formulation and execution of strategies that help to push the organization on a progress path(Nur & Muafi, 2025). They guide the development of actionable plans, ensuring that the organization is on a route associated with its long-term goals(Grant & Baden-Fuller, 2018). The absence of Leaders may result in a lack of solid planning, with ad-hoc decision-making prevailing over a systematic approach, leading to disorganized efforts and suboptimal outcomes(Abu Mostafa et al., 2021).

5. Strategic leaders the Decision-Makers:

Strategic leaders are responsible for making important decisions that guide the organization to achieve its goals. They have a thorough understanding of the external environment and the possible consequences of their decisions(Ellinger & Ellinger, 2021; Jose & Buchanan, 2025). By doing so, leaders guarantee that decisions not only address instant challenges but also help to achieve the long-term desired objectives of the organization. Without strategic leadership, organizations may make volatile decisions that prioritize short-term benefits over long-term success.

6. Risk management ability:

Every business involves risks and uncertainties that may affect the outcomes. Strategic leaders are skilled at identifying, examining, and controlling risks that can come with new steps taken under strategic management. They design risk-justified strategies to protect the organizational welfare. Without strategic leadership, companies may have difficulty dealing with unforeseen challenges, resulting in possible setbacks and crises that could have been prevented with a proactive risk management approach(Geier, 2023).

7. Outcome of Organizational Culture:

Strategic leaders are important in shaping and maintaining the culture of any organization. They represent the values and principles that support the strategic vision and help to create an optimistic work environment. A healthy organizational culture improves employee engagement, commitment, and dedication to strategic goals. In the absence of Leaders organizations may face a disorganised culture that fails to support and meet the desired objectives. As a result, there may be a lack of unity and shared purpose among workers (Irnawati & Prasetyo, 2020; Shao, 2019).

8. Talent Expansion and Succession Planning:

Leaders play a central role in talent development of included factors and succession planning. Leaders invest in developing a team of skilled individuals, ensuring that the organization owns the necessary human capital to tackle the possible challenges effectively. Succession planning helps ensure a smooth leadership evolution, avoiding any disturbances to strategic desired goals. In the absence of strategic leadership, organizations may face difficulties in filling talent gaps, and leadership crises, and may not be sufficiently prepared for the future(Rolla, 2025; Yasin et al., 2022).

9. Stakeholder Bonds and Relationship Building:

Developing a strong and keen relationship with important stakeholders is a fundamental aspect of strategic leadership. Leaders must cooperate with their employees, customers, investors, and communities to maintain an understanding of their needs and expectations. The involvement of leader assurance the interests of stakeholders into account and prioritized when making strategic decisions for building trust and loyalty with important elements. if Leaders fails to communicate with stakeholders that can lead to a loss of support, damage to status, or other supervisory issues (Adoli & Kilika, 2020).

10. Innovations and improvements:

Strategic leaders understand that continuous improvement and innovation are critical factors for achieving success. They adopt a culture that places high value on creativity, research, and learning from successes and failures as well as past experiences. This practical approach to novelty allows organizations to stay ahead in the market and allow them to point out customer preferences. Without strategic leadership, organizations may become stagnant, fail to embrace new ideas and technological changes, and ultimately lose their competitive edge (Cortes & Herrmann, 2021; Geier, 2023).

11. Ethical Leadership with Social Responsibilities:

Maintaining ethical standards is a significant part of strategic leadership. Leaders should act as role models by displaying ethical behaviours and honesty in their decision-making and actions. Their reputation as a personality should be crystal clear and attractive to followers. In addition, strategic leaders should hold social responsibility, admitting the impact of their organization on the wider community and environment. Ethical leadership helps to build the organization's reputation, fosters trust, and enhances long-term sustainability (Barbar et al., 2025; Yazıcı & Çiçeklioğlu, 2025).

12. Performance assessment and Responsibility:

Effective leaders create key performance indicators (KPI) to track progress toward achieving strategic goals. Regular performance analyses and assessments help to keep everyone responsible and provide visions for making adjustments to strategies and designed policies. Without strategic leadership, organizations may face a lack of an organized approach to monitoring performance. Good leadership will lead to effective ways of assessing what needs improve(Ellinger & Ellinger, 2021).

CHALLENGES OF INTEGRATING TECHNOLOGY INTO LEADERSHIP

There some challenges which a leader have to tackle some following challenges in the age of digitalization

Figure 2. Challenges of leadership

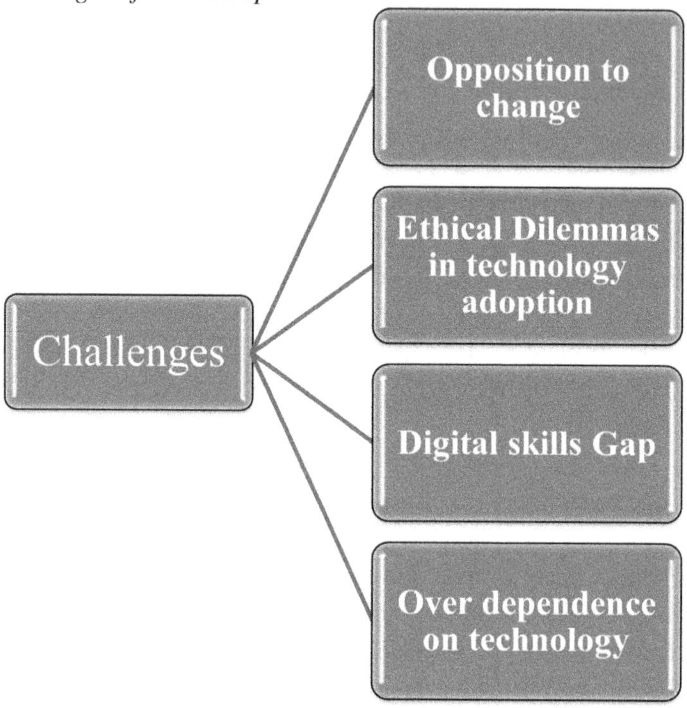

1. Opposition to change

Leaders have to face some challenges and one of the important challenges is to participate technology into leadership is disabling opposition to change among organizations. Workers and leaders have fear to loss control the situation and consequences related with digital technology. This inactivity stops from an absence of knowledge in new technologies. Leaders must bring this resistance through giving education and highlighting the long-run profit of technological implementation. Clear discussion and including workers in the variation procedure are important to modifying and confirming smoother changes(Kouzes & Posner, 2023).

2. Ethical Dilemmas in technology adoption

The adoption of technology usually drives ethical tasks that leaders direct wisely. These dilemmas involve concerns about cyber security. Using artificial instruments is the example of it that can be accidentally broadcast partialities. Leadership must equal innovation with moral deliberation by creating rules and guaranteeing amenability with data fortification laws. Leaders can establish trust with workers and consumers by addressing these moral issues(Bhatta, 2021).

3. Digital skills Gap

By developing reliance on digital technology shows the gap in digital skill within leaders and workers. Organizations try to keep pace with quick update because of the lack of technical capabilities in their workforce. Leaders have to tackle with problem of upskilling teams to successfully use developing technologies. Spending money in training programs and making opportunities for development is important step in filling this gap. Leaders must continue to improving their own digital skill(Reddy et al., 2023).

4. Overdependence on technology

Digital technology has become embedded in decision-making and task managements. There is a danger of overreliance on digital instruments. This challenge can decrease decision and critical thinking. Digital technology can improve efficiency that cannot substitute understanding. Leaders must struggle to attack equality by implementing technology as an instrument to supplement rather than replace human skills(Singh, 2021).

OPPORTUNITIES AT THE CONNECTION OF LEADERSHIP AND TECHNOLOGY

There are following opportunities for the leaders to adopt the digital technologies in the work place.

Figure 3. Opportunities of leader for using digital tools

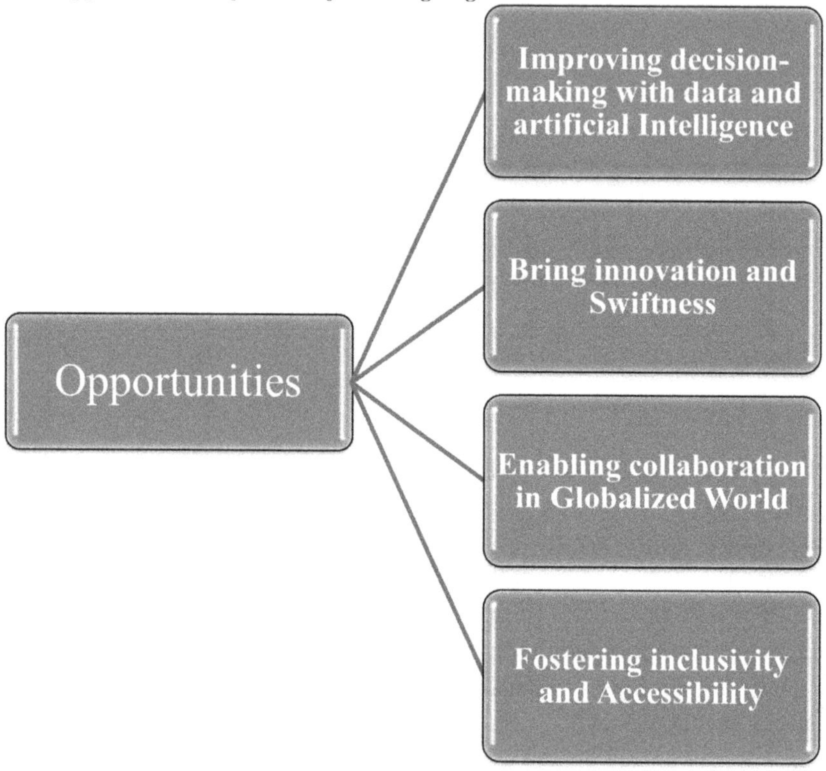

1. Improving decision-making with data and artificial Intelligence

Leadership has the accessibility to large amount of data or updated AI instruments, which encourages them to make strong decisions. Proficient leaders may recognize tendencies or improve operations. Artificial intelligence improves decision-making process by presenting routine tasks. AI also offer data driven visions and gives actual results. This opportunity allows leaders to pay attention on challenges and grow forward-thinking policies personalized to market wants(Haleem et al., 2024).

2. Bring innovation and Swiftness

Digital technology plays an important role in promoting innovation or confirming organization remains swift in competitive situation. Leadership may influence digital instruments to analyze with new vision and follow agile to varying situation. Swiftness facilitated by technology as it allows businesses to spindle in reaction to market competition. Innovation driven thorough technologies help businesses grow products and improve consumer knowledge(Jasim et al., 2024).

3. Enabling collaboration in Globalized World

The growth of digital platforms has designed the pathway leaders connect team in different areas. Instruments like video conferencing and project management allow continuous collaboration. Leaders can make organized atmosphere for team force and confirming association on aims and prompting a sense of collaboration by using these digital instruments. This opportunity is important in globalized world where different viewpoint give to organizational development(Newman & Ford, 2021).

4. Fostering inclusivity and Accessibility

Digital technology is an important element for fostering inclusivity and accessibility in leadership. Leaders can use digital instruments to bring different viewers. Leaders can bend up limitations and can make balanced prospects by using technologies which include comprehensive platforms and screen readers. Inclusivity also inspires diverse viewpoints and it lead to best problem-solving ideas and innovation(Ismail et al., 2023).

Navigation of the Challenges and Opportunities

In current speedily growing digital landscape, leaders cultivate a diverse set of skills and capabilities to navigate the challenges and opportunities showed by technology (Badada et al., 2025). Getting the essential skills for progress in this digital world needs a commitment to learning, and strategic foresight (Stein et al., 2025). Here's a deeper look at leaders obtain the opportunities and skills they require to succeed in the digital era:

1. Continuous Learning and Education

Leaders follow specified courses and certifications connected to digital technologies, like data analytics, cyber security, and digital marketing (Daouk, 2025). Some of the higher universities and organizations provide online courses and certifications in evolving technologies. Joining industry-specific workshops, sessions, and boot camps permit leaders to be informed with the advance methods, tendencies, and technologies in their field. For intense, contributing in workshops on artificial intelligence, and cloud calculating will support leaders to know about these technologies from an applied perspective (Gupta & Jaiswal, 2025). Linking with digital thought leaders and impacts by meeting, or sessions support leaders to be updated on practices, case studies, and upcoming tendencies. This also provides them the chance to network with industry upper class and learn from their practices (Yusof et al., 2025).

2. Developing a Growth Mindset

Embrace modification and view it as a chance for developments is one of the main skills for leaders which they need in the digital era (Subrahmanyam, 2025). Leaders should inspire a mindset of non-stop betterment and flexibility across the institution. Leaders are ready for discovering advance technologies and methodologies even if leaders tackle with traditional methods of running a business. A growth mindset inspired leaders to take risks with advance technologies and approaches. In the digital era, innovation derives from trying advance things, and leaders require modeling this behavior among their institution by promoting an atmosphere where research and knowledge from failure are part of the development process (de Vasconcelos Gomes et al., 2025).

3. Building Technological Literacy

Leaders do not need to be specialists in every technology, having knowledge of main digital tendencies are important. This involves getting information of areas like cloud computing, AI, machine learning, data analytics, mechanization, and block chain (Senapati & Rawal, 2025). Leaders establish knowledgeable decisions about leveraged to determine business worth. Leaders grow the capability to efficiently cooperate with their information technology, data science, and software progress teams (Subrahmanyam, 2025). This process is not for that they want to be technical specialists, but they know the language and task of technology to enable smooth communication and association in business and technology teams (Al-Tarawneh & Al-Badawi, 2025).

4. Data-Driven Decision Making

Leaders overcome with data in this digital era. Learning to understand and influence this data to make informed, independent decisions is an important ability skill (Sutarman et al., 2025). Leaders have courses on data visualization tools and data analytics platforms to know about to develop visions from huge datasets. Data-driven and decision-making process allows leaders to increase performance, and forecast upcoming tendencies (Ebepu et al.). Leaders can promote data-driven culture in their institution by encouraging for data collection, analysis, and transparency. Leaders confirm that decisions are based on realities rather than expectations by inspiring their workforce to depend on data to update their approaches (MAHABUB et al., 2025).

5. Developing Digital Leadership Skills

Digital leadership is not only about the knowledge of technology but also about teaching people by digital transformation (Singun, 2025). Emotional intelligence (EQ) supports leaders to navigate the tasks that come with organizational modification. Leaders with huge emotional intelligence understand with workforce, connect efficiently, and promote a sympathetic work atmosphere, which is important during periods of fast digital modification (Yadav & Hung, 2025). Leaders give information to their team members by the use of advance technologies, confirming that the change is smooth and that workers feel helped. This includes training workers, and establishing the case for the advantages of digital acceptance (Hossain et al., 2025).

CASE STUDY ON DIGITAL TRANSFORMATION

Nike's Digital Transformation

Nike is one of the greatest brands in the world. The leadership of this company's leadership transfer from CEO Mark Paker to Jhon Doahoe this step and acceptance of technology has shaped the future of the company. They sketched a strong digital transformation approach that would permit Nike to associate directly with customers, identify experiences as well as continue control over their brand and product circulation(Dolles & Santomier, 2025; Fransisca et al., 2025).

Digital Transformation as Acceptance of Technology

Nike has accepted the digital technology in different way. This company has focused on the structure of vigorous e-commerce policy which became a vital part of its business plan. The company invested greatly in its own online store and mobile apps, such as the Nike app and SNKRS app, to generate a continuous online shopping experience for consumers. These platforms enabled Nike to sidestep outmoded retail channels and reach customers directly(Kaur et al., 2025).

Furthermore, the Nike leveraged data analytics and artificial intelligence (AI) to better recognize consumer behavior. Nike increased deeper insights into customers' first choice, workout behaviors, and purchasing behaviors. This allowed the business to engrave marketing campaigns, create targeted offers, and optimize product assortments (Ganesha & Hemalatha, 2025).

Moreover, Nike also accepted digital expertise in its supply chain. The company initiated the using of 3D printing and other progressive manufacturing techniques to rapid up product prototyping and decreases costs. Nike also invested in automation to make its supply chain more agile and approachable to demand (Ganesha & Hemalatha, 2025; Kaur et al., 2025).

Theories on Leadership

There are some theories are supportive to understand the real importance and categories of the leadership. These theories also lead to recognize that how the leadership works efficiently.

Following are the leader ship theories

1. Great Man Theory
2. Trait Theory
3. Contingency Theories
4. Path Goal theories
5. Transformational Theory
6. Theory X and Theory Y
    1. Great man theory 1840

The Great Man theory developed around 19th century. This theory is about the personalities of leadership. This theory simply explains that great leaders are born, they are not made. Furthermore, it was believed that great leaders would flourish when faced with an appropriate situation. The theory was popularized by Thomas Carlile, a writer and instructor. In 1860, Herbert Spencer, an English philosopher confirmed the great man theory, stating that these heroes are only products of their time and that their actions are the result of social situations

2. Trait theory:

Trait theory is one of the precise attempts of thought leadership (Northhouse, 1997). It is one of the early efforts to understand the leadership process that highlights the employee traits of leaders. The most recognizable parts of the theory are that fruitful leaders everywhere and through history conceive fruitful leaders with innate traits, for example, identity traits, social traits, competence traits and physical attributes. Leadership traits have been explicitly sorted by Jago (1982) and Silli (199), isolating them into four groups, specifically identity, social, competence, and physical traits (Tangle, 2008). The doctrine is exceptionally helpful for separating leaders from devotees, succeeding ineffectual leaders. The theory focuses entirely around the leader's part in leadership and subsequently has the potential to give a deeper and more nuanced understanding of how the leader and his or her identity are identified with the leadership process (Tangle, 2008).

The trait theory is condemned for different reasons. The most important issue is that despite the fact that various investigations have long been led on trait theory, there is no standard extension of familiarity properties that can be used to characterize leadership viability. The second disappointment is the failure of the trait theory which confines itself to a realm of virtues. Third, it is associated with the suspicion that a leader is conceived, if a person has certain qualities, that he is a leader. In this theory, the assurance of leadership adequacy depends exclusively on the quality of stay and not on the situation. This makes it difficult to view the feasibility of leadership in light of the pre-characterized rundown of symptoms in different circumstances (Tangle, 2008).

CONTINGENCY THEORY

History of Contingency Principles

This theory is developed by Fred Fiedler in 1958 in the research on the leader effect in group. Fiedler believed that the effectiveness of being dependent on one's leadership position and style of leadership. In contrast to the situational theory of leadership, the leader effect corresponds to the leader's style, which matches the situation, not accepting it. A leader is most effective when his characteristics and style of leadership coincide with the situation and environment around him (Gupta, 2009).

Contingency theory use to generate leadership for organizations, in which certain styles can be matched to situations that have proved successful (Gupta, 2009). Companies can know what type of person will fit in each position of the organization whenever there is an opening. While this principle is complex but very useful for professionals to match the right conditions and determines the best person for the job (Gupta, 2009).

TRANSFORMATIONAL LEADERSHIP THEORY

Transformational leadership is a relatively new approach to leadership that focuses on how leaders can bring valuable and positive modification to their workers. James McGregor Burns first offered the ideas of transformational leadership for studying political leaders, but in the current time of period this term is also used in the study of organizations. Burns described two leadership styles: transactional and transformational. The Supporters of a transformational leader use to respond by feeling trust, gratitude, faithfulness and veneration for the leader and are ready to work harder than formerly expected. This theory solidified the need to study followers in leadership research. Transformational leadership was the first developed and validated theory to emphasis morals and values in leadership. However, research on the theory is primarily based on the multifactor leadership questionnaire, which has produced inconsistent results. Research has also focused heavily on senior-level leaders. Nevertheless, this theory is a appreciated and extensively used approach to studying and teaching leadership.

PATH GOAL THEORIES

This theory helps to the supporters by selecting style of leadership that motivates followers as well as helps them to move toward the desired reward. In short, it helps the followers to fulfill that goal through management, training and determine the path. Path-goal theory is a contingency philosophy that forecasts the leader's style of communication with a follower's wants and the nature of the task. It argues instructional leadership for ambiguous tasks, supportive leadership for repetitive tasks, participatory leadership for vague tasks, achievement-oriented leadership for autonomous tasks and challenging tasks.

Path-goal theory provides leaders with a practical yet theoretical basis for understanding which leadership style to choose. It also constructs a motivational principle as its foundation. However, path-goal theory is challenging to apply to organizations because it uses multiple, interrelated assumptions. Despite the formulation of a motivational theory, path-goal theory does not fully explain how the style of leadership affects follower motivation, which is one of several reasons why the lack of a strong research supporting its claims is.

THEORY X AND THEORY Y

The advocate of this theory is MC Gregor (1966). This theory clarifies two clashing perceptions of employees at a job that will impact leadership style. The directors are a view to take after either perspective of their workforce. Theory X is view as a conventional perspective of bearing and control. Theory Y includes a more self-coordinated workforce that appreciates the objectives of their organization and fuses their very own portion objectives into these.

Theory X accept that the normal employee aversions job and will maintain a strategic distance from it unless specifically administered, the employees must be pressured, controlled and coordinated to guarantee the organizational goals are met; the danger of discipline must exist inside an organization and they want to be dealt with thusly to stay away from obligation. It likewise expects that employees are moderately undriven and their prime main thrust is the want for security (Tangle, 2008).

On the other hand, Theory Y is the extraordinary inverse and views employees to be spurred, quick to take more noteworthy responsibility and apply both poise and heading: the employees will condition job towards organizational goals and that dedication will in itself be remunerated for so doing. The employees will practice their considerations and creative energy in their jobs if given the shot and this will give a public door for more noteworthy efficiency. Theory Y expect that the basic employee will, under the adequate conditions, assume liability as well as search for additional, and the absence of aspiration and the traits of Theory X are no intrinsic human Traits however learned in working situations that suffocate or don't advance theory Y practices (Okumbe,1998) Mcgregor hypothesized that understanding the suppositions by which administrators job enables leaders to end up more powerful in their workplace which thus impacts on their employees(Thrush, 2012).

CONCLUSION

The leaders are important for the administration of companies and they play important role for the decision making in critical situation. This chapter explains the definition of the leaders and digital leader by different scholar. This chapter elaborates the challenges in the context of opposition to change, ethical dilemmas of leaders in adoption of technology, digital skill gap and over dependence on technology.

Furthermore, this chapter explains the importance of leaders and its different types and how the different situations call for different leadership styles. In the digital time of period, the leaders have to develop its knowledge and experience in the field where implication of new technologies is important. Therefore, this chapter elaborated the opportunities for the leader in improving decision making with data and artificial intelligence; bring innovation and swiftness in the production and service process, enabling collaboration in globalization world and fostering the inclusivity and accessibility which leaders to the problem solving ideas in the organization. Besides, this chapter gives details on the important theories related to leadership such as great man theory, trait theory, contingency theories, path goal theories, x, y theory and transformational theory. These theories give the strong theoretical perceptions to the reader.

Moreover, In an emergency when there is little time to converge on an agreement and where a designated authority has significantly more experience or expertise than the rest of the team, an autocratic leadership style may be most effective; however, in a highly motivated and aligned team with a homogeneous level of expertise, a more democratic or laissez-faire style may be more effective. Any leadership style adopted should be the one that most effectively achieves the objectives of the group while balancing the interests of its individual members. This chapter is very beneficial for the future studies, administrative authority of organization and policy makers

REFERENCES

Abu Mostafa, Y., Salama, A. A., Abu Amuna, Y. M., & Aqel, A. (2021). The Role of Strategic Leadership in Activating Time Management Strategies to Enhance Administrative Creativity Skills. [IJAMSR]. *International Journal of Academic Management Science Research*, *5*, 36–48.

Adie, B. U., Tate, M., Cho, W., & Valentine, E. (2022). Digital leaders and digital leadership: a literature review and research agenda.

Adoli, H. L., & Kilika, J. M. (2020). Conceptualizing the role of leadership strategy in the context of strategic management process: A review of literature. *Journal of Economics and Business*, *3*(4). Advance online publication. DOI: 10.31014/aior.1992.03.04.307

Afsar, B., & Umrani, W. A. (2020). Transformational leadership and innovative work behavior: The role of motivation to learn, task complexity and innovation climate. *European Journal of Innovation Management*, *23*(3), 402–428. DOI: 10.1108/EJIM-12-2018-0257

Ahern, S., & Loh, E. (2021). Leadership during the COVID-19 pandemic: Building and sustaining trust in times of uncertainty. *BMJ Leader*, *5*(4), 266–269. DOI: 10.1136/leader-2020-000271

Al-Tarawneh, A., & Al-Badawi, M. (2025). Effective Strategies for Managing Multilingual Teams in Human Resources. In *From Machine Learning to Artificial Intelligence: The Modern Machine Intelligence Approach for Financial and Economic Inclusion* (pp. 1341-1351). Springer. DOI: 10.1007/978-3-031-76011-2_100

Ali, J., Vanchapo, A. R., Suharyatun, S., & Subasman, I. (2023). Analysis of The Effectiveness of School Principles' Democratic Leadership in Improving Teacher Professionalism. *Mudir: Jurnal Manajemen Pendidikan*, *5*(2), 471–476.

Badada, B., Delina, G., Krishnaraj, R., & Thiruthuvanathan, M. M. (2025). Navigating Leadership and Technology Integration in the Digital Age: Success Factors and Determinants. *Insights Into Digital Business, Human Resource Management, and Competitiveness*, 349-376.

Barbar, J., Abualigah, A., Dahleez, K., Abou-Al-Ross, S., & Aboramadan, M. (2025). Ethical leadership and public healthcare organizational and employee outcomes: The role of psychological meaningfulness. *Leadership in Health Services (Bradford, England)*, *38*(1), 32–53. DOI: 10.1108/LHS-04-2024-0039

Bhatta, N. (2021). Emerging ethical challenges of leadership in the digital era: A multi-vocal literature review. *EJBO. Electronic Journal of Business Ethics and Organization Studies*, *26*(1).

Bwalya, A. (2023). Leadership styles. *Global Scientific Journal, 11*(8).

Ciulla, J. B., & Ciulla, J. B. (2020). The importance of leadership in shaping business values. *The search for ethics in leadership, business, and beyond*, 153-163.

Cortes, A. F., & Herrmann, P. (2021). Strategic leadership of innovation: A framework for future research. *International Journal of Management Reviews*, *23*(2), 224–243. DOI: 10.1111/ijmr.12246

Curseu, P. L., & Schruijer, S. G. (2024). Leading without position power: Preliminary validation of the multiparty collaborative leadership scale (MCLS). *International Journal of Conflict Management*, *35*(2), 411–426. DOI: 10.1108/IJCMA-01-2023-0014

Daouk, A. (2025). Navigating the Digital Transformation Landscape: Education, Opportunities, and Challenges for Entrepreneurs. *Entrepreneurship-Digital Transformation, Education, Opportunities and Challenges: Digital Transformation, Education, Opportunities and Challenges*, 113.

de Vasconcelos Gomes, L. A., Chaparro, X. A. F., Maniçoba, R. F., Borini, F. M., & Silva, L. E. (2025). Transformation of the governance of failure for radical innovation: The role of strategic leaders. *Research Policy*, *54*(1), 105108. DOI: 10.1016/j.respol.2024.105108

Den Hartog, D. N. (2023). Transformational leadership. In *Encyclopedia of business and professional ethics* (pp. 1776–1780). Springer. DOI: 10.1007/978-3-030-22767-8_57

Dolles, H., & Santomier, J. (2025). Transformational digital leadership and organizational strategy: the case of the US National Basketball Association. In *Digital Leadership* (pp. 78-91). Edward Elgar Publishing. Ebepu, O. O., Okpeseyi, S. B. A., John-Ogbe, J., & Emmanuel, E. Harnessing Data-Driven Strategies For Sustained United States Business Growth: A Comparative Analysis Of Market Leaders. DOI: 10.4337/9781035321247.00012

Ellinger, A. D., & Ellinger, A. E. (2021). Providing strategic leadership for learning: Optimizing managerial coaching to build learning organizations. *The Learning Organization*, *28*(4), 337–351. DOI: 10.1108/TLO-05-2020-0070

Explainers, M. (2022). What is leadership? In: August.

Fransisca, L., Renaldo, N., Chandra, T., Augustine, Y., & Musa, S. (2025). Digital Innovation Capability and Customer Value Co-Creation on New Product Performance with Digital Transformation Maturity as a Moderating Variable in Trading Companies in Indonesia. *Luxury: Landscape of Business Administration, 3*(1), 1–15.

Gabriel, O. D., De Alwi, C. D. T. V., Jayang, E. A., & Wai, S. L. C. (2022). The impact of transformational leadership on generation Z employee retention and innovative behaviour: A case of Malaysian hotel industry. *International Journal of Multicultural and Multireligious Understanding*, *9*(4), 35–53.

Ganesha, K., & Hemalatha, K. (2025). Digital Transformation in Advertising after COVID-19: Routing the New Landscape. In *Handbook of Digital Innovation, Transformation, and Sustainable Development in a Post-Pandemic Era* (pp. 384–406). CRC Press.

Geier, M. T. (2023). Strategic thinking: Theoretical development and assessment. *Journal of Strategy and Management.*

Gkintoni, E., Halkiopoulos, C., & Antonopoulou, H. (2022). Neuroleadership an asset in educational settings: An overview. *Emerging Science Journal.Emerging Science Journal*, *6*(4), 893–904. DOI: 10.28991/ESJ-2022-06-04-016

Gono, T., & April, K. (2022). Adaptive Leadership During Covid-19 Pandemic. *Effective Executive*, *25*(2), 46–79.

Grant, R. M., & Baden-Fuller, C. (2018). How to develop strategic management competency: Reconsidering the learning goals and knowledge requirements of the core strategy course. *Academy of Management Learning & Education*, *17*(3), 322–338. DOI: 10.5465/amle.2017.0126

Gupta, S., & Jaiswal, R. (2025). A deep learning-based hybrid PLS-SEM-ANN approach for predicting factors improving AI-driven decision-making proficiency for future leaders. *Journal of International Education in Business.*

Haleem, A., Javaid, M., & Singh, R. P. (2024). Perspective of leadership 4.0 in the era of fourth industrial revolution: A comprehensive view. *Journal of Industrial Safety*, 100006.

Herath, S. K., & White, S. L. (2025). Digital Transformation and the Future of Accounting: A Comparative Analysis of Asia, Europe, and the Gulf Region. In *Insights Into Digital Business, Human Resource Management, and Competitiveness* (pp. 1-34). IGI Global Scientific Publishing.

Hossain, M. K., Sutanto, J., Handayani, P. W., Haryanto, A. A., Bhowmik, J., & Frings-Hessami, V. (2025). An exploratory study of electronic medical record implementation and recordkeeping culture: The case of hospitals in Indonesia. *BMC Health Services Research*, *25*(1), 1–20. DOI: 10.1186/s12913-025-12399-0 PMID: 39953485

Hussein, H., Albadry, O. M., Mathew, V., Al-Romeedy, B. S., Alsetoohy, O., Abou Kamar, M., & Khairy, H. A. (2024). Digital leadership and sustainable competitive advantage: Leveraging green absorptive capability and eco-innovation in tourism and hospitality businesses. *Sustainability (Basel)*, *16*(13), 5371. DOI: 10.3390/su16135371

Irnawati, J. E., & Prasetyo, J. H. (2020). The Influence Over the Transformational of Leadership Style, the Organizational Culture, and Employee Empowerment towards Achievement of Organizational Strategies in one the Central Government Organization. *International Journal of Innovative Science and Research Technology*, *5*(3), 917–927.

Ismail, A., Hidajat, T., Dora, Y. M., Prasatia, F. E., & Pranadani, A. (2023). *Leading the digital transformation: Evidence from Indonesia*. Asadel Publisher.

Jasim, T. A., Khairy, H. A., Fayyad, S., & Al-Romeedy, B. S. (2024). Digital leadership and creative performance in tourism and hotel enterprises: Leveraging strategic agility and organizational learning culture. *Geo Journal of Tourism and Geosites*, *54*(2 supplement), 872–884. DOI: 10.30892/gtg.542spl11-1262

Jose, S., & Buchanan, F. R. (2025). Strategic factors in SME leadership orientation towards initiating exports: India context. *Measuring Business Excellence*, *29*(1), 150–167. DOI: 10.1108/MBE-02-2024-0023

Kainde, S. J., & Mandagi, D. (2023). A systematic review of servant leadership outcomes in education context. *EDUKASIA: Jurnal Pendidikan dan Pembelajaran*, *4*(2), 2563-2574.

Karlsen, J. T., & Berg, M. E. (2020). Coaching leadership style: A learning process. *International Journal of Knowledge and Learning*, *13*(4), 356–368. DOI: 10.1504/IJKL.2020.111143

Karwan, D. H., Hariri, H., & Ridwan, R. (2021). *Visionary leadership: what, why, and how*. European Union Digital Library.

Kaur, D., Ahsan, M., & Gill, G. S. (2025). Digital Transformation in the Sports Industry: Driving Circular Economy in Sports Equipment and Infrastructure. In *Innovating Sustainability Through Digital Circular Economy* (pp. 65-90). IGI Global Scientific Publishing.

Kouzes, J. M., & Posner, B. Z. (2023). *The leadership challenge: How to make extraordinary things happen in organizations*. John Wiley & Sons.

Kozioł-Nadolna, K. (2020). The role of a leader in stimulating innovation in an organization. *Administrative Sciences*, *10*(3), 59. DOI: 10.3390/admsci10030059

Kule, J., Muhammad, T., Joseph, W. G., Johnson, A., & Ugwu, J. N. (2024). The Relationship between Head Teachers' Authoritarian Leadership Style and Teachers' Burnout in Secondary Schools in Ibanda Municipality, Ibanda District, Uganda. [NIJCIAM]. *Management*, *5*(1).

Latukha, M., Yakovleva, P., & Yan, K. (2025). Adaptive Leadership for Multilevel Resilience in the Context of Disruptions. *Thunderbird International Business Review*, *67*(2), 149–167. DOI: 10.1002/tie.22416

Lester, I. (2021). *Employee expectations and perceptions of leadership styles in a chemical manufacturing facility in South Africa*. North-West University.

MahabubMD Russel HossainEsrat Zahan Snigdha. (2025). Data-Driven Decision-Making and Strategic Leadership: AI-Powered Business Operations for Competitive Advantage and Sustainable Growth. *Journal of Computer Science and Technology Studies*, *7*(1), 326–336. DOI: 10.32996/jcsts.2025.7.1.24

Mansaray, H. E. (2019). The role of leadership style in organisational change management: A literature review. *Journal of Human Resource Management*, *7*(1), 18–31. DOI: 10.11648/j.jhrm.20190701.13

Newman, S. A., & Ford, R. C. (2021). Five steps to leading your team in the virtual COVID-19 workplace. *Organizational Dynamics*, *50*(1), 100802. DOI: 10.1016/j.orgdyn.2020.100802 PMID: 36536689

Nur, S. A., & Muafi, M. (2025). Link between dynamic capability and sustainable entrepreneurship: The mediation role of digital networking. *Jurnal Siasat Bisnis*, 1-14.

Ohemeng, F. L., Obuobisa Darko, T., & Amoako-Asiedu, E. (2020). Bureaucratic leadership, trust building, and employee engagement in the public sector in Ghana: The perspective of social exchange theory. *International Journal of Public Leadership*, *16*(1), 17–40. DOI: 10.1108/IJPL-05-2019-0018

Reddy, P., Chaudhary, K., & Hussein, S. (2023). A digital literacy model to narrow the digital literacy skills gap. *Heliyon, 9*(4), e14878. DOI: 10.1016/j.heliyon.2023.e14878 PMID: 37025876

Rolla, A. (2025). Talent Management in Learning Organizations: Designing Curriculum for Business Schools. In *Handbook of Talent Management and Learning Organizations* (pp. 85-104). CRC Press.

Ross, C., Smith, C., & Pulley, T. W. (2023). Equity Fluent Leadership: Implementation.

Sağbaş, M., & Erdoğan, F. A. (2022). Digital leadership: a systematic conceptual literature review. *İstanbul Kent Üniversitesi İnsan ve Toplum Bilimleri Dergisi, 3*(1), 17-35.

Samimi, M., Cortes, A. F., Anderson, M. H., & Herrmann, P. (2022). What is strategic leadership? Developing a framework for future research. *The Leadership Quarterly, 33*(3), 101353. DOI: 10.1016/j.leaqua.2019.101353

Senapati, B., & Rawal, B. S. (2025). Distributed Hybrid Quantum Computing Applications into Battery Cell Manufacturing Industries as per the Industries 5.0. *Cloud Computing and Data Science*, 136-165.

Shao, Z. (2019). Interaction effect of strategic leadership behaviors and organizational culture on IS-Business strategic alignment and Enterprise Systems assimilation. *International Journal of Information Management, 44*, 96–108. DOI: 10.1016/j.ijinfomgt.2018.09.010

Singh, K. (2021). *Intelligent decision support system for selection of Learning Apps to promote critical thinking in first year programming students*

Singun, A. J. (2025). Unveiling the barriers to digital transformation in higher education institutions: A systematic literature review. *Discover Education, 4*(1), 37. DOI: 10.1007/s44217-025-00430-9

Stein, S., Ghantous, D., Chandler, Z., Simpson, A., & Udupi, I. (2025). Evolving Foresight Skills: How Will We Shape the Future of Strategic Foresight? Subrahmanyam, S. (2025). The Paradigm Shift in Leadership Owing to Technological Development. In *Leadership Paradigms and the Impact of Technology* (pp. 381-406). IGI Global Scientific Publishing.

Suryawan, I. W. K., Gunawan, V. D., & Lee, C.-H. (2025). The role of local adaptive capacity in marine ecotourism scenarios. *Tourism Management, 107*, 105039. DOI: 10.1016/j.tourman.2024.105039

Sutarman, A., Aprianto, R., Mitrev, R., Adyatama, R., & Yusup, M. (2025). Influence of Digital Technology & Data Analytics on Strategic Decision Making. [SABDA Journal]. *Startupreneur Business Digital*, *4*(1), 12–23. DOI: 10.33050/sabda.v4i1.685

Vargo, D., Zhu, L., Benwell, B., & Yan, Z. (2021). Digital technology use during COVID-19 pandemic: A rapid review. *Human Behavior and Emerging Technologies*, *3*(1), 13–24. DOI: 10.1002/hbe2.242

Wang, Y., Toseef, M., & Gong, Y. (2021). It process alignment in business strategy: Examining the role of transactional leadership and organization culture. *Information (Basel)*, *12*(6), 237. DOI: 10.3390/info12060237

Yadav, M., & Hung, T. H. (2025). Role of Emotional Intelligence in Crisis Leadership. In *Emotionally Intelligent Methods for Meaningful Leadership* (pp. 149–172). IGI Global Scientific Publishing.

Yasin, A., Hussain, S., Hali, S. M., & Iqbal, S. (2022). Digitalization and firm performance: Mediating role of smart technologies. *Journal of Tianjin University Science and Technology*, *55*(4).

Yazıcı, A. M., & Çiçeklioğlu, H. (2025). The moderating role of environmental ethics in the effect of green innovation awareness on corporate social responsibility. *Social Responsibility Journal*, *21*(4), 826–854. DOI: 10.1108/SRJ-05-2024-0306

Yusof, F. M., Majid, M., Fadzil, A. S., & Ramli, M. F. (2025). The Conceptualisation Of Work Integrated Learning Practices In Hospitality Education To Develop Students'career Preparedness: A Preliminary Paper. *The Insight Journal*, *12*(1), 1–12. DOI: 10.24191/ij.v12i1.3902

Compilation of References

Abbas, G., & Joseph, C. (2025). Cost-Effective Cloud Strategies for SMEs: Solving Technology Challenges and Driving Competitiveness.

Abbas, Q., & Yaqoob, S. (2009). Effect of leadership development on employee performance in Pakistan. *Pakistan Economic and Social Review*, •••, 269–292.

Abu Mostafa, Y., Salama, A. A., Abu Amuna, Y. M., & Aqel, A. (2021). The Role of Strategic Leadership in Activating Time Management Strategies to Enhance Administrative Creativity Skills. [IJAMSR]. *International Journal of Academic Management Science Research*, *5*, 36–48.

Acar, O. (2020). *Yapay Zekâ Fırsat Mı, Yoksa Tehdit Mi?* [Is Artificial Intelligence an Opportunity or a Threat?]. Kriter Yayınevi. [Kriter Publishing House]

Accenture. (2021). AI: Built to Scale – Unleashing the Power of AI across the Enterprise. https://www.accenture.com

Adie, B. U., Tate, M., Cho, W., & Valentine, E. (2022). Digital leaders and digital leadership: a literature review and research agenda.

Adoli, H. L., & Kilika, J. M. (2020). Conceptualizing the role of leadership strategy in the context of strategic management process: A review of literature. *Journal of Economics and Business*, *3*(4). Advance online publication. DOI: 10.31014/aior.1992.03.04.307

Adriyanto, A. (2023). Evaluation of Employee Engagement Level in Improving Productivity and Retention in the Company. *Atestasi: Jurnal Ilmiah Akuntansi*, *6*(1), 583–598. DOI: 10.57178/atestasi.v6i1.1105

Aeon, X. Digital. (n.d.). How Gopal Namkeen modernized its order processing system to improve dealer experience. https://www.aeonx.digital/how-gopal-namkeen-modernized-its-order-processing-system-to-improve-dealer-experience

Afsar, B., & Umrani, W. A. (2020). Transformational leadership and innovative work behavior: The role of motivation to learn, task complexity and innovation climate. *European Journal of Innovation Management*, *23*(3), 402–428. DOI: 10.1108/EJIM-12-2018-0257

Agarwal, T., Gopalkrishnan, S., Kale, V., Periwal, D., Kulkarni, A. A., Tharkude, D., & Jaiwani, M. (2023, November). Transforming Advertising: Harnessing AI for Personalised Customer-Centricity. In *2023 IEEE International Conference on Technology Management, Operations and Decisions (ICTMOD)* (pp. 1-8). IEEE. DOI: 10.1109/ICTMOD59086.2023.10438160

Aggarwal, S., Bharti, V., & Badhon, A. J. (2024). Quantum Computing. In *Quantum Computing and Cryptography in Future Computers* (pp. 1–32). IGI Global. DOI: 10.4018/978-1-7998-9522-0.ch001

Aghaunor, C. T., Eshua, P., Obah, T., & Aromokeye, O. (2025). Data security strategies to avoid data breaches in modern information systems.

Agrawal, A., Catalini, C., & Goldfarb, A. (2015). Crowdfunding: Geography, social networks, and the timing of investment decisions. *Journal of Economics & Management Strategy*, *24*(2), 253–274. DOI: 10.1111/jems.12093

Agrawal, A., Gans, J., & Goldfarb, A. (2018). *Prediction Machines: The Simple Economics of Artificial Intelligence*. Harvard Business Review Press.

Ahern, S., & Loh, E. (2021). Leadership during the COVID-19 pandemic: Building and sustaining trust in times of uncertainty. *BMJ Leader*, *5*(4), 266–269. DOI: 10.1136/leader-2020-000271

Ahlers, G. K. C., Cumming, D., Günther, C., & Schweizer, D. (2015). Signaling in equity crowdfunding. *Entrepreneurship Theory and Practice*, *39*(4), 955–980. DOI: 10.1111/etap.12157

Ahmed, F., Hasan, M., Hossain, M. S., & Andersson, K. (2023). Comparative Performance of Tree Based Machine Learning Classifiers in Product Backorder Prediction. *Lecture Notes in Networks and Systems, 569 LNNS*, 572–584. DOI: 10.1007/978-3-031-19958-5_54

Ahmed, S. (2024). Artificial Intelligence (AI) Technology Adoption in SME. [AI]. *Artificial Intelligence*, *17*(01).

Ajanaku, O. J., & Mutula, S. (2018). The relationship between knowledge management and nursing care performance. *South African Journal of Library and Information Science*, *84*(2), 39–51.

Akash, C. R., Vivekanandhan, P. K., Adam Khan, M., Ebenezer, G., Vinoth, K., Prithivirajan, J., & Kishan, V. J. P. (2024). Assessment of ridge regression-based machine learning model for the prediction of automotive sales based on the customer requirements. *Interactions (Cham)*, *245*(1), 289. Advance online publication. DOI: 10.1007/s10751-024-02132-4

Akhavan, P., Ramezan, M., Yazdi Moghaddam, J., & Mehralian, G. (2014). Exploring the relationship between ethics, knowledge creation and organizational performance: Case study of a knowledge-based organization. *VINE Journal of Information and Knowledge Management Systems*, *44*(1), 42–58.

Al Breiki, M., & Nobanee, H. (2019). The Role of Financial Management in Promoting Sustainable Business Practices and Development. SSRN *Electronic Journal*. https://doi.org/DOI: 10.2139/SSRN.3472404

Al Khatib, I., Ahmed, V., & Ndiaye, M. (2024). Integrated blockchain systems are paving the way to SMART logistics. *AIP Conference Proceedings*, *3034*(1), 070001. DOI: 10.1063/5.0194698

Al Shraah, A., Abu-Rumman, A., Al Madi, F., Alhammad, F. A. F., & AlJboor, A. A. (2022). The impact of quality management practices on knowledge management processes: A study of a social security corporation in Jordan. *The TQM Journal*, *34*(4), 605–626. DOI: 10.1108/TQM-08-2020-0183

Alabdulatif, A., Khalil, I., & Saidur Rahman, M. (2022). Security of blockchain and AI-empowered smart healthcare: Application-based analysis. *Applied Sciences (Basel, Switzerland)*, *12*(21), 11039. DOI: 10.3390/app122111039

Alazazi, M., Wang, B., & Allan, T. (2020). *Success factors of donation-based crowdfunding campaigns: A machine learning approach.*

Ali, J., Vanchapo, A. R., Suharyatun, S., & Subasman, I. (2023). Analysis of The Effectiveness of School Principles' Democratic Leadership in Improving Teacher Professionalism. *Mudir: Jurnal Manajemen Pendidikan*, *5*(2), 471–476.

Ali, S, S., I, H., & S, A. (2016). Easypaisa: An innovative Pakistani model for mobile banking. *J.D.A*, *50*(6), 277–285.

Ali, S., Haq, S., & Anjum, S. (2020). Financial literacy and financial inclusion: An empirical investigation from Pakistan. *Journal of Financial Services Marketing*, *25*(3), 155–167.

Alkan, D. (2020). *İnsan Kaynakları Yönetiminin Yapay Zekâ Teknolojileri ile Dönüşümü [Transformation of Human Resources Management with Artificial Intelligence Technologies]. Oyunu Değiştiren Güç Yapay Zekâ* İçinde [The Power That Changes is in Artificial Intelligence]. İstanbul. 269-295.

Allam, M., Cai, S., Ganesh, S., Venkatesan, M., Doodhwala, S., Song, Z., Hu, T., Kumar, A., Heit, J., Study Group, C., & Coskun, A. F. (2020). COVID-19 diagnostics, tools, and prevention. *Diagnostics (Basel), 10*(6), 409. DOI: 10.3390/diagnostics10060409 PMID: 32560091

Allioui, H., & Mourdi, Y. (2023). Unleashing the potential of AI: Investigating cutting-edge technologies that are transforming businesses. [IJCEDS]. *International Journal of Computer Engineering and Data Science, 3*(2), 1–12.

Almatrooshi, B., Singh, S. K., & Farouk, S. (2016). Determinants of organizational performance: A proposed framework. *International Journal of Productivity and Performance Management, 65*(6), 844–859. DOI: 10.1108/IJPPM-02-2016-0038

Alnofeli, K., Akter, S., & Yanamandram, V. (2023). Understanding the Future trends and innovations of AI-based CRM systems. In *Handbook of Big Data Research Methods* (pp. 279–294). Edward Elgar Publishing. DOI: 10.4337/9781800888555.00021

Al-Tarawneh, A., & Al-Badawi, M. (2025). Effective Strategies for Managing Multilingual Teams in Human Resources. In *From Machine Learning to Artificial Intelligence: The Modern Machine Intelligence Approach for Financial and Economic Inclusion* (pp. 1341-1351). Springer. DOI: 10.1007/978-3-031-76011-2_100

Amazon. (2023). How Amazon fulfilment centers work. Amazon. https://www.aboutamazon.com/news/operations/how-amazon-fulfillment-centers-work

Amershi, S.. (2019). Guidelines for Human-AI Interaction. *CHI Conference on Human Factors in Computing Systems*. DOI: 10.1145/3290605.3300233

Amit, R., & Schoemaker, P. J. (1993). Strategic assets and organizational rent. *Strategic Management Journal, 14*(1), 33–46.

Amjad, F., Baig, S. A., Jamil, K., & Amjad, A. (2017). Impact of service quality on Loyalty & Mediating role of Trust: An empirical investigation of Restaurants. *Journal of Education and Vocational Research, 8*(4), 6–14. DOI: 10.22610/jevr.v8i4.2156

Amoozad Mahdiraji, H., Razavi Hajiagha, S. H., Jafari-Sadeghi, V., Busso, D., & Devalle, A. (2024). Towards financing the entrepreneurial SMEs: Exploring the innovation drivers of successful crowdfunding via a multi-layer decision-making approach. *European Journal of Innovation Management, 27*(7), 2275–2301. DOI: 10.1108/EJIM-12-2021-0618

Andaru, F. M., & Aryani, Y. A. (2023). Big data adoption: Does it have a great impact on crowdfunding success in SMEs? *Proyecciones (Antofagasta).*

Antunes, H. J. G., & Pinheiro, P. G. (2020). Linking knowledge management, organizational learning and memory. *Journal of Innovation & Knowledge*, *5*(2), 140–149. DOI: 10.1016/j.jik.2019.04.002

Anzion, L. J., Schaafsma, F. G., Boot, C. R., Formanoy, M. A., & Schelvis, R. M. (2025). An exploration of changes in the mental models of middle management and their association with activities to implement a dialogue tool to address mental health in the workplace. *BMC Public Health*, *25*(1), 623. DOI: 10.1186/s12889-025-21702-x PMID: 39953447

Appiah-Otoo, I., & Song, N. (2021). The Impact of Fintech on Poverty Reduction: Evidence from China. *Sustainability (Basel)*, *13*(9), 1–17. https://www.mdpi.com/2071-1050/13/9/5225. DOI: 10.3390/su13095225

Aprilina, V., Dompak, T., Salsabila, L., & Lodan, K. T. (2025). The Role Of Digitalization In Enhancing Public Service Efficiency: Challenges And Opportunities In Managing Public Complaints Through E-Government In Indonesia. *International Journal of Social Welfare and Family Law*, *2*(1), 57–66. DOI: 10.62951/ijsw.v2i1.183

Areed, S., Salloum, S. A., & Shaalan, K. (2020). The role of knowledge management processes for enhancing and supporting innovative organizations: a systematic review. *Recent advances in intelligent systems and smart applications*, 143-161.

Arner, D. W., Barberis, J., & Buckley, R. P. (2015). The evolution of Fintech: A new post-crisis paradigm. *SSRN*, *47*, 1271. DOI: 10.2139/ssrn.2676553

Arrieta, A. B., Díaz-Rodríguez, N., Del Ser, J., Bennetot, A., Tabik, S., Barbado, A., García, S., Gil-López, S., Molina, D., & Benjamins, R. (2020). Explainable Artificial Intelligence (XAI): Concepts, taxonomies, opportunities and challenges toward responsible AI. *Information Fusion*, *58*, 82–115. DOI: 10.1016/j.inffus.2019.12.012

Arya.ag. (n.d.). *Arya agri-tech solutions.* Retrieved from https://www.arya.ag

Ashta, A., & Biot-Paquerot, G. (2018). FinTech evolution: Strategic value management issues in a fast changing industry. *Strategic Change*, *27*(4), 301–311. DOI: 10.1002/jsc.2203

Atalar, G. D. (2019). *Teknolojinin gelişimi ve hukuktaki yansımaları* [The development of technology and its reflections in law]. Ankara ve İzmir Baroları Çalıştay Raporu.

Atienza-Barba, M., del Río, M. de la C., Meseguer-Martínez, Á., & Barba-Sánchez, V. (2024). Artificial intelligence and organizational agility: An analysis of scientific production and future trends. *European Research on Management and Business Economics*, *30*(2), 100253. DOI: 10.1016/j.iedeen.2024.100253

Aviv, I., Hadar, I., & Levy, M. (2021). Knowledge management infrastructure framework for enhancing knowledge-intensive business processes. *Sustainability (Basel)*, *13*(20), 11387. DOI: 10.3390/su132011387

Awais, M., Afzal, A., Firdousi, S., & Hasnaoui, A. (2023). Is fintech the new path to sustainable resource utilisation and economic development? *Resources Policy*, *81*, 103309. https://doi.org/https://doi.org/10.1016/j.resourpol.2023.103309. DOI: 10.1016/j.resourpol.2023.103309

Aydın, İ. H., & Değirmenci, C. (2020). *Yapay Zekâ* [Artificial intelligence]. Girdap Kitap.

Azam, T., & Jamil, K. (2024). Studying the role of corporate social responsibility, green HRM and green innovation to improve green performance of SMEs. *Journal of Business and Industrial Marketing*, *39*(12), 2620–2637. DOI: 10.1108/JBIM-02-2023-0087

Azer, M. A., & Samir, R. (2024). Overview of the Complex Landscape and Future Directions of Ethics in Light of Emerging Technologies. *International Journal of Advanced Computer Science and Applications*, *15*(7). Advance online publication. DOI: 10.14569/IJACSA.2024.01507142

Badada, B., Delina, G., Krishnaraj, R., & Thiruthuvanathan, M. M. (2025). Navigating Leadership and Technology Integration in the Digital Age: Success Factors and Determinants. *Insights Into Digital Business, Human Resource Management, and Competitiveness*, 349-376.

Balarezo, J. D., Foss, N. J., & Nielsen, B. B. (2023). Organizational learning: Understanding cognitive barriers and what organizations can do about them. *Management Learning*. Advance online publication. DOI: 10.1177/13505076231210635

Balasubramanian, N., Ye, Y., & Xu, M. (2022). Substituting Human Decision-Making with Machine Learning: Implications for Organizational Learning. Https://Doi.Org/10.5465/Amr.2019.0470, *47*(3), 448–465. DOI: 10.5465/amr.2019.0470

Balasubramanian, S., Devarajan, H. R., Raparthi, M., Dodda, S. B., Maruthi, S., & Adnyana, I. M. D. M. (2023). Ethical Considerations in AI-assisted Decision-Making for End-Of-Life Care in Healthcare. *Power System Technology*, *47*(4), 167–182.

Balducci, B., & Marinova, D. (2018). Unstructured data in marketing. *Journal of the Academy of Marketing Science*, *46*(4), 557–590. DOI: 10.1007/s11747-018-0581-x

Balducci, F., Impedovo, D., & Pirlo, G. (2018). Machine learning applications on agricultural datasets for smart farm enhancement. *Machines (Basel)*, *6*(3), 38. Advance online publication. DOI: 10.3390/machines6030038

Banuari, N., Absah, Y., & Siahaan, E. (2021). Analyze the Influence of Talent Management and Knowledge Management on Employee Performance through Employee Retention as Intervening Variable at PT Bhanda Ghara Reksa Divre I Medan. *International Journal of Research and Review*, *8*(9), 189–204. DOI: 10.52403/ijrr.20210926

Barbar, J., Abualigah, A., Dahleez, K., Abou-Al-Ross, S., & Aboramadan, M. (2025). Ethical leadership and public healthcare organizational and employee outcomes: The role of psychological meaningfulness. *Leadership in Health Services (Bradford, England)*, *38*(1), 32–53. DOI: 10.1108/LHS-04-2024-0039

Barney, J. B. (1986). Strategic Factor Markets: Expectations, Luck and Business Strategy. Management Science, Vol. 32, No. 10, ss. 1231-1241.

Barney, J. B. (1991). Firm resources and sustained competitive advantage. Journal of Management, Vol. 17, No. 1, ss. 99-120.

Batra, R., & Keller, K. L. (2016). Integrating marketing communications: New findings, new lessons, and new ideas. *Journal of Marketing*, *80*(6), 122–145. DOI: 10.1509/jm.15.0419

Becker, B., & Hoyer, P. (2024). The anatomy of clinical decision-making: Aligning AI design with ICU routines. *Journal of Organizational Ethnography*, *13*(3), 427–451. Advance online publication. DOI: 10.1108/JOE-03-2024-0011

Behl, A., Dutta, P., Luo, Z., & Sheorey, P. (2022). Enabling artificial intelligence on a donation-based crowdfunding platform: A theoretical approach. *Annals of Operations Research*, *319*(1), 1–29. DOI: 10.1007/s10479-020-03906-z

Belbe, S., Gomez, L., Stanca, L., Wenzlaff, K., Mare, C., Elitzur, R., Bolesta, K., Huang, X., Yilmaz, G. N., & Bernard, F. S. (2024). [*Crowdfunding: A hands-on roadmap to study and understand crowdfunding data using critical thinking AI.*]. *AI*, •••, 4.

Belleflamme, P., Lambert, T., & Schwienbacher, A. (2021). Spillovers in crowdfunding. *Available atSSRN* 3259191.

Ben Romdhane, Y., Kammoun, S., & Loukil, S. (2024). The impact of Fintech on inflation and unemployment: The case of Asia. *Arab Gulf Journal of Scientific Research, 42*(1), 161–181. DOI: 10.1108/AGJSR-08-2022-0146

Berliner, L. S., & Kenworthy, N. J. (2017). Producing a worthy illness: Personal crowdfunding amidst financial crisis. *Social Science & Medicine, 187*, 233–242. DOI: 10.1016/j.socscimed.2017.02.008 PMID: 28274601

Bertsimas, D., & Kallus, N. (2020). From predictive to prescriptive analytics. *Management Science, 66*(3), 1025–1044. DOI: 10.1287/mnsc.2018.3253

Bess, J. L., Johnstone, D. B., & Dee, J. R. (2012). *Understanding college and university organization: Theories for effective policy and practice: Volume II—Dynamics of the system*. Routledge.

Bhat, A. K.Aparna Krishna Bhat. (2024). Application And Impact of Artificial Intelligence in Financial Decision Making. *International Journal of Scientific Research in Science, Engineering and Technology, 11*(5), 57–63. DOI: 10.32628/IJSRSET2411417

Bhatta, N. (2021). Emerging ethical challenges of leadership in the digital era: A multi-vocal literature review. *EJBO. Electronic Journal of Business Ethics and Organization Studies, 26*(1).

Bhatt, G. D. (2001). Knowledge management in organizations: Examining the interaction between technologies, techniques, and people. *Journal of Knowledge Management, 5*(1), 68–75. DOI: 10.1108/13673270110384419

Binns, R. (2018). Fairness in machine learning: Lessons from political philosophy. *Proceedings of the 2018 Conference on Fairness, Accountability and Transparency*, 149–159. DOI: 10.1145/3287560.3287598

Bock, L. (2015). *Work Rules!* Insights from Inside Google That Will Transform How You Live and Lead. Twelve.

Bostrom, N. (2018). *Süper Zekâ, Yapay Zekâ Uygulamaları, Tehlikeler ve Stratejiler [Super Intelligence, Artificial Intelligence Applications, Dangers and Strategies]*. Koç Üniversitesi Yayınları [Koç University Publications].

Brewer, J., Patel, D., Kim, D., & Murray, A. (2024). Navigating the challenges of generative technologies: Proposing the integration of artificial intelligence and blockchain. *Business Horizons, 67*(5), 525–535. DOI: 10.1016/j.bushor.2024.04.011

Brynjolfsson, E., & McAfee, A. (2017). The Business of Artificial Intelligence: The Next Frontier for Competition. Harvard Business Review.

Brynjolfsson, E., & McAfee, A. (2017). *Machine, platform, crowd: Harnessing our digital future*. W. W. Norton & Company.

Bughin, J., Hazan, E., Ramaswamy, S., Chui, M., Allas, T., Dahlström, P., . . . Trench, M. (2017). Artificial Intelligence: The Next Digital Frontier? McKinsey & Company. https://www.mckinsey.com

Bughin, J., Seong, J., Manyika, J., Chui, M., & Joshi, R. (2018). Notes from the AI frontier: Modeling the impact of AI on the world economy. McKinsey Global Institute. https://www.mckinsey.com

Bughin, J., Seong, J., Manyika, J., Chui, M., & Joshi, R. (2019). *Notes from the AI frontier: Modeling the impact of AI on the world economy*. McKinsey Global Institute. Retrieved from https://www.mckinsey.com

Bughin, J., Hazan, E., Ramaswamy, S., Chui, M., Allas, T., Dahlström, P., & Trench, M. (2017). *Artificial Intelligence: The Next Digital Frontier?* McKinsey Global Institute.

Butt, J. (2024). Analytical Study of the World's First EU Artificial Intelligence (AI) Act. *International Journal of Research and Publications*, *5*(3), 7343–7364. DOI: 10.55248/gengpi.5.0324.0914

Büyükgöze, S., & Dereli, E. (2020). Dijital sağlık uygulamalarında yapay zeka [Artificial intelligence in digital health applications]. VI. Uluslararası Bilimsel ve Mesleki Çalışmalar Kongresi-Fen ve Sağlık [6th International Scientific and Professional Studies Congress-Science and Health], 7(10).

Bwalya, A. (2023). Leadership styles. *Global Scientific Journal, 11*(8).

Calp, M. H., & Doğan, A. (2019). Insan Kaynaklari Yönetiminde Dijital Dönüşüm [Digital Transformation in Human Resources Management].

Calvard, T. S. (2016). Big data, organizational learning, and sensemaking: Theorizing interpretive challenges under conditions of dynamic complexity. *Management Learning*, *47*(1), 65–82. DOI: 10.1177/1350507615592113

Camisón-Zornoza, C., Forés-Julián, B., Puig-Denia, A., & Camisón-Haba, S. (2020). Effects of ownership structure and corporate and family governance on dynamic capabilities in family firms. *The International Entrepreneurship and Management Journal*, *16*(4), 1393–1426. DOI: 10.1007/s11365-020-00675-w

Cao, X., Ali, A., Pitafi, A. H., Khan, A. N., & Waqas, M. (2021). A socio-technical system approach to knowledge creation and team performance: Evidence from China. *Information Technology & People, 34*(7), 1976–1996. DOI: 10.1108/ITP-10-2019-0536

Carroll, A. B., & Shabana, K. M. (2010). The business case for corporate social responsibility: A review of concepts, research and practice. *International Journal of Management Reviews, 12*(1), 85–105. DOI: 10.1111/j.1468-2370.2009.00275.x

Carter, C. R., & Rogers, D. S. (2008). A framework of sustainable supply chain management: Moving toward new theory. *International Journal of Physical Distribution & Logistics Management, 38*(5), 360–387. DOI: 10.1108/09600030810882816

Castelnovo, A. (2024). *Towards Responsible AI in Banking: Addressing Bias for Fair Decision-Making*. https://arxiv.org/abs/2401.08691v1

Cavaliere, L. P. L., Khan, R., Sundram, S., Jainani, K., Bagale, G., Chakravarthi, M. K., Regin, R., & Rajest, S. S. (2021). The Impact of customer relationship management on customer satisfaction and retention: The mediation of service quality. *Turkish Journal of Physiotherapy and Rehabilitation, 32*(3), 22107–22121.

Cazzaniga, M., Jaumotte, M. F., Li, L., Melina, M. G., Panton, A. J., Pizzinelli, C., Rockall, E. J., & Tavares, M. M. M. (2024). *Gen-ai: Artificial intelligence and the future of work*. International Monetary Fund. DOI: 10.5089/9798400262548.006

Çelen, A. İ. (2020). Dijital Dönüşüm Sürecinde Yükselen Bir Değer: Dijital Liderlik [A Rising Value in the Digital Transformation Process: Digital Leadership]. *Proceedings E-Book*, 449-461.

Chatman, J. A., & Cha, S. E. (2003). Leading by leveraging culture. *California Management Review, 45*(4), 20–34. DOI: 10.2307/41166186

Chatterjee, S., Rana, N. P., Tamilmani, K., & Sharma, A. (2021). The future of AI and customer engagement: A study of predictive customer behavior using machine learning. *Journal of Business Research, 124*, 353–365. DOI: 10.1016/j.jbusres.2020.11.048

Chen, H., Chiang, R. H. L., & Storey, V. C. (2012). Business Intelligence and Analytics: From Big Data to Big Impact. *Management Information Systems Quarterly, 36*(4), 1165–1188. DOI: 10.2307/41703503

Chen, K. Q., & He, Y. ve Zhong, G. Q. (2018). The Information Literacy Connotation Transformation and the Orientation of AI Education in the Perspective of Artificial Intelligence: Also on the Al Curriculum and Teaching Implementation Path in the Basic Education Stage. *Journal of Distance Education, 36*, 61–71.

Chen, N., Liu, W., Bai, R., & Chen, A. (2019). Application of computational intelligence technologies in emergency management: A literature review. *Artificial Intelligence Review*, *52*(3), 2131–2168. DOI: 10.1007/s10462-017-9589-8

Cheong, B. C. (2024). Transparency and accountability in AI systems: Safeguarding wellbeing in the age of algorithmic decision-making. *Frontiers in Human Dynamics*, *6*, 1421273. DOI: 10.3389/fhumd.2024.1421273

Chin, T., Ghouri, M. W. A., Jin, J., & Deveci, M. (2024). AI technologies affording the orchestration of ecosystem-based business models: The moderating role of AI knowledge spillover. *Humanities & Social Sciences Communications*, *11*(1), 1–13. DOI: 10.1057/s41599-024-03003-7

Chokshi, N. (2022, November 25). How Amazon's logistics empire is preparing for Black Friday. The New York Times. https://www.nytimes.com/2022/11/25/business/amazon-black-friday.html

Chowdhury, A., Kabir, K. H., McQuire, M., & Bureau, D. P. (2025). The dynamics of digital technology adoption in rainbow trout aquaculture: Exploring multi-stakeholder perceptions in Ontario using Q methodology and the theory of planned behaviour. *Aquaculture (Amsterdam, Netherlands)*, *594*, 741460. DOI: 10.1016/j.aquaculture.2024.741460

Chowdhury, S., Budhwar, P., Dey, P. K., Joel-Edgar, S., & Abadie, A. (2022). AI-employee collaboration and business performance: Integrating knowledge-based view, socio-technical systems and organisational socialisation framework. *Journal of Business Research*, *144*, 31–49. DOI: 10.1016/j.jbusres.2022.01.069

Chui, M., & Francisco, S. (2017). Artificial intelligence the next digital frontier. *McKinsey and Company Global Institute, 47*(3.6), 6-8.

Chui, M., Harryson, M., Manyika, J., Roberts, R., Chung, R., van Heteren, A., & Nel, P. (2018). Applying artificial intelligence for social good. McKinsey & Company. https://www.mckinsey.com

Chui, M., & Malhotra, S. (2018). *AI adoption advances, but foundational barriers remain*. McKinsey & Company.

Chukwuemeke, H. E., & Igbinedion, V. (2021). Relationship between knowledge dissemination, learning self-efficacy and task performance of business educators. *Nau Journal Of Technology and Vocational Education*, *6*(1), 13–21.

Ciulla, J. B., & Ciulla, J. B. (2020). The importance of leadership in shaping business values. *The search for ethics in leadership, business, and beyond*, 153-163.

Clayton, P. R., & Clopton, J. (2019). Business curriculum redesign: Integrating data analytics. *Journal of Education for Business, 94*(1), 57–63. DOI: 10.1080/08832323.2018.1502142

Cohen, W. M., & Levinthal, D. A. (1990). Absorptive Capacity: A New Perspective on Learning and Innovation. *Administrative Science Quarterly, 35*(1), 128. DOI: 10.2307/2393553

Copeland, B. J. (2019). "Artificial Intelligence". https://www.britannica.com/technology/artificial-intelligence. 21.03.2023.

Cordova, A., Dolci, J., & Gianfrate, G. (2015). The determinants of crowdfunding success: Evidence from technology projects. *Procedia: Social and Behavioral Sciences, 181*, 115–124. DOI: 10.1016/j.sbspro.2015.04.872

Cortes, A. F., & Herrmann, P. (2021). Strategic leadership of innovation: A framework for future research. *International Journal of Management Reviews, 23*(2), 224–243. DOI: 10.1111/ijmr.12246

Coughlin, R. (2022). Designing Ethical AI Systems for the Future of Business. In Ethical, A. I. (Ed.), *Principles and Practice*. Springer.

Cox, A. M., Pinfield, S., & Rutter, S. (2019). The intelligent library: Thought leaders' views on the likely impact of artificial intelligence on academic libraries. *Library Hi Tech, 37*(3), 418–435.

Cristofaro, M., Giardino, P. L., & Barboni, L. (2025). Growth hacking: A scientific approach for data-driven decision making. *Journal of Business Research, 186*, 115030. Advance online publication. DOI: 10.1016/j.jbusres.2024.115030

Cukurova, M., Kent, C., & Luckin, R. (2019). Artificial intelligence and multimodal data in the service of human decision-making: A case study in debate tutoring. *British Journal of Educational Technology, 50*(6), 3032–3046. DOI: 10.1111/bjet.12829

Curseu, P. L., & Schruijer, S. G. (2024). Leading without position power: Preliminary validation of the multiparty collaborative leadership scale (MCLS). *International Journal of Conflict Management, 35*(2), 411–426. DOI: 10.1108/IJCMA-01-2023-0014

Dahiyat, S. E., Khasawneh, S. M., Bontis, N., & Al-Dahiyat, M. (2023). Intellectual capital stocks and flows: Examining the mediating roles of social capital and knowledge transfer. *VINE Journal of Information and Knowledge Management Systems, 53*(1), 11–42. DOI: 10.1108/VJIKMS-06-2020-0110

Daouk, A. (2025). Navigating the Digital Transformation Landscape: Education, Opportunities, and Challenges for Entrepreneurs. *Entrepreneurship-Digital Transformation, Education, Opportunities and Challenges: Digital Transformation, Education, Opportunities and Challenges*, 113.

Dash, R., McMurtrey, M., Rebman, C., & Kar, U. K. (2019). Application of artificial intelligence in automation of supply chain management. *Journal of Strategic Innovation and Sustainability*, *14*(3), 43–53.

Dastin, J. (2021, June 13). Amazon unveils warehouse robots to reduce workplace injuries. Reuters. https://www.reuters.com/technology/amazon-unveils-warehouse-robots-reduce-workplace-injuries-2021-06-13/

Daugherty, P., & Wilson, H. J. (2018). *Human + Machine: Reimagining Work in the Age of AI*. Harvard Business Review Press.

Davenport, T. H., & Ronanki, R. (2018). Artificial intelligence for the real world. *Harvard Business Review*, *96*(1), 108–116.

Davies, R. (2024). Guided choices: The ethics of using algorithmic systems to shape philanthropic decision-making. In *The Routledge Handbook of Artificial Intelligence and Philanthropy* (pp. 451–470). Routledge. DOI: 10.4324/9781003468615-32

De Cremer, D., & Kasparov, G. (2021). AI should augment human intelligence, not replace it. *Harvard Business Review*, *18*(1).

de Laat, P. B. (2018). Algorithmic Decision-Making Based on Machine Learning from Big Data: Can Transparency Restore Accountability? *Philosophy & Technology*, *31*(4), 525–541. DOI: 10.1007/s13347-017-0293-z PMID: 30873341

De Luca, P., & Cano Rubio, M. (2019). The curve of knowledge transfer: A theoretical model. *Business Process Management Journal*, *25*(1), 10–26. DOI: 10.1108/BPMJ-06-2017-0161

de Vasconcelos Gomes, L. A., Chaparro, X. A. F., Maniçoba, R. F., Borini, F. M., & Silva, L. E. (2025). Transformation of the governance of failure for radical innovation: The role of strategic leaders. *Research Policy*, *54*(1), 105108. DOI: 10.1016/j.respol.2024.105108

Deloitte. (2015). "Global Power of Retailing 2015: Embracing Innovation",https://www2.deloitte.com/content/dam/Deloitte/global/Documents/Consumer-Business/gx-cb-global-powers-of-retailing. pdf

Deloitte. (2020). Artificial Intelligence Innovation Report. https://www2.deloitte.com/content/dam/Deloitte/de/Documents/Innovation/Artificial-Intelligence-Innovation-Report-2018-Deloitte.pdf

Deloitte. (2023). State of AI in the Enterprise – 5th Edition. https://www.deloitte.comUse Case Examples & Business Practices

Demir, A., Budur, T., Omer, H. M., & Heshmati, A. (2023). Links between knowledge management and organisational sustainability: Does the ISO 9001 certification have an effect? *Knowledge Management Research and Practice*, *21*(1), 183–196. DOI: 10.1080/14778238.2020.1860663

Den Hartog, D. N. (2023). Transformational leadership. In *Encyclopedia of business and professional ethics* (pp. 1776–1780). Springer. DOI: 10.1007/978-3-030-22767-8_57

Deng, H., Duan, S. X., & Wibowo, S. (2023). Digital technology driven knowledge sharing for job performance. *Journal of Knowledge Management*, *27*(2), 404–425. DOI: 10.1108/JKM-08-2021-0637

Deng, L., Ye, Q., Xu, D., Sun, W., & Jiang, G. (2022). A literature review and integrated framework for the determinants of crowdfunding success. *Financial Innovation*, *8*(1), 41. DOI: 10.1186/s40854-022-00345-6

Deng, L., & Yu, D. (2014). Deep Learning: Methods and Applications. *Foundations and Trends in Signal Processing*, *7*(3–4), 197–387. DOI: 10.1561/2000000039

DFIN. (2024). AI in Financial Reporting. Retrieved November 10, 2024, from https://www.dfinsolutions.com/knowledge-hub/thought-leadership/knowledge-resources/ai-in-financial-reporting

Dhamija, P., Bag, S., & Debnath, R. M. (2021). Artificial intelligence (AI)-based digital transformation and dynamic capabilities: Mediating role of organizational agility. *Technological Forecasting and Social Change*, *166*, 120636. DOI: 10.1016/j.techfore.2021.120636

Díaz-Rodríguez, N., López-Pernas, S., & Hernández-Leo, D. (2023). Responsible AI: Ethical principles and guidelines. *AI & Society*, *38*(1), 12–28. DOI: 10.1007/s00146-023-01586-5

Dierickx, I., & Cool, K. (1989). Asset stock accumulation and sustainability of competitive advantage. *Management Science*, *35*(12), 1504–1511.

Dolles, H., & Santomier, J. (2025). Transformational digital leadership and organizational strategy: the case of the US National Basketball Association. In *Digital Leadership* (pp. 78-91). Edward Elgar Publishing. Ebepu, O. O., Okpeseyi, S. B. A., John-Ogbe, J., & Emmanuel, E. Harnessing Data-Driven Strategies For Sustained United States Business Growth: A Comparative Analysis Of Market Leaders. DOI: 10.4337/9781035321247.00012

Dorfleitner, G., Hornuf, L., Schmitt, M., Weber, M., Dorfleitner, G., Hornuf, L., Schmitt, M., & Weber, M. (2017). *The fintech market in Germany*. Springer. DOI: 10.1007/978-3-319-54666-7

Du Plessis, M. (2007). The role of knowledge management in innovation. *Journal of Knowledge Management*, *11*(4), 20–29. DOI: 10.1108/13673270710762684

Du, H.-S., Ma, J.-J., & Li, M. (2016). High-quality health information provision for stroke patients. *Chinese Medical Journal*, *129*(17), 2115–2122. DOI: 10.4103/0366-6999.189065 PMID: 27569241

Durojaiye, A. T., Ewim, C. P.-M., & Igwe, A. N. (2024). *Developing a crowdfunding optimization model to bridge the financing gap for small business enterprises through data-driven strategies.*

Eboigbe, E. O., Farayola, O. A., Olatoye, F. O., Nnabugwu, O. C., & Daraojimba, C. (2023). Business intelligence transformation through AI and data analytics. *Engineering Science & Technology Journal*, *4*(5), 285–307. DOI: 10.51594/estj.v4i5.616

Efrat, K., Gilboa, S., & Wald, A. (2021). The emergence of well-being in crowdfunding: A study of entrepreneurs and backers of reward and donation campaigns. *International Journal of Entrepreneurial Behaviour & Research*, *27*(2), 397–415. DOI: 10.1108/IJEBR-12-2019-0685

ElBaih, M. (2023). The role of privacy regulations in ai development (A Discussion of the Ways in Which Privacy Regulations Can Shape the Development of AI). *Available atSSRN* 4589207. DOI: 10.2139/ssrn.4589207

Ellinger, A. D., & Ellinger, A. E. (2021). Providing strategic leadership for learning: Optimizing managerial coaching to build learning organizations. *The Learning Organization*, *28*(4), 337–351. DOI: 10.1108/TLO-05-2020-0070

Enebeli, J. P. (2024). Information And Communication Technology (Ict), Globalization And Inpeneding Challenges. *Global Journal of Pure and Applied Sciences*, *30*(1), 95–100. DOI: 10.4314/gjpas.v30i1.9

Ennajeh, L., Najjar, T., & Aloui, A. (2025). Digital Transformation through Artificial Intelligence in Organizations: A Systematic Literature Review. *Journal of Information Technology Management, 17*(Special Issue on Strategic, Organizational, and Social Issues of Digital Transformation in Organizations), 53-78.

Erdoğan, G. (2021). Yapay Zekâ ve Hukukuna Genel Bir Bakış [An Overview of Artificial Intelligence and Its Law]. *Adalet Dergisi [Justice Magazine]*, (66), 117–192.

Eşitti, Ş. (2020). *Sosyal Medya ve Yapay Zekâ* [Social Media and Artificial Intelligence]. Artificial Intelligence Transforms Disciplines–Are We Ready for Change.

European Commission. (2018). DigComp into action: Get inspired, make it happen. JRC Science For Policy Report, EUR 29115 EN, Publications Office of the European Union, Luxembourg. http://publications.jrc.ec.euro-pa.eu/repository/bitstream/JRC110624/deguidemay18.pdf

European Commission. (2020). *Ethics guidelines for trustworthy AI.* High-Level Expert Group on AI. https://digital-strategy.ec.europa.eu/en/library/ethics-guidelines-trustworthy-ai

European Parliament. (2024), Artificial Intelligence Act: MEPs adopt landmark law. (website). https://www.europarl.europa.eu/news/en/press-room/20240308IPR19015/artificial-intelligence-act-meps-adoptlandmark-law Accessed 7 October 2024.

Explainers, M. (2022). What is leadership? In: August.

Fabrègue, B. F. G., & Bogoni, A. (2023). Privacy and Security Concerns in the Smart City. *Smart Cities 2023, Vol. 6, Pages 586-613, 6*(1), 586–613. DOI: 10.3390/smartcities6010027

Fanea-Ivanovici, M. (2018). Transparency of financial information on crowdfunding platforms–a prerequisite for successful funding campaigns. *International Conference Knowledge-Based Organization, 24*(2), 37–42. DOI: 10.1515/kbo-2018-0063

Fannin, R. (2021, November 11). *How Alibaba redefined Singles' Day—and what it means for global e-commerce. Forbes.* https://www.forbes.com/sites/rebeccafannin/2021/11/11/how-alibaba-redefined-singles-day-and-what-it-means-for-global-e-commerce/

Farahani, M. S., & Esfahani, A. (2022). Opportunities and challenges of applying artificial intelligence in the financial sectors and startups during the coronavirus outbreak. International Journal of Innovation in Management. *Economics and Social Sciences*, *2*(4), 33–55.

Feng, S. C., Bernstein, W. Z., Hedberg, T.Jr, & Barnard Feeney, A. (2017). Toward knowledge management for smart manufacturing. *Journal of Computing and Information Science in Engineering*, *17*(3), 031016. DOI: 10.1115/1.4037178 PMID: 28966561

Fenwick, M., Vermeulen, E. P. M., & Compagnucci, M. C. (2024). Business and regulatory responses to artificial intelligence: Dynamic regulation, innovation ecosystems an d the strategic management of disruptive technology. *arXiv preprint arXiv:2407.19439*. Retrieved from https://arxiv.org/abs/2407.19439

Fiksel, J., & Fiksel, J. R. (2015). *Resilient by design: Creating businesses that adapt and flourish in a changing world*. Island Press. DOI: 10.5822/978-1-61091-588-5

Fleming, P. (2019). Robots and organization studies: Why robots might not want to steal your job. *Organization Studies*, *40*(1), 23–38. DOI: 10.1177/0170840618765568

Floridi, L., & Cowls, J. (2019). A unified framework of five principles for AI in society. *Harvard Data Science Review*, *1*(1). Advance online publication. DOI: 10.1162/99608f92.8cd550d1

Forbes Finance Council. (2024). *The Impact of Artificial Intelligence on Financial Decision Making*. Retrieved March 22, 2025, from https://councils.forbes.com/blog/artificial-intelligence-and-financial-decision-making

Frank, A. G., Dalenogare, L. S., & Ayala, N. F. (2019). Industry 4.0 technologies: Implementation patterns in manufacturing companies. *International Journal of Production Economics*, *210*, 15–26. DOI: 10.1016/j.ijpe.2019.01.004

Fransisca, L., Renaldo, N., Chandra, T., Augustine, Y., & Musa, S. (2025). Digital Innovation Capability and Customer Value Co-Creation on New Product Performance with Digital Transformation Maturity as a Moderating Variable in Trading Companies in Indonesia. *Luxury: Landscape of Business Administration*, *3*(1), 1–15.

Gabriel, O. D., De Alwi, C. D. T. V., Jayang, E. A., & Wai, S. L. C. (2022). The impact of transformational leadership on generation Z employee retention and innovative behaviour: A case of Malaysian hotel industry. *International Journal of Multicultural and Multireligious Understanding*, *9*(4), 35–53.

Ganesha, K., & Hemalatha, K. (2025). Digital Transformation in Advertising after COVID-19: Routing the New Landscape. In *Handbook of Digital Innovation, Transformation, and Sustainable Development in a Post-Pandemic Era* (pp. 384–406). CRC Press.

García, J., Amescua, A., Sánchez, M.-I., & Bermón, L. (2011). Design guidelines for software processes knowledge repository development. *Information and Software Technology*, *53*(8), 834–850. DOI: 10.1016/j.infsof.2011.03.002

Gartner. (2023). Top Strategic Technology Trends for 2024. https://www.gartner.com

Gashaw Kettema, W., Tefera Ayele, Z., Assefaw Geremew, M., Temesgen Assefa, K., Ayalew Yimer, S., Dessie Liyew, A., Berihun Erega, B., & Habtie Dagnaw, E. (2023). Knowledge, Utilization, and Associated Factors of Nonpneumatic Antishock Garments for Management of Postpartum Hemorrhage among Maternity Ward Health Care Professionals in South Wollo Zone Health Facilities, Ethiopia, 2021: A Cross-Sectional Study Design. *Obstetrics and Gynecology International*, *2023*, 2023. DOI: 10.1155/2023/8247603 PMID: 36691431

Geier, M. T. (2023). Strategic thinking: Theoretical development and assessment. *Journal of Strategy and Management*.

Gigante, G., & Cozzio, G. (2021). Equity crowdfunding: An empirical investigation of success factors in real estate crowdfunding. *Journal of Property Investment & Finance*, *40*(6), 532–547. DOI: 10.1108/JPIF-06-2021-0055

Gil, D., Hobson, S., Mojsilović, A., Puri, R., & Smith, J R. (2019, September 22). AI for Management: An Overview. Springer Nature, 3-19. DOI: 10.1007/978-3-030-20680-2_1

Gill, A., & Mathur, A. (2024). Emotional Intelligence in the Age of AI: Enhancing Workforce Development for Human-Machine Collaboration. In *Sustainable Innovation for Industry 6.0* (pp. 263-285). IGI Global.

Gillani, S. A., Alvi, A. R., Ahmad, H., Gillani, S. A., & Tanveer, Y. (2025). FinTech Adoption for SMEs: Innovation and Opportunities Worldwide. In *Algorithmic Training, Future Markets, and Big Data for Finance Digitalization* (pp. 105–120). IGI Global Scientific Publishing.

Giuggioli, G., Pellegrini, M. M., & Giannone, G. (2024). Artificial intelligence as an enabler for entrepreneurial finance: A practical guide to AI-driven video pitch evaluation for entrepreneurs and investors. *Management Decision*. Advance online publication. DOI: 10.1108/MD-10-2023-1926

Gkintoni, E., Halkiopoulos, C., & Antonopoulou, H. (2022). Neuroleadership an asset in educational settings: An overview. *Emerging Science Journal.Emerging Science Journal*, *6*(4), 893–904. DOI: 10.28991/ESJ-2022-06-04-016

Gleasure, R. (2023). Contrasting the response to past and future oriented appeals for help on donation-based crowdfunding platforms. *European Journal of Information Systems*, •••, 1–22.

Gleasure, R., & Feller, J. (2016). Does heart or head rule donor behaviors in charitable crowdfunding markets? *International Journal of Electronic Commerce*, *20*(4), 499–524. DOI: 10.1080/10864415.2016.1171975

Gobble, M. (2018). Dijitalleşme, Dijitalleşme ve Yenilik [Digitalization, Digitalization and Innovation]. *Araştırma-Teknoloji Yönetimi [Research-Technology Management]*, *61*(4), 56–59.

Gökşin, E. (2017). *Dijital Pazarlama Temelleri [Digital Marketing Fundamentals]*. Abaküs Yayınları [Abacus Publications].

Gong, Q., Fan, D., & Bartram, T. (2024). Algorithmic human resource management: Toward a functional affordance perspective. *Personnel Review*. Advance online publication. DOI: 10.1108/PR-01-2024-0099

Gono, T., & April, K. (2022). Adaptive Leadership During Covid-19 Pandemic. *Effective Executive*, *25*(2), 46–79.

Google Cloud. (2021). Edge AI and IoT: Transforming Industry. https://cloud.google.com/blogs, Books & Book Chapters

Gopal Snacks Pvt. Ltd. (n.d.). Infrastructure. https://gspl.7technosoftsolutions.com/infrastructure

Goralski, M. A., & Tan, T. K. (2020). Artificial intelligence and sustainable development. *International Journal of Management Education*, *18*(1), 100330. DOI: 10.1016/j.ijme.2019.100330

Görener, A., & Toker, K. (2020). Yapay zekâda evrimsel algoritmalar: Lojistik sektöründe bir genetik algoritma uygulaması [Evolutionary algorithms in artificial intelligence: A genetic algorithm application in the logistics sector]. Oyun Değiştiren Güç Yapay Zekâ [Game-Changing Power: Artificial Intelligence], (Editörler: Mustafa K. Yılmaz, N. Öykü İyigün), Beta Basım Yayım Dağıtım, 1-40.

Grant, R. M., & Baden-Fuller, C. (2018). How to develop strategic management competency: Reconsidering the learning goals and knowledge requirements of the core strategy course. *Academy of Management Learning & Education*, *17*(3), 322–338. DOI: 10.5465/amle.2017.0126

Gray, M., & Zhang, B. (2017). Crowdfunding: understanding diversity. In *Handbook on the Geographies of Money and Finance* (pp. 580–609). Edward Elgar Publishing. DOI: 10.4337/9781784719005.00034

Green, B. (2022). The flaws of policies requiring human oversight of government algorithms. *Computer Law & Security Review, 45*, 105681. DOI: 10.1016/j.clsr.2022.105681

Grover, P., Kar, A. K., & Dwivedi, Y. K. (2022). Understanding artificial intelligence adoption in operations management: Insights from the review of academic literature and social media discussions. *Annals of Operations Research, 308*(1), 177–213. DOI: 10.1007/s10479-020-03683-9

Grover, V., Chiang, R. H. L., Liang, T. P., & Zhang, D. (2018). Creating Strategic Business Value from Big Data Analytics: A Research Framework. *Journal of Management Information Systems, 35*(2), 388–423. DOI: 10.1080/07421222.2018.1451951

Guide, V. D. R.Jr, & Vanwassenhove, L. N. (2001). Managing product returns for remanufacturing. *Production and Operations Management, 10*(2), 142–155. DOI: 10.1111/j.1937-5956.2001.tb00075.x

Gülşen, İ. (2019). İşletmelerde Yapay Zeka Uygulamaları ve Faydaları: Perakende Sektöründe Bir Derleme [Applications and Benefits of Artificial Intelligence in Business: A Compilation in the Retail Industry]. *Tüketici ve Tüketim Araştırmaları Dergisi [Journal of Consumer and Consumption Research], 11*(2), 407–436.

Gupta, S., & Jaiswal, R. (2025). A deep learning-based hybrid PLS-SEM-ANN approach for predicting factors improving AI-driven decision-making proficiency for future leaders. *Journal of International Education in Business.*

Güvener, A. (2019). *Dijital dönüşüm sürecinde çalışanların teknolojik hazıroluş seviyelerinin belirlenmesi. Yüksek Lisans Tezi [Determining the technological readiness levels of employees in the digital transformation process. Master's Thesis].* Bahçeşehir Üniversitesi SBE.

Haddad, C., & Hornuf, L. (2023). How do fintech start-ups affect financial institutions' performance and default risk? *European Journal of Finance, 29*(15), 1761–1792. DOI: 10.1080/1351847X.2022.2151371

Haenlein, M., & Kaplan, A. (2019). A brief history of artificial intelligence:on the past, present, and future of artificial intelligence. *California Management Review, 61*(4), 5–14. DOI: 10.1177/0008125619864925

Haenlein, M., Kaplan, A., Tan, C. W., & Zhang, P. (2023). Artificial Intelligence in Business: Myths, Ethics, and Reality. *Business Horizons*, *66*(1), 85–96. DOI: 10.1016/j.bushor.2022.07.003

Haleem, A., Javaid, M., & Singh, R. P. (2024). Perspective of leadership 4.0 in the era of fourth industrial revolution: A comprehensive view. *Journal of Industrial Safety*, 100006.

Hallin, A., Andersson, C., Crevani, L., Ingvarsson, C., Ivory, C., Lammi, I., Lindell, E., & Uhlin, A. (2025). Creating the Future of Work: Imaginaries in an Era of Digitalization. In *Creating the Future of Work*. Edward Elgar Publishing. DOI: 10.4337/9781035324484

Han, F. Ö., & Sarı, E. B. (2021). Enerji Sektörünün Dijital Dönüşüm Projeleri-ni Yürüten Araştırmacıların Dijital Yeterliliklerine Yönelik İçerik Analizi [Content Analysis of Digital Competencies of Researchers Carrying Out Digital Transformation Projects in the Energy Sector]. *Scientific Journal of Innovation and Socia Sciences Research*, *1*(1), 1–25.

Hashem, G., Aboelmaged, M., & Ahmad, I. (2024). Proactiveness, knowledge management capability and innovation ambidexterity: An empirical examination of digital supply chain adoption. *Management Decision*, *62*(1), 129–162. DOI: 10.1108/MD-02-2023-0237

Hassija, V., Chamola, V., Mahapatra, A., Singal, A., Goel, D., Huang, K., Scardapane, S., Spinelli, I., Mahmud, M., & Hussain, A. (2024). Interpreting black-box models: A review on explainable artificial intelligence. *Cognitive Computation*, *16*(1), 45–74. DOI: 10.1007/s12559-023-10179-8

Hassija, V., Chamola, V., & Zeadally, S. (2020). BitFund: A blockchain-based crowd funding platform for future smart and connected nation. *Sustainable Cities and Society*, *60*, 102145. DOI: 10.1016/j.scs.2020.102145

Hawkins, A. J. (2021, October 20). *Tesla's Full Self-Driving beta is here, and it's terrifying. The Verge*. https://www.theverge.com/2021/10/20/22735673/tesla-full-self-driving-beta-safety-issues

Heikkinen, T. H. (2019) "How Does the Use of Artificial Intelligence Affect the Concept of Fair Trial?", Faculty Of Law Lund University, Master Thesis-International Human Rights Law, Lund, https://lup.lub. lu.se/ student- papers/search/publication/8980709 (03.04.2023).

Herath, S. K., & White, S. L. (2025). Digital Transformation and the Future of Accounting: A Comparative Analysis of Asia, Europe, and the Gulf Region. In *Insights Into Digital Business, Human Resource Management, and Competitiveness* (pp. 1-34). IGI Global Scientific Publishing.

Heyn, H. M., Mohr, D., Neugebauer, R., Schumacher, A., & Weking, J. (2021). AI readiness in manufacturing—Toward a maturity model. *Procedia CIRP*, *104*, 1256–1261. DOI: 10.1016/j.procir.2021.11.211

Hiniduma, T. A., Nguyen, T. H., & Dhinakaran, A. (2024). A strategic framework for evaluating AI readiness in SMEs. *Journal of Business Research*, *172*, 114016. DOI: 10.1016/j.jbusres.2023.114016

Holbeche, L. (2023). *The agile organization: how to build an engaged, innovative and resilient business.* Kogan Page Publishers.

Hoque, M. M. (2024). Crowdfunding for innovation: A comprehensive empirical review. *Future Business Journal*, *10*(1), 102. DOI: 10.1186/s43093-024-00387-5

Hornuf, L., & Schwienbacher, A. (2017). Should securities regulation promote equity crowdfunding? *Small Business Economics*, *49*(3), 579–593. DOI: 10.1007/s11187-017-9839-9

Hossain, M. K., Sutanto, J., Handayani, P. W., Haryanto, A. A., Bhowmik, J., & Frings-Hessami, V. (2025). An exploratory study of electronic medical record implementation and recordkeeping culture: The case of hospitals in Indonesia. *BMC Health Services Research*, *25*(1), 1–20. DOI: 10.1186/s12913-025-12399-0 PMID: 39953485

Howard, A., Zhang, C., & Horvitz, E. (2017). Addressing bias in machine learning algorithms: A pilot study on emotion recognition for intelligent systems. *Proceedings of IEEE Workshop on Advanced Robotics and Its Social Impacts, ARSO*. DOI: 10.1109/ARSO.2017.8025197

Huang, A. H., & You, H. (2023). Artificial intelligence in financial decision-making. *Handbook of Financial Decision Making*, 315–335. DOI: 10.4337/9781802204179.00029

Huang, M.-H., & Rust, R. T. (2018). Artificial intelligence in service. *Journal of Service Research*, *21*(2), 155–172. DOI: 10.1177/1094670517752459

Hua, X., Huang, Y., & Zheng, Y. (2019). Current practices, new insights, and emerging trends of financial technologies. *Industrial Management & Data Systems*, *119*(7), 1401–1410. DOI: 10.1108/IMDS-08-2019-0431

Hui, X., Reshef, O., & Zhou, L. (2024). The Short-Term Effects of Generative Artificial Intelligence on Employment: Evidence from an Online Labor Market. *Organization Science*, *35*(6), 1977–1989. DOI: 10.1287/orsc.2023.18441

Hu, L., Zhou, J., Zhang, J. Z., & Behl, A. (2024). Blockchain technology adaptation and organizational inertia: Moderating role between knowledge management processes and supply chain resilience. *Kybernetes*, *53*(2), 515–542. DOI: 10.1108/K-12-2022-1661

Hussain, N., Di Pietro, F., & Rosati, P. (2023). Crowdfunding for Social Entrepreneurship: A systematic review of the literature. *Journal of Social Entrepreneurship*, •••, 1–24. DOI: 10.1080/19420676.2023.2236637

Hussain, Z., Jusoh, A., Jamil, K., Rehman, A. U., & Gul, R. F. (2022). Analyzing the role of knowledge management process to enhance sustainable corporate performance: A mediation moderation model. *Knowledge and Process Management*, *29*(3), 205–220. DOI: 10.1002/kpm.1679

Hussein, H., Albadry, O. M., Mathew, V., Al-Romeedy, B. S., Alsetoohy, O., Abou Kamar, M., & Khairy, H. A. (2024). Digital leadership and sustainable competitive advantage: Leveraging green absorptive capability and eco-innovation in tourism and hospitality businesses. *Sustainability (Basel)*, *16*(13), 5371. DOI: 10.3390/su16135371

Iansiti, M., & Lakhani, K. R. (2020). *Competing in the Age of AI: Strategy and Leadership When Algorithms and Networks Run the World*. Harvard Business Review Press.

IBM. (2021). What is blockchain and artificial intelligence (AI)? IBM. Retrieved November 10, 2024, from https://www.ibm.com/topics/blockchain-ai

IBM. (2022). AI and Ethics in Business: A Responsible Approach. https://www.ibm.com/research

Imran, M. K., Ilyas, M., Aslam, U., & Fatima, T. (2018). Knowledge processes and firm performance: The mediating effect of employee creativity. *Journal of Organizational Change Management*, *31*(3), 512–531. DOI: 10.1108/JOCM-10-2016-0202

Iqbal, S., Ullah, S., Rizwan, A., Nazeer, N., Rasheed, M., & Siddiqi, A. F. I. (2025). Building competitive advantage: how organizational culture shapes absorptive capacity through knowledge sharing. *Journal of Organizational Effectiveness: People and Performance*.

Irnawati, J. E., & Prasetyo, J. H. (2020). The Influence Over the Transformational of Leadership Style, the Organizational Culture, and Employee Empowerment towards Achievement of Organizational Strategies in one the Central Government Organization. *International Journal of Innovative Science and Research Technology*, *5*(3), 917–927.

Islam, M. T., Mission, M. R., Refat, T. K., & Kynatun, M. (2025). Cybersecurity risk assessment frameworks for engineering databases: A systematic literature review. *Strategic Data Management and Innovation*, *2*(01), 224–243.

Islam, S., & Amin, S. H. (2020). Prediction of probable backorder scenarios in the supply chain using Distributed Random Forest and Gradient Boosting Machine learning techniques. *Journal of Big Data*, *7*(1), 1–22. DOI: 10.1186/s40537-020-00345-2

Ismail, A., Hidajat, T., Dora, Y. M., Prasatia, F. E., & Pranadani, A. (2023). *Leading the digital transformation: Evidence from Indonesia*. Asadel Publisher.

Ismail, M., Mustafa, Ö., Slađana, Đ., & Stefan, J. (2019). Influence of financial technology (fintech) on financial industry. *Agricultural Economics*, *04*, 1003–1021.

Itoe Mote, N. J., & Karadas, G. (2022). The impact of automation and knowledge workers on employees' outcomes: Mediating role of knowledge transfer. *Sustainability (Basel)*, *14*(3), 1377. DOI: 10.3390/su14031377

Iyelolu, T. V., Agu, E. E., Idemudia, C., & Ijomah, T. I. (2024). Improving Customer Engagement and CRM for SMEs with AI Driven Solutions and Future Enhancements. *International Journal of Engineering Research and Development*, *20*(8).

Jamil, K., Anwar, A., & Baig, S. A. (2025). Building Brand Authenticity and Strategies for Genuine Destination Experiences. In Destination Branding and Bias in Ecotourism (pp. 75-104). IGI Global Scientific Publishing.

Jamil, K., Anwar, A., & Mohsin, M. (2025). Crafting Digital Destinations via Effective Social Media Strategies for Hospitality Industry. In Marketing Technology-Infused Hospitality: Upskilling Frontline Employees for Competitiveness (pp. 205-230). IGI Global Scientific Publishing. DOI: 10.4018/979-8-3693-7127-5.ch008

Jariwala, M. (2025). Artificial Intelligence and Blockchain and the Growth of the FinTech Industry. In *Driving Socio-Economic Growth With AI and Blockchain* (pp. 113–146). IGI Global Scientific Publishing. DOI: 10.4018/979-8-3693-8664-4.ch006

Jarrahi, M. H. (2018). Artificial intelligence and the future of work: Human-AI symbiosis in organizational decision making. *Business Horizons*, *61*(4), 577–586. DOI: 10.1016/j.bushor.2018.03.007

Jasim, T. A., Khairy, H. A., Fayyad, S., & Al-Romeedy, B. S. (2024). Digital leadership and creative performance in tourism and hotel enterprises: Leveraging strategic agility and organizational learning culture. *Geo Journal of Tourism and Geosites*, *54*(2 supplement), 872–884. DOI: 10.30892/gtg.542spl11-1262

Jayanth Balaji, A., Harish Ram, D. S., & Nair, B. B. (2018). Applicability of deep learning models for stock Price forecasting an empirical study on BANKEX data. *Procedia Computer Science*, *143*, 947–953. DOI: 10.1016/j.procs.2018.10.340

Jensen, K. (2024). *The Ethics of Entrepreneurship Education*. MIT Press. DOI: 10.7551/mitpress/15073.001.0001

Jobin, A., Ienca, M., & Vayena, E. (2019). The global landscape of AI ethics guidelines. *Nature Machine Intelligence*, *1*(9), 389–399. DOI: 10.1038/s42256-019-0088-2

Jordan, M. I., & Mitchell, T. M. (2015). Machine learning: Trends, perspectives, and prospects. *Science*, *349*(6245), 255–260. DOI: 10.1126/science.aaa8415 PMID: 26185243

Jose, S., & Buchanan, F. R. (2025). Strategic factors in SME leadership orientation towards initiating exports: India context. *Measuring Business Excellence*, *29*(1), 150–167. DOI: 10.1108/MBE-02-2024-0023

Jung, J. H., Yoo, J. J., & Arnold, T. J. (2021). The influence of a retail store manager in developing frontline employee brand relationship, service performance and customer loyalty. *Journal of Business Research*, *122*, 362–372. DOI: 10.1016/j.jbusres.2020.09.010

Kainde, S. J., & Mandagi, D. (2023). A systematic review of servant leadership outcomes in education context. *EDUKASIA: Jurnal Pendidikan dan Pembelajaran*, *4*(2), 2563-2574.

Kalia, P. (2021). Artificial intelligence in e-commerce: a business process analysis. In *Artificial Intelligence* (pp. 9–19). CRC Press. DOI: 10.1201/9781003095910-2

Kareem, O., Aliyu, O. A., & Salimon, M. G. (2025). Does the Islamic work ethic moderate the relationship between organizational culture and enterprise performance? *Journal of Small Business and Enterprise Development*, *32*(2), 298–324. DOI: 10.1108/JSBED-11-2022-0480

Karlsen, J. T., & Berg, M. E. (2020). Coaching leadership style: A learning process. *International Journal of Knowledge and Learning*, *13*(4), 356–368. DOI: 10.1504/IJKL.2020.111143

Kar, S., Kar, A. K., & Gupta, M. P. (2021). Modeling Drivers and Barriers of Artificial Intelligence Adoption: Insights from a Strategic Management Perspective. *International Journal of Intelligent Systems in Accounting Finance & Management, 28*(4), 217–238. DOI: 10.1002/isaf.1503

Karwan, D. H., Hariri, H., & Ridwan, R. (2021). *Visionary leadership: what, why, and how*. European Union Digital Library.

Kaur, D., Ahsan, M., & Gill, G. S. (2025). Digital Transformation in the Sports Industry: Driving Circular Economy in Sports Equipment and Infrastructure. In *Innovating Sustainability Through Digital Circular Economy* (pp. 65-90). IGI Global Scientific Publishing.

Kazancoglu, I., Ozbiltekin-Pala, M., Mangla, S. K., Kazancoglu, Y., & Jabeen, F. (2022). Role of flexibility, agility and responsiveness for sustainable supply chain resilience during COVID-19. *Journal of Cleaner Production, 362*, 132431. DOI: 10.1016/j.jclepro.2022.132431

Khan, S., & Iqbal, M. (2020, June). AI-Powered Customer Service: Does it optimize customer experience? In 2020 8th International Conference on Reliability, Infocom Technologies and Optimization (Trends and Future Directions)(ICRITO) (pp. 590-594). IEEE.

Khan, S. M., Abbas, Q., & Shah, S. (2020). Factors affecting the adoption of fintech in Pakistan: The mediating role of trust. *Journal of Financial Services Marketing, 25*(4), 137–149.

Khattak, M. A., & Ullah, M. (2019). Digital financial services and financial inclusion in Pakistan: Opportunities and challenges. *J.A-P.B, 20(2)*, 106-118.

Khneyzer, C., Boustany, Z., & Dagher, J. (2024). AI-Driven Chatbots in CRM: Economic and Managerial Implications across Industries. *Administrative Sciences, 14*(8), 182. DOI: 10.3390/admsci14080182

Khosravi, K., Shahabi, H., Pham, B. T., Adamowski, J., Shirzadi, A., Pradhan, B., Dou, J., Ly, H. B., Gróf, G., Ho, H. L., Hong, H., Chapi, K., & Prakash, I. (2019). A comparative assessment of flood susceptibility modeling using Multi-Criteria Decision-Making Analysis and Machine Learning Methods. *Journal of Hydrology (Amsterdam), 573*, 311–323. DOI: 10.1016/j.jhydrol.2019.03.073

Kiessling, T., Maley, J. F., Moeller, M., & Dabić, M. (2021). Managing global knowledge transfer: Inpatriate manager embeddedness and firm innovation. *International Business Review*, •••, 101868.

Kim, P. T., & Bodie, M. T. (2020). Artificial intelligence and the challenges of workplace discrimination and privacy. *ABAJ Lab. & Emp. L.*, *35*, 289.

Kırmızısaç, E. (2021). Yeni Nesil İnsan Kaynakları Yönetiminde Dijital Dönüşüm [Digital Transformation in New Generation Human Resources Management], *European Journal of Educational and Social Sciences*, *6*(2), 156–169.

Knights, D., & Morgan, G. (1991). Corporate strategy, organizations, and subjectivity: A critique. *Organization Studies*, *12*(2), 251–273. DOI: 10.1177/017084069101200205

Kolkman, D., Lee, G. K., & van Witteloostuijn, A. (2024). Data science and automation in the process of theorizing: Machine learning's power of induction in the co-duction cycle. *PLoS One*, *19*(11), e0309318. DOI: 10.1371/journal.pone.0309318 PMID: 39495739

Kordon, A K. (2020, August 1). Applied Artificial Intelligence-Based Systems as Competitive Advantage. DOI: 10.1109/IS48319.2020.9200097

Korzynski, P., Haenlein, M., & Rautiainen, M. (2021). Impression management techniques in crowdfunding: An analysis of Kickstarter videos using artificial intelligence. *European Management Journal*, *39*(5), 675–684. DOI: 10.1016/j.emj.2021.01.001

Kotsiantis, S. B., Zaharakis, I. D., & Pintelas, P. E. (2006). Machine learning: A review of classification and combining techniques. *Artificial Intelligence Review*, *26*(3), 159–190. DOI: 10.1007/s10462-007-9052-3

Kouzes, J. M., & Posner, B. Z. (2023). *The leadership challenge: How to make extraordinary things happen in organizations*. John Wiley & Sons.

Kozioł-Nadolna, K. (2020). The role of a leader in stimulating innovation in an organization. *Administrative Sciences*, *10*(3), 59. DOI: 10.3390/admsci10030059

Kraus, M., Feuerriegel, S., & Oztekin, A. (2020). Deep learning in business analytics and operations research: Models, applications and managerial implications. *European Journal of Operational Research*, *281*(3), 628–641. DOI: 10.1016/j.ejor.2019.09.018

Kühl, N., Mühlthaler, M., & Goutier, M. (2020). Supporting customer-oriented marketing with artificial intelligence: Automatically quantifying customer needs from social media. *Electronic Markets*, *30*(2), 351–367. DOI: 10.1007/s12525-019-00351-0

Kule, J., Muhammad, T., Joseph, W. G., Johnson, A., & Ugwu, J. N. (2024). The Relationship between Head Teachers' Authoritarian Leadership Style and Teachers' Burnout in Secondary Schools in Ibanda Municipality, Ibanda District, Uganda. [NIJCIAM]. *Management*, *5*(1).

Kumari, S. (2021). Context-Aware AI-Driven CRM: Enhancing Customer Journeys Through Real-Time Personalization and Predictive Analytics. *ESP Journal of Engineering and Technology Advancements*, *1*(1), 7–13.

Kumar, J., Rani, M., Rani, G., & Rani, V. (2024). Crowdfunding adoption in emerging economies: Insights for entrepreneurs and policymakers. *Journal of Small Business and Enterprise Development*, *31*(1), 55–73. DOI: 10.1108/JSBED-05-2023-0204

Kumar, V., Ashraf, A. R., & Nadeem, W. (2024). AI-powered marketing: What, where, and how? *International Journal of Information Management*, *77*, 102783. DOI: 10.1016/j.ijinfomgt.2024.102783

Kumar, V., Dixit, A., Javalgi, R. G., & Dass, M. (2016). Digital transformation of business-to-business marketing: Framework and research agenda. *Journal of Business and Industrial Marketing*, *31*(8), 1151–1160. DOI: 10.1108/JBIM-12-2016-0276

Kun, M. (2022). Linkages between Knowledge Management Process and Corporate Sustainable Performance of Chinese SMEs: Mediating role of Frugal Innovation. *Frontiers in Psychology*, •••, 1172.

Kuo, Y.-F., Lin, C. S., & Liu, L.-T. (2022). The effects of framing messages and cause-related marketing on backing intentions in reward-based crowdfunding. *Journal of Retailing and Consumer Services*, *64*, 102799. DOI: 10.1016/j.jretconser.2021.102799

Kushwaha, A. K., Kar, A. K., & Dwivedi, Y. K. (2021). Applications of big data in emerging management disciplines: A literature review using text mining. *International Journal of Information Management Data Insights*, *1*(2), 100017. Advance online publication. DOI: 10.1016/j.jjimei.2021.100017

Kusmawan, A., Rahman, R., Anis, N., & Arifudin, O. (2025). The Relationship Between Teacher Involvement in Curriculum Development and Student Learning Outcomes. *International Journal of Educatio Elementaria and Psychologia*, *2*(1), 1–12.

Lambert, F. (2023, February 13). *Tesla pushes new safety features with software update. Electrek.* https://electrek.co/2023/02/13/tesla-pushes-new-safety-features-software-update/

Lambert, T. (2024). The Rise of Crowdfunding. In *Oxford Research Encyclopedia of Economics and Finance*. DOI: 10.1093/acrefore/9780190625979.013.1002

Latukha, M., Yakovleva, P., & Yan, K. (2025). Adaptive Leadership for Multilevel Resilience in the Context of Disruptions. *Thunderbird International Business Review, 67*(2), 149–167. DOI: 10.1002/tie.22416

Lee, J., Suh, T., Roy, D., & Baucus, M S. (2019, September 1). Emerging Technology and Business Model Innovation: The Case of Artificial Intelligence. Springer Science+Business Media, 5(3), 44-44. https://doi.org/DOI: 10.3390/joitmc5030044

Lee, I., & Shin, Y. J. (2020). Machine learning for enterprises: Applications, algorithm selection, and challenges. *Business Horizons*, *63*(2), 157–170. DOI: 10.1016/j.bushor.2019.10.005

Leslie, D. (2020). Tackling COVID-19 through responsible AI innovation: Five steps in the right direction. *Harvard Data Science Review*, •••, 10.

Lester, I. (2021). *Employee expectations and perceptions of leadership styles in a chemical manufacturing facility in South Africa*. North-West University.

Liang, C., Chang, C.-C., Liang, C.-T., & Liu, Y.-C. (2017). Imagining future success: Imaginative capacity on the perceived performance of potential agrisocio entrepreneurs. *Thinking Skills and Creativity*, *23*, 161–174. DOI: 10.1016/j.tsc.2016.12.007

Liao, S., Chen, C., & Hu, D. (2018). The role of knowledge sharing and LMX to enhance employee creativity in theme park work team: A case study of Taiwan. *International Journal of Contemporary Hospitality Management*, *30*(5), 2343–2359. DOI: 10.1108/IJCHM-09-2016-0522

Li, H., Yang, Z., Jin, C., & Wang, J. (2023). How an industrial internet platform empowers the digital transformation of SMEs: Theoretical mechanism and business model. *Journal of Knowledge Management*, *27*(1), 105–120. DOI: 10.1108/JKM-09-2022-0757

Liu, Y., Zhang, K., Xue, W., & Zhou, Z. (2024). Crowdfunding innovative but risky new ventures: The importance of less ambiguous tone. *Financial Innovation*, *10*(1), 27. DOI: 10.1186/s40854-023-00529-8

Li, Y.-H., Huang, J.-W., & Tsai, M.-T. (2009). Entrepreneurial orientation and firm performance: The role of knowledge creation process. *Industrial Marketing Management*, *38*(4), 440–449. DOI: 10.1016/j.indmarman.2008.02.004

Long, S. (2023). Optimizing Knowledge Management During Crises. In *Health Informatics and Patient Safety in Times of Crisis* (pp. 77–94). IGI Global.

Lv, Y. (2025). Support vector machine (SVM) algorithm optimization and innovative talent matching model for employment needs. *Journal of Computational Methods in Sciences and Engineering*, 14727978251325084.

Macharla, S. L., & Raghavendra, G. S. (2025). Leveraging AI for E-Business Transformation. In Business Transformation in the Era of Digital Disruption (pp. 29-58). IGI Global.

Magill, E., Siegel, Z., & Pike, K. M. (2020). The mental health of frontline health care providers during pandemics: A rapid review of the literature. *Psychiatric Services (Washington, D.C.)*, *71*(12), 1260–1269. DOI: 10.1176/appi.ps.202000274 PMID: 33019857

MahabubMD Russel HossainEsrat Zahan Snigdha. (2025). Data-Driven Decision-Making and Strategic Leadership: AI-Powered Business Operations for Competitive Advantage and Sustainable Growth. *Journal of Computer Science and Technology Studies*, *7*(1), 326–336. DOI: 10.32996/jcsts.2025.7.1.24

Mahdi, O. R., Nassar, I. A., & Almsafir, M. K. (2019). Knowledge management processes and sustainable competitive advantage: An empirical examination in private universities. *Journal of Business Research*, *94*, 320–334. DOI: 10.1016/j.jbusres.2018.02.013

Makridakis, S., Spiliotis, E., & Assimakopoulos, V. (2018). Statistical and Machine Learning forecasting methods: Concerns and ways forward. *PLoS One*, *13*(3), e0194889. DOI: 10.1371/journal.pone.0194889 PMID: 29584784

Mansaray, H. E. (2019). The role of leadership style in organisational change management: A literature review. *Journal of Human Resource Management*, *7*(1), 18–31. DOI: 10.11648/j.jhrm.20190701.13

Margaryan, P. (2019). Antik Yunan Mitlerinde Yapay Zekâ [Artificial Intelligence in Ancient Greek Myths], Arkeofili. https://arkeofili.com/antik-yunanmitlerinde-yapay-zeka/

Markauskaite, L., Marrone, R., Poquet, O., Knight, S., Martinez-Maldonado, R., Howard, S., Tondeur, J., De Laat, M., Shum, S. B., & Gašević, D. (2022). Rethinking the entwinement between artificial intelligence and human learning: What capabilities do learners need for a world with AI? *Computers and Education: Artificial Intelligence*, *3*, 100056. DOI: 10.1016/j.caeai.2022.100056

Marr, B. (2020). *Artificial Intelligence in Practice: How 50 Companies are Using AI to Grow Business and Solve Problems*. Wiley.

Mbiti, I., & Weil, D. N. (2015). Mobile banking: The impact of M-Pesa in Kenya. In *African successes, Volume III: Modernization and development* (pp. 247-293). University of Chicago Press.

McCorduck, P., Minsky, M., Selfridge, O. G., & Simon, H. A. (1977, August). History of artificial intelligence. In IJCAI (pp. 951-954).

McKinsey & Company. (2023, January 11). Artificial intelligence in strategy. Retrieved from https://www.mckinsey.com/capabilities/strategy-and-corporate-finance/our-insights/artificial-intelligence-in-strategy

McNeill, S. (2019). Artificial intelligence in the classroom. Education Blog. https://educationblog.microsoft.com/en-au/2019/01/artificial-intelligence-in-theclassroom/ (03.04.2023).

McQuade, E., Sjoer, E., Fabian, P., Nascimento, J. C., & Schroeder, S. (2007). Will you miss me when I'm gone? A study of the potential loss of company knowledge and expertise as employees retire. *Journal of European Industrial Training, 31*(9), 758–768. DOI: 10.1108/03090590710846701

Mei, C. W., Konar, R., & Kumar, J. (2024). The Role of AI Chatbots in Transforming Guest Engagement and Marketing in Hospitality. In *Integrating AI-Driven Technologies Into Service Marketing* (pp. 595–620). IGI Global. DOI: 10.4018/979-8-3693-7122-0.ch029

Mert, Y. L. (2018). Dijital Pazarlama Ekseninde İnfluencer Marketing Uygulamaları. *Gümüşhane Üniversitesi İletişim Fakültesi Elektronik Dergisi* [Influencer Marketing Applications in the Axis of Digital Marketing. Gümüşhane University Faculty of Communication Electronic Journal*], 6*(2), 1299–1328.

Microsoft. (2023). Generative AI: The Next Frontier in Product Innovation. https://www.microsoft.com

Migdadi, M. M. (2022). Knowledge management processes, innovation capability and organizational performance. *International Journal of Productivity and Performance Management, 71*(1), 182–210. DOI: 10.1108/IJPPM-04-2020-0154

Mikalef, P., & Gupta, M. (2021). Artificial intelligence capability: Conceptualization, measurement calibration, and empirical study on its impact on organizational creativity and firm performance. *Information & Management, 58*(3), 103434. DOI: 10.1016/j.im.2021.103434

Mikalef, P., Krogstie, J., Pappas, I. O., & Giannakos, M. (2018). Investigating the effects of big data analytics capabilities on firm performance: The mediating role of dynamic capabilities. *Information & Management*, *55*(8), 103176. DOI: 10.1016/j.im.2018.03.004

Millo, Y., Spence, C., & Xu, R. (2024). Algorithmic self-referentiality: How machine learning pushes calculative practices to assess themselves. *Accounting, Organizations and Society*, *113*, 101567. Advance online publication. DOI: 10.1016/j.aos.2024.101567

Minzhi, W., Tortosa-Ausina, E., Peiró-Palomino, J., & Arribas, I. (2023). Fintech and Regional Economic Performance in China (2012-2019). *Available atSSRN* 4225041.

Mitra, A., Jain, A., Kishore, A., & Kumar, P. (2023). A Comparative Study for Machine Learning Models in Retail Demand Forecasting. *Smart Innovation. Systems and Technologies*, *316*, 273–282. DOI: 10.1007/978-981-19-5403-0_23

Mittelstadt, B. D., Allo, P., Taddeo, M., Wachter, S., & Floridi, L. (2016). The ethics of algorithms: Mapping the debate. *Big Data & Society*, *3*(2), 1–21. DOI: 10.1177/2053951716679679

Modupe, J. (2023). The role of artificial intelligence in financial decision making. Medium. Retrieved November 6, 2024, from https://medium.com/@jamesmodupe75/the-role-of-artificial-intelligence-in-financial-decision-making-57befaccfb4f

Mollick, E. (2014). The dynamics of crowdfunding: An exploratory study. *Journal of Business Venturing*, *29*(1), 1–16. DOI: 10.1016/j.jbusvent.2013.06.005

Morgan, B. (2019), "The 7 Best Examples of Artificial Intelligence to Improve Personalization", Forbes. https://www.forbes.com/sites/ blakemorgan/2019/01/24/the-7-best-examples-of-artificial-intelligence-to-improve-personalization

Mosier, K. L., Fischer, U., Burian, B. K., & Kochan, J. A. (2017). Autonomous, context-sensitive, task management systems and decision support tools I: Human-autonomy teaming fundamentals and state of the art.

Mullangi, M. K., Yarlagadda, V. K., Dhameliya, N., & Rodriguez, M. (2018). Integrating AI and Reciprocal Symmetry in Financial Management: A Pathway to Enhanced Decision-Making. *Int. J. Reciprocal Symmetry Theor. Phys*, *5*(1), 42–52.

Murray, A., Rhymer, J., & Sirmon, D. G.Murray. (2021). Humans and technology: Forms of conjoined agency in organizations. *Academy of Management Review*, *46*(3), 552–571. DOI: 10.5465/amr.2019.0186

Murthy, & Bhojanna, U. (2009). 2nd ed.). Business Research Methods.

Mushinzimana, L., Faisal, A., & Teressia, A. (2025). Strategy For Evaluating the Strengths, Weaknesses, Opportunities, And Threats of The Business Community in Rwanda in Adopting Digital Transformation to Increase Financial Benefits. *Indiana Journal of Economics and Business Management*, *5*(1), 64–96.

Nagy, J., Oláh, J., Erdei, E., Máté, D., & Popp, J. (2018). The role and impact of Industry 4.0 and the internet of things on the business strategy of the value chain—The case of Hungary. *Sustainability (Basel)*, *10*(10), 3491. DOI: 10.3390/su10103491

Napoli, P. M. (2011). *Audience evolution: New technologies and the transformation of media audiences*. Columbia University Press.

Nawaz, N., Arunachalam, H., Pathi, B. K., & Gajenderan, V. (2024). The adoption of artificial intelligence in human resources management practices. *International Journal of Information Management Data Insights*, *4*(1), 100208. DOI: 10.1016/j.jjimei.2023.100208

Newman, S. A., & Ford, R. C. (2021). Five steps to leading your team in the virtual COVID-19 workplace. *Organizational Dynamics*, *50*(1), 100802. DOI: 10.1016/j.orgdyn.2020.100802 PMID: 36536689

Nguyen, Q. K. (2022). The effect of FinTech development on financial stability in an emerging market: The role of market discipline. *Research in Globalization*, *5*, 100105. DOI: 10.1016/j.resglo.2022.100105

Ni, V. (2022, July 14). *Inside Alibaba's tech-driven e-commerce empire. The Guardian*. https://www.theguardian.com/technology/2022/jul/14/inside-alibabas-tech-driven-e-commerce-empire

Nike. (2022). How AI is Changing the Future of Footwear. Nike Innovation Blog. https://news.nike.com

Nonaka, I., Toyama, R., & Konno, N. (2000). SECI, Ba and leadership: A unified model of dynamic knowledge creation. *Long Range Planning*, *33*(1), 5–34. DOI: 10.1016/S0024-6301(99)00115-6

Nur, S. A., & Muafi, M. (2025). Link between dynamic capability and sustainable entrepreneurship: The mediation role of digital networking. *Jurnal Siasat Bisnis*, 1-14.

Nwaogbe, G., Ekpenyong, E., & Urhoghide, O. (2025). Managing workforce productivity in the post-pandemic construction industry.

Oakley, T., Vaz, J., da Silva, F., Allan, R., Almeida, D., Champlin, K., da Silva, E. S., Tilman, A. J., Marr, I., Smith-Vaughan, H., Yan, J., & Francis, J. R. (2025). Implementation of a Laboratory Information Management System (LIMS) for microbiology in Timor-Leste: Challenges, mitigation strategies, and end-user experiences. *BMC Medical Informatics and Decision Making*, *25*(1), 32. DOI: 10.1186/s12911-024-02831-6 PMID: 39825312

Obeso, M., Hernández-Linares, R., López-Fernández, M. C., & Serrano-Bedia, A. M. (2020). Knowledge management processes and organizational performance: The mediating role of organizational learning. *Journal of Knowledge Management*, *24*(8), 1859–1880. DOI: 10.1108/JKM-10-2019-0553

OECD. (2019). Hello, World: Artificial Intelligence and its use in the Public Sector. [OPSI]. *OECD Observatory of Public Sector Innovation*, *36*, 1–148.

Ogunode, O. A., & Akintoye, R. I. (2023). Financial Technologies and Financial Inclusion in Emerging Economies: Perspectives from Nigeria. *Asian J. Econ. Bus. Acc*, *23*(1), 38–54.

Ohemeng, F. L., Obuobisa Darko, T., & Amoako-Asiedu, E. (2020). Bureaucratic leadership, trust building, and employee engagement in the public sector in Ghana: The perspective of social exchange theory. *International Journal of Public Leadership*, *16*(1), 17–40. DOI: 10.1108/IJPL-05-2019-0018

Okine, A. N. D., Li, Y., Djimesah, I. E., Zhao, H., Budu, K. W. A., Duah, E., & Mireku, K. K. (2023). Analyzing crowdfunding adoption from a technology acceptance perspective. *Technological Forecasting and Social Change*, *192*, 122582. DOI: 10.1016/j.techfore.2023.122582

Olatoye, F. O., Awonuga, K. F., Mhlongo, N. Z., Ibeh, C. V., Elufioye, O. A., & Ndubuisi, N. L. (2024). AI and ethics in business: A comprehensive review of responsible AI practices and corporate responsibility. *International Journal of Science and Research Archive*, *11*(1), 1433–1443.

Open, A. I. (2023). Introducing GPT-4 Technical Report. https://openai.com/research/gpt-4

Ordanini, A., Miceli, L., Pizzetti, M., & Parasuraman, A. (2011). Crowd-funding: Transforming customers into investors through innovative service platforms. *Journal of Service Management*, *22*(4), 443–470. DOI: 10.1108/09564231111155079

Ordu, A., & Nayır, F. (2021). Dijital Liderlik Nedir? Bir Tanım Önerisi [What is Digital Leadership? A Proposed Definition]. E-International Journal of Educational Research, 12(3).

Ozay, D., Jahanbakht, M., Shoomal, A., & Wang, S. (2024). Artificial Intelligence (AI)-based Customer Relationship Management (CRM): A comprehensive bibliometric and systematic literature review with outlook on future research. *Enterprise Information Systems, 18*(7), 2351869. DOI: 10.1080/17517575.2024.2351869

Özmen, Ö. N., Eriş, E., & Özer, P. (2020). Dijital liderlik çalişmalarina bir bakiş. Süleyman Demirel Üniversitesi İktisadi ve İdari Bilimler Fakültesi Dergisi [A look at digital leadership studies. Süleyman Demirel University Faculty of Economics and Administrative Sciences Journal], 25(1), 57-69.

Packin, N. G., & Lev-Aretz, Y. (2018). Learning algorithms and discrimination. In *Research handbook on the law of artificial intelligence* (pp. 88–113). Edward Elgar Publishing. DOI: 10.4337/9781786439055.00014

Pala, F. K. (2020). *Makine öğrenmesi ve eğitim sistemine getirdikleri. Eğitimde Yapay Zeka Kuramdan Uygulamaya içinde*. Pegem Yayıncılık. [Machine learning and what it brings to the education system. In Artificial Intelligence in Education: From Theory to Application. Ankara: Pegem Publishing]

Pan, X., & Dong, L. (2023). What Determines the Success of Charitable Crowdfunding Campaigns? Evidence from China During the COVID-19 Pandemic. *Voluntas, 34*(6), 1–15. DOI: 10.1007/s11266-023-00557-z PMID: 36743475

Parayitam, S., Usman, S. A., Namasivaayam, R. R., & Naina, M. S. (2021). Knowledge management and emotional exhaustion as moderators in the relationship between role conflict and organizational performance: Evidence from India. *Journal of Knowledge Management, 25*(6), 1456–1485. DOI: 10.1108/JKM-03-2020-0184

Passos, D. M. A., Sarmento, A. M., & Gonçalves, P. J. P. (2021). Knowledge Management and Individual Job Performance in Higher Education: Proposal of a Conceptual Model. In *Perspectives and Trends in Education and Technology: Selected Papers from ICITED 2021* (pp. 367-382). Springer.

Paul, P., & Singh, B. (2023). Healthcare Employee Engagement Using the Internet of Things: A Systematic Overview. *The Adoption and Effect of Artificial Intelligence on Human Resources Management, Part A*, 71-97.

Peng, Y., Ahmad, S. F., Ahmad, A. Y. A. B., Al Shaikh, M. S., Daoud, M. K., & Alhamdi, F. M. H. (2023). Riding the Waves of Artificial Intelligence in Advancing Accounting and Its Implications for Sustainable Development Goals. *Sustainability (Basel), 15*(19), 14165. Advance online publication. DOI: 10.3390/su151914165

PENROSE E. (2003). The Theory of The Growth of The Firm. In Nicolai, J. (Ed.), *Resources Firms and Strategies: A Reader in the Resource-Based Perspective, Oxford Management Readers*. FOSS.

Peteraf, M. A. (1993). "The cornerstones of competitive advantage: A resource-based view", Strategic Management Journal, Vol. 14, No 3, ss. 179-191.

Pietruszka-Ortyl, A., Ćwiek, M., Ziębicki, B., & Wójcik-Karpacz, A. (2021). Organizational culture as a prerequisite for knowledge transfer among IT professionals: The case of energy companies. *Energies*, *14*(23), 8139. DOI: 10.3390/en14238139

Pinheiro, J., Silva, G. M., Dias, Á. L., Lages, L. F., & Preto, M. T. (2020). Fostering knowledge creation to improve performance: The mediation role of manufacturing flexibility. *Business Process Management Journal*, *26*(7), 1871–1892. DOI: 10.1108/BPMJ-10-2019-0413

Poalelungi, D. G., Mu at, C. L., Fulga, A., Neagu, M., Neagu, A., Piraianu, A. I., & Fulga, I. (2023, July 31). Advancing Patient Care: How Artificial Intelligence Is Transforming Healthcare. *Journal of Personalized Medicine*, *13*(8), 1214–1214. DOI: 10.3390/jpm13081214 PMID: 37623465

Pólvora, A., Nascimento, S., Lourenço, J. S., & Scapolo, F. (2020). Blockchain for industrial transformations: A forward-looking approach with multi-stakeholder engagement for policy advice. *Technological Forecasting and Social Change*, *157*, 120091. DOI: 10.1016/j.techfore.2020.120091

Potla, R. T. (2023). Enhancing Customer Relationship Management (CRM) through AI-Powered Chatbots and Machine Learning. *Distributed Learning and Broad Applications in Scientific Research*, *9*, 364–383.

Priyono, A., Shukor, S. A., Moin, A., & Salikin, N. How does a firm leverage dynamic capabilities to pioneer a 2 business ecosystem and serve as the orchestrator? Lessons 3 learned from coffee shop industry 4.

Pyo, S. (2005). Knowledge map for tourist destinations—Needs and implications. *Tourism Management*, *26*(4), 583–594. DOI: 10.1016/j.tourman.2004.03.001

Quadra Wealth. (2024). *How AI Investment Advisors are transforming Financial Advice*. Retrieved from https://quadrawealth.com/articles/the-rise-of-ai-investment-advisors/

Rahimi, R., & Kozak, M. (2017). Impact of customer relationship management on customer satisfaction: The case of a budget hotel chain. *Journal of Travel & Tourism Marketing*, *34*(1), 40–51. DOI: 10.1080/10548408.2015.1130108

Rai, A., & Mishra, A. K. (2022). The Role of Artificial Intelligence in the Automation of Human Resources. In *Adoption and Implementation of AI in Customer Relationship Management* (pp. 166–176). IGI Global. DOI: 10.4018/978-1-7998-7959-6.ch011

Raisch, S., & Krakowski, S. (2021). Artificial intelligence and management: The automation–augmentation paradox. *Academy of Management Review*, *46*(1), 192–210. DOI: 10.5465/amr.2018.0072

Rajagopal, N. K., Qureshi, N. I., Durga, S., Ramirez Asis, E. H., Huerta Soto, R. M., Gupta, S. K., & Deepak, S. (2022). Future of Business Culture: An Artificial Intelligence-Driven Digital Framework for Organization Decision-Making Process. *Complexity*, *2022*(1), 7796507. DOI: 10.1155/2022/7796507

Raji, I. D., Smart, A., White, R. N., Mitchell, M., Gebru, T., Hutchinson, B., Smith-Loud, J., Theron, D., & Barnes, P. (2020). Closing the AI accountability gap: Defining an end-to-end framework for internal algorithmic auditing. Proceedings of the 2020 conference on fairness, accountability, and transparency, Rane, N., Choudhary, S., & Rane, J. (2023). Hyper-personalization for enhancing customer loyalty and satisfaction in Customer Relationship Management (CRM) systems. *Available at SSRN 4641044*.

Rana, R., & Hatibaruah, P. D. (2024). Revolutionizing Customer Service and Experience: The Impact of Artificial Intelligence. In Leveraging AI and Emotional Intelligence in Contemporary Business Organizations (pp. 253-275). IGI Global.

Rane, N. (2023). Role and Challenges of ChatGPT and Similar Generative Artificial Intelligence in Finance and Accounting. SSRN *Electronic Journal*. https://doi.org/ DOI: 10.2139/SSRN.4603206

Ransbotham, S., Candelon, F., Kiron, D., LaFountain, B., & Khodabandeh, S. (2021). The cultural benefits of artificial intelligence in the Enterprise. *MIT Sloan Management Review and Boston Consulting Group, 1*.

Ransbotham, S., Khodabandeh, S., Kiron, D., LaFountain, B., & Kiron, D. (2020). *The Cultural Benefits of Artificial Intelligence in the Enterprise*. MIT Sloan Management Review and Boston Consulting Group.

Ratcliffe, J. S. (2006). Challenges for corporate foresight: Towards strategic prospective through scenario thinking. *Foresight*, *8*(1), 39–54. DOI: 10.1108/14636680610647138

Raudeliūnienė, J., Davidavičienė, V., & Jakubavičius, A. (2018). Knowledge management process model. *Entrepreneurship and Sustainability Issues*, *5*(3), 542–554. DOI: 10.9770/jesi.2018.5.3(10)

Reddy, P., Chaudhary, K., & Hussein, S. (2023). A digital literacy model to narrow the digital literacy skills gap. *Heliyon*, *9*(4), e14878. DOI: 10.1016/j.heliyon.2023.e14878 PMID: 37025876

Renaldo, N., Junaedi, A. T., Musa, S., Wahid, N., & Cecilia, C. (2024). Mapping the Financial Technology Industry in Indonesia. *Journal of Applied Business and Technology*, *5*(1), 61–66. DOI: 10.35145/jabt.v5i1.162

Riahi, E., & Islam, M. S. (2025). Employees' information security awareness (ISA) in public organisations: Insights from cross-cultural studies in Sweden, France, and Tunisia. *Behaviour & Information Technology*, *44*(1), 79–101. DOI: 10.1080/0144929X.2024.2311734

Ritala, P., Aaltonen, P., Ruokonen, M., & Nemeh, A. (2024). Developing industrial AI capabilities: An organisational learning perspective. *Technovation*, *138*, 103120. Advance online publication. DOI: 10.1016/j.technovation.2024.103120

Rizwan, M., & Bruneau, C. (2019). Microfinance, financial inclusion and ICT: Implications for poverty and inequality. *Technology in Society*, *59*, 101154. DOI: 10.1016/j.techsoc.2019.101154

Rogers, M. E. (2003). *Diffusion of innovation* (5th ed.). The Free Press.

Rolla, A. (2025). Talent Management in Learning Organizations: Designing Curriculum for Business Schools. In *Handbook of Talent Management and Learning Organizations* (pp. 85-104). CRC Press.

Rooke, D., & Torbert, W. R. (2005). Welcome: Background Material 7 Transformations of Leadership Making the case for a developmental perspective The Hidden Talent Essay 7: Emergent Leadership: Linking Competency, Cognitive Processes, Adaptability, an Innovation. *Harvard business review*.

Rosário, A. T., & Casaca, J. A. (2025). How Artificial Intelligence Can Leverage Relationship Marketing Strategies. In Leveraging AI for Effective Digital Relationship Marketing (pp. 1-34). IGI Global.

Ross, C., Smith, C., & Pulley, T. W. (2023). Equity Fluent Leadership: Implementation.

Russell, S., & Norvig, P. (2021). *Artificial Intelligence: A Modern Approach* (4th ed.). Pearson Education.

Russo, D. (2024). Navigating the complexity of generative ai adoption in software engineering. *ACM Transactions on Software Engineering and Methodology*, *33*(5), 1–50. DOI: 10.1145/3652154

Sackstein, S., & Laing, A. (2025). *Solving School Challenges: The Everything Guide to Transformative Change*. Taylor & Francis. DOI: 10.4324/9781003508960

Saeed, I., Khan, J., Zada, M., & Zada, S. (2024). Employee sensemaking in organizational change via knowledge management: Leadership role as a moderator. *Current Psychology (New Brunswick, N.J.), 43*(7), 6657–6671. DOI: 10.1007/s12144-023-04849-x

Sağbaş, M., & Erdoğan, F. A. (2022). Digital leadership: a systematic conceptual literature review. *İstanbul Kent Üniversitesi İnsan ve Toplum Bilimleri Dergisi, 3*(1), 17-35.

Sahibzada, U. F., Jianfeng, C., Latif, K. F., Shah, S. A., & Sahibzada, H. F. (2023). Refuelling knowledge management processes towards organisational performance: Mediating role of creative organisational learning. *Knowledge Management Research and Practice*, *21*(1), 1–13. DOI: 10.1080/14778238.2020.1787802

Şahin, E., & Kaya, F. (2019). *Pazarlamada Yeni Dönem Endüstri 4.0. Yapay Zeka ve Akıllı Asistanlar*. Çizgi Kitabevi. [New Era in Marketing Industry 4.0. Artificial Intelligence and Smart Assistants: Konya: Çizgi Bookstore]

Saini, V., & Bhati, S. (2019). Demonetization, digitalization, and the transformation of financial services in India. *Journal of Financial Services Marketing*, *24*(3-4), 119–126.

Salehi, H., & Burgueno, R. (2018). Emerging Artificial Intelligence Methods in Structural Engineering. *Engineering Structures*, *171*, 170–189. DOI: 10.1016/j.engstruct.2018.05.084

Salem, I. E., Fathy, E. A., Magdy, A., Elsaqqa, M. A., & Kamal Abdien, M. (2025). Unlocking organizational ambidexterity via the role of cross-functional coopetition in quick-service restaurants. *Tourism and Hospitality Research*, •••, 14673584241313353. DOI: 10.1177/14673584241313353

Salido-Andres, N., Rey-Garcia, M., Alvarez-Gonzalez, L. I., & Vazquez-Casielles, R. (2021). Mapping the field of donation-based crowdfunding for charitable causes: Systematic review and conceptual framework. *Voluntas*, *32*(2), 288–302. DOI: 10.1007/s11266-020-00213-w

Salman, A., Fakhraldeen, S. A., Chun, S., Jamil, K., Gasana, J., & Al-Hunayan, A. (2020). Enhancing Research and Development in the Health Sciences as a Strategy to Establish a Knowledge-Based Economy in the State of Kuwait: A Call for Action. *Health Care*.

Salzmann-Erikson, M., Olsson, A., Rezagholi, M., Fjellström, D., & Osarenkhoe, A. (2024). Bridging technostress and continuous learning in knowledge-intensive organizations: A socio-technical systems approach for the future of healthy working life. *Journal of Infrastructure, Policy and Development, 8*(13).

Sa, M. L. L., Choon-Yin, S., Chai, Y. K., & Joo, J. H. A. (2020). Knowledge creation process, customer orientation and firm performance: Evidence from small hotels in Malaysia. *Asia Pacific Management Review, 25*(2), 65–74. DOI: 10.1016/j.apmrv.2019.07.002

Samawi, G. A., Bwaliez, O. M., Jreissat, M., & Kandas, A. (2025). Advancing Sustainable Development in Jordan: A Business and Economic Analysis of Electric Vehicle Adoption in the Transportation Sector. *World Electric Vehicle Journal, 16*(1), 45. DOI: 10.3390/wevj16010045

Samimi, M., Cortes, A. F., Anderson, M. H., & Herrmann, P. (2022). What is strategic leadership? Developing a framework for future research. *The Leadership Quarterly, 33*(3), 101353. DOI: 10.1016/j.leaqua.2019.101353

Sánchez-Polo, M. T., Cegarra-Navarro, J.-G., Cillo, V., & Wensley, A. (2019). Overcoming knowledge barriers to health care through continuous learning. *Journal of Knowledge Management, 23*(3), 508–526. DOI: 10.1108/JKM-10-2018-0636

Sanford, C. (2011). *The responsible business: Reimagining sustainability and success*. John Wiley & Sons.

Sarfo, C., Zhang, J. A., O'Kane, P., & O'Kane, C. (2024). Crowdfunding's impact on small business performance through exploitative and exploratory search strategies: An entrepreneurial resourcefulness perspective. *Strategic Change, 33*(5), 355–369. DOI: 10.1002/jsc.2584

Sarıel, S. (2017). *Günümüzde Yapay Zekâ*, İstanbul Teknik Üniversitesi Vakfı Yayını, İnsanlaşan Makinalar ve Yapay Zekâ [Artificial Intelligence Today, Istanbul Technical University Foundation Publication, Humanized Machines and Artificial Intelligence], 75.

Sarpong, B., & Nketiah-Amponsah, E. (2022). Financial inclusion and inclusive growth in sub-Saharan Africa. *Cogent Economics & Finance, 10*(1), 2058734. DOI: 10.1080/23322039.2022.2058734

Say, C. (2018). *50 Soruda Yapay Zekâ*. Bilim ve Gelecek Yayınevi. [Artificial Intelligence in 50 Questions. Science and Future Publishing House]

Schallmo, D. R. A., & Williams, C. A. (2018). *Digital transformation now*. Springer International Publishing. DOI: 10.1007/978-3-319-72844-5

Schmitt, M. (2024). Strategic integration of artificial intelligence in the C-suite: The role of the Chief AI Officer. *arXiv preprint arXiv:2407.10247*. Retrieved from https://arxiv.org/abs/2407.10247

Schmitt, M. (2022). Deep Learning vs. Gradient Boosting: Benchmarking state-of-the-art machine learning algorithms for credit scoring. *ArXiv*. DOI: 10.48550/ARXIV.2205.10535

Schmitt, M. (2023a). Automated machine learning: AI-driven decision making in business analytics. *Intelligent Systems with Applications*, *18*, 200188. DOI: 10.1016/j.iswa.2023.200188

Schmitt, M. (2023b). Deep learning in business analytics: A clash of expectations and reality. *International Journal of Information Management Data Insights*, *3*(1), 100146. Advance online publication. DOI: 10.1016/j.jjimei.2022.100146

Schot, J., & Geels, F. W. (2013). Strategic niche management and sustainable innovation journeys: theory, findings, research agenda, and policy. *The Dynamics of Sustainable Innovation Journeys*, 17-34.

Schueffel, P. (2016). Taming the beast: A scientific definition of fintech. *Journal of Innovation Management*, *4*(4), 32–54. DOI: 10.24840/2183-0606_004.004_0004

Scott, H., Ujvari, M. M., Bakeer, A., & Shanaa, K. (2025). Sumud as connected learning: towards a collective digital commons in Palestine.

Senapati, B., & Rawal, B. S. (2025). Distributed Hybrid Quantum Computing Applications into Battery Cell Manufacturing Industries as per the Industries 5.0. *Cloud Computing and Data Science*, 136-165.

Senyapar, H. N. D. (2024). Artificial Intelligence in Marketing Communication: A Comprehensive Exploration of the Integration and Impact of AI. *Technium Social Sciences Journal*, *55*, 64–81. DOI: 10.47577/tssj.v55i1.10651

Shaik, A. S., Jain, M., Mendiratta, A., Alarifi, G., & Arrigo, E. (2024). Role of strategic knowledge management practices in enhancing strategic perspectives of an organisation to improve entrepreneurial performance. *Journal of Knowledge Management*, *28*(6), 1648–1675. DOI: 10.1108/JKM-04-2023-0300

Shankar, V. (2018). How Artificial Intelligence (AI) Is Resha- ping Retailing. *Journal of Retailing*, *94*(4), 5–11. DOI: 10.1016/S0022-4359(18)30076-9

Shannak, R., Maqableh, M., & Tarhini, A. (2017). The impact of knowledge management on job performance in higher education: The case of the University of Jordan. *Journal of Enterprise Information Management*, *30*(2), 244–262. DOI: 10.1108/JEIM-09-2015-0087

Shao, Z. (2019). Interaction effect of strategic leadership behaviors and organizational culture on IS-Business strategic alignment and Enterprise Systems assimilation. *International Journal of Information Management*, *44*, 96–108. DOI: 10.1016/j.ijinfomgt.2018.09.010

Shedden, P., Scheepers, R., Smith, W., & Ahmad, A. (2011). Incorporating a knowledge perspective into security risk assessments. *Vine*, *41*(2), 152–166. DOI: 10.1108/03055721111134790

Shimizu, K., & Hitt, M. A. (2004). Strategic flexibility: Organizational preparedness to reverse ineffective strategic decisions. *The Academy of Management Perspectives*, *18*(4), 44–59. DOI: 10.5465/ame.2004.15268683

Shim, Y., & Shin, D.-H. (2016). Analyzing China's fintech industry from the perspective of actor–network theory. *Telecommunications Policy*, *40*(2-3), 168–181. DOI: 10.1016/j.telpol.2015.11.005

Shortliffe, E. (2012). *Computer-based medical consultations: MYCIN* (Vol. 2). Elsevier.

Shrestha, Y. R., Ben-Menahem, S. M., & von Krogh, G. (2019). Organizational Decision-Making Structures in the Age of Artificial Intelligence. *California Management Review*, *61*(4), 66–83. DOI: 10.1177/0008125619862257

Shrestha, Y. R., Krishna, V., & von Krogh, G. (2021). Augmenting organizational decision-making with deep learning algorithms: Principles, promises, and challenges. *Journal of Business Research*, *123*, 588–603. DOI: 10.1016/j.jbusres.2020.09.068

Siemens. (2022). AI at the Edge: Transforming Industrial Automation. Siemens Digital Industries. https://new.siemens.com

Simchi-Levi, D., Kaminsky, P., Simchi-Levi, E., & Shankar, R. (2008). *Designing and managing the supply chain: concepts, strategies and case studies*. Tata McGraw-Hill Education.

Singh, K. (2021). *Intelligent decision support system for selection of Learning Apps to promote critical thinking in first year programming students*

Singh, H., Schiff, G. D., Graber, M. L., Onakpoya, I., & Thompson, M. J. (2017). The global burden of diagnostic errors in primary care. *BMJ Quality & Safety*, *26*(6), 484–494. DOI: 10.1136/bmjqs-2016-005401 PMID: 27530239

Singun, A. J. (2025). Unveiling the barriers to digital transformation in higher education institutions: A systematic literature review. *Discover Education*, *4*(1), 37. DOI: 10.1007/s44217-025-00430-9

Sitalaksmi, S., Indarti, N., Anggadwita, G., & Sambudi, A. D. (2024). Knowledge leakage and collaborative innovation: A systematic literature review. *Knowledge Management Research and Practice*, •••, 1–17. DOI: 10.1080/14778238.2024.2431111

Smith, A. (2018). "Three Ways AI Can Help Build Customer Relationships", Forbes. https://www.forbes.com/sites/anthonysmith/2018/03/12/

Smith, J. The Impact of AI on Business Models. Journal of Technology Management, 15, 45-62.

Soares, J., Miguel, I., Venâncio, C., Lopes, I., & Oliveira, M. (2021). On the path to minimize plastic pollution: The perceived importance of education and knowledge dissemination strategies. *Marine Pollution Bulletin*, *171*, 112890. DOI: 10.1016/j.marpolbul.2021.112890 PMID: 34500371

Son, H. (2024). This AI-powered financial advisor has quickly gained $20 billion in assets. CNBC. https://www.cnbc.com/2024/07/31/portfoliopilot-ai-powered-financial-advisor-has-20-billion-in-assets.html

Song, N., & Appiah-Otoo, I. (2022). The impact of fintech on economic growth: Evidence from China. *Sustainability (Basel)*, *14*(10), 6211. DOI: 10.3390/su14106211

Soomro, R. B., Al-Rahmi, W. M., Dahri, N. A., Almuqren, L., Al-Mogren, A. S., & Aldaijy, A. (2025). A SEM–ANN analysis to examine impact of artificial intelligence technologies on sustainable performance of SMEs. *Scientific Reports*, *15*(1), 5438. DOI: 10.1038/s41598-025-86464-3 PMID: 39948417

Spaska, A., Kozub, H., Abylasynova, G., Kozub, V., & Koval, Y. (2025). Evaluation of innovative teaching methods using modern information technologies. *Jurnal Ilmiah Ilmu Terapan Universitas Jambi*, *9*(1), 422–440. DOI: 10.22437/jiituj.v9i1.38107

Srikanth, D. R. K., Ragini, M., Tripathi, G., Rajesh, K., Giri, A., Pandey, S. K., & Verma, L. K. (2024). The Impact of Emerging Technologies on Sustainable Agriculture and Rural Development. *International Journal of Environment and Climate Change*, *14*(1), 253–263. DOI: 10.9734/ijecc/2024/v14i13830

Stein, S., Ghantous, D., Chandler, Z., Simpson, A., & Udupi, I. (2025). Evolving Foresight Skills: How Will We Shape the Future of Strategic Foresight? Subrahmanyam, S. (2025). The Paradigm Shift in Leadership Owing to Technological Development. In *Leadership Paradigms and the Impact of Technology* (pp. 381-406). IGI Global Scientific Publishing.

STM ThinkTech. (2019). "İleri Sağlık Teknolojileri I Akıllı Sağlık Uygulamaları ve Veri Analizi İle İle Sağlık Sorunlarını Tanımlamak" [Identifying Health Problems with Advanced Health Technologies I Smart Health Applications and Data Analysis]. https://thinktech.stm.com.tr/uploads/docs/1608905321_stm-ileri-saglik-teknolojileri-1.pdf

Stone, M. L., & Stidham, R. W. (2023). Artificial Intelligence in IBD: How Will It Change Patient Management? *Current Treatment Options in Cardiovascular Medicine*, *21*(4), 365–377. DOI: 10.1007/s11938-023-00437-x

Suryawan, I. W. K., Gunawan, V. D., & Lee, C.-H. (2025). The role of local adaptive capacity in marine ecotourism scenarios. *Tourism Management*, *107*, 105039. DOI: 10.1016/j.tourman.2024.105039

Sutarman, A., Juliastuti, D., Yati, I., & Pasha, L. P. (2025). Enhancing Security and Privacy in Blockchain Systems for Tax Administration. *Blockchain Frontier Technology, 4*(2), 145~ 155-145~ 155.

Sutarman, A., Aprianto, R., Mitrev, R., Adyatama, R., & Yusup, M. (2025). Influence of Digital Technology & Data Analytics on Strategic Decision Making. [SABDA Journal]. *Startupreneur Business Digital*, *4*(1), 12–23. DOI: 10.33050/sabda.v4i1.685

Swanson, E., Kim, S., Lee, S.-M., Yang, J.-J., & Lee, Y.-K. (2020). The effect of leader competencies on knowledge sharing and job performance: Social capital theory. *Journal of Hospitality and Tourism Management*, *42*, 88–96. DOI: 10.1016/j.jhtm.2019.11.004

Syed-Ikhsan, S. O. S., & Rowland, F. (2004). Knowledge management in a public organization: A study on the relationship between organizational elements and the performance of knowledge transfer. *Journal of Knowledge Management*.

Teece, D. J. (2007). Explicating dynamic capabilities: The nature and microfoundations of (sustainable) enterprise performance. *Strategic Management Journal*, *28*(13), 1319–1350. DOI: 10.1002/smj.640

Teece, D. J. (2018). Business models and dynamic capabilities. *Long Range Planning*, *51*(1), 40–49. DOI: 10.1016/j.lrp.2017.06.007

Teece, D. J., & Pisano, G. (1994). The dynamic capabilities of firms: An introduction. *Industrial and Corporate Change, 3*(3), 537556. DOI: 10.1093/icc/3.3.537-a

Tegmark, M. (2017). *Life 3.0: Being Human in the Age of Artificial Intelligence*. Penguin.

Telli, G. (2019). Yapay zeka ve geleceğin meslekleri. Yapay zeka ve gelecek içinde [Artificial intelligence and the professions of the future]. (ss. 186-197). İstanbul: Doğu Kitapevi.

Tenca, F., & Franzoni, C. (2019). Crowdfunding: Risk, fraud and regulation. In *Handbook of research on crowdfunding* (pp. 323–355). Edward Elgar Publishing.

Thalheimer, L., Simperingham, E., & Jjemba, E. W. (2022). The role of anticipatory humanitarian action to reduce disaster displacement. *Environmental Research Letters, 17*(1), 014043. DOI: 10.1088/1748-9326/ac4292

Tien, N. H., Diem, P. T., Van On, P., Anh, V. T., Van Dat, N., Hung, N. T., & Tam, B. Q. (2021). The formation and development of CRM system at Thien Hoa electronics supermarket in Vietnam. *International Journal of Research and Growth Evaluation, 2*(4), 752–760.

Tierno, P. (2024). *Artificial Intelligence and Machine Learning in Financial Services*. https://crsreports.congress.gov

Timms, M. J. (2016). Letting artificial intelligence in education out of the box: Educational cobots and smart classrooms. *International Journal of Artificial Intelligence in Education, 26*(2), 701–712. DOI: 10.1007/s40593-016-0095-y

Tomé, E., & Gromova, E. (2021). Development of emergent knowledge strategies and new dynamic capabilities for business education in a time of crisis. *Sustainability (Basel), 13*(8), 4518. DOI: 10.3390/su13084518

Toniolo, A., Cerutti, F., Norman, T. J., Oren, N., Allen, J. A., Srivastava, M., & Sullivan, P. (2023). Human-machine collaboration in intelligence analysis: An expert evaluation. *Intelligent Systems with Applications, 17*, 200151. Advance online publication. DOI: 10.1016/j.iswa.2022.200151

Topol, E. (2019). *Deep medicine: How artificial intelligence can make healthcare human again*. Basic Books.

Tornatzky, L. G., & Fleischer, M. (1990). *The processing of technological innovation*. Lexington Books.

Trivedi, K., & Srivastava, K. B. (2025). Is improvisation a mediating link driving knowledge management processes towards innovativeness in Indian IT firms? *Management Research Review*. Advance online publication. DOI: 10.1108/MRR-06-2024-0488

Tuğluk, M. N., & Gök-Çolak, F. (2019). Sanayi toplumu ve eğitimi. Eğitimde ve endüstride [Industrial society and education. In education and industry], 21, 305-335.

Ünal, A., & Kılınç, İ. (2020). Yapay zekâ işletme yönetimi ilişkisi üzerine bir değerlendirme. Yönetim Bilişim Sistemleri Dergisi [An evaluation on the relationship between artificial intelligence and business management. Journal of Management Information Systems], 6(1), 51-78.

van Teunenbroek, C., Dalla Chiesa, C., & Hesse, L. (2023). The contribution of crowdfunding for philanthropy: A systematic review and framework of donation and reward crowdfunding. *Journal of Philanthropy and Marketing*, *28*(3), e1791. DOI: 10.1002/nvsm.1791

Vargo, D., Zhu, L., Benwell, B., & Yan, Z. (2021). Digital technology use during COVID-19 pandemic: A rapid review. *Human Behavior and Emerging Technologies*, *3*(1), 13–24. DOI: 10.1002/hbe2.242

Varona, D., & Suárez, J. L. (2022). Discrimination, bias, fairness, and trustworthy AI. *Applied Sciences (Basel, Switzerland)*, *12*(12), 5826. DOI: 10.3390/app12125826

Venkateswaran, N. (2023). AI-driven personalization in customer relationship management: Challenges and opportunities. *Journal of Theoretical and Applied Information Technology*, *101*(18), 7392–7399.

Villani, C., Bonnet, Y., & Rondepierre, B. (2018). *For a meaningful artificial intelligence: Towards a French and European strategy*. Conseil national du numérique.

Vincent, O., & Evans, O. (2019). Can cryptocurrency, mobile phones, and internet herald sustainable financial sector development in emerging markets? *Journal of Transnational Management*, *24*(3), 259–279. DOI: 10.1080/15475778.2019.1633170

Vučinić, M. (2020). Fintech and financial stability potential influence of FinTech on financial stability, risks and benefits. *Journal of Central Banking Theory and Practice*, *9*(2), 43–66. DOI: 10.2478/jcbtp-2020-0013

Wagner, D N. (2020, March 27). Strategically managing the artificially intelligent firm. Emerald Publishing Limited, 48(3), 19-25. https://doi.org/DOI: 10.1108/SL-08-2019-0119

Wald, H. S., Dube, C. E., & Anthony, D. C. (2007). Untangling the Web—The impact of Internet use on health care and the physician–patient relationship. *Patient Education and Counseling*, *68*(3), 218–224. DOI: 10.1016/j.pec.2007.05.016 PMID: 17920226

Wall, S. (2020). *Exploration of factors that influence the adoption and utilization of knowledge management systems*. Capella University.

Wang, Y., Mohsin, M., & Jamil, K. (2024). Customer trust and willingness to use shopping assistant humanoid chatbot. *Service Industries Journal*, •••, 1–25. DOI: 10.1080/02642069.2024.2432935

Wang, Y., Toseef, M., & Gong, Y. (2021). It process alignment in business strategy: Examining the role of transactional leadership and organization culture. *Information (Basel)*, *12*(6), 237. DOI: 10.3390/info12060237

Warwick, K. (2012). *Artificial Intelligence: The Basics*. Routledge.

Wasti, S. M. H. A., Ahmed, J., & Khan, M. H. (2024). Role of successive round as a quality signal in equity crowdfunding: Novel evidence from the perspective of investors' preferences. *PLoS One*, *19*(3), e0297820. DOI: 10.1371/journal.pone.0297820 PMID: 38452130

Watson, R., Wilson, H. N., Smart, P., & Macdonald, E. K. (2018). Harnessing difference: A capability-based framework for stakeholder engagement in environmental innovation. *Journal of Product Innovation Management*, *35*(2), 254–279. DOI: 10.1111/jpim.12394

Wei, J. (2019). China uses AI assistive tech on court trial for first time. https://www.chinadaily.com.cn/a/201901/24/WS5c4959f9a3106c65c34e64ea.html (11.04.2021).

Wernerfelt, B. (1984). A Resource-Based View of the Firm. *Strategic Management Journal*, *5*(2), 171–180. DOI: 10.1002/smj.4250050207

Westerman, G., Bonnet, D., & McAfee, A. (2014). *Leading Digital: Turning Technology into Business Transformation*. Harvard Business Review Press.

Wilson, H. J., & Daugherty, P. R. (2018). Feature Collaborative Intelligence: Humans And AI Are Joining Forces. *Harvard Business Review*.

Wong, L.-W., Tan, G. W.-H., Ooi, K.-B., Lin, B., & Dwivedi, Y. K. (2024). Artificial intelligence-driven risk management for enhancing supply chain agility: A deep-learning-based dual-stage PLS-SEM-ANN analysis. *International Journal of Production Research*, *62*(15), 5535–5555. DOI: 10.1080/00207543.2022.2063089

World Economic Forum. (2020). AI Governance: A Holistic Approach to Implement Ethics into AI. https://www.weforum.org

Wuest, T., Weimer, D., Irgens, C., & Thoben, K. D. (2016). Machine learning in manufacturing: Advantages, challenges, and applications. *Production & Manufacturing Research*, *4*(1), 23–45. DOI: 10.1080/21693277.2016.1192517

Wu, S., Ramli, M. Z., Ngian, S. P., Qiao, G., & Jiang, B. (2025). Review on parametric building information modelling and forward design approaches for sustainable bridge engineering. *Discover Applied Sciences*, *7*(2), 127. DOI: 10.1007/s42452-025-06543-y

Wu, Y. H., Bai, L., & Chen, X. (2023). How does the development of fintech affect financial efficiency? Evidence from China. *Ekonomska Istrazivanja*, *36*(2), 2106278. DOI: 10.1080/1331677X.2022.2106278

Xiaohui, C., Teng, L., & Chen, W. (2022). How does FinTech affect the development of the digital economy? Evidence from China. *The North American Journal of Economics and Finance*, *61*, 101697. https://doi.org/https://doi.org/10.1016/j.najef.2022.101697. DOI: 10.1016/j.najef.2022.101697

Xu, J. (2017). China's Internet Finance: A Critical Review. *China & World Economy*, *25*(4), 78–92. https://doi.org/https://doi.org/10.1111/cwe.12207. DOI: 10.1111/cwe.12207

Yadav, M., & Hung, T. H. (2025). Role of Emotional Intelligence in Crisis Leadership. In *Emotionally Intelligent Methods for Meaningful Leadership* (pp. 149–172). IGI Global Scientific Publishing.

Yaiprasert, C., & Hidayanto, A. N. (2024). AI-powered in the digital age: Ensemble innovation personalizes the food recommendations. *Journal of Open Innovation*, *10*(2), 100261. Advance online publication. DOI: 10.1016/j.joitmc.2024.100261

Yang, X., Ye, H. J., & Wang, X. (2021). Social media use and work efficiency: Insights from the theory of communication visibility. *Information & Management*, *58*(4), 103462. DOI: 10.1016/j.im.2021.103462

Yasin, A., Hussain, S., Hali, S. M., & Iqbal, S. (2022). Digitalization and firm performance: Mediating role of smart technologies. *Journal of Tianjin University Science and Technology*, *55*(4).

Yazıcı, A. M., & Çiçeklioğlu, H. (2025). The moderating role of environmental ethics in the effect of green innovation awareness on corporate social responsibility. *Social Responsibility Journal*, *21*(4), 826–854. DOI: 10.1108/SRJ-05-2024-0306

Yeh, Y. J., Lai, S. Q., & Ho, C. T. (2006). Knowledge management enablers: A case study. *Industrial Management & Data Systems*, *106*(6), 793–810. DOI: 10.1108/02635570610671489

Ye, S., & Zhao, T. (2023). Team knowledge management: How leaders' expertise recognition influences expertise utilization. *Management Decision*, *61*(1), 77–96. DOI: 10.1108/MD-09-2021-1166

Ye, T., Zheng, J., Jin, J., Qiu, J., Ai, W., & Mei, Q. (2024). Using Artificial Intelligence to Unlock Crowdfunding Success for Small Businesses. *Available atSSRN* 4806426. DOI: 10.2139/ssrn.4806426

Yin, F., Jiao, X., Zhou, J., Yin, X., Ibeke, E., Iwendi, M. G., & Biamba, C. (2022). Fintech application on banking stability using Big Data of an emerging economy. *Journal of Cloud Computing (Heidelberg, Germany)*, *11*(1), 43. DOI: 10.1186/s13677-022-00320-7 PMID: 36093281

Yoon, S. S., Lee, H., & Oh, I. (2023). Differential impact of Fintech and GDP on bank performance: Global evidence. *Journal of Risk and Financial Management*, *16*(7), 304. DOI: 10.3390/jrfm16070304

Younus, M., Purnomo, E. P., Nurmandi, A., Mutiarin, D., Manaf, H. A., Mumtaz, F., & Khairunnisa, T. (2025). Analyzing the trend of government support for cloud computing usage in e-government architecture. *Journal of Cloud Computing (Heidelberg, Germany)*, *14*(1), 14. DOI: 10.1186/s13677-025-00735-y

Yusof, F. M., Majid, M., Fadzil, A. S., & Ramli, M. F. (2025). The Conceptualisation Of Work Integrated Learning Practices In Hospitality Education To Develop Students'career Preparedness: A Preliminary Paper. *The Insight Journal*, *12*(1), 1–12. DOI: 10.24191/ij.v12i1.3902

Zafar, J., Shaukat, M., & Mat, N. (2010). An analysis of e-human resource management practices: A case study of State Bank of Pakistan. *European Journal of Social Sciences*, *15*(1), 18–26.

Zaidi, S. A. M., & Shah, S. A. A. (2023). Fintech contribution towards economic prosperity in Pakistan. [PRSS]. *Pakistan Review of Social Sciences*, *4*(1), 1–14.

Zamiri, M., & Esmaeili, A. (2024). Methods and technologies for supporting knowledge sharing within learning communities: A systematic literature review. *Administrative Sciences*, *14*(1), 17. DOI: 10.3390/admsci14010017

Zawacki-Richter, O., Marín, V. I., Bond, M., & Gouverneur, F. (2019). Systematic review of research on artificial intelligence applications in higher education – where are the educators? *International Journal of Educational Technology in Higher Education, 16*(1), 39. DOI: 10.1186/s41239-019-0171-0

Zeebaree, M., Ismael, G. Y., Nakshabandi, O. A., Saleh, S. S., & Aqel, M. (2020). Impact of innovation technology in enhancing organizational management. *Studies of Applied Economics, 38*(4). Advance online publication. DOI: 10.25115/eea.v38i4.3970

Zhang, P. (2024). *Gig Working Relationships: A Grounded Theory Study on the Dynamics between Gig Workers and Digital Platforms in the US*. University of Minnesota.

Zhang, X., Liu, X., Wang, X., Zhao, H., & Zhang, W. (2022). Exploring the effects of social capital on crowdfunding performance: A holistic analysis from the empirical and predictive views. *Computers in Human Behavior, 126*, 107011. DOI: 10.1016/j.chb.2021.107011

Zhang, Y.. (2021). Edge AI: On-Demand Deep Learning Model Co-Inference with Device-Edge Synergy. [Industry Reports & White Papers]. *ACM Transactions on Computer Systems, 39*(1), 1–27.

Zhao, L., & Li, Y. (2020). Crowdfunding in China: Turmoil of global leadership. *Advances in Crowdfunding: Research and Practice*, 273–296.

Zhou, Q., Wang, S., Wang, L., & Xu, W. (2025). Knowledge governance and innovation ambidexterity in the platform context: Exploring the role of knowledge transformation. *Journal of Knowledge Management, 29*(4), 1301–1329. DOI: 10.1108/JKM-03-2024-0256

Zizic, M. C., Mladineo, M., Gjeldum, N., & Celent, L. (2022). From industry 4.0 towards industry 5.0: A review and analysis of paradigm shift for the people, organization and technology. *Energies, 15*(14), 5221. DOI: 10.3390/en15145221

About The Contributors

Sajjad Baig is an Associate Professor in the faculty of Management Sciences. Currently, He is working as Dean/Director of faculty of Management science. Dr. Sajjad Baig has earned his Doctorate Degree in Total Quality Management from University of the Punjab, Lahore. His main research areas are Micro Economics, Total Quality Management, Operation Management, Human Resource Management, Organizational Behavior and Business Ressearch Methods.

Muhammad Mohsin is an associate professor at the Faculty of Business School at Hunan University of Humanities, Science and Technology (HUHST). He has earned his Doctorate Degree in Management Sciences (Finance) from Liaoning Technical University (LNTU), Fuxin, China. and Postdoctoral from PUTRA Business School, Universiti Putra Malaysia. Dr. Muhammad Mohsin has been an academic researcher whose valuable publications have contributed exceptionally to the discipline of Business and Finance. His academic profile is remarkable, and he has participated in SCI/SSCl research articles, international conferences, and seminars. The research work is admired by thousands of global readers and cited by hundreds of researchers in their fieldwork. He also received the "Outstanding Foreigner Student Award" 2018 from the China Scholarship Council (CSC). He has experience of conducting numerous training sessions or seminars regarding Advanced Research Methods, Data Analysis Techniques, and Business Analytics & efficiencies. He is a member of many research societies and leads a departmental board of studies at renowned universities in Pakistan. He has been working on divergent dimensions of Digitalization as a leading & guest Editor in different special issues of renowned SCI/SSCI journals. He also provided the services of reviewing research articles for many SCI/SSCI Journals. Based on technical & theoretical knowledge, he received many certificates from the journals. His discipline in research and teaching explores new dimensions of Green Finance, Sustainable development, and Digital Finance.

Rab Nawaz Lodhi is an Associate Professor at Hailey College of Commerce, University of the Punjab, Lahore, Pakistan. He is also a Visiting Research Scholar at the M3 Center of Muma College of Business, University of South Florida, USA. QSR International (Pty) Ltd. Melbourne, Australia certified him in 2013 as an International Trainer and Consultant for NVivo 9/10. Previously, He served as Chairman of UE Business School at the University of Education, Lahore, Pakistan. He has contributed significantly to academia with over 100 research publications, many in impact factor journals. He served as a Guest Editor for the Journal of Hospitality and Tourism Technology by Emerald for a special issue on Qualitative Research in Hospitality and Tourism Management. He is proficient in qualitative and quantitative data analysis tools including NVivo, Atlas- ti, SPSS, AMOS, Smart PLS, and MPlus. His areas of interest encompass Effective Leadership and Change Management, Artificial Intelligence (AI) and Business Transformation, Business Strategy, Enterprise Resource Planning (ERP) Systems Success Evaluation, and e-business.

***

Aliya Anwar doctoral is scholar at College of Economics and Management, Beijing University of Technology, Beijing, China and is a dedicated academic with over five years of teaching experience, notably serving as a lecturer and Head of Commerce at one of the well-known educational institutes in Pakistan. Currently pursuing her MS in Business Administration at North China Electric Power University under a Chinese Government Scholarship, her research focuses on sustainability, green innovation, and management practices. With multiple publications in SSCI and SCIE journals, her work has contributed to advancing knowledge in lean manufacturing and green market orientation. Aliya is proficient in research methodology and primary data analysis, complemented by strong communication and leadership skills.

Hilal Gökdağ Çelik was born in Istanbul in 1982. She completed her high school education at Beykent Private High School as the top student. With the success she showed in the university exam, she won the Department of Mathematics - Computer Science, Faculty of Arts and Sciences, Beykent University with a full scholarship. She graduated from Beykent University as the top student of her faculty and department in 2004. Since she aimed for an academic life in 2004, she started working as a lecturer at Beykent University. In 2011, she successfully completed the Business Management and Organization PhD program at Istanbul University. Dr.Hilal Çelik served as the head of the Foreign Trade Department at Beykent University Vocational School between 2013-2019. Hilal is proficient in research strategic management, management and technology, organizational behavior, management and organization, businesses, digital transformation, organizational culture. She has various international book chapters, international articles, Ulakbim publications and international congress papers. She currently serves as an Assistant Professor at the Department of Business Administration, Faculty of Economics and Administrative Sciences, Istanbul Beykent University. She is married and the mother of 2 boys.

Khalid Jamil is a distinguished academic with over five years of teaching experience at leading universities in Pakistan. Currently pursuing a post-doctoral fellowship at the College of Economics and Management, Beijing University of Technology, China, he holds a Ph.D. in Business Administration from North China Electric Power University. Dr. Jamil's research spans marketing, management, and sustainability, with numerous publications in high-impact SSCI and SCIE journals. His expertise extends to social media marketing, green innovation, and environmental performance. A recipient of the Chinese Government Scholarship, Dr. Jamil is also actively engaged in international research projects and academic collaborations.

Sohaib Mustafa is an assistant professor at College of Economics and Management, Beijing University of Technology, Beijing, China. He got his doctoral degree from the same college. His research work is published in high quality journals like international journal of human-computer interaction, electronic commerce research and applications and behavior and information technology. His research interests are human computer interaction, artificial intelligence, online communities, online knowledge sharing, live stream sales.

Dhartiben Patel is working with Indukaka Ipcowala Institute of Management, Faculty of Management Studies, as an Assistant Professor. She carries 1 year of experience in banking field , 4 years of experience in corporate field and 4 years of experience in education field. Her teaching interest lie in the areas of Finance, Accounts and Logical Thinking. Her educational background includes Pursuing PhD in management, Masters in Business Administration (MBA-FINANCE), Bachelors in Commerce (B. Com).She is dedicated to advancing knowledge in the field through both teaching and research.

Reshma G Sable is working with Indukaka Ipcowala Institute of management, Faculty of Management Studies, as I/C Dean and Associate Professor. She carries 17 years of experience education field. Her teaching interest lie in the areas of Organizational Behaviour, Human Resource Management, General Management, Critical Thinking and Logic and Emotional Intelligence. Her educational background includes Doctorate in Management (PhD – Learning Organization), Masters in Business Administration (MBA-HR), Masters in Education (MEd), Masters in Inorganic Chemistry (MSc), Bachelors in Education (BEd) and Bachelors in Chemistry (BSc). She has qualified NET in Human Resource Management and Education and SET in Education. In addition, she is also an Accredited Management Teacher (AMT) certified by All India Management Association, New Delhi. She has also published quite a good number of research papers in journals of repute. She is proficient in English, Hindi and Marathi and her strengths lie in the areas of critical thinking, interpersonal and analytical skills.

Index

A

B

C

D

E

R

S

W

www.ingramcontent.com/pod-product-compliance
Lightning Source LLC
LaVergne TN
LVHW081349300926
849161LV00008B/2111